Computational Methods in Wind Engineering

Computational Methods in Wind Engineering

Guest Editor

Ali Cemal Benim

Basel • Beijing • Wuhan • Barcelona • Belgrade • Novi Sad • Cluj • Manchester

Guest Editor
Ali Cemal Benim
Department of Mechanical
and Process Engineering
Düsseldorf University of
Applied Sciences
Düsseldorf
Germany

Editorial Office
MDPI AG
Grosspeteranlage 5
4052 Basel, Switzerland

This is a reprint of the Special Issue, published open access by the journal *Computation* (ISSN 2079-3197), freely accessible at: https://www.mdpi.com/journal/computation/special_issues/ Computational_Methods_in_Wind_Engineering.

For citation purposes, cite each article independently as indicated on the article page online and as indicated below:

Lastname, A.A.; Lastname, B.B. Article Title. *Journal Name* **Year**, *Volume Number*, Page Range.

ISBN 978-3-7258-3849-3 (Hbk)
ISBN 978-3-7258-3850-9 (PDF)
https://doi.org/10.3390/books978-3-7258-3850-9

Contents

Preface

Wind engineering is a truly interdisciplinary area encompassing many branches, such as meteorology, geographic information systems, fluid dynamics, structural dynamics, urban planning, energy, and the environment, as well as probability and statistics. Wind loads on structures (buildings, towers, and bridges), pedestrian comfort, city ventilation, wind effects on ventilation in buildings and vehicles, pollution dispersion in urban areas, and wind energy harvesting have been typical focal areas in wind engineering. Beyond this non-exhaustive list, issues related to climate change are gaining significance.

In wind engineering, in parallel to all other engineering disciplines, the impact of computational methods is rapidly increasing. As far as computational aspects are concerned, wind engineering embodies a series of specific challenges, including the availability of suitable validation data, the definition of boundaries and boundary conditions, scale disparities, and fluid–structure interaction.

The present Special Issue aims to present the recent advances in the development and application of computational methods in wind engineering.

Ali Cemal Benim
Guest Editor

Review

A Review of Numerical Modelling of Multi-Scale Wind Turbines and Their Environment

Katrina Calautit [1,*], Angelo Aquino [2], John Kaiser Calautit [1,*], Payam Nejat [3], Fatemeh Jomehzadeh [3] and Ben Richard Hughes [2]

[1]   Department of Architecture and Built Environment, University of Nottingham, Nottingham NG7 2JA, UK
[2]   Department of Mechanical Engineering, University of Sheffield, Sheffield S10 2TN, UK;
      aiaquino1@sheffield.ac.uk (A.A.); ben.hughes@sheffield.ac.uk (B.R.H.)
[3]   Faculty of Civil Engineering, Universiti Teknologi Malaysia, UTM, Skudai 81310, Malaysia;
      payam.nejaat@gmail.com (P.N.); Fjomehzadeh@gmail.com (F.J.)
*   Correspondence: calautitkatrina@gmail.com (K.C.); john.calautit1@nottingham.ac.uk (J.K.C.);
      Tel.: +44-0787-3928-164 (K.C.); +44-780-268-5370 (J.K.C.)

Received: 14 January 2018; Accepted: 2 March 2018; Published: 5 March 2018

Abstract: Global demand for energy continues to increase rapidly, due to economic and population growth, especially for increasing market economies. These lead to challenges and worries about energy security that can increase as more users need more energy resources. Also, higher consumption of fossil fuels leads to more greenhouse gas emissions, which contribute to global warming. Moreover, there are still more people without access to electricity. Several studies have reported that one of the rapidly developing source of power is wind energy and with declining costs due to technology and manufacturing advancements and concerns over energy security and environmental issues, the trend is predicted to continue. As a result, tools and methods to simulate and optimize wind energy technologies must also continue to advance. This paper reviews the most recently published works in Computational Fluid Dynamic (CFD) simulations of micro to small wind turbines, building integrated with wind turbines, and wind turbines installed in wind farms. In addition, the existing limitations and complications included with the wind energy system modelling were examined and issues that needs further work are highlighted. This study investigated the current development of CFD modelling of wind energy systems. Studies on aerodynamic interaction among the atmospheric boundary layer or wind farm terrain and the turbine rotor and their wakes were investigated. Furthermore, CFD combined with other tools such as blade element momentum were examined.

Keywords: Computational Fluid Dynamic (CFD); micro to small wind turbine; building integrated with wind turbine; wind farm; aerodynamic interaction; wind energy systems; atmospheric boundary layer (ABL); blade element momentum (BEM)

---

1. Introduction

Over the last decade, the production of renewable energy has rapidly increased and this development is expected to continue. Wind energy generation contributed a great share to this expansion and has attracted institutional investors. Wind resource is one of the most used sources of energy and about 50 GW have been installed in the year 2014 [1]. The global warming effect, increasing price of fossil products, instability of the energy market, and desire for clean-smart cities are the main drivers for increasing awareness in renewable technologies. Creating an environment which is clean and sustainable for the future is one of the greatest challenges of our time. As conventional sources like coal, oil, and other fossil fuels are limited and continue to be depleted, it is very important to search for renewable energy sources and develop technologies [2]. Researchers continue to develop and optimise wind turbines to eliminate the drawbacks associated with these devices. Due to all of these issues, the trend of increasing production from wind power resulted in wind farm constructions in locations with highly complex orography and, therefore, predicting its performance using simplified and linear models may not be adequate or accurate enough. The installation of wind turbines in complex terrain landscapes represents a major challenge due to the combination of uncertain wind resources and the flow accelerations from the surrounding terrain and wake effects from other turbines [3]. Another example is the installation of wind turbines in buildings or building-integrated wind turbines (BIWT), where the wind resource and condition are uncertain due to the surrounding buildings.

The profitability of energy production from wind resource is dependent on the turbine productivity, price of energy and generation costs, taking into account the total cost over the entire lifetime [4,5]. Micro-siting or the selection of the most efficient and effective type of wind turbine and exact location are very important factors that should be considered during the planning stage of a wind energy project. A lot of present tools/methods are not sufficient to completely predict the wind flow multifaceted and complex settings where the estimation of acceleration–deceleration wind effects is challenging. The error associated with the energy data presents a growing issue as the accuracy concerning the quantity of the energy which could be commercialised is even greater. Recent studies have shown that the integration of numerical Computational Fluid Dynamics (CFD) modelling with other tools such as wind tunnel or field measurements could provide a solution for the assessment of wind power in complex conditions [6,7]. Complex conditions, specifically in urban areas, presents substantial challenges for the integration of wind turbines. Also, there is lack of understanding and uncertainty concerning the impact of turbulence on the effectiveness of wind turbines in urban areas.

Figure 1 shows the different sizes and capacities of wind turbines [7]. A number of exhaustive studies have been made in small and medium scale wind turbine blades and most of them have used CFD and traditional BEM or blade element momentum to design the blades and compute the forces that act on it. Many studies on searching the optimum chord lengths have been prepared using different evolutionary optimising strategies. Issues including high turbulence, low wind velocity, and frequent direction of the wind change can affect the performance of HAWT or Horizontal-Axis Wind Turbine. Some VAWT or Vertical-Axis Wind Turbine designs can operate well in complex operating conditions however many possess low power coefficient [8,9].

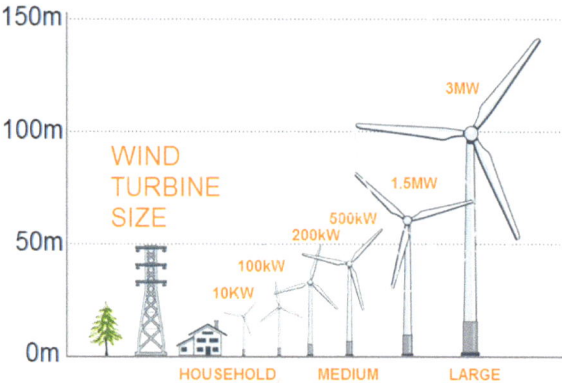

Figure 1. Different sizes and capacity of wind turbines.

Buildings or roofs integrated with micro-wind turbines are also creating great attention for decentralised power production and promising low cost renewable energy devices in populated areas, but, there is an uncertainty concerning the viability of these wind turbines. In high density urban/suburban areas, the installation of wind turbines is fairly limited because of problems including high turbulence intensity, low wind speeds, and possibly of greater levels of noise produced by the turbine. In order to make use of the application of micro-small renewable-energy production, particularly smaller turbines, allowing for tower heights that permits max utilisation of the accessible wind resource is important [10]. Between the different classifications of wind systems, small-scale VAWT showed the greatest potential for the generation of power in off-grid locations [11]. But the wind turbines are mostly being utilised in wind power farms or high-rise buildings where the wind with high speed is available. Few studies focus on the micro-wind utilisation in low-rise buildings due to the bottleneck i.e., wind speed cannot meet the minimal speed requirement of small wind turbines.

Recently, the optimisation of wind farms using CFD has received much attention in literature. For uniform terrains, the wind farm layout optimisation has been addressed through many works using various strategies; but currently, optimising the layout of wind farm on non-uniform/complex terrains is a challenge because of the absence of accurate and computationally tractable wake models for the assessment of the layout of wind farm. CFD modelling solutions such as actuator-disk and -line were established to predict the interaction with non-uniform terrains and phenomena of wake though these methods are computationally expensive particularly during the process of optimisation.

There is an ongoing debate on the health effects of wind turbines, especially in terms of aerodynamic noise, coming from the rotational motion of the blades of these devices. Therefore, set-back distances have been reported globally in order to avoid or minimise possible criticisms or impacts from the population located nearby the turbines [12]. The noise coming from the wind turbine has been an issue for years which resulted in barrier to widespread the use of wind turbines [13]. It is one of the most typical obstacles to the application of wind turbines, it is necessary to design the wind turbine rotors as quiet as possible. Currently, there is limited work available to examine the sources of noise for these devices, in particular, smaller wind turbines. The noise can create a negative influence on people nearby wind turbine [14]. In addition, these devices can also have adversative impact on animals, specifically by collision with the turbine blades [15].

Large scale wind turbines were found to affect the local climatic conditions and the atmosphere, while smaller wind turbines can provide a good possibility for providing power that could be sufficient for local demands without changing the local conditions. The growing attention on the installation of sustainable energy systems has led to a wide range of micro-wind turbine methods introduced in the market. Though most of the commercially used wind turbines are the HAWT, vertical axis is recognised to have a potential technology for the future. The application of micro-small-scale wind turbine is increasing with also the legislation and support encouraging further development [16].

It is known that the environmental impacts produced in the operational process of wind turbines are lower compared to the ones produced by fossil fuels-based systems [17], however, the overall contribution of smaller wind turbines may be limited. The environmental effects of small-micro turbines and their capability to contribute to climate change targets in the UK was examined by [18]. Installation of small wind turbines in the domestic sector would only save around 0.6–1% of greenhouse emissions of 2009. So, its potential to contribute to the climate change targets of the UK is limited.

CFD modelling has been used by several researchers to predict the wind energy systems' performance over the last few decades. With the growing computing capacity of modern computers, CFD modelling has developed to a substantial tool to numerically assess the wind conditions within the investigated site or environment [19–21]. Current developments in wind turbine using CFD simulation have shown progress from flow modelling of flow around two-dimensional aerofoils to ABL or atmospheric boundary layer flow by arrangements of turbines or wind farms. The velocity profile of the wind depends on the boundary layer based on a complex terrain layout that varies significantly on the roughness of surface and local Reynolds number. Accuracy of CFD simulations of wind flow is important for choosing wind farm locations and the design of suitable wind turbines. The rising computational resource and power in the past few years permitted the CFD simulation of the sites containing the wind turbines.

To respond to the challenges associated with the modelling of wind turbines in various scales, this study will review the state of the art and most recent literature (2010–2018) on the CFD modelling of wind turbine energy systems. Different types of wind turbine categories will be investigated: micro to small-scale, building mounted, and large-scale wind turbines based on the analysis of performance of these devices using CFD simulations. To identify articles for this review, a computerised literature search using terms such as "Wind Turbine", "Micro to Small Wind Turbine", "Building Mounted with Wind Turbine", "Wind Turbine installed in Wind Farm", and "CFD" in the Sciencedirect, Researchgate, and Springer database for publications available to date. These databases include scientific books, journals, articles, and papers from conference proceedings. Several publications were removed due to duplicates or unrelated to the CFD simulation. Moreover, only articles that were written in English were selected.

2. Micro-Small Scale

Decentralised or on-site energy generation by exploiting various types of energy resources has the prospective to deliver extensively applicable low carbon electricity generation at the urban or built environment level [22,23]. Generation of power at the point of use can minimise the energy loss associated with the transmission of electricity. Due to these, micro to small-scale renewables such as solar panels and wind turbines have gained increasing attention. Small micro-wind turbines are generally classified based on swept area (<25 m^2) and have rated power of up to 6 kW [24,25]. Different types of small micro wind turbine are shown in Figure 2. This section will review the recent studies that assess the wind energy systems in the micro-small scale using CFD and addresses the challenges associated with its applications, including design, optimisation, low velocity and high turbulence of urban wind, vibration and noise problems.

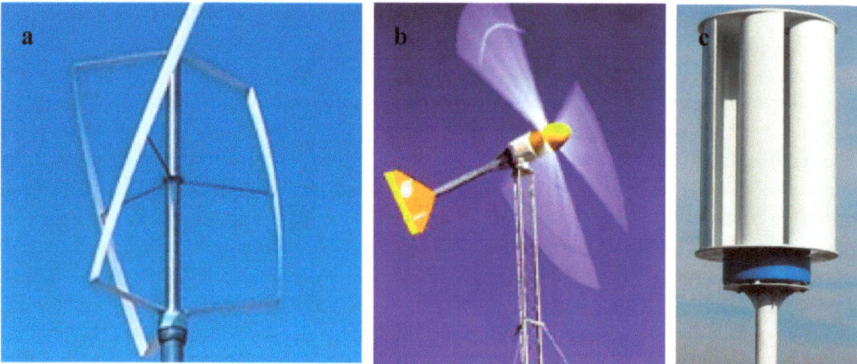

Figure 2. Different types of micro wind turbine: (**a**) Twisted H-Darrieus VAWT; (**b**) Three-blade propeller HAWT; (**c**) Savonius VAWT [24].

De-Santoli et al. [26] conducted CFD and experimental analysis of an AM300 vertical axis micro-wind turbine with an electrical power of 3.7 kW. The study assessed the viability and energy generation in low wind speed locations. The initial energy results demonstrated that the electricity production of the prototype was higher than that generated by a typical generator with the same technical features. Hence, a lower cut in wind speed for the power curve was achieved. The CFD analysis highlighted that adding the convergent duct to the H-rotor Darrieus turbine (see Figure 3) improved its energy generation. The percentage of power rises at roughly 125% for wind speed equal to 8 m/s. Although the CFD model was able to evaluate the speed amplification effect due to the convergent duct, experiments were conducted to assess the power increase.

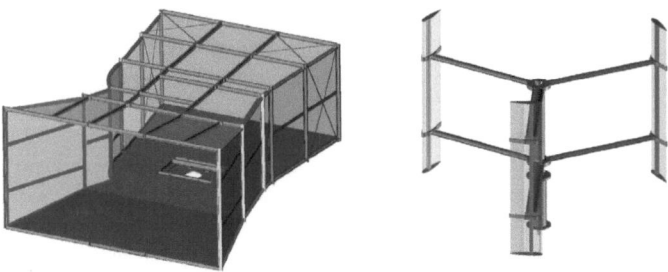

Figure 3. Schematic of the AM300: A micro VAWT with convergent duct [26].

A similar study by El-Zahaby et al. [27] used a 2-D axisymmetric CFD model based on standard k-ε turbulence model to investigate a micro wind turbine contained in a diffuser with flanges to enhance power generation. The work focused on the influence of flange's angles on velocity at diffuser entrance. The verification of the present model showed good agreement among earlier published experimental data. The numerical results demonstrated the vortices which were generated at the leeward side of the flange which caused a drop in pressure and increased the diffuser's flow rate. The work concluded that the right flange with 15° angle was the most effective in terms of accelerating the flow at the inlet of diffuser. The work only focused on the diffuser geometry and did not consider the rotor of the turbine.

Several recent studies have focused on optimizing the blades of micro scale wind turbines using CFD modelling. A 3D CFD analysis of the performance of a lotus shape wind turbine based on the Savonius type VAWT was studied by Wang and Zhan [28]. Using CFD based on unsteady continuity RANS with realisable k-ε turbulence model, three types of configurations were compared as shown in Figure 4; wind turbine with semi-circular blades, Savonius type with helically-twisted blades or semi-cylindrical. Its rotation was simulated using the sliding mesh method in CFD. The results showed that the performance of the semi-circular blade configuration was equivalent to that of the semi-cylindrical configuration and was lower as compared to the helically-twisted type. The study, however, ignored the influence of the guide blades on the systems performance.

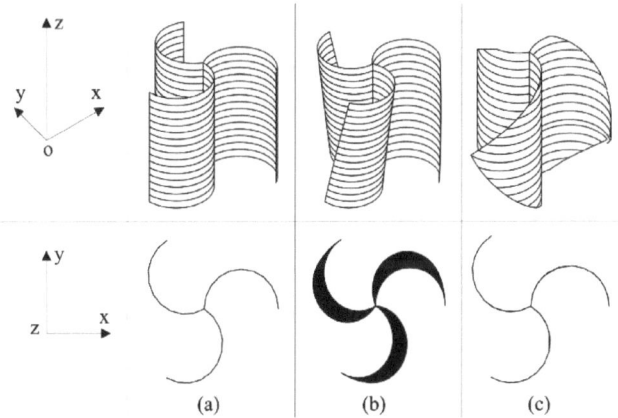

Figure 4. Model of the rotors with (**a**) semi-cylindrical (**b**) helically-twisted and (**c**) semi-circular blades [28].

Mohamed et al. [29] used CFD based on the SST k-ω and Realisable k-ε models in order to investigate 25 different types of blade aerofoil sections and blade pitch angles (−10–10°) of a small

H-rotor Darrieus turbine. The results showed that LS (1)-0413 aerofoil had a power coefficient 10% higher than the NACA 0018. In another study [30], the same author compared the performance of 20 different symmetrical and unsymmetrical aerofoil shapes (Figure 5) to maximise the power and torque coefficient. The results indicated that the S-1046 aerofoil section led to a 27% increase in maximum power output coefficient compared to the standard symmetrical NACA aerofoils. Elkhoury et al. [31] used CFD based on LES or large eddy simulation with the dynamic SGS or Smagorinsky–Subgrid scale model to investigate the micro VAWT's performance with variable-pitch. The variable-pitch mechanism was simulated using the sliding mesh method. The results showed that thicker aerofoils had improved performance for the studied high-solidity ratio fixed pitch wind turbine. Furthermore, good consistency was seen among the LES numerical model and experimental results, both for the variable and fixed pitch mechanisms as detailed in Figure 6.

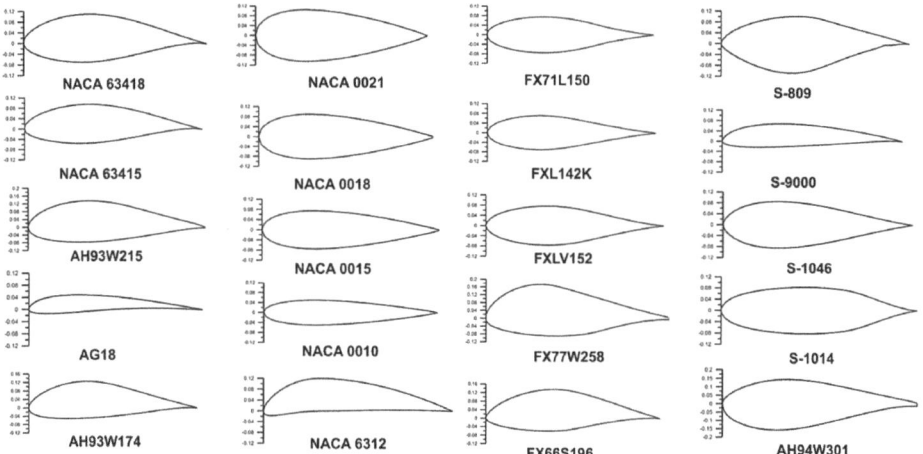

Figure 5. Different symmetric and non-symmetric aerofoils investigated in [30].

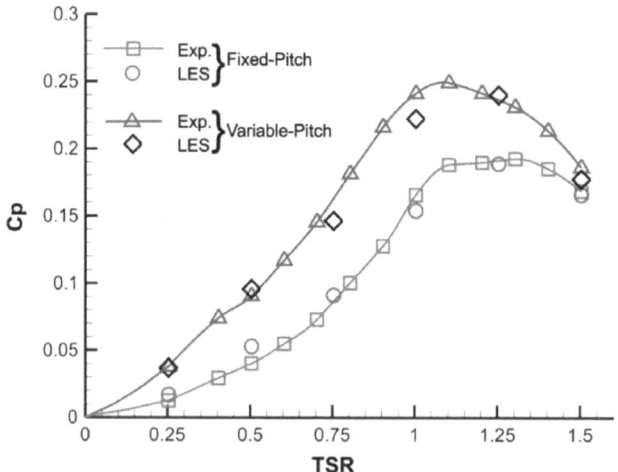

Figure 6. Comparison between experiment and CFD LES model prediction of the average power coefficient for an adjustable- and fixed-pitch angle, NACA0018 [31].

VAWTs such as H-Darrieus rotor can be effective in low wind speed conditions but since blades with symmetrical profiles are generally used, it had poor self-starting capabilities. Its starting performance can be improved by using high solidity cambered or unsymmetrical blades. Bausas and Danao [32] used CFD modelling to study the overall performance of a camber-bladed VAWT under varying wind conditions. The CFD analysis highlighted that variable wind causes a negative effect on the VAWT's performance with up to 9% drop in pressure coefficient. In addition, the camber slightly improved VAWT's performance. Similarly, Sengupta et al. [33] also conducted a CFD investigation to evaluate the self-starting features and efficiency of a H-Darrieus turbine with unsymmetrical blades under low wind conditions. The study concluded that the unsymmetrical blades had a higher power and static and dynamic torque coefficient than the evaluated symmetrical blades. Li et al. [34] conducted 3D transient CFD analysis of a straight-bladed turbine to assess the influence of near-wake and thrust coefficient. The results showed that the momentum amount is minimum at the tip of blade and maximum at the centre of the blade. Furthermore, the CFD model based on the k-epsilon SST transport model provided reasonable predictions as compared to the experimental results. In another study, Li et al. [35] predicted the aerodynamic performance of the same VAWT model in the span-wise direction. Based on the evaluation of the experimental and CFD data, it was seen that the fluid force reduced as the spanwise position increased.

The study of Abdalrahman et al. [36] focused on investigating an intelligent controller for blade pitch of a small H-type VAWT for optimising its power production. CFD was used to examine the performance at various tip speed ratios. The flow was investigated using two methods: sliding mesh and MRF or multiple reference frame method. The power coefficient was solved for each configuration and validated with available experimental data. Due to the complexity related to the dynamic response modelling of the turbine rotor, the numerical data was used for mapping the rotor's variable- and fixed-pitch angle system models using an artificial neural network. Results showed that the proposed technique improved the output by up to 25%, as compared to a fixed blade configuration.

One of the benefits of the VAWT is its capability to extract wind power from any wind angle or direction and hence it does not require costly pitch and yaw system [37]. Although this also results in deceleration because of the torque (negative) on the returning blades, which then decreases performance. To address this, Stout et al. [38] examined the efficiency improvement of a small VAWT as a result of the addition of an upstream deflector or guide vanes. A 2D VAWT was simulated using ANSYS Fluent CFD to calculate the unsteady Navier–Stokes equation and the k-epsilon RNG model. At the initial process, the performance was enhanced by modifying the pitch angle and orientation, before assessing the impact on increasing wind velocity had on the turbine efficiency. Results showed that it reached 19% maximum efficiency and employed as the design for open rotor. Installed deflectors redirected the fluid flow from the returning turbine blade, thus minimising the negative torque on the device. Moreover, deflectors with width angles between 36 and 45° were observed to enhance the performance of the turbine by up to 1.27%.

CFD simulations were conducted by Arpino et al. [39] to examine the optimal formation of straight-blade Darrieus type VAWT, particularly designed for energy conversion at low wind velocities. The system consisted of three aerofoilpairs, composed of primary and secondary blades with various chord lengths. Analyses were conducted using CFD OpenFOAM, taking into account various turbulence models and using the moving mesh method. The simulation data were compared to the results gathered from the experimental wind tunnel tests of a scaled model and it was concluded that the most accurate model for the analysis of the investigated turbine was the Spalart–Allmaras one equation model.

Various numerical models were developed over the years to accurately simulate the aerodynamic performance of VAWTs. The numerical models can be categorised into the main types, stream-tube, vortex method and CFD modelling. The study of Delafin et al. [40] compared the RANS CFD modelling method with other two low order aerodynamic models (double multiple streamtube model and free-wake vortex mode) based on the prediction of VAWT's performance, examined by Sandia National

Laboratories. The models were assessed based on the prediction of the power coefficient, power, thrust, lateral force and instantaneous turbine torque. All the models agreed well with the test at the optimum tip speed ratio (see Figure 7), but away from the optimal value, the stream tube model greatly differs from other numerical models and experimental data. The RANS CFD model results compared well with the conducted tests, but to some extent underestimating the power coefficient values.

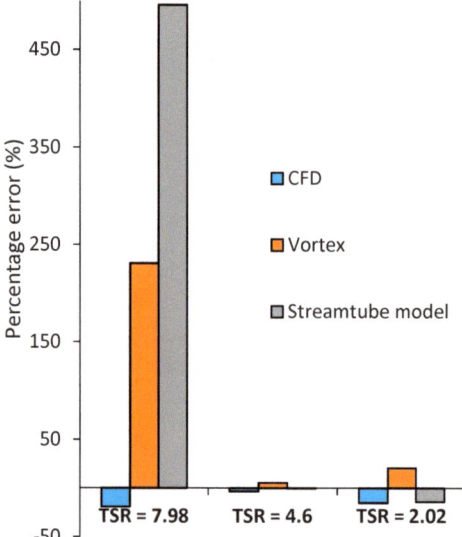

Figure 7. Error of the predicted power by CFD, stream-tube, vortex methods from the experiments at several tip speed ratios (TSR) [40].

Accurate prediction of the performance of turbines by means of CFD necessitates an adequately fine grid or mesh resolution and azimuthal increment in order to capture important flow details. The size of the computational domains also requires to be adequately large to minimise the impact of blockage caused by the device in the domain. The work of Rezaeiha et al. [41] examined the effect of the aforementioned computational parameters on a small two-bladed VAWT operating at 4.5 tip speed ratio using CFD with the uRANS or unsteady Reynolds averaged Navier–Strokes. Figure 8 shows the sizing of the computational domain. The study highlighted that a distance from the turbine center to the domain inlet *di* and outlet *do* of 10 D (10 × diameter of turbine) each, a 20D domain width W and a diameter of the rotating core dc of 1.5D were seen to be safe choices to reduce the effects of blockage and uncertainty in the boundary conditions on the results. Klein et al. [42] used CFD modelling to investigate the impact of blockage on the blade performance. The study compared the results of the CFD code with a LLFVW or Lifting Line Free Vortex Wake code and wind tunnel experiment. Good comparison was observed between the numerical and wind tunnel data.

In the study of Chowdhury et al. [43], a parametric investigation of turbulence models, time step, and mesh independence were conducted for accurate simulation of an upright and tilted small VAWT. Based on the results, the Spalart–Allmaras turbulence model had the worst performance in regards to vortices capturing. While the SST k-omega modelled the vortices in wake better compared to Spalart–Allmaras and RNG k-epsilon turbulence models. The analysis proved that CFD was better as compared to BEM in terms of aerodynamic feature predictions. Furthermore, the tilted VAWT configuration produced better downwind torque than the upright VAWT configuration.

Yang et al. [44] examined the effect of tip vortex on small VAWT wake using CFD simulations based on the k omega SST or shear-stress transport model at various TSRs. To accurately study the tip vortex formation, the grid which had a substantial effect on the vortex evolution was concentrated in the rotor blade area, as shown in Figure 9. The vortex structure distribution was more complex with the span wise direction at a lower TSR and the tip vortex had an extended dissipation distance at a high TSR. Moreover, the average wind velocity results demonstrated a small value beside the blade and large value behind the blade tip, due to the vortex effect.

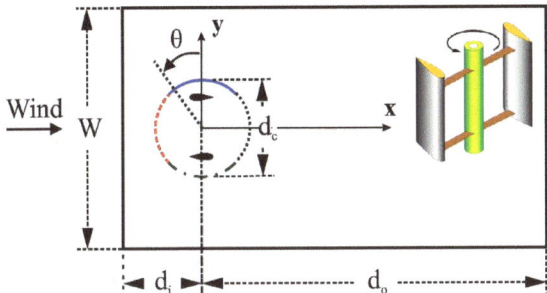

Figure 8. 2D Computational domain for the analysis of VAWT.

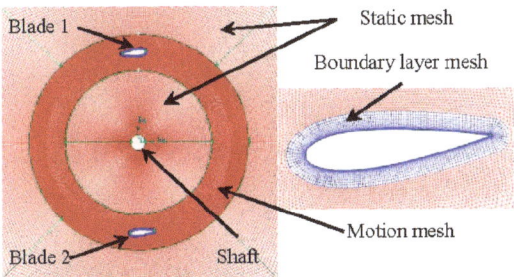

Figure 9. Meshing strategy for the VAWT rotor investigated in [44].

Small VAWTs can be easily integrated into urban areas for decentralised power generation. Due to its size, it is generally considered to be sufficiently quiet assuming that its utilisation in urban environments means that the noise output will hardly exceed that of the surroundings, hence only a small number of work has studied its noise output. However, it is still important to conduct noise prediction during the early stage turbine design so that its integration into urban environments can be approved. Botha et al. [45] developed on optimised technique for calculating aerodynamically produced noise by a small VAWT. This technique enhances the current prediction of noise and integrates currently established aerofoil prediction models. The self-noise methods and inflow turbulence were considered. Time-dependent CFD simulations were conducted to calculate or the aerodynamic solution and noise predictions were reliant on the input data. The analytical flow approaches were also compared against the CFD results to quantity errors in the previous method. The results showed that the dominant source of noise was the inflow turbulence. The work concluded that the integration with CFD enhanced the prediction accuracy when compared with analytic methods. While Ghasemian and Nejat [46] and Wasala et al. [47] also employed CFD but using LES to predict the flow field in combination with FW-H or Ffowcs Williams and Hawkings method to predict the generated noise by a wind turbine at different tip speed ratios.

Several recent studies (Bremseth and Duraisamy [48], Dabiri [49], Giorgetti et al. [50]) suggested that unlike HAWTs, VAWTs demand less stringent spacing requirements and optimising the positioning and rotation (co-/counter-rotating) of the closely spaced multi VAWT arrangement, could lead to improved performance. Giorgetti et al. [50] used CFD to investigate the enhancement in power that can be achieved by setting medium to high solidity and thus low TSR Darrieus micro turbines in close proximity. CFD simulations were conducted to assess the aerodynamic interferences in two- and four-rotor formations as shown in Figure 10. In addition, the performance of counter-rotating and co-rotating arrangements was compared. The results of the simulations demonstrated a rise in production of around 10% as compared to an isolated turbine. The study concluded that acceleration of the freestream flow among the turbines was the reason of the improvement of power extraction through re-energisation and contraction of the turbine wakes.

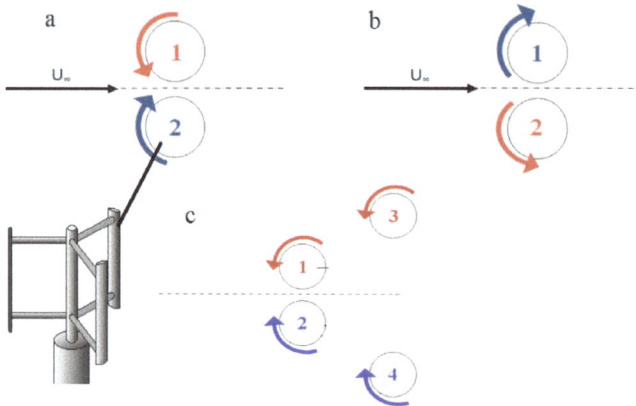

Figure 10. Schematic diagram of close proximity VAWT in (**a**) inward counter-rotating; (**b**) outward counter-rotating; (**c**) 4-rotors configuration.

A similar CFD study was conducted by Zanforlin and Nishino [51] to investigate the enhancement of power generation due to the pairing of counter-rotating VAWTs. They concluded that two main mechanisms contribute to the power increase of a side by side counter-rotating VAWTs: (1) modification of lateral velocity in the windward pathway due to the existence of the adjacent wind turbine and (2) wake contraction in the downwind path. Ghasemian et al. [52] emphasised that the grouping of VAWTs results in distributed flows downwind of rotors with reduced wind speed and the optimum arrangement can enhance the power generation.

Table 1 summarises the different CFD studies on wind turbines in the micro to small scale including augmentation using guide vanes and shrouds, blade profile modification optimisation, wind turbine wake interaction, aeroacoustics of wind turbines, unsteady wind flow conditions and self-starting characteristics. The effects of different geometrical and operating parameters including tip speed ratio, blade number and blade shapes, wind speed, solidity on the wind turbine performance and self-starting characteristics were investigated. Several studies highlighted the importance of CFD in accelerating the design process of micro to small scale wind turbines and bringing down the overall cost of design. Many research on micro to small scale wind turbines have used CFD for designing the blades and computing the forces acting on it. Various numerical models were established over the years to accurately simulate the aerodynamic performance of micro to small scale wind turbines. The numerical models can be mainly categorised into stream-tube, vortex method and CFD modelling. Many of the CFD studies carried out used low order models including the k-epsilon, SST k-ω, or Spalart–Allmaras models and few investigations used models such as LES and Reynolds Stress Transport models. Few studies have studied the noise output of small scale wind turbines. Several studies have employed CFD to predict the turbulent flow field in combination with analytical method to accurately predict the noise generation by a wind turbine.

Table 1. Wind Turbine Assessment—Small Wind Turbine.

Author	Type	No of WT	Capacity	Tool/Method	Key Findings
De-Santoli et al. (2014)	VAWT Micro WT (AM300)	1	Nominal electric power of 3.7 kW	FLUENT, 3D	The proposed WT's electricity production is 6000 kWh annually. The electricity generation is improved by 50% with the use of PV array to the device.
Wang and Zhan (2013)	Savonius VAWT	2	-	FLUENT, RANS, 3D, Realizable k-ε	The wind rotor performance integrated with semi-circular blades was almost similar to the semi-cylindrical wind rotor and slower compared to the shape of spiral twisted wind rotor but the semi-circular wind rotor operates more smoothly.
El-Zahaby et al. (2016)	Diffuser augmented wind turbines (DAWT)	-		FLUENT, 2D, standard k-ε	Expected power increase level at optimal flange angle reaches a value of 1.953 related to the expected power of standard turbine, whereas the estimated power increase ratio of normal flange reaches 1.903 which means that the improvement in power generation is about 5% due to the optimal flange angle.
Abdalrahman et al. (2017)	Darrieus VAWT (H-type VAWT)	-		FLUENT, 2D	Blade pitch angle method increases the power output of the H-type VAWT, an average 25% improvement.
Mohamed (2012)	Darrieus turbine (H-rotor VAWT)	-		FLUENT, URANS, Realizable к-ε	The investigation on aerodynamic was conducted for 20 different aerofoils (Symmetric and Non-symmetric) by 2-dimensional CFD to maximise output torque and output power coefficient. An improvement of the H-rotor Darrieus turbine performance can be achieved in this method.
Elkhoury et al. (2015)	VAWT with low aspect ratio 3 straight blades with struts	-		FLUENT, LES, 3D	The greatest power coefficient distribution changes were found in the tests at low level of wind speeds of 6 m/s and 4 m/s for the NACA0018 fixed-pitch and aerofoils NACA 634-221.
Bausas and Danao (2015)	VAWT	-	5kW	FLUENT, 2D, standard k-ε	Despite of the increase in wind energy because of varying wind at 233.13 W in a wind cycle compared to 229.69 W for the stable 5 m/s wind speed, generated power by the camber-bladed VAWT decreased to 74.96 W from the steady 78.32 W wind rotor power.
Sengupta et al. (2016)	VAWT (H-Darrieus rotor)	-	-	FLUENT, 2D, RNG k-ε	The investigation showed that asymmetrical blade rotor had greater vital torque and greater power level compared to the asymmetrical EN0005 and even blade H-Darrieus rotors.
Li et al. (2016)	Straight-bladed VAWT	-	-	FLUENT, 3D, RANS, SST k-ε	The fluid force was reduced with the increase of span wise positions excluding the position of support structure.
Stout et al. (2017)	VAWT with an Upstream Deflector	2	-	FLUENT 14.0	The application of small, curve upstream deflectors were seen to enhance the turbine performance up to 1.266%; with the WT that requiring decreased rotational speed to offer optimal performance values.

Table 1. *Cont.*

Author	Type	No of WT	Capacity	Tool/Method	Key Findings
Arpino et al. (2017)	VAWT	2	-	Open FOAM	The simulation of the power coefficient-TSR curves of a VAWT and the moving mesh method combined with SpalartAllmaras turbulence model provided acceptable results, in spite of few discrepancies among experimental and numerical data.
Yang et al. (2017)	VAWT	1	-	WAsP, LES, RANS	The vortex structure distribution with the span wise direction was more complicated at a lower tip speed ratio and the tip vortex had a longer dissipation distance at a highertip speed ratio. Moreover, the average wind speed demonstrated a higher value near the tip of the blade and a small value close to the blade due to the vortex effect.
Delafin et al. (2017)	VAWT	-	-	ANSYS CFX, CACTUS, 3D, RANS k-omega SST	Double Multi-Streamtube method was seen to be less accurate compared to the vortex method, which itself was seen to be less accurate than the RANS CFD. For all the tip speed ratios tested, the Double Multi-Streamtube method over-predicted the torque amplitude while the RANS CFD gave a good prediction of this amplitude.
Rezaeiha et al. (2017)	VAWT	-	-	FLUENT, SIMPLE, 2D URANS	A domain width of 20 × diameter and a rotating core of 1.5 × diameter were seen to be safe choices to reduce uncertainty in the boundary conditions and effects of blockage on the results.
Klein et al. (2017)	HAWT and VAWT	-	450 kW fan	FLOWer, 3D, URANS, SST turbulence	Good accordance was seen for the flow fields, the on-blade speed and the angle between the line of the chord of an aero foil and relative airflow. Deviations occulted for the bending moments.
Chowdhury et al. (2016)	VAWT upright and tilted positions	-	-	URANS, SST k-omega	It was seen that in the situation of tilted structure the wake stream shifts downward. This characteristics of VAWT in tilted state may result into effective sea surface application in floating offshore wind farms.
Botha et al. (2017)	VAWT	2	2 and 5 kW	FLUENT, 2D, 3D, RANS, DES	Calculations from the CFD was found to enhance the accurateness of noise projections when compared to the analytical flow solution; for the inflow-turbulence noise sources, blade produced turbulence dominates the atmospheric inflow turbulence.
Ghasemian and Nejat (2015)	H-Darrieus VAWT	-	-	Incompressible LES	The study showed direct relation among the strength of the rotational speed and the radiated noise. Moreover, the effect of receiver distance on the Overall Sound Pressure Level was investigated and it was concluded that it varies with a logarithmic trend with the receiver distance.
Wasala et al. (2015)	HAWT CART-2	-	660 kW	LES, 3D	The study showed that noise evaluations can be achieved with less computational expense as compared to carrying out full WT models, and with greater accurateness compared to using semi empirical noise anticipated codes. Moreover, the study recommended that the expected 0 radial flow was used for computing the farfield noise at high TSR.

Table 1. *Cont.*

Author	Type	No of WT	Capacity	Tool/Method	Key Findings
Bremseth and Duraisamy (2016)	VAWT	-	-	OVERTURNS, URANS, e-Spalart–Allmaras turbulence	Studies of VAWT in multiple columns demonstrated that the downstream columns may be more effective than the leading column, a proposition which could result to radical enhancement in productivity of small scale wind farm.
Dabiri (2011)	Counter-rotating VAWT	6	-	Numerical Simulations	Results recommended an alternative method to small scale wind farming that could concurrently lessen the cost, size, and environmental effects of wind farms.
Giorgetti et al. (2015)	Straight-bladed Darrieus Vertical Axis micro-turbines	2	1.2kW VAWT	Fluent, 2D, URANS, k-ω SST	The accelerated free-stream flow between the turbines was the main cause of the power extraction improvement by means of re-energisation and contraction of the turbine wakes. CFD projections of a four-rotor configuration proved this hypothesis, also the wind direction greatly affects the overall efficiency
Zanforlin and Nishino (2016)	VAWT	2	1.2 kW	Unsteady (URANS), 2D	Results demonstrated that the total power of a staggered pair of turbines cannot surpass that of a side-by-side pair of turbines.
Ghasemian et al. (2017)	Darrieus vertical axis wind turbines	-	-	FLUENT, k-ε turbulence k- ω (SST), RANS-LES	Power variation decreased through increasing the blade number. Greater number of blades allows the maximum power coefficient to be reach at lower angular velocities. The guide vane is a good strategy to increase the performance of wind turbines and enhance their self-starting ability specifically at lower level of wind speeds.

3. Building Scale

There has been renewed interest by architects, built environment engineers, developers and governments regarding the installation of wind turbines into urban or built environments due to their capability to provide delocalised power which could provide a solution to the increasing urbanisation and renewable energy demand and interest in low energy and sustainable buildings [53,54]. Wind turbines positioned at the rooftop of a tall building to extract wind energy, in theory, could take advantage of a higher area of the wind velocity profile (see Figure 11) which is not significantly affected by the surface roughness [55,56]. Prominent examples include, the World Trade Centre in Bahrain, Strata Tower in London, and Pearl River Tower in Guangzhou which have building-integrated wind turbines [57].

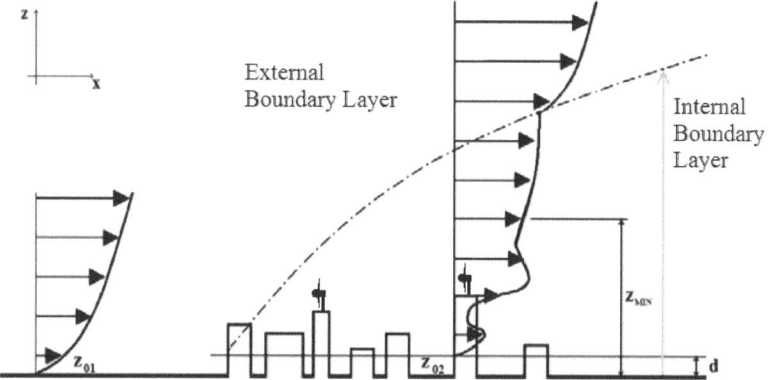

Figure 11. Wind velocity profile in the internal boundary layer in an urban area.

Currently, there are several challenges to installing wind turbines in urban areas, particularly turbines near an urban environment. The main challenge is the availability of adequate wind resource in these environments. The wind conditions in urban areas are highly complex due to surface roughness and the presence of obstacles, i.e., buildings and structures, characterised by low wind speed and high turbulence which are not desirable regarding power production by WTs [58,59]. Furthermore, the wind turbines in buildings also raise other concerns such as aesthetic dissatisfaction, vibration and aerodynamic noise [60].

Several researchers have employed CFD modelling to establish the feasibility of building integrated turbines. CFD can investigate how the wind flows over a building, the effect of the speed, direction and turbulence of flow and the interference effects of surrounding buildings or structures. It is important to carefully assess the position of the WT on a building so that the great volume of power can be gathered. Figure 12 illustrates examples of the incorporation of large scale wind turbines (roof, between buildings, within the structure) and small-scale wind turbines into buildings.

Ayhan and Sağlam [20] conducted an investigation of wind turbine installations in buildings using CFD modelling. The wind flows and aerodynamics were examined according to the local meteorological data and local buildings features. To achieve the greatest potential resource of wind energy and prevent turbulent places, CFD was used to simulate the annual wind flows with buildings to assist in locating, analysing, and designing wind turbines around and on buildings. The work highlighted that the height of mounted WT was essential as wind can be extremely strong at rooftop height. Moreover, smaller VAWTs are more advisable to use in urban areas. The typical Darrieus WT was not suitable because it was observed to be too noisy, while the Savonious rotor has the drawback of low power levels. Through improvement of the initial design of Darrieus by decreasing the TSR, the noise can be minimised.

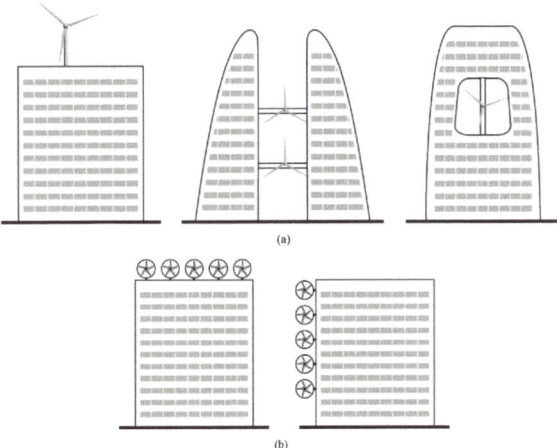

Figure 12. Building integration of (**a**) large scale WTs and (**b**) small scale WTs.

The size of WTs for building integration is constrained by the available space. To highlight this issue, a number of studies have tried to increase power by forcing air through a duct with a turbine which accelerates velocity and increases the kinetic energy of the air. This acceleration can also be attained by locating the wind turbine between two buildings. These increases in wind velocity occurring between two buildings are also known as the Venturi effects [61] or building augmented wind turbine (BAWT) [62]. Heo et al. [63] conducted CFD analysis of a 110-kW BAWT with different reference wind speed and flow angles. Figure 13 shows the structure of the wind turbine and sky bridge on the buildings. The turbulence model used was the RANS-SST. Results showed that aerodynamic power production of 110 kW BAWT was more compared to 110 kW stand-alone WT because of the concentration effect produced by the wind acceleration among buildings when flow angle is between −30 and 15°. Because of the steady rotational direction of the WT, the impact of flow angle showed unsymmetrical nature.

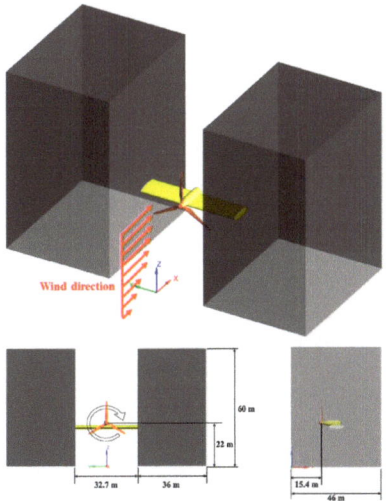

Figure 13. Configuration of the 110-kW wind turbine and buildings with a sky bridge studied in [63].

A similar study by Chaudhry et al. [64] also used CFD to analyse the efficiency of BAWT but focused on the shape or structural morphology of the building. The performance of the turbines integrated into buildings with triangular, square and circular cross-sections (see Figure 14) was analysed and compared with a benchmark model which was based on the Bahrain Trade Centre. Based on the simulated conditions, the results showed that the circular building shape was the most effective orientation, particularly in the areas with a dominant wind direction. Wang et al. [65] established the relationship between potential of wind energy and two perpendicular building configurations (converging and diverging) by conducting CFD analysis. The results showed that, in a converging configuration, the wind energy potential at the rooftop normally increased when the corner separation became bigger, while in a separating configuration, it decreased gradually with corner enlargement. Veena et al. [66] conducted research on the optimal sitting of wind turbines with high rise buildings using CFD simulations. Two configurations were compared: wind turbines in between twin towers and building with roof top wind turbines. The use of realistic wind profiles gathered from a weather projection model was the focus of the study. Results have shown that for a standalone high-rise building, there was a substantial fraction on which winds were enough to be used in wind power production. In the case of twin buildings, WTs wind can be positioned also in between the buildings and not only at the roof top. The velocity of 2 m/s can be achieved for a separation distance of fraction 0.2 and 2–2.8 m/s for 0.5.

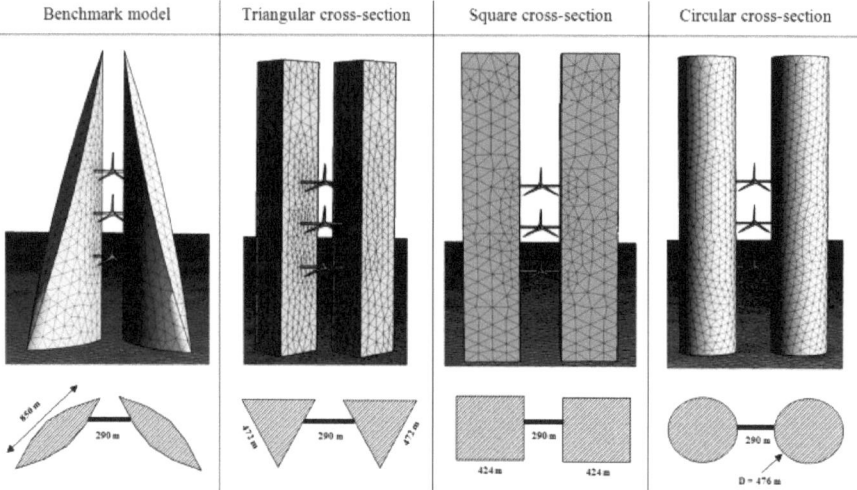

Figure 14. Integration of wind turbines into buildings with different shapes.

Locating a roof-mounted wind turbines where there is a significant separated zone will subject the WT to low wind velocity and positioning it where there is high turbulence intensity could cause early blade failure. Hence, CFD simulation of the wind flow around the building rooftop with wind turbines could help mitigate the issues during the early stages of the design. Ledo et al. [10] studied the wind flow characteristics around three typical suburban roof profiles including flat, pyramidal, pitched roofs.

The wind flow in such areas was simulated using CFD based on SST k-ω turbulence model and to search the most effective and efficient turbine place of installation. Findings showed that power outputs of WT installed on flat roofs were more consistent and with higher power as compared to some roof profiles. The work of Balduzzi et al. [55,67] presented a comprehensive CFD analysis of the suitability of rooftop installation of Darrieus wind. The effects of geometric proportion, roof shape, and building height on the performance were evaluated. Padmanabhan [68] used CFD to investigate the feasibility of wind turbines on an adjustable roof to increase power production and wind velocity of small WTs positioned in urban environments.

A CFD study was conducted by Abohela et al. [69,70] to investigate wind flow on top of six different roof shapes including vaulted, flat, gabled, wedged, domed, and pyramidal roofs, to identify the most efficient location of the WT and the most efficient roof shape for installing WTs, as shown in Figure 15. Results showed that the vaulted roof was the most effective roof shape as the WT generated 56% more electricity compared to a stand-alone WT at the exact place with similar flow settings. In contrary, the wedged roof showed the least accelerating effect on wind on top of it. The Tabrizi et al. [71] study also investigated the performance of a WT installation on a rooftop of a warehouse using CFD. The analysis also included the surrounding buildings to a radius of 200 m.

Although many studies [72–75] have shown that Large Eddy Simulation (LES) presents better agreement with experiments than RANS in particular when predicting the behaviour of the separated flows around buildings, its computational cost for modelling full scale geometries is very high. Hence RANS models are still widely used. Toja-Silva et al. [72] performed CFD simulations based on several RANS turbulence models of the airflow around different types of roof-mounted wind turbines (HAWT, VAWT and ducted). The focus was to replicate actual measurements data for both airflow velocity and turbulence kinetic energy around the roof of a building. The work provided guidelines on the optimum positioning of wind turbines on top of an isolated building model. Mohamed and Wood [73] modified the standard k-ε model by developing new formulation of the eddy viscosity and compared with previous modifications designed for stagnation regions around buildings. The results showed that the developed model provided more accurate k values and displayed comparable results for stream-wise mean velocity predicted by the SST model. Furthermore, combination of the developed model and eddy viscosity model provided the most accurate estimation of the velocities and turbulence. Many of the RANS models showed substantial over estimation of the k or normal stresses at the windward side of the building while other RANS models that accurately reproduced the windward side k or normal stresses showed significant under estimation of the k or normal stresses above the centre or leeward side of the building [74].

Toja-Silva et al. [75] expanded their work by studying the impact of roof solar panels on wind turbines. The solar panels were simulated with tilt angles of 10–30°. The study highlighted that the recirculation vortex among the upstream edge of the roof and the first array of solar panel had the highest velocity and the study recommended to position the Vertical Axis Wind Turbine in a horizontal position inside this vortex.

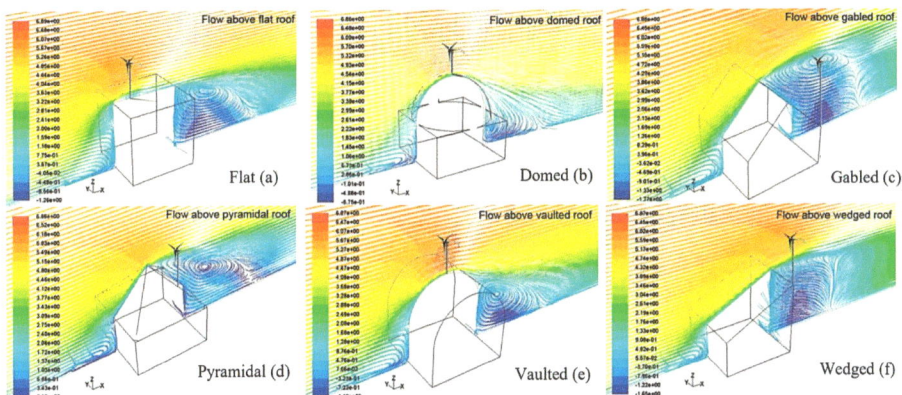

Figure 15. Vertical stream wise velocity path lines along the central plan for the investigated roof shapes [69].

Wang et al. [76] studied the effect of different forms (flat, trough, double-pitched, gable) of a canopy roof on the airflow over the roof and the potential wind energy generation using CFD simulation. The results showed that under the flat type canopy there is minimal amplification of wind energy amplification. The addition of an overhang to the upstream of the flat canopy slightly improved the wind concentration under the canopy, however, it was disadvantageous for the region above it (no concentration of wind). The trough configuration showed improved wind concentration compared to the flat type mainly under its canopy while the gable configuration mainly above its canopy. The double pitched type with a 20° pitch angle was found to be the best in terms of wind concentration.

CFD was used to evaluate the impacts of heights and simple house shapes on the air flow reaching wind turbines in the study of White and Wakes [77]. Municipal governments in New Zealand have authority to impose height of the building constraint in rural areas, including the WTs. Currently, there is no sufficient information to understand which height limitations may reduce wind resource use by small WTs placed in these areas. The study found that permitted structure height is not high, forcing either acceptance of sub-optimal turbine output or length planning consent process. Municipal governments can minimise the barriers to small wind turbine installation through taking taller towers into account, in the range of 15–20 m. This range is transferrable to all rural area, where a small number of small turbines are recognised for installation near dwellings.

Several studies focused on the impact of surrounding buildings on the performance of BIWT [78–82]. Zhou et al. [19] focused on finding the most efficient and effective design that could accelerate the speed of wind flow for wind turbines in low-rise residential buildings. Figure 16 shows an example of the wind amplification effect of the designed building shape in a sample building. According to the assessment between different building shapes and CFD assessment using Phoenics software, the building shape of composite prism can enable the harvesting of most of the wind power. The tested building shape was later tested in a simulated environment of a residential area in China. The long-term community system, local wind conditions, and the comfort level needed were all considered in the simulation model. The result of the study showed that using wind energy harvesting in low rise residential buildings by adopting the proposed building composite prism shape has a great potential.

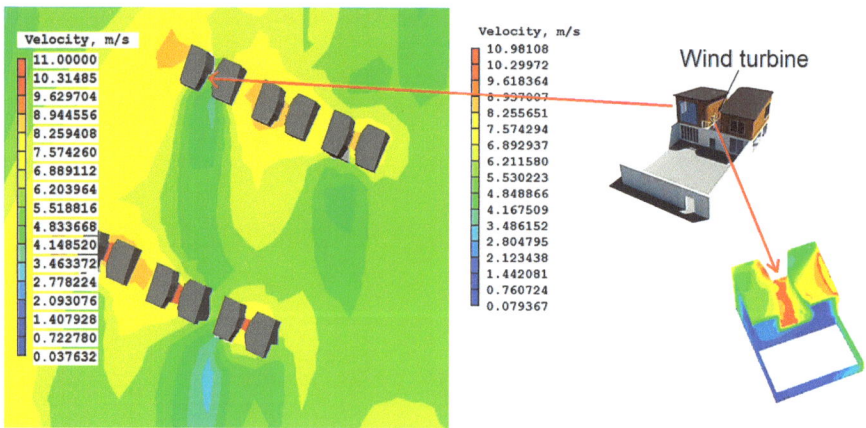

Figure 16. Wind amplification effect of the designed building shape in sample building(s) [19].

Micro sitting of wind turbines installed at the rooftop in an urban environment was investigated in Wang et al. [81] study using CFD simulation to analysed the wind turbulence behaviours on the Engineering and Technology Building (ETB) on campus according to the urban ABL inflow, and the outcomes were validated by lidar measurements. The micrositing method of roof mounted WT was developed based on the CFD simulations that contains accurate and preliminary micrositings.

The results suggested that the optimum installation height was 1.51–1.70 times theheight range of building and the best locations were at the front position where the acceleration of the wind reaches the maximum, as the wind direction changes. The methods proposed in this study could offer a viable schem for micrositing of WT installed at the rooftop in urban areas.

Sunderland et al. [6] presented two models which can consider issues such as wind velocity variation and how it affects the turbine and wind velocity variation which are entirely based on the standard deviation within successive 10-min time intervals and observed mean wind speed. These approaches were based on turbulence intensity, appreciation of the standards metric, and in conjunction with the power curve of a 2.5-kW WT. The first method was an adaptation of a model based on the initial results to measure the loss of power performance of turbines with the use of Gaussian probability distribution to stimulate turbulence. The second method overcomes these barriers by the novel application of the Weibull Distribution. The first and second models were assessed at suburban and urban locations in Ireland, where sonic anemometry was installed at around 1.5 times the standard height of the buildings at particular areas. According to the results of the investigation, it was suggested that both methods can replicate this.

Yang et al. [82] developed an assessment methodology based on CFD to identify the potential mounting locations of WTs and calculate the generation while considering the impact of the local terrain. The CFD model was validated with field experiments and the results of the realisable k-ε model agreed well with the experimental data. The authors highlighted the difference between the method they proposed and those recommended in the literature which had flaws in offering optimum mounting locations in small-scale environments.

Several authors [83,84] explored the potential of unconventional methods of incorporation of wind energy systems into the built environment. Park et al. [83] proposed and assessed a BIWT systems incorporated into the building façade which combines a series of guide vanes to re-direct and accelerate the wind into a rotor. The work used CFD to simulate and optimise the system configuration which was also validated by scaled experiments. The results showed that the system can accelerate the wind velocity to satisfactory levels and, therefore, increases power production. Hassanli et al. [84] used CFD modelling to assess the characteristics of the flow in a Double-Skin Façade (DSF) system with openings for harvesting wind energy in high rise buildings. The model was assessed with wind tunnel experiments and a good agreement was found between the results (15% discrepancy). The results showed that the uniformity of the flow improved while the turbulence progressively decays as the flow progressed through the DSF cavity.

Table 2 summarises the different CFD studies on building integrated wind turbines in urban areas. The studies highlighted the complex wind conditions in urban areas which presents major challenges for the installation of WTs. The wind conditions in urban locations are very complex due to surface roughness and the presence of obstacles, i.e., buildings and structures, characterised with low wind speed and high turbulence which are not desirable with regards to power generation by wind turbines. Also, there is uncertainty and limited understanding regarding how the turbulence within urban areas affects the WT effectiveness. Several researchers have employed CFD modelling to establish the feasibility of roof- or building-integrated turbines. CFD was utilised to study how the wind flows on a building or a roof, the effect of the speed, direction and turbulence of flow and the interference effects of surrounding buildings or structures on the wind turbine. Many studies used CFD simulation on WTs integrated in a building to understand the wind flow around the building and use the result to optimise the positioning of the wind turbines and maximise the power generation. Similar to the small-scale wind turbines, many of the CFD studies used low order models and few investigations used models such as LES and Reynolds Stress Transport models.

Table 2. Wind Turbine Assessment—Building Mounted Wind Turbine.

Author	Type/Integration	Number of WT	Capacity	Method/Tool	Key Findings
Ayhan and Saglam (2012)	Building mounted wind power systems	-	1.4 kW	FLUENT, 3D, standard k-ε	The typical Darrieus WT was not suitable as it was too noisy. Savonius WT rotor shortcoming was its low per power coefficient. Decreasing the design TSR and through using blade sweep, noise level can be reduced. Standard dimensions were 10–20% of the characteristic building height.
Heo et al. (2016)	Between two buildings	2	110 kW	CFX, URANS, 3D, SST k-ε	The aerodynamic power production of 110 kW wind turbine installed on a building was higher as compared to a stand-alone 110 kW WT because of the concentration effect caused by the wind speed acceleration between buildings. Moreover, this advantage showed in flow angle between −30 and 15°. Because of the fixed rotational direction of the WT, the effect of flow angle demonstrated asymmetric condition. It is also shown that to exceed Betz limit of 0.593 is possible by the effect of buildings similar to the ducts and shrouds.
Chaudhry et al. (2014)	Between two buildings	3	-	FLUENT RANS, 3D, standard k-ε	Results of the investigation showed that circular building morphology was the most effective buildingshape, specifically suitable to areas with a dominant prevailing wind direction.
Wang et al. (2015)	Between two buildings	2	-	FLUENT RANS, 3D, standard k-ε	The results demonstrated that in converging inlet mode, wind energy potential on the roof rises reasonably as the corner separation becomes larger, whereas in diverging inlet mode it reduces gradually with corner enlargement. When compared with isolated building, most of the corner configurations investigated demonstrated more wind energy density over the roof.
Veena et al. (2013)	WT on high rise buildings	3	-	Open FOAM, GAMBIT	Reattachment length decreases on increasing the separation distance. The highest velocity rate on the second building was almost similar to that of the first building for non-dimensional separation distance up to 0.2 while for greater separations, the velocity reduces to 75%.
Zhou et al. (2017)	Micro-wind utilisation in low-rise buildings	-	-	FLUENT, k-ε turbulence	The potential of applying wind energy in low-rise residential buildings is enormous through implementing the proposed building shape of composite prism. Results showed great potential for wind energy implementation in built environment.
Balduzzi 2012	Darrieus VAWT installed at the rooftop of a building	-	-	OpenFOAM, 2D, SIMPLE, Standard ke 3 turbulence	The study showed 70%notable increase of the capacity factor in the rooftop area of installation building can be reached it was reasonably higher compared to the surrounding buildings and optimum geometric proportions of the building itself with respect to its upwind building were achieved; if not, a continuous detriment of the potential energy was observed.
Tabrizi, 2014	Rooftop wind turbines	-	-	ANSYS CFX 14, WAsP	Analysis of the model demonstrated that the outcome was mainly sensitive to building height and shape, roof shape, turbine installation height and location, and wind direction.
Toja-Silva, 2015	HAWT, VAWT	-	-	OpenFOAM LES, RANS	The most practical areas to install HAWT were above z/0.1 H = 9 from the roof surface upstream and above z/0.3 H = 1 downstream. It was suggested to incline the HAWT by 5° downwards at the upstream region below z/0.3 H = 1. The application of VAWT was suggested below these heights. The VAWT installation in horizontal position at the central-upstream area near to the roof surface was also taken into consideration, to make use of the recirculation of the flow.

Table 2. *Cont.*

Author	Type/Integration	Number of WT	Capacity	Method/Tool	Key Findings
White and Wakes (2014)	Small wind-turbine to be installed on a tower	-	-	FLUENT	The existing permitted structure heights are not sufficiently high, hence lengthy planning consent processes and acceptance of sub-optimal turbine output were still needed. It was suggested that the Municipal councils in New Zealand may decrease barriers to small wind-turbine installations by considering taller towers, in the 15–20 m range, acceptable.
Wang et al. (2018)	Roof mounting wind turbine	1	-	FLUENT, k-ε turbulence, SIMPLEC	Optimal installation height is from 1.51 to 1.79 times the height of building and the best locations are at the forefront where the wind acceleration reaches its highest point, as the wind direction varies.
Ledo et al., 2011	Building-integrated micro-wind turbines	-	-	FLUENT	The study demonstrated how the wind flow features are highly dependent on the shape of the roofs. It was seen that turbines integrated on flat roofs are possibly to produce higher and more steady power for the similar turbine hub elevation than the other roof shapes.
Abohela et al. (2011)	Roof Mounted Wind Turbine	1	-	FLUENT 12.1, 3D, RANS, k-ε turbulence.	The vaulted roof was the optimum roof shape for wind turbines installed on the rooftop as the WT would generate 56% higher electricity compared to stand alone WT in the similar places under similar flow situations. Whereas the wedged roof showed least performance with regards to the accelerating effect on wind above it.
Toja-Silva et al. (2013)	BAWT, HAWT, VAWT	-	-	ANSYS FLUENT, 2D	The results demonstrated that HAWT had better performance in flat-terrain installations, while in high-density building surroundings, the dominance of VAWT was shown.
Yang et al. (2016)	VAWT	-	-	ANSYS/Fluent, 3D, RANS, k-ε model	The high-rise buildings in the upstream direction of the investigated area have a tendency to block the incoming wind and create greater turbulence intensity on specific areas of the objective building. It was seen to be promising to increase the hub height and place micro turbines on the windward side of the building to obtain greater wind power production.
Park et al. (2015)	Facade-integrated wind turbine (BIWT)	-	0.248 kWh/day for a year	SIMPLE, Navier-Stokes, 2D/Steady, k-omega (Standard), SIMPLE	It was seen from performance assessment that the model with the guide vane design and rotor for the Building Integrated Wind Turbine system accelerated the wind velocity to a satisfactory level and therefore enhances the power coefficient considerably. It was proven that the recommended configuration was promising for the sustainable and renewable energy production for urban areas.
Hassanli et al. (2017)	Small-scale wind turbines installed on a building-high with double Skin Façade, VAWT and VAWT	-	-	FLUENT, SST-SAS, k-ω is, Eddy-viscosity, defaults to a URANS	The flow became more uniform while the turbulence gradually declines as flow develops through the cavity for all wind directions. Therefore, the areas in the middle of the leading and trailing sides of the cavity were promising locations for installing small-scale, building-mounted wind turbines. Also, the DSF system with a strategic opening can efficiently improve the flow within the cavity for a wide-ranging incident wind angles and can be used for wind energy harvesting purposes.

4. Large Scale

The primary aim of a wind farm is to maximise energy production and at the same time reduce the cost. Power generation of a wind farm is reliant on the wind speed, which is reliant on atmospheric conditions, terrain landscape, and upstream wakes of the turbine. The loss of power production because of the wake intervention of upstream wind turbines, namely wake losses can reduce the yearly energy production of a wind farm by 10–20% [85,86]. CFD simulation is an important tool in wind farm layout optimisation and allows the examination of potential wind turbine sites to be carried out in advance [86]. CFD models such as actuator disk and line have been developed to simulate complex wake phenomena and their interactions with terrain. For the actuator disk and line approach, the modelling of the turbine is carried out by imposing aerodynamic forces through a disk representative of the rotor or lines representative of the blades. A more accurate simulation of the aerodynamic effects is the direct blade modelling approach [87] in which the geometry of the wind turbine is incorporated into the domain. However, these simulations are computationally expensive and must be used sparingly during the wind farm optimisation process. Studies on detailed wind farm-ABL simulation and turbine-wake interactions based on LES have increased over the years. While it is computationally expensive for LES to resolve all the complete flow physics in wind farm simulations, such as the blade boundary layers, it does lead to quite accurate predictions of wakes. However, LES modelling of wind farms involves extensive computational times (several hours to days for a single condition) and, hence, require super-computing. Hence, LES models are not useful for the purpose of wind farm layout optimisation.

Traditionally, wind farm layout is designed based on simple rules that lead to regular, straight-lined layouts, where turbines are often organised in identical rows and separated by a large distance. It is a very challenging task to have several design objectives and constraints due to multiple wake phenomena. Many researches have reported that irregular layouts result in a higher expected energy production than regular grids [86]. There are three main issues that are vital for the wake behaviour, these include the yaw angle, energy extraction, and atmospheric stratification. During evaluations and generalisations of models, knowledge of the behaviour of full-scale turbines plays a significant factor. The blade's design will create a specific wake that will be unique for every turbine, so the momentum transport in the wake will also be unique. Examinations of the near wake of full-scale turbines are important to simplify the results from far wake measurements on these devices [88].

The cost of onshore wind turbine energy production is amongst the lowest, although it is often positioned in complex terrains where there is uncertainty in terms of the available wind resources due to the surrounding topography [86]. Full-size turbines in a complex topography was studied by Castellani et al. [3] using CFD and experiments. The aim of their research was to test the vibrations at the structure and drive train level. Figure 17 demonstrates the inter-turbine distance and layout of the sub-cluster in in the study. The data was gathered through the on-board situation examining system were assessed and considering wind situations and working constraints gathered by the supervisory control and data acquisition (SCADA) [89,90]. CFD simulation was used, which allowed for better interpretation of the vibration assessment. The most important result was the interpretation of how wakes and flow turbulences appear in the vibration signals, at the structural and drive train levels. Hence, this wind to gear system created links among flow and mechanical phenomena in the aspect of vibrations, indicating an important tool for analysing loads in various working conditions. In another study, Castellani et al. [91] investigated the combined impact of wakes and terrain-driven flow on the performance of WT. The subcluster of four turbines in a very complex terrain was evaluated through CFD simulations and experimental SCADA data mining. Researchers within the Project Wakebench developed a framework for the evaluation of wind farm flow models operating at the micro-scale level. The study [92,93] highlighted the verification and validation method applied to wake models of wind farm including benchmarking and data processing methods for SCADA datasets.

The neutral atmospheric and wind turbine wind flow over complex terrain were examined by Makridis and Chick [94] using CFD Fluent software. An actuator disc model built based on the BEM

Theory was used for the model of the rotor effects. The 3D RANS calculations with RSM was used to investigate the atmospheric turbulence. The results have shown that predicted wake deficit was in good agreement with the measurements at hub height. Also, few discrepancies were shown in the vertical velocity deficit profile, it is due to the CFD model overestimating the wake deficit above the turbine axis by the maximum 17.5% and underestimated near the ground by a maximum of 30%. Wake turbulence was also over predicted by 13% to 14% close to the wake centerline by 2.5 and 4D downwind, and 20–23% at 6D and 7.5 downwind.

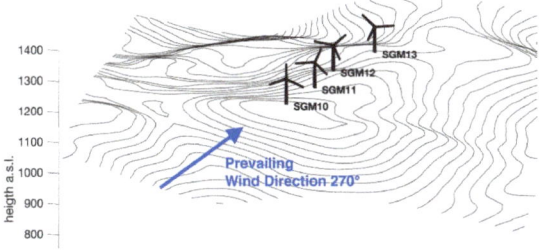

Figure 17. The layout and the inter-turbine distance of the sub-cluster investigated [3].

Yan and Li [95] proposed an integrated CFD/on-site measurement-based method to simulate the spatial changes of wind velocity for different areas with complex terrains. Figure 18 shows the methodology for potential wind energy assessment. The wind resource assessment involved statistical analysis, CFD simulations and on-site measurement. Also, a case study on wind resource assessment for an offshore island with complex terrain structures was equipped with anemometers for long-term wind measurement was implemented. A detailed wind resource map of the offshore island was achieved over the wind data from a single measurement site coupled with the simulations and showed a great use for future wind farm sitting and turbine micro-sitting.

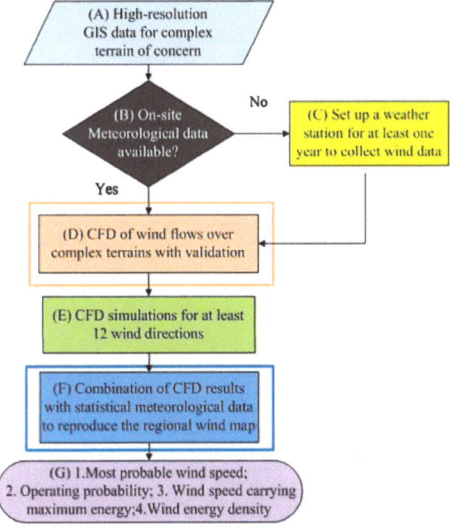

Figure 18. The methodology used for potential wind energy assessment with coupled CFD/on-site measurement [95].

The study of Nedjari et al. [96] focused on the WT wake evolution in a wind farm over complex and flat topography. The aerodynamic, nonlinear interaction among the wind farm terrain and rotor wake was modelled using the Hybrid technique and CFD with the actuator disk model. The initial CFD calculations were carried out for flat topography by changing the WT hub height. For the second arrangement concerning the complex terrain, the suggested hybrid technique was adapted to local wind field greatly disturbed by the topography singularities. The flow field gathered at the hub level was analysed and applied to define the corresponding actuator disk model. The results gathered from different cases provided remarkable information about wind farm layout.

Kuo et al. [84] proposed an algorithm that combines mixed-integer programming (MIP) and Computational Fluid Dynamics (CFD) to optimise wind farm layouts for complex topographies. The MIP solvers' ability to search solutions was essential for capturing the effects of optimised wake deficit projections on the quality of wind farm layout solutions. The recommended algorithm was used on a wind farm area in Canada. The results have shown that the proposed algorithm can produce great layouts in complex terrains.

Wang et al. [97] proposed a novel computational optimisation strategy to take into account the effect of wind velocity differences on irregular land plot boundary and non-flat terrain (Figure 19). The irregular boundaries were addressed over a novel constraint handling strategy in an open coordinated optimisation formulation. While the standard analytical wake simulations were improved through a wind multiplier, gathered from the simulation software, to account for the effect of variations in altitude. This approach was used for actual wind farms with great different altitude: The Grasmere, Albany and Gokceada Island wind farm. The Grasmere and Albany wind farm demonstrated less reduction in cost of energy on conventional optimisation. This inconsistency can be attributed to the wind behaviour in each site. While the augmented Gokceada wind farm layout showed significant reduction of energy cost when topography was taken into consideration. The Gokceada wind farm has a steady wind direction and the optimisation may use topography to prevent wake interactions. In contrast, the Grasmere and Albany wind farm with unsteady wind directions shows no clear strategy to get rid of wakes when using topography. As a result, this shows that recognising wind farm topography can produce great advantages and the wake interactions can significantly decrease by positioning the wind turbines carefully where strong narrow wind direction is present.

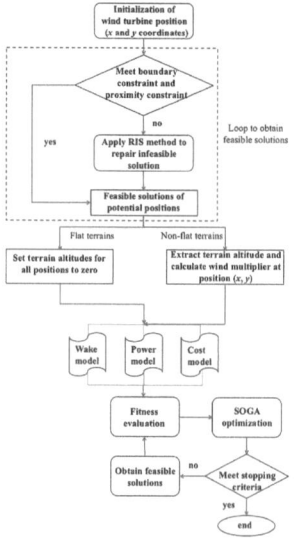

Figure 19. The optimisation process of wind farm layout in flat and non-flat terrains recommended by [97].

The work of Dhunny et al. [98] investigated the mean wind power predicted through the WindSim tool with on-site computation from nine meteorological positions all over a very complex topography at various heights. The research focused on in depth examination of different computational parameters such as the turbulence models, grid dependency test, the order of the Standard k-ε, k-ε with Yap corrections, RNG k-ε and Modified k-ε and the iterative convergence standards. The results have proven that WindSim is an effective tool to investigate the wind flow in a very complex topography with acceptable accuracy. The model was employed to investigate feasibility of major wind farm hot spots in Mauritius. The tool produced wind maps at various heights which can be applied in the process of farm decision making.

Akin and Kara [99] investigated the potential of wind power in the coastal region in Turkey. The study focused on searching for the feasible location for installing the wind power plants in the shore of Turkey. In order to convince the policy makers and investors for developing wind potential of the area, a wind power plant feasibility research for Gemlik area linked to Bursa was shown through using WindSim CFD tool. The annual production of energy and capacity factor measured, and power and energy curves of chosen wind turbines were obtained as output. The findings showed that through using Vestas V90 WTs in Gemlik Narki area, institution of an economic wind power plant that has forty gigawatt hours per year annual energy production volume was viable.

Troldborg et al. [100] assessed the wake interaction among two turbines in various inflow situations with the actuator line strategy and full Navier–Stokes equation calculations. The work compared the results for changing distances among the WTs. Moreover, simulations were used at various degrees of ambient turbulence intensity presenting laminar, onshore, and offshore situations. The results showed a complicated wake interaction process in which the individual wakes initially were visible with the mixed wake structure, however, further downstream effects were created into what was recognised as a single far wake where the axial velocity follows a nearly Gaussian shape. Therefore, the simulations showed potential in providing more understanding about the wake interaction phenomenon and in what way it affects the exterior aerodynamic loads on WTs.

Schulz et al. [101] investigated various methods of incorporating a WT including the nacelle, hub, fully meshed blades and tower in a complex topography area as shown in Figure 20. The research focused on the challenges of meshing the WT in a complex terrain and how to overcome them. The simulation process started with a benchmark flat terrain model with uniform flow and then was increasingly made complex by increasing atmospheric turbulence to a model of a spinning three-dimensional WT. The complex terrain showed three major effects including a mean wind speed increase and as a result load and power increase, a correlation between the inclination angle and load and power behaviour and increase of turbulence and consequently of load and power fluctuations.

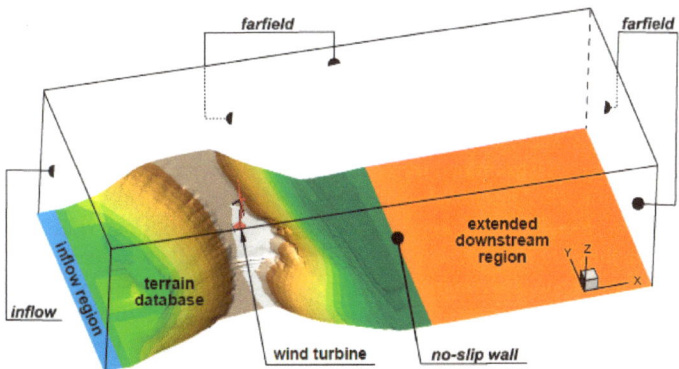

Figure 20. Computational domain of a wind turbine in a complex terrain [100].

Schmidt and Stoevesandt [102] examined the flow over several types of hill geometries using RANS CFD models. The results for every hill studied were transformed into numerical models that converted arbitrary uninterrupted inlet flow behaviour by rescaling the obstacle effects. The result of these models were analysed by comparing them to the full results of CFD; initially for the ABL flow and later a single WT wake in the presence of a hill. The incorporation of such models into the flapFOAM wind farm software was investigated, developing their inclusion to a complete modular wind farm layout optimisation procedure.

The effect of atmospheric stability on a WT wake was investigated numerically and experimentally in the study of Machefaux et al. [103]. The modelling was conducted using the actuator disk rotor and large eddy simulation. The model was validated using data obtained from full-size experiments based on pulsed lidar calculations of the wake flow ground of a stall with 500 kW WT and a reasonable agreement was observed between the results. A spectral tensor model with buoyancy effects was developed and employed to adapt turbulence interaction of the approaching wind flow to the thermal stratification. Discrepancies were studied for future model advancement.

Liu et al. [104] examined a wind farm in southwest China in a mountainous area using numerical CFD modelling. A newly developed actuator disk technique using rotor data which includes blade geometry data, pitch and attack angle was employed to examine the flow behaviour of the wind farm, specifically the developing wake beside the WTs. When comparing the in situ measurements and actuator disk technique, the newly developed actuator disk method demonstrated better agreement with the measurements. The results showed that the stable simulation integrated with optimised actuator disk method was capable of evaluating the wind resource very well and provided better balance among accuracy and efficiency compared to costly computation methods including actuator-line/actuator-surface transient models, or a less accurate approach including the linear velocity reduced wake model.

Politis et al. [105] used CFD methods to estimate the full wind farms production in complex topography and investigate the development and patterns of wake flow. The work used two types of solvers; in-house developed CRES–flowNS and FLUENT's CFDWake and CFD Navier–Stokes solvers to evaluate the large wind farm performance. Without any wind turbines, similar results were obtained from both models while significant variances increase when wind turbine modelling was presented. The prediction of CFD wake was satisfactory, although the method was only possible when the direction of wind is almost upright to the wind turbine rows. The CRES–flowNS employed two types of approximations for estimating the reference wind velocity which needs a single calculation for the full wind farm.

A study of wind farm layout optimisation on a Gaussian hill was presented in Feng and Shen [106] research. Jensen wake model and CFD simulation were combined and an RS algorithm was employed to optimise the power production of a wind farm, taking account of wind farm boundary restraint and minimal distance constraint among any two wind turbines. It was shown in the case study that the optimised approach had a promising performance in various conditions. While in practice, it is usual to apply an expert guess layout for improvement of a wind farm that is highly based on wind resource and not on appropriate wake modelling. This study concluded that layout development issues in complex topography must be examined through further realistic problem formulation and effective numerical computations. The Jensen Wake model also required further adjustments and validations.

Parada et al. [107] focused on the approach of designing highly efficient wind farms, which was further compared to different arrangements of standard arrayed layout considering a number of wind turbines and different spacing. This method maximises the wind farm power and efficiently integrates the use of real wind data and irregular terrain boundaries. It was found that standard arrayed wind farms were sub optimal and can produce high wake losses, especially for some wind directions. For this approach, 4.09% and 2.18% higher efficiencies were gathered compared to staggered and aligned layouts.

Table 3 summarises different CFD studies on the simulation and optimisation of large size WT and wind farms. The wind farm layout optimisation on terrains has been addressed by many studies through a number of strategies; but currently, optimising wind farm layouts on complex topographies is very difficult because of missing computationally manageable and accurate wake models to assess the wind farm layouts. CFD models such as actuator line and disk have been used to simulate the interaction with challenging topographies and wake occurrences although these methods are computationally expensive and must be used economically during the process of optimisation. Methods proposed for large wind farms were able to see wake width to a certain level and reduction of power output around the wind farm. In spite of few uncertainties, it showed a very promising approach which allows to consider the slowdown in large wind farms. It was also seen that simple methods of location assessment make it possible to remove estimations of the future WT behaviour. Complex topography conditions showed great effects such as turbulence increase and, as a result, load of power fluctuation, a mean wind speed increase and, consequently, power and load rise, and relation among the power behaviour and inclination angle. Moreover, the research about wind farm layouts obtained using guess methods from the experts were very different compared to the optimum ones that result in a great area of improvement for wind farm layout optimisation. The turbulence intensity and velocity behaviour depend on the complex terrain, which creates a more reliable experimental assessment important to validate the micrositing layout. The losses of power production due to the wake effects simply reach 20% of the overall power. The turbulence and atmospheric inflow turbulence produced in orographic variations and interaction among atmospheric turbulence and WT in the case of wind farm concerns. Further study in improving the novel approach for Wind Farm Layout coupled with mathematical programming with CFD simulations of the wake behaviour is necessary to examine the scalability of the algorithm to greater issues concerning wind farms with more potential wind turbine sites.

Table 3. Wind Turbine Assessment—Large Scale Wind Turbine.

Author	Type	No of WT	Capacity	Tool/Method	Key Findings
Da-Costa et al. (2006)	Wind farm within forests	-	-	WAsP, RANS, LES, k-ε	The existence of the canopy may increase the levels of turbulence by almost 2 levels of magnitude, when compared to the outcome gathered without the model of canopy.
Castellani et al. (2017)	Full-scale wind turbines working in a complex topography	4	-	WindSim, RANS, LES	The main purpose of the study is to interpret in what way flow turbulences and wakes appeared in the vibration signals, both at the drive-train and structural level. Hence, this method creates link among mechanical and flow occurrences formed through vibrations, presenting a precious approach for calculating loads in various operating situations.
Palma et al. (2008)	Wind turbine micro-siting in complex terrain	3	-	WAsP	Gust factors and turbulence intensity showed to be unreliable estimators and highly dependent on sampling level and mean time period. Despite of great variances among the average wind speed at each of the 5 areas, the field measurements at one location, after appropriate investigations, added to the confidence in results and improved knowledge of the field of wind flow.
Makridis and Chick (2013)	Wind turbine wakes with terrain effects	1	-	WAsP, Fluent, VBM	The assessment of stream wise variations of turbulence and speed demonstrated a better agreement for both the downstream and upstream of the hilltop; the only main discrepancies were an underestimation of the velocity increase at the hilltop which was approximately 13% and an under prediction of the turbulence power at a hill around the lee side which was approximately 35%.
Yan and Li (2016)	Wake effects of wind turbines	-	-	LES, WAsP, RANS, Navier-Stokes	The clear characteristics of the wind potential distribution was altitude-dependent and thus more wind energy was anticipated to be harvested with the rising elevation.
Nedjari et al. (2017)	Wind turbine wake growth in farm over flat and complex topography	-	2 MW horizontal axis wind turbine	FLUENT, RANS, 2D, 3D	The wind turbine design including the rotor diameter and mast height applied in the wake ground interaction showed to be an important factor to be considered when identifying the optimum distance in a wind farm. The effects of the terrain on the wake were decreased at the top hub level with symmetrical wake sizes downstream the rotor.
Kuo et al. (2016)	Wind farm layout optimisation on complex topographies	-	-	LES, RANS	Incorporating a CFD wake model with mixed-integer programming demonstrated that it can produce optimum layouts in complex terrains.
Wang et al. (2017)	Wind farm layout	-	Flat terrain 10.2–11.8 MW Non-flat terrain 10.3–11.9 MW	FLUENT, Wind Multiplier, RIS	Consideration of wind farm topography can generate important advantages and the wake interactions can be highly decreased by carefully positioning of wind turbines in the situations where a narrow wind direction was dominant.
Dhunny et al. (2017)	Wind farm for a highly complex terrain	-	1500–2500 MWh/m²/year at 110 m	WindSim, CDS, Standard k-ε, k-ε with Yap corrections, RNG k-ε and Modified k-ε	The WindSim was an ideal software to investigate the flow of the wind on a very complex topography like in the studied locations in Mauritius with reasonable accuracy. Topographical distribution of seasonal wind velocity was highly affected by the local topography.
Li et al. (2016)	Wind Turbine Operation with Low Roughness Topography	-	-	Fluent, GAMBIT, 3D, SST k-ω turbulence, SIMPLIC	The wind-turbine wakes improved the vertical mixing, resulting in changes to the flow. As compared to the original velocity distribution, the wind speed decreased rapidly when passing the wind turbine and then rising slowly, however it still cannot achieve the initial speed at 17 rotor diameters. The distribution of the turbulent kinetic energy after the wind turbines was a bit diverse, particularly at top-tip level near the wind turbines. The turbulent kinetic energy behind the turbine rises rapidly, and later decreases with the extension of the downstream.

Table 3. *Cont.*

Author	Type	No of WT	Capacity	Tool/Method	Key Findings
Tromeur et al. (2016)	Wind Turbine model in a large wind farm	-	-	WindFarmer, ECN-Wakefar, WAsP, NTUA, Meteodyn WT, k-ε	All the proposed large wind farm models had the ability to capture width of the wake to a degree and the reduced power output moving through the wind farm. In spite of uncertainties, this promising model integration allows to take into account the slowdown in large wind farms.
Schulz et al. (2014)	Wind turbine in Complex Topography in Atmospheric Inflow Situations	-	-	FLOWer,3D, DES, BEM	The complex terrain condition showed overall three main effects including the rise of turbulence and subsequently of load and power variations, mean wind speed increase and as a result load and power increase, and a correlation among the load and power behaviour and inclination angle.
Schmidt and Stoevesandt (2014)	Wind farm layout optimisation in complex terrain	64	2.5 MW nominal power	OpenFOAM, RANS, FLAPROAM, k-ε EKM	The positioning of turbines was highly constraint for real-life on-shore developments. However, optimisation codes can provide vital input during the design phase, particularly for complex terrain locations where the optimum layout may not always be obvious.
Liu et al. (2017)	Onshore wind farm in Southwest China	33 site,	1.5 MW of assessed power	FLUENT, RANS, SST k-ω	Stable CFD model with improved actuator disk technique was capable of examining wind resource well and provide better balance among calculating accuracy and efficiency, in contrary to more expensive computation methods including actuator-surface/actuator-line transient model, or fewer accurate approaches including linear speed reduction wake model.
Feng and Shen (2014)	Wind farm layout optimisation in complex terrain	25–30	17.76 19.28 17.76 19.28 MW	WAsP, LES, EllipSys3D	Wind farm layouts obtained using experts guess methods were very different compared to the optimum ones that result in great area of improvement for wind farm layout optimisation. Random Search algorithm showed many good features including effectiveness in developing primary layouts in several situations, robust in multiple runs.

5. Summary and Conclusions

Wind power is one of the most rapidly growing renewable sources of energy and with the decreasing costs due to advancements in technology and manufacturing, the rising concerns over energy security and environmental issues, the trend is expected to continue. CFD modelling has been widely used by several researchers to predict the wind energy systems' performance over the last few decades. With the growing computing capacity of modern computers, CFD modelling became a significant tool to numerically investigate the wind flow within the investigated site conditions. As a result, tools and methods to measure and optimise the performance of new innovative sources of wind energy must also continue to advance. Current developments in wind turbines using CFD simulation have shown progress from flow modelling of flow around two-dimensional aerofoils to ABL flow by wind turbine arrangements or wind farms.

This paper reviewed recently published studies (2010–2018) on CFD simulations of micro to small wind turbines, buildings integrated with wind turbines, and wind turbines positioned in a wind farm. Guidelines and recommendations were investigated for numerical schemes and algorithms, computational domain size, turbulence modelling, and spatial and temporal discretisation. Current development of CFD simulation of wind turbine systems and different variables affecting its performance such as wind turbine wake interaction in wind farms, blade profile, augmentation using guide vanes, dynamic stall control and self-starting characteristics were discussed.

Although current CFD models already perform well in predicting and optimising the performance of small scale wind turbines (much better than simpler methods) the complex nature of turbulent flow means that continuous improvement of models would be an ongoing challenge. Several studies have highlighted the importance of CFD in accelerating the design process of small scale wind turbines and bringing down the overall cost of design. Different numerical models were developed over the years to accurately predict the aerodynamic performance of small scale wind turbines. Many of the CFD studies used low order models including SST k-ω, k-epsilon, or Spalart–Allmaras models and few investigations used models such as LES, DES and Reynolds Stress Transport models. Complexity and computational cost are still noted as the main obstacles when using high-fidelity models, hence, RANS models are still widely used. For the simulation of wind turbine in buildings, many of the RANS models showed substantial over estimation of the k or normal stresses at the windward side of the building while other RANS models that accurately reproduced the windward side k or normal stresses showed significant under estimation of the k or normal stresses above the centre or leeward side of the building. More research should also be focused on conducting and validating unsteady and transient simulations of wind turbines which also requires additional computational effort.

Studies have shown that the integration of CFD modelling with other tools such as wind tunnel or field measurements could provide a solution for the assessment of wind power in complex conditions. Combining CFD with other tools like blade element momentum has also proved effective for investigating the wind turbine performance. Most of the micro to small wind turbine used the traditional BEM theory for designing the blades and computing the forces acting on it. Complex conditions, specifically in urban areas, present great challenges for the installation of small turbines. The wind conditions in urban locations are very complex due to surface roughness and the presence of obstacles i.e., buildings and structures, characterised with low wind speed and high turbulence which are not desirable with regards to power generation by wind turbines. Also, there is uncertainty and lack of understanding regarding how turbulence under urban areas which contribute to the effectiveness of the wind turbine. Several researchers have employed CFD modelling to establish the feasibility of roof- or building-integrated wind turbines. CFD was utilised to examine the effect of the speed, direction and turbulence of wind flow and the interference of surrounding buildings or structures on the wind turbine's performance. Although many studies have shown that Large Eddy Simulation (LES) presents better agreement with experiments than RANS when predicting the behaviour of the separated flows around buildings, its computational cost for modelling full scale geometries is very high. Hence, RANS models are still widely used. Many of the RANS models showed substantial over estimation of the turbulence kinetic energy or normal stresses at the windward side of the building while other RANS models that accurately reproduced the windward side turbulence kinetic energy or normal stresses showed significant under estimation of the k or normal stresses above the centre or leeward side of the building. More research should also be focused on conducting and validating unsteady and transient simulations of wind turbines which also requires additional computational effort. The lack of available experimental data for wind turbines installed in urban areas makes it difficult to validate the CFD modelling and compare the viability of different BIWT. Although some small-scale wind turbines already show good results, it should be further optimised for urban applications. Power augmentation concepts around standard wind turbines promise performance increase and, hence, should be further investigated. Furthermore, more research should be focused on the noise output of small scale wind turbines. Several studies have employed CFD to predict the turbulent flow field in combination with analytical methods to predict the noise generation by a wind turbine.

Methods proposed for large wind farms were capable of capturing wake width to some level and reduction of power production within the wind farm. In spite of few uncertainties, it showed a very promising approach which allows to consider the slowdown in large wind farms. It was also been seen that simple methods of location assessment make it possible to extract estimations on later behaviour of the turbines. The complex topography conditions showed main effects such as turbulence intensity increase and as a result load of power fluctuation, a mean wind speed increase and consequently power and load rise, and connection among angle of inclination and power behaviour. Moreover, research about the layouts gathered using expert guess methods were far from the optimal ones, which leaves large areas of improvement for wind farm layout optimisation. The turbulence intensity and velocity profiles vary over the complex terrain, which makes an accurate experimental assessment important to validate the micrositing layout.

The optimisation of wind farms using CFD has received much attention in the literature. The wind farm layout optimisation on terrains has been addressed by many works through a number of strategies; but currently, optimising wind farm layouts in a complex topography is complicated because of the absence of tractable computations and accurate wake simulations to assess wind farm layouts. CFD models such as actuator line and actuator disk have been developed to investigate the interaction with complex terrains and wake occurrences though these methods are computationally expensive and must be used economically during the process of optimisation. Studies on detailed wind farm-ABL simulation and turbine-wake interactions based on LES have increased over the years. While it is computationally expensive for LES to resolve all the complete flow physics in wind farm simulations, it does lead to accurate predictions of wakes. However, LES modelling of wind farms involves extensive computational times (several hours to days for a single condition) and hence, require super-computing. Hence, LES models are not useful for the purpose of wind farm layout optimisation. However, as computing resource and power increase and as wind turbine modelling further develops, it is expected that LES will become more feasible and continue its transition from academic environment towards the wind industry and research and development laboratories. With improved and more accurate tools, operators of wind farms will maximise their investments, optimally design wind turbines and minimise the upstream turbines' turbulent wakes.

Future research on the CFD modelling of wind turbines and wind farms should quantify the computational uncertainties associated with the predictions, which is not only a result of errors with discretisation and turbulence modelling but the variables, assumptions and set boundary conditions such as the blade and topography geometry, atmospheric inflow, stratification, etc. This would enable the fair comparison with experiments and show the areas that require improvement. Furthermore, future work should provide more details on the required computational cost for the different optimisation methods and wind farm dimensions. In addition, more research should be focused on the calculation of the energy production of wind farms in complex terrains.

Author Contributions: All the authors have contributed extensively to the presented investigation. K.C. conducted a comprehensive literature review on small scale and building scale wind turbines and participated in writing. A.A. and F.J. conducted the comprehensive literature review of large scale wind farms and participated in writing. P.N., B.R.H. and J.K.C. participated in the writing of the review.

Conflicts of Interest: The authors declare no conflict of interest.

Abbreviations

ABL	Atmospheric Boundary Layer
ANN	Artificial Neural Network
BEM	Blade Element Momentum
BIWT	Building Integrated Wind Turbines
CFD	Computational Fluid Dynamic
GW	Gigawatt
DSF	Double-Skin Façade
HAWT	Horizontal Axis Wind Turbine
IEA	International Energy Agency
k-ε	k-epsilon
k-ω	k-omega
kW	Kilowatt
LES	Large Eddy Simulation
LLFV	Lifting Line Free Vortex
MRF	Multiple Reference Frame
RANS	Reynolds-averaged Navier–Stokes equations
RNG	Re-Normalisation Group
RSM	Reynolds stress model
SCADA	Supervisory Control and Data Acquisition
SST	Shear Stress Transport
TSR	Tip Speed Ratio
URANS	Unsteady Reynolds-averaged Navier–Stokes equations
VAWT	Vertical Axis Wind Turbine
WT	Wind Turbine
2D	Two-dimensional
3D	Three-dimensional

References

1. Global Wind Energy Council (CWEC). *Global Wind Report: Annual Market Update*; GWEC: Brussels, Belgium, 2014.
2. Gupta, R.K.; Warudkar, V.; Purohit, R.; Rajpurohit, S.S. Modeling and Aerodynamic Analysis of Small Scale, Mixed Airfoil Horizontal Axis Wind Turbine Blade. *Mater. Today Proc.* **2017**, *4*, 5370–5384. [CrossRef]
3. Castellani, F.; Marco, B.; Davide, A.; Gianluca, D.; Giorgio, D.; Terzi, L. Wind Turbine Loads Induced by Terrain and Wakes: An Experimental Study through Vibration Analysis and Computational Fluid Dynamics. *Energies* **2017**, *10*, 1839. [CrossRef]
4. Pieralli, S.; Ritter, M.; Odening, M. Efficiency of wind power production and its determinants. *Energy* **2015**, *90*, 429–438. [CrossRef]
5. Fletcher, T.M. *Wind Energy Engineering: A Handbook for Onshore and Offshore Wind Turbine*; Academic Press: London, UK, 2017.
6. Sunderland, K.; Woolmington, T.; Blackledge, J.; Conlon, M. Small wind turbines in turbulent (urban) environments: A consideration of normal and Weibull distributions for power prediction. *J. Wind Eng. Ind. Aerodyn.* **2013**, *121*, 70–81. [CrossRef]
7. Tummala, A.; Velamati, R.K.; Sinha, D.K.; Indraja, V.; Hari Krishna, V. A review on small scale wind turbines. *Renew. Sustain. Energy Rev.* **2016**, *56*, 1351–1371. [CrossRef]
8. Aquino, A.; Calautit, J.K.; Hughes, B.R. Urban Integration of Aeroelastic Belt for Low-Energy Wind Harvesting. *Energy Procedia* **2017**, *105*, 738–743. [CrossRef]

9. Chong, W.T.; Wong, K.H.; Wang, C.T.; Gwani, M.; Chu, Y.J.; Chia, W.C.; Poh, S.C. Cross-Axis-Wind-Turbine: A Complementary Design to Push the Limit of Wind Turbine Technology. *Energy Procedia* **2017**, *105*, 973–979. [CrossRef]

10. Ledo, L.; Kosasih, P.B.; Cooper, P. Roof mounting site analysis for micro-wind turbines. *Renew. Energy* **2011**, *36*, 1379–1391. [CrossRef]

11. Pearson, C. Vertical Axis Wind Turbine Acoustics. Ph.D. Thesis, Cambridge University Engineering Department, Cambridge, UK, 2014.

12. Knopper, L.D.; Ollson, C.A. Health effects and wind turbines: A review of the literature. *Environ. Health* **2011**, *10*, 78. [CrossRef] [PubMed]

13. Taylor, J.; Eastwick, C.; Lawrence, C.; Wilson, R. Noise levels and noise perception from small and micro wind turbines. *Renew. Energy* **2013**, *55*, 120–127. [CrossRef]

14. Lee, S.; Lee, S. Numerical and experimental study of aerodynamic noise by a small wind turbine. *Renew. Energy* **2014**, *65*, 108–112. [CrossRef]

15. Lombardi, L.; Mendecka, B.; Carnevale, E.; Wojciech, S. Environmental impacts of electricity production of micro wind turbines with vertical axis. *Renew. Energy* **2017**. [CrossRef]

16. Greening, B.; Azapagic, A. Environmental impacts of micro-wind turbines and their potential to contribute to UK climate change targets. *Energy* **2013**, *59*, 454–466. [CrossRef]

17. Carrete, M.; Sánchez-Zapata, J.A.; Benítez, J.R.; Lobón, M.; Donázar, J.A. Large scale risk-assessment of wind-farms on population viability of a globally endangered long-lived raptor. *Biol. Conserv.* **2009**, *142*, 2954–2961. [CrossRef]

18. Peacock, A.D.; Jenkins, D.; Ahadzi, M.; Berry, A.; Turan, S. Micro wind turbines in the UK domestic sector. *Energy Build.* **2008**, *40*, 1324–1333. [CrossRef]

19. Zhou, H.; Lu, Y.; Liu, X.; Chang, R.; Wang, B. Harvesting wind energy in low-rise residential buildings: Design and optimization of building forms. *J. Clean. Prod.* **2017**, *167*, 306–316. [CrossRef]

20. Aquino, A.; Calautit, J.K.; Hughes, B.R. Integration of aero-elastic belt into the built environment for low-energy wind harnessing: Current status and a case study. *Energy Convers. Manag.* **2017**, *149*, 830–850. [CrossRef]

21. Aquino, A.; Calautit, J.K.; Hughes, B.R. Evaluation of the integration of the Wind-Induced Flutter Energy Harvester (WIFEH) into the built environment: Experimental and numerical analysis. *Appl. Energy* **2017**, *207*, 61–77. [CrossRef]

22. Aquino, A.; Calautit, J.K.; Hughes, B.R. A Study on the Wind-Induced Flutter Energy Harvester (WIFEH) Integration into Buildings. *Energy Procedia* **2017**, *142*, 321–327. [CrossRef]

23. Chaudhry, H.N.; Calautit, J.K.; Hughes, B.R. Design and aerodynamic investigation of dynamic architecture. *Innov. Infrastruct. Solut.* **2016**, *1*, 7. [CrossRef]

24. Ayhan, D.; Sağlam, S. A technical review of building-mounted wind power systems and a sample simulation model. *Renew. Sustain. Energy Rev.* **2012**, *16*, 1040–1049. [CrossRef]

25. Department for Business, Energy & Industrial Strategy. *Energy and Climate Change: Evidence and Analysis*; BEIS: London, UK, 2013.

26. De-Santoli, L.; Albo, A.; Garcia, D.A.; Bruschi, D.; Cumo, F. A preliminary energy and environmental assessment of a micro wind turbine prototype in natural protected areas. *Sustain. Energy Technol. Assess.* **2014**, *8*, 42–56. [CrossRef]

27. El-Zahaby, A.; Kabeel, A.E.; Elsayed, S.S.; Obiaa, M.F. CFD analysis of flow fields for shrouded wind turbine's diffuser model with different flange angles. *Alexandra Eng. J.* **2017**, *56*, 171–179. [CrossRef]

28. Wang, Y.F.; Zhan, M.S. 3-Dimensional CFD simulation and analysis on performance of a micro-wind turbine resembling lotus in shape. *Energy Build.* **2013**, *65*, 66–74. [CrossRef]

29. Mohamed, M.H.; Ali, A.M.; Hafiz, A.A. CFD analysis for H-rotor Darrieus turbine as a low speed wind energy converter. *Eng. Sci. Technol. Int. J.* **2015**, *18*, 1–13. [CrossRef]

30. Mohamed, M.H. Performance investigation of H-rotor Darrieus turbine with new airfoil shapes. *Energy* **2012**, *47*, 522–530. [CrossRef]

31. Elkhoury, M.; Kiwata, T.; Aoun, E. Experimental and numerical investigation of a three-dimensional vertical-axis wind turbine with variable-pitch. *J. Wind Eng. Ind. Aerodyn.* **2015**, *139*, 111–123. [CrossRef]

32. Bausas, M.; Danao, L.A. The aerodynamics of a camber-bladed vertical axis wind turbine in unsteady wind. *Energy* **2015**, *93*, 1155–1164. [CrossRef]

33. Sengupta, A.R.; Biswas, A.; Gupta, R. Studies of some high solidity symmetrical and unsymmetrical blade H-Darrieus rotors with respect to starting characteristics, dynamic performances and flow physics in low wind streams. *Renew. Energy* **2016**, *93*, 536–554. [CrossRef]
34. Li, Q.; Maeda, T.; Kamada, Y.; Murata, J.; Kawabata, T.; Shimizu, K.; Ogasawara, T.; Nakai, A.; Kasuya, T. Wind tunnel and numerical study of a straight-bladed vertical axis wind turbine in three-dimensional analysis (Part I: For predicting aerodynamic loads and performance). *Energy* **2016**, *106*, 443–452. [CrossRef]
35. Li, Q.; Maeda, T.; Kamada, Y.; Murata, J.; Kawabata, T.; Shimizu, K.; Ogasawara, T.; Nakai, A.; Kasuya, T. Wind tunnel and numerical study of a straight-bladed Vertical Axis Wind Turbine in three-dimensional analysis (Part II: For predicting flow field and performance). *Energy* **2016**, *104*, 295–307. [CrossRef]
36. Abdalrahman, G.; Melek, W.; Lien, F.S. Pitch angle control for a small-scale Darrieus vertical axis wind turbine with straight blades (H-Type VAWT). *Renew. Energy* **2017**, *114*, 1353–1362. [CrossRef]
37. Howell, R.; Qin, N.; Edwards, J.; Durrani, N. Wind tunnel and numerical study of a small vertical axis wind turbine. *Renew. Energy* **2010**, *35*, 412–422. [CrossRef]
38. Stout, C.; Islam, S.; White, A.; Arnott, S.; Kollovozi, E.; Shaw, M.; Droubi, G.; Sinha, Y.; Bird, B. Efficiency Improvement of Vertical Axis Wind Turbines with an Upstream Deflector. *Energy Procedia* **2017**, *118*, 141–148. [CrossRef]
39. Arpino, F.; Cortellessa, G.; Dell-Isola, M.; Scungio, M.; Focanti, V.; Profili, M.; Rotondi, M. CFD simulations of power coefficients for an innovative Darrieus style vertical axis wind turbine with auxiliary straight blades. *J. Phys. Conf. Ser.* **2017**, *923*, 012036. [CrossRef]
40. Delafin, P.L.; Kolios, N.; Wang, L. Comparison of low-order aerodynamic models and RANS CFD for full scale 3D vertical axis wind turbines. *Renew. Energy* **2017**, *109*, 564–575. [CrossRef]
41. Rezaeiha, A.; Kalkman, I.; Blocken, B. CFD simulation of a vertical axis wind turbine operating at a moderate tip speed ratio: Guidelines for minimum domain size and azimuthal increment. *Renew. Energy* **2017**, *107*, 373–385. [CrossRef]
42. Klein, A.C.; Bartholomay, S.; Marten, D.; Lutz, T.; Pechlivanoglou, G.; Nayeri, C.N.; Paschereit, C.O.; Krämer, E. About the suitability of different numerical methods to reproduce model wind turbine measurements in a wind tunnel with high blockage ratio. *Wind Energy Sci.* **2017**. [CrossRef]
43. Chowdhury, A.M.; Akimoto, H.; Hara, Y. Comparative CFD analysis of Vertical Axis Wind Turbine in upright and tilted configuration. *Renew. Energy* **2016**, *85*, 327–337. [CrossRef]
44. Yang, Y.; Guo, Z.; Zhang, Y.; Ho, J.; Li, Q. Numerical Investigation of the Tip Vortex of a Straight-Bladed Vertical Axis Wind Turbine with Double-Blades. *Energies* **2017**, *10*, 1721. [CrossRef]
45. Botha, J.D.M.; Shahroki, A.; Rice, H. An implementation of an aeroacoustic prediction model for broadband noise from a vertical axis wind turbine using a CFD informed methodology. *J. Sound Vib.* **2017**, *410*, 389–415. [CrossRef]
46. Ghasemian, M.; Nejat, A. Aero-acoustics prediction of a vertical axis wind turbine using Large Eddy Simulation and acoustic analogy. *Energy* **2015**, *88*, 711–717. [CrossRef]
47. Wasala, S.; Storey, R.; Norris, S.; Cater, J. Aeroacoustic noise prediction for wind turbines using Large Eddy Simulation. *J. Wind Eng. Ind. Aerodyn.* **2015**, *145*, 17–29. [CrossRef]
48. Bremseth, J.; Duraisamy, K. Computational analysis of vertical axis wind turbine arrays Theory. *Comput. Fluid Dyn.* **2016**, *30*, 387–401. [CrossRef]
49. Dabiri, J. Potential order-of-magnitude enhancement of wind farm power density via counter-rotating vertical-axis wind turbine arrays. *J. Renew. Sustain. Energy* **2011**, *3*, 043104. [CrossRef]
50. Giorgetti, S.; Pellegrini, G.; Zanforlin, S. CFD Investigation on the Aerodynamic Interferences between Medium-solidity Darrieus Vertical Axis Wind Turbines. *Energy Procedia* **2015**, *81*, 227–239. [CrossRef]
51. Zanforlin, S.; Nishino, T. Fluid dynamic mechanisms of enhanced power generation by closely spaced vertical axis wind turbines. *Renew. Energy* **2016**, *99*, 1213–1226. [CrossRef]
52. Ghasemian, M.; Ashrafi, N.; Sedaghat, A. A review on computational fluid dynamic simulation techniques for Darrieus vertical axis wind turbines. *Energy Convers. Manag.* **2017**, *149*, 87–100. [CrossRef]
53. Li, Q.S.; Shu, Z.R.; Chen, F.B. Performance assessment of tall building-integrated wind turbines for power generation. *Appl. Energy* **2016**, *165*, 777–788. [CrossRef]
54. Cao, J.; Man, X.; Liu, J.; Liu, L.; Shui, T. Preliminary assessment of the wind power resource around the thousand-meter scale megatall building. *Energy Build.* **2017**, *142*, 62–71. [CrossRef]

55. Balduzzi, F.; Bianchini, A.; Carnevale, E.; Ferrari, L.; Magnani, S. Feasibility analysis of a Darrieus vertical-axis wind turbine installation in the rooftop of a building. *Appl. Energy* **2012**, *97*, 921–929. [CrossRef]

56. Walker, S.L. Building mounted wind turbines and their suitability for the urban scale—A review of methods of estimating urban wind resource. *Energy Build.* **2011**, *43*, 1852–1862. [CrossRef]

57. Neofytou, P.; Venetsanos, A.G.; Vlachogiannis, D.; Bartzis, J.G.; Scaperdas, A. CFD simulations of the wind environment around an airport terminal building. *Environ. Model. Softw.* **2006**, *21*, 520–524. [CrossRef]

58. Chaudhry, H.N.; Calautit, J.K.S.; Hughes, B.R. Computational Analysis to Factor Wind into the Design of an Architectural Environment. *Model. Simul. Eng.* **2015**, *2015*, 234601. [CrossRef]

59. Mithraratne, N. Roof-top wind turbines for microgeneration in urban houses in New Zealand. *Energy Build.* **2009**, *41*, 1013–1018. [CrossRef]

60. James, P.A.B.; Sissons, M.F.; Bradford, J.; Myers, L.E.; Bahaj, A.S.; Anwar, A.; Green, S. Implications of the UK field trial of building mounted horizontal axis micro-wind turbines. *Energy Policy* **2010**, *38*, 6130–6144. [CrossRef]

61. Sharpe, T.; Proven, G. Crossflex: Concept and early development of a true building integrated wind turbine. *Energy Build.* **2010**, *42*, 2365–2375. [CrossRef]

62. Petković, D.; Shamshirband, S.; Ćojbašić, Ž.; Nikolić, V.; Anuar, N.B.; Sabri, A.Q.M.; Akib, S. Adaptive neuro-fuzzy estimation of building augmentation of wind turbine power. *Comput. Fluids* **2014**, *97*, 188–194. [CrossRef]

63. Heo, Y.G.; Choi, N.K.; Choi, K.H.; Ji, H.S.; Kim, K.C. CFD study on aerodynamic power output of a 110 kW building augmented wind turbine. *Energy Build.* **2016**, *129*, 162–173. [CrossRef]

64. Chaudhry, H.N.; Calautit, J.K.S.; Hughes, B.R. The influence of structural morphology on the efficiency of building integrated wind turbines (BIWT). *AIMS Energy* **2014**, *2*, 219–236. [CrossRef]

65. Wang, B.; Cot, L.D.; Adolphe, L.; Geoffroy, S.; Morchain, J. Estimation of wind energy over roof of two perpendicular buildings. *Energy Build.* **2015**, *88*, 57–67. [CrossRef]

66. Veena, K.; Asha, V.; Shameem, C.A.; Venkatesh, T.N. CFD analysis for siting of wind turbines on high-rise buildings. *J. Phys. Conf. Ser.* **2017**, *822*, 012013. [CrossRef]

67. Balduzzi, F.; Bianchini, A.; Ferrari, L. Microeolic turbines in the built environment: Influence of the installation site on the potential energy yield. *Renew. Energy* **2012**, *45*, 163–174. [CrossRef]

68. Padmanabhan, K.K. Study on increasing wind power in buildings using TRIZ Tool in urban areas. *Energy Build.* **2013**, *61*, 344–348. [CrossRef]

69. Abohela, I.; Hamza, N.; Dudek, S. Effect of roof shape, wind direction, building height and urban configuration on the energy yield and positioning of roof mounted wind turbines. *Renew. Energy* **2013**, *50*, 1106–1118. [CrossRef]

70. Abohela, I.; Hamza, N.; Dudek, S. Effect of Roof Shape on Energy Yield and Positioning of Roof Mounted Wind Turbines. In Proceedings of the Building Simulation 2011, 12th Conference of International Building Performance Simulation Association, Sydney, Australia, 14–16 November 2011.

71. Tabrizi, A.B.; Whale, J.; Lyons, T.; Urmee, T. Performance and safety of rooftop wind turbines: Use of CFD to gain insight into inflow conditions. *Renew. Energy* **2014**, *67*, 242–251. [CrossRef]

72. Toja-Silva, F.; Peralta, C.; Lopez-Garcia, O.; Navarro, J.; Cruz, I. Roof region dependent wind potential assessment with different RANS turbulence models. *J. Wind Eng. Ind. Aerodyn.* **2015**, *142*, 258–271. [CrossRef]

73. Mohamed, M.A.; Wood, D.H. Modifications to Reynolds-averaged Navier–Stokes turbulence models for the wind flow over buildings. *Int. J. Sustain. Energy* **2017**, *36*, 225–241. [CrossRef]

74. Kono, T.; Kogaki, T.; Kiwata, T. Numerical Investigation of Wind Conditions for Roof-Mounted Wind Turbines: Effects of Wind Direction and Horizontal Aspect Ratio of a High-Rise Cuboid Building. *Energies* **2016**, *9*, 907. [CrossRef]

75. Toja-Silva, F.; Peralta, C.; Lopez-Garcia, O.; Navarro, J.; Cruz, I. Effect of roof-mounted solar panels on the wind energy exploitation on high-rise buildings. *J. Wind Eng. Ind. Aerodyn.* **2015**, *145*, 123–138. [CrossRef]

76. Wang, B.; Cot, L.D.; Adolphe, L.; Geoffroy, S. Estimation of wind energy of a building with canopy roof. *Sustain. Cities Soc.* **2017**, *35*, 402–416. [CrossRef]

77. White, L.V.; Wakes, S.J. Permitting best use of wind resource for small wind-turbines in rural New Zealand: A micro-scale CFD examination. *Energy Sustain. Dev.* **2014**, *21*, 1–6. [CrossRef]

78. Toja-Silva, F.; Colmenar-Santos, A.; Castro-Gil, M. Urban wind energy exploitation systems: Behaviour under multidirectional flow conditions—Opportunities and challenges. *Renew. Sustain. Energy Rev.* **2013**, *24*, 364–378. [CrossRef]

79. Ishugah, T.F.; Li, Y.; Wang, R.Z.; Kiplagat, J.K. Advances in wind energy resource exploitation in urban environment: A review. *Renew. Sustain. Energy Rev.* **2014**, *37*, 613–626. [CrossRef]

80. Wang, Q.; Wang, J.; Hou, Y.; Yuan, R.; Luo, K.; Fan, J. Micrositing of roof mounting wind turbine in urban environment: CFD simulations and lidar measurements. *Renew. Energy* **2018**, *115*, 1118–1133. [CrossRef]

81. Yang, A.S.; Su, Y.M.; Wen, C.Y.; Juan, Y.H.; Wang, W.S.; Cheng, C.H. Estimation of wind power generation in dense urban area. *Appl. Energy* **2016**, *171*, 213–230. [CrossRef]

82. Park, J.; Jung, H.J.; Lee, S.W.; Park, J. A New Building-Integrated Wind Turbine System Utilizing the Building. *Energies* **2015**, *8*, 11846–11870. [CrossRef]

83. Hassanli, S.; Hu, G.; Kwok, K.C.S.; Fletcher, D. Utilizing cavity flow within double skin façade for wind energy harvesting in buildings. *J. Wind Eng. Ind. Aerodyn.* **2017**, *167*, 114–127. [CrossRef]

84. Kuo, J.Y.J.; Romero, D.; Beck, J.; Amon, C. Wind farm layout optimization on complex terrains—Integrating a CFD wake model with mixed-integer programming. *Appl. Energy* **2016**, *178*, 404–414. [CrossRef]

85. Gaumond, M.; Réthoré, P.E.; Ott, S.; Pena, A.; Bechmann, A.; Hansen, K.S. Evaluation of the wind direction uncertainty and its impact on wake modeling at the Horns Rev offshore wind farm. *Wind Energy* **2014**, *17*, 1169–1178. [CrossRef]

86. Göçmen, T.; van der Laan, P.; Réthoré, P.; Diaz, A.P.; Larsen, G.; Ott, S. Wind turbine wake models developed at the technical university of Denmark: A review. *Renew. Sustain. Energy Rev.* **2016**, *60*, 752–769. [CrossRef]

87. Mo, J.; Choudhry, A.; Arjomandi, M.; Lee, Y. Large eddy simulation of the wind turbine wake characteristics in the numerical wind tunnel model. *J. Wind Eng. Ind. Aerodyn.* **2013**, *112*, 11–24. [CrossRef]

88. Da-Costa, L.; Castro, F.A.; Palma, J.M.L.M.; Stuart, P. Computer simulation of atmospheric flows over real forests for wind energy resource evaluation. *J. Wind Eng. Ind. Aerodyn.* **2006**, *94*, 603–620. [CrossRef]

89. Astolfi, D.; Castellani, F.; Terzi, L. A study of wind turbine wakes in complex terrain through RANS simulation and SCADA data. *J. Sol. Energy Eng.* **2018**, *140*, 031001. [CrossRef]

90. Castellani, F.; Astolfi, D.; Piccioni, E.; Terzi, L. Numerical and experimental methods for wake flow analysis in complex terrain. *J. Phys. Conf. Ser.* **2015**, *625*, 012042. [CrossRef]

91. Castellani, F.; Astolfi, D.; Mana, M.; Piccioni, E.; Becchetti, M.; Terzi, L. Investigation of terrain and wake effects on the performance of wind farms in complex terrain using numerical and experimental data. *Wind Energy* **2017**, *20*, 1277–1289.

92. Rodrigo, J.; Gancarski, P.; Arroyo, R.; Moriarty, P.; Chuchfield, M.; Naughton, J.; Hansen, K.; Machefaux, E.; Koblitz, T.; Maguire, E.; et al. IEA-Task 31 WAKEBENCH: Towards a protocol for wind farm flow model evaluation. Part 1: Flow-over-terrain models. *J. Phys. Conf. Ser.* **2014**, *524*, 012105. [CrossRef]

93. Moriarty, P.; Rodrigo, J.; Gancarski, P.; Chuchfield, M.; Naughton, J.; Hansen, K.; Machefaux, E.; Maguire, E.; Castellani, F.; Terzi, L.; et al. IEA-Task 31 WAKEBENCH: Towards a protocol for wind farm flow model evaluation. Part 2: Wind farm wake models. *J. Phys. Conf. Ser.* **2014**, *524*, 012185. [CrossRef]

94. Makridis, A.; Chick, J. Validation of a CFD model of wind turbine wakes with terrain effects. *J. Wind Eng. Ind. Aerodyn.* **2013**, *123*, 12–29. [CrossRef]

95. Yan, B.W.; Li, Q.S. Coupled on-site measurement/CFD based approach for high-resolution wind resource assessment over complex terrains. *Energy Convers. Manag.* **2016**, *117*, 351–366. [CrossRef]

96. Nedjari, H.D.; Guerri, O.; Saighi, M. CFD wind turbines wake assessment in complex topography. *Energy Convers. Manag.* **2017**, *138*, 224–236. [CrossRef]

97. Wang, L.; Cholette, M.; Tan, A.C.C.; Gu, Y. A computationally-efficient layout optimization method for real wind farms considering altitude variations. *Energy* **2017**, *132*, 147–159. [CrossRef]

98. Dhunny, A.Z.; Lollchund, M.R.; Rughooputh, S.D.D.V. Wind energy evaluation for a highly complex terrain using Computational Fluid Dynamics (CFD). *Renew. Energy* **2017**, *101*, 1–9. [CrossRef]

99. Akin, S.; Kara, Y. An Assessment of Wind Power Potential along the Coast of Bursa, Turkey: A Wind Power Plant Feasibility Study for Gemlik Region. *J. Clean Energy Technol.* **2017**, *5*, 101–106. [CrossRef]

100. Troldborg, N.; Larsen, G.C.; Madsen, H.A.; Hansen, K.S.; Sørensen, J.N.; Mikkelsen, R. Numerical simulations of wake interaction between two wind turbines at various inflow conditions. *Wind Energy* **2011**, *14*, 859–876. [CrossRef]

101. Schulz, C.; Klein, L.; Weihing, P.; Lutz, T.; Krämer, E. CFD Studies on Wind Turbines in Complex Terrain under Atmospheric Inflow Conditions. *J. Phys. Conf. Ser.* **2014**, *524*, 012134. [CrossRef]

102. Schmidt, J.; Stoevesandt, B. Modelling complex terrain effects for wind farm layout optimization. *J. Phys. Conf. Ser.* **2014**, *524*, 012136. [CrossRef]

103. Machefaux, E.; Larsen, G.C.; Koblitz, T.; Troldborg, N.; Kelly, M.C.; Chougule, A.; Hansen, S.K.; Rodrigo, J.S. An experimental and numerical study of the atmospheric stability impact on wind turbine wakes. *Wind Energy* **2016**, *19*, 1099–1824. [CrossRef]

104. Liu, X.; Yan, S.; Mu, Y.; Chen, X.; Shi, S. CFD and Experimental Studies on Wind Turbines in Complex Terrain by Improved Actuator Disk Method. *J. Phys. Conf. Ser.* **2017**, *854*, 012028. [CrossRef]

105. Politis, E.S.; Prospathopoulos, J.; Cabezon, D.; Hansen, K.S.; Chaviaropoulos, P.K.; Barthelmie, R.J. Modeling wake effects in large wind farms in complex terrain: The problem, the methods and the issues. *Wind Energy* **2012**, *15*, 161–182. [CrossRef]

106. Feng, J.; Shen, W.Z. Wind farm layout optimization in complex terrain: A preliminary study on a Gaussian hill. *J. Phys. Conf. Ser.* **2014**, *524*, 012146. [CrossRef]

107. Parada, L.; Herrera, C.; Flores, P.; Parada, V. Assessing the energy benefit of using a wind turbine micro-siting model. *Renew. Energy* **2017**, *118*, 591–601. [CrossRef]

Article

A Localized Meshless Technique for Generating 3-D Wind Fields

Darrell W. Pepper * and Maria Ramos Gonzalez

Department of Mechanical Engineering, University of Nevada, 89154 Las Vegas, NV, USA;
ramosm27@unlv.nevada.edu
* Correspondence: darrell.pepper@unlv.edu; Tel.: +1-702-895-1056

Received: 22 December 2017; Accepted: 1 February 2018; Published: 8 February 2018

Abstract: A localized meshless method is used to simulate 3-D atmospheric wind fields for wind energy assessment and emergency response. The meshless (or mesh-free) method with radial basis functions (RBFs) alleviates the need to create a mesh required by finite difference, finite volume, and finite element methods. The method produces a fast solution that converges with high accuracy, establishing 3-D wind estimates over complex terrain. The method does not require discretization of the domain or boundary and removes the need for domain integration. The meshless method converges exponentially for smooth boundary shapes and boundary data, and is insensitive to dimensional constraints. Coding of the method is very easy and can be done using MATLAB or MAPLE. By employing a localized RBF procedure, 3-D wind fields can be established from sparse meteorological data. The meshless method can be easily run on PCs and hand-held mobile devices. This article summarizes previous work where the meshless method has successfully simulated 3D wind fields over various environments, along with the equations used to obtain the simulations.

Keywords: meshless; 3-D wind field; localized RBF; radial basis functions

1. Introduction

Wind energy continues to be a limited resource in the Southwestern U.S. A preliminary wind energy study conducted by Pepper [1] and later by the National Renewable Energy Laboratory (NREL) and AWS Truewind (now AWS Truepower, Albany, NY, USA) [2] showed that Nevada has wind resource potential (Figure 1a). Detailed wind energy resource data is difficult to obtain, requiring data gathering equipment to reach remote ridges and mountain tops where higher-class winds may exist. Previous efforts indicated that Nevada has significant wind resource potential, mostly on ridge tops in rural areas [3]. Numerical simulations based on extensive mesh-based models are typically conducted to estimate the potential of wind energy over extended areas of interest. These models can be time consuming to setup and require extensive computational resources. A fast, alternative approach to these more conventional models is the use of meshless methods.

Sufficient wind resources may be available to provide both electric power and economic development opportunities for rural areas, as shown in Figure 1. Efforts were undertaken by the University of Nevada Las Vegas (UNLV) and Desert Research Institute (DRI) to examine wind energy potential within the central and upper Northern regions of the state. The UNLV-DRI study resulted in a revised, more refined estimate of wind resources within the central portion of the state with placement of four meteorological towers near Whitney Mountain.

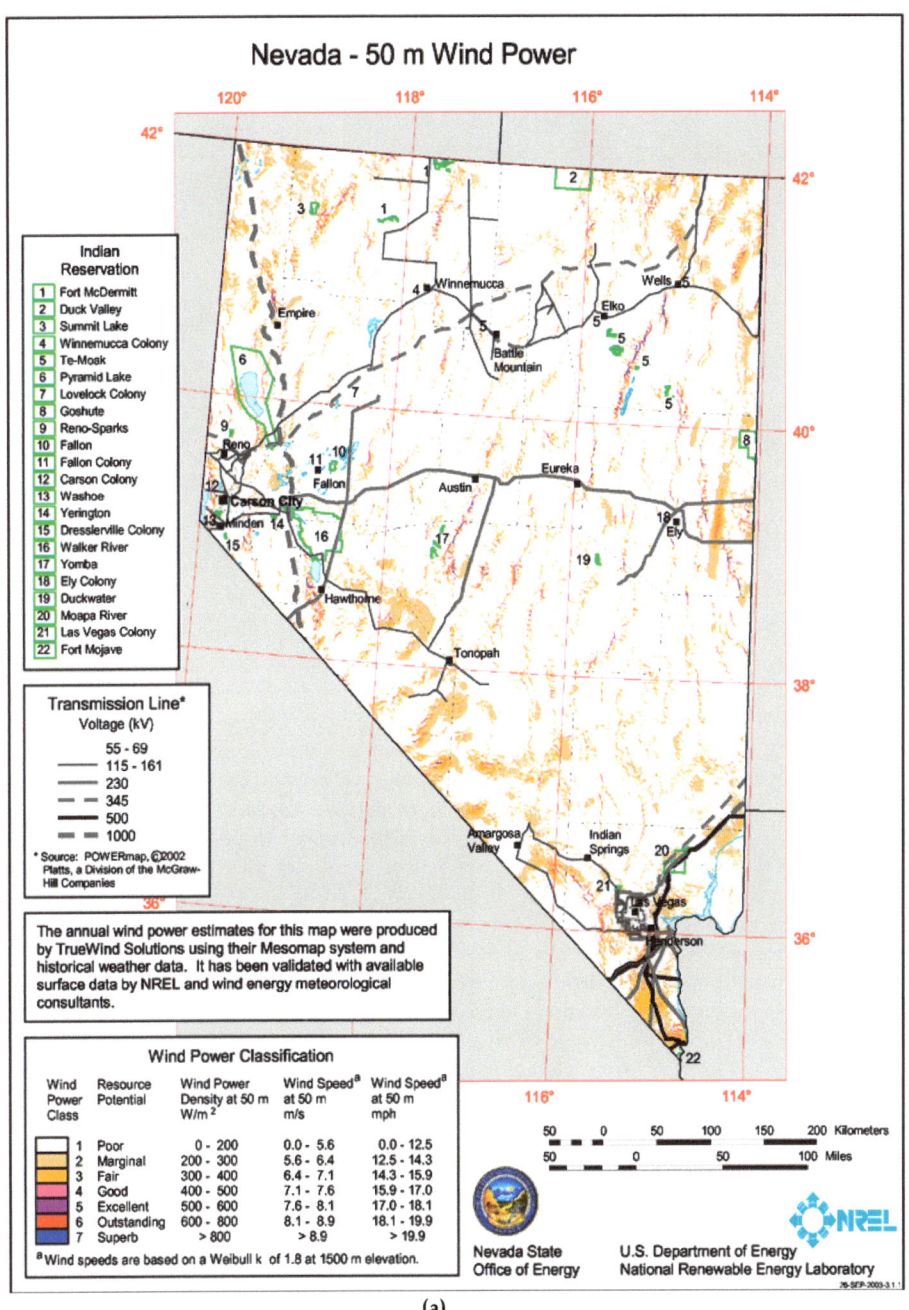

Figure 1. *Cont.*

 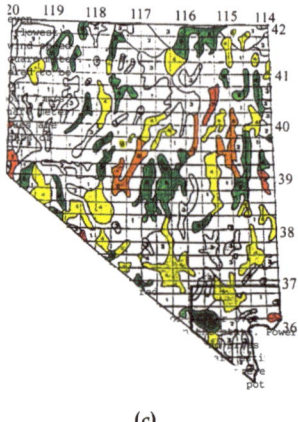

(b)   (c)

Figure 1. (**a**) National Renewable Energy Laboratory and AWS Truepower—Nevada 50 m wind power map; (**b,c**) University of Nevada Las Vegas (UNLV) assessment (red-Class 7, Orange-Class 6, Yellow-Class 5, Green-Class 4)—1998 study.

2. Mass Consistent Winds

In order to create realistic 3-D wind fields, a mass consistent model must first be established. The basis for the model employed in this study follows the earlier works of Sherman [4] and later applied by Pepper [5]. The mass consistent model minimizes the differences between observed and computed velocity values. Simulation values are calculated at all the nodes within the computational domain utilizing weighted averaging around each measured meteorological data point, i.e., data obtained from an instrumented meteorological tower, to fill in values to all the nodes. This interpolated wind field is then minimized to reduce error and satisfy mass conservation. In this situation, the limitations of the incompressible approach should be noted. In reality, the atmosphere is compressible and the differences in density can lead to issues affecting temperature, humidity, and pressure (e.g., nocturnal drainage winds). In this approach, we have kept the simulations simple to provide quick estimates of the wind fields. A more detailed approach should include compressibility. However, the procedure would essentially be the same.

Inverse squared weighting is first used to create a preliminary surface wind field employing a fixed radius from the tower and the values interpolated to all grid points in the first level above the terrain. The remaining upper level winds are then constructed using inverse weighting from the initial surface generated values. If measured vertical velocities are not available, the equation of continuity is then used to calculate the remaining velocities, i.e.,

$$w = -\int_0^z \left(\frac{\partial u}{\partial x} + \frac{\partial v}{\partial y} \right) dz \tag{1}$$

which stems from the conservation of mass for atmospheric (incompressible) flow [6],

$$\frac{\partial u}{\partial x} + \frac{\partial v}{\partial y} + \frac{\partial w}{\partial z} = 0 \tag{2}$$

A variational technique originally employed by Sasaki [7] is used to create an equation for Lagrange multipliers, $\lambda(x, y, z)$, which are used to adjust velocities. This Poisson equation contains the observed velocity values (u_0, v_0, and w_0 obtained from meteorological tower or SODAR-SOnic Detection and Ranging-data), along with Gauss moduli (α) that can be tuned to adjust for more horizontal or vertical effects (e.g., rough terrain may create more vertical influence). The resulting Euler-Lagrange equation for $\lambda(x, y, z)$ written as

$$\frac{\partial^2 \lambda}{\partial x^2} + \frac{\partial^2 \lambda}{\partial y^2} + \left(\frac{\alpha_1}{\alpha_2}\right)^2 \frac{\partial^2 \lambda}{\partial z^2} = -2\alpha_1^2 \left(\frac{\partial u_0}{\partial x} + \frac{\partial v_0}{\partial y} + \frac{\partial w_0}{\partial z}\right) \tag{3}$$

where u_0, v_0, w_0 are the measured velocity values in the x, y, and z directions and α_i are the Gauss precision moduli, where $\alpha_i^2 \equiv 1/(2\sigma_i^2)$ (with the deviation errors from the observed and desired fields defined by σ_i). Sherman [4] points out that these moduli are important in establishing non-divergent wind fields over irregular terrain, where $(\alpha_1/\alpha_2)^2$ is proportional to $(w/u)^2$. Pepper and Wang [8] set α_1 (the horizontal adjustment) = 0.01 and α_2 (the vertical adjustment) = 0.1.

Once λ is calculated at each node, the velocities are adjusted to satisfy continuity, keeping the measured tower velocities fixed, i.e.,

$$u = u_0 + \frac{1}{2\alpha_1^2} \frac{\partial \lambda}{\partial x} \tag{4}$$

$$v = v_0 + \frac{1}{2\alpha_1^2} \frac{\partial \lambda}{\partial y} \tag{5}$$

$$w = w_0 + \frac{1}{2\alpha_2^2} \frac{\partial \lambda}{\partial z} \tag{6}$$

Measured velocities are typically collected and averaged every 10–15 min, generating a new 3-D wind field. Equations (3)–(6) are updated once per cycle. Setting $\lambda = 0$ accounts for open or "flow-through" boundaries; setting $\partial\lambda/\partial n = 0$ on the boundary defines closed or "no-flow-through" boundaries. Both Sherman [4] and Dickerson [9] employed this technique to produce realistic wind fields using very sparse measured values.

3. Wind Power Density Calculation

Wind power density ranges from Class 1 (lowest) to Class 7 (highest), defined on a vertical extrapolation of wind speed based on the 1/7 power law. The Battelle Wind Energy Resource Atlas provides the source for classification data [10]. Satisfactory power-generating winds are typically Class 4 winds and higher, but as wind turbine technology advances, Class 3 winds are becoming viable. Table 1 shows wind class versus power density for winds at 50 m.

Table 1. Wind Class versus Power Density.

Class	Power Density (W/m^2)	Mean Speed(m/s)
1	<200	<5.6
2	200–300	5.6–6.4
3	300–400	6.4–7.0
4	400–500	7.0–7.5
5	500–600	7.5–8.0
6	600–700	5.6–8.8
7	>800	>8.8

The wind power density calculations are obtained by calculating the wind speed at each grid point on an hourly basis.

$$Speed_i = \sqrt{u_i^2 + v_i^2 + w_i^2} \tag{7}$$

The hourly wind power density at each grid point is then obtained using the simple expression,

$$WPD_i = 0.5 \cdot \rho \cdot Speed_i^3 \tag{8}$$

with wind power in Watts, area is m^2, wind velocity is m/s, and the density for air is 1.225 kg/m^3 at sea level. To account for density variation at elevation Z (above sea level in m), density is obtained using

$$\rho = 1.225 - (1.194 \times 10^{-4}) \cdot Z \tag{9}$$

The monthly average wind power density is then calculated using the relation

$$WPD_{monthly\_avg} = \frac{\sum\limits_{i=1}^{N} WPD_i}{N} \tag{10}$$

where N is the total number of hours in a selected month.

4. The Meshless Method

The meshless method is a unique numerical technique that does not require discretization with a mesh [11,12]. In addition, the method can easily handle complex geometrical problems with inhomogeneous or variable properties employing a general-purpose algorithm. Applications of meshless (or mesh-free) methods have continued to increase over the past few years to solve a wide range of problems [13–16]. In many situations, the meshless method can serve as a viable alternative to problems involving complex or extensive mesh generation. Atluri and Zhu [13,17,18] discuss the issue of node placement in mesh-free methods. In this work, radial basis functions (RBF) are used since issues dealing with nodal placement are not critical.

The concept of a meshless approach to obtain approximate solutions to differential equations began in the 1970s [19]. The method began to take more notice in the ensuing years due to their ease in implementation, bypassing the need for nodal connectivity required in the more widely used conventional mesh-based numerical methods. Mesh discretization using finite elements as well as non-structured polygonal mesh techniques used in finite volume methods can become troublesome when encountering complex geometries. While a variety of meshless approaches now exist, they have the common property of not requiring a nodal mesh. This is a unique feature of the method, and truly eliminates the effort typically required to produce a refined and optimal mesh (to ensure mesh independence solutions including refined local adaptations—both time consuming). The more common forms of meshless methods include smoothed particle hydrodynamics, reproducing kernel particle, meshless Petrov–Galerkin, local radial point interpolation, finite point, and finite differences with arbitrary irregular grids. Each method has benefits and drawbacks. Further details describing the unique properties of meshless methods are given in Liu [15].

An example illustrating the placement of nodes in a uniform pattern versus a random pattern is shown in Figure 2a,b. The nodes do not need to be distributed uniformly, and in fact can be scattered and grouped within the problem domain to more accurately capture information in regions of greater interest.

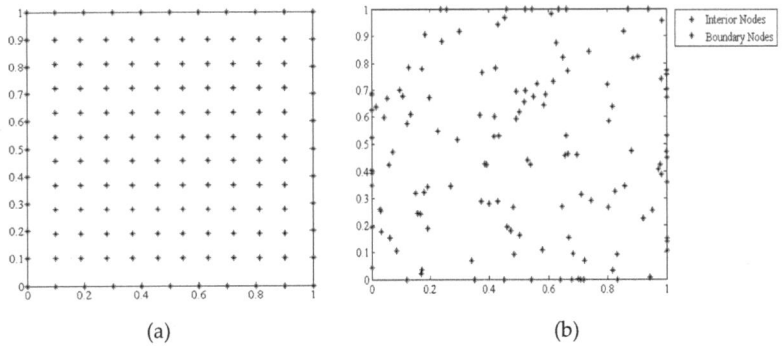

(a)   (b)

Figure 2. Nodal placement for (**a**) uniform mesh and (**b**) random nodal placement.

Shape functions relate the influences from all the nodes within the domain on each individual node. These functions act as support domains for each node, and can have weighted influence. In this instance, the Lagrange multipliers, $\lambda(\mathbf{x})$, are interpolated using the displacements at their nodes within the support domain. For example, a PDE is discretized into a nodal matrix form, and the global matrix solved using a simple elimination procedure.

4.1. Radial Basis Functions (RBF)

The RBF method employs a basis function that relates the influence of surrounding nodes to the node of interest, i.e., a distance, d, with the nodes closest to the node of interest having the greatest influence. This distance between the radial positions, r, can be expressed as:

$$d_i = \left[(r - r_i)^2 \right]^{1/2} \tag{11}$$

Hardy [20] introduced a basis function based on multi-quadratics (MQ). The MQ is a popular function used to construct approximate solutions to PDEs, and is used in this study. Incorporating the relation for distance, a basis function, ϕ, can be established such that:

$$\phi_j = \left[(r - r_j)^2 + c_j^2 \right]^{1/2}, j = 1, 2 \ldots N \tag{12}$$

where N is the total number of nodes. The Lagrange multipliers, $\lambda(\mathbf{x})$, are then expressed as:

$$\lambda(\mathbf{x}) = \sum_{j=1}^{N} \phi_j(\mathbf{x})\lambda_j \tag{13}$$

where λ_j is the Lagrange coefficient defined at each point.

In order to solve the Poisson equation for $\lambda(\mathbf{x})$, a linear operator ($L \equiv \nabla^2$) is applied to the interior domain, Ω. Thus,

$$L\lambda(\mathbf{x}) = \sum_{j=1}^{N} L\phi_j(\mathbf{x})\lambda_j \tag{14}$$

where the linear operator (the PDE) is applied to the basis function. First and second derivatives of the basis function are used to solve Equation (3). A boundary operator, B, is used to account for either Dirichlet or Neumann conditions applied to the boundaries, Γ, i.e.,

$$B\lambda(\mathbf{x}) = \sum_{j=1}^{N} B\phi_j(\mathbf{x})\lambda_j \tag{15}$$

The procedure used in this study is based on the approach used by Kansa [21]. Note that different constants for the shape parameter can be used for the interior, Ω, and the boundary, Γ.

Equation (3) can be expressed as:

$$\frac{\partial^2 \lambda}{\partial x^2} + \frac{\partial^2 \lambda}{\partial y^2} + \left(\frac{\alpha_1}{\alpha_2}\right)^2 \frac{\partial^2 \lambda}{\partial z^2} = f(\mathbf{x}) \quad \mathbf{x} \in \Omega \tag{16}$$

where $\mathbf{x} \equiv (x,y,z)$ with

$$f(\mathbf{x}) = -2\alpha_1^2 \left(\frac{\partial u_0}{\partial x} + \frac{\partial v_0}{\partial y} + \frac{\partial w_0}{\partial z}\right) \tag{17}$$

at all interior points, and

$$\lambda(\mathbf{x}) = g(\mathbf{x}) \quad \mathbf{x} \in \Gamma \tag{18}$$

where $g(\mathbf{x})$ denotes the divergence of the observed velocity values at the boundaries, Γ. Introducing the MQ form of the basis function for $\phi_j(\mathbf{x})$,

$$\phi_j(\mathbf{x}) = \sqrt{r_j^2 + c^2} = \sqrt{(x - x_j)^2 + (y - y_j)^2 + (z - z_j)^2 + c^2} \tag{19}$$

the derivatives can be written as

$$\begin{aligned}
&\frac{\partial \phi_j}{\partial x} = \frac{x - x_j}{\sqrt{r_j^2 + c^2}}, \quad \frac{\partial \phi_j}{\partial y} = \frac{y - y_j}{\sqrt{r_j^2 + c^2}}, \quad \frac{\partial \phi_j}{\partial z} = \frac{z - z_j}{\sqrt{r_j^2 + c^2}} \\
&\frac{\partial^2 \phi_j}{\partial x^2} = \frac{(y - y_j)^2 + (z - z_j)^2 + c^2}{\sqrt[3]{r_j^2 + c^2}}, \quad \frac{\partial^2 \phi_j}{\partial y^2} = \frac{(x - x_j)^2 + (z - z_j)^2 + c^2}{\sqrt[3]{r_j^2 + c^2}}, \quad \frac{\partial^2 \phi_j}{\partial z^2} = \frac{(x - x_j)^2 + (y - y_j)^2 + c^2}{\sqrt[3]{r_j^2 + c^2}}
\end{aligned} \tag{20}$$

Substituting Equation (20) into Equations (16) and (18),

$$\sum_{j=1}^{N} \left(\frac{\partial^2 \phi_j(x_i)}{\partial x^2} + \frac{\partial^2 \phi_j(x_i)}{\partial y^2} + \left(\frac{\alpha_1}{\alpha_2}\right)^2 \frac{\partial^2 \phi_j(x_i)}{\partial z^2}\right) \lambda_j(x_i) = f(x_i) \quad i = 1, 2, \cdots, N_I \tag{21}$$

$$\sum_{j=1}^{N} \phi_j(x_i) \lambda_j = g(x_i) \quad i = N_{I+1}, N_{I+2}, \cdots N \tag{22}$$

an $N \times N$ linear system of equations is created for the unknown, λ_j.

The introduction of the shape parameter, c, assists in enhancing the accuracy of the RBFs. The shape parameter is based on the number of nodes, N, and distance, d, where $d = \frac{1}{N_I} \sum_{i=1}^{N} d_i$, and d_i is the distance between the i th data point and its nearest neighbor. The shape parameter depends on the number and distribution of nodes, the choice of basis function, and computer precision [22].

4.2. Local RBF Approach

The two techniques commonly used in RBF-based methods are based on global versus local collocation. The global approach collocates over the total number of nodes within the computational domain, i.e., the global matrix is defined by the total number of nodes, N, creating an $N \times N$ matrix that must be solved. The local approach employs only local collocation, creating a series of overlapping matrices defined by m x m nodes surrounding the node of interest. This creates a small series of linear equations that must be solved for each node. Providing the problem domain and number of nodes are not huge, the global RBF approach works well for simple and small problems. Pepper et al. [23] describes the use of the global RBF approach for 3-D wind fields. More detailed discussion on implementation of the local approach is given in Waters and Pepper [24]. Since the localized RBF method collocates a small number of points for each subdomain, the method is ideal for use as an app on mobile devices.

In order to approximate $\lambda(\mathbf{x})$ of Equation (16), a series of local subdomains are solved that overlap within the problem domain. Figure 3 shows a set of subdomains with the dark points serving as the center node points. Each node serves as a center node of interest until all the nodes are resolved. This permits $\lambda(\mathbf{x})$ to be solved at every point, i.e.,

$$\lambda(x_i) = \sum_{k=1}^{m} \phi_k(x_i)\lambda_{k,j}, \quad x_i \in \Omega_j \tag{23}$$

where $\lambda_{k,j}$ are the coefficients of the RBFs. The RBF, ϕ_k, are the shape functions. Substituting Equation (23) into Equation (21), an m x m linear algebraic system is obtained for each local domain with an interior point, i.e.,

$$\sum_{k=1}^{m} \left(\frac{\partial^2 \phi_k(x_i)}{\partial x^2} + \frac{\partial^2 \phi_k(x_i)}{\partial y^2} + \left(\frac{\alpha_1}{\alpha_2}\right)^2 \frac{\partial^2 \phi_k(x_i)}{\partial z^2} \right) \lambda_{k,j}(x_i) = f(x_i) \quad i = 1, 2, \cdots, m \quad x_i \in \Omega_j \tag{24}$$

with the boundary conditions:

$$\sum_{k=1}^{m} \phi_k(x_i)\lambda_{k,j}(x_i) = g(x_i) \quad i \in N_{I+1}, N_{I+2}, \cdots, N \quad x_i \in \Omega_j \tag{25}$$

An $m \times m$ linear system consisting of the unknown multipliers, $\left\{\lambda_{k,j}\right\}_{k=1}^{m}$ is produced from Equations (24) and (25) for each local domain defined by the interior center points where Equation (24) applies to interior points $(x_i, \ i = 1, 2, \ldots, N_I)$ and Equation (25) applies to the boundary points.

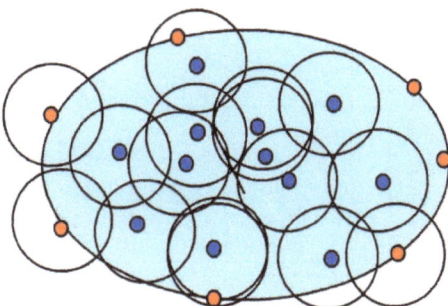

Figure 3. Node placement and circle of influence (from Pepper, D.W., et al. [25]).

Figure 4a,b shows a localized domain on a simple rectangular field with the center point surrounded by 8 nodes, and a randomized array consisting of 30 points. Various test cases were examined as to the optimal number of surrounding nodes, ranging from 5 to 30. It was found that the best number with regards to acceptable accuracy and speed was nine nodes per local domain. The global matrix involving $N \times N$ nodes in the global technique reduces to a simple $m \times m$ matrix that can be quickly solved, and does not create matrix conditioning issues.

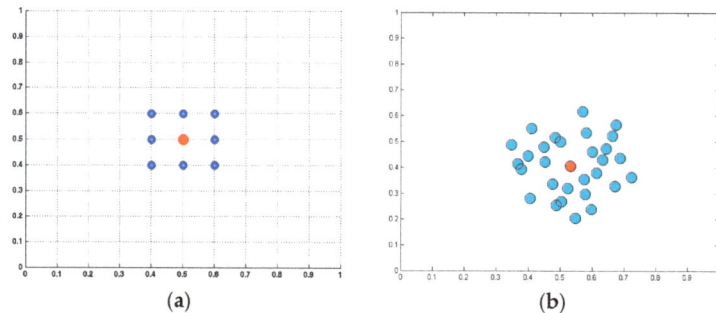

Figure 4. Localized stencil, (a) 9-point and (b) random 30-point array (from Waters, J., et al. [24]).

As an example, to illustrate the accuracy of the meshless method, a simple test case was used to solve for heat conduction in a two-dimensional plate subjected to prescribed temperatures along each boundary [25], as shown in Figure 5. The temperature at the mid-point (1,0.5) was used to compare numerical solutions with the analytical solution. The analytical solution is given as

$$\theta(x,y) \equiv \frac{T-T_1}{T_2-T_1} = \frac{2}{\pi}\sum_{n=1}^{\theta}\frac{(-1)^{n+1}+1}{n}\sin\left(\frac{n\pi x}{L}\right)\frac{\sinh(n\pi y/L)}{\sinh(n\pi W/L)}$$

which yields $\theta(1,0.5) = 0.445$, or $T(1,0.5) = 94.5$ °C. Table 2 lists the final exact temperatures at the mid-point compared with a finite element and the meshless method.

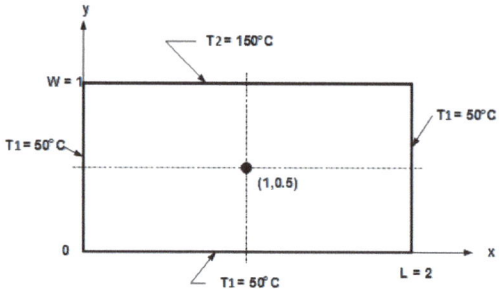

Figure 5. Steady-state conduction in a two-dimensional plate (from Waters, J., et al. [24]).

Table 2. Comparison of results for Exact, FEM, and Meshless Method (from Pepper, D.W., et al. [25]).

Method	Mid-Point (°C)	Elements	Nodes
Exact	94.512	0	0
FEM	94.605	256	289
Meshless	94.514	0	325

5. Comparison Results

The Nevada Test Site (NTS) is located within the southern part of Nevada, about 100 miles northwest of Las Vegas. The NTS was used principally for nuclear weapons testing. The terrain and 26 wind tower locations are shown in Figure 6.

An h-adaptive finite element model was initially developed by Pepper and Wang [8] utilizing the UNLV supercomputer system to simulate 3-D winds over the NTS, as shown in Figure 6. The initial meshes were constructed using USGS and DEM data.

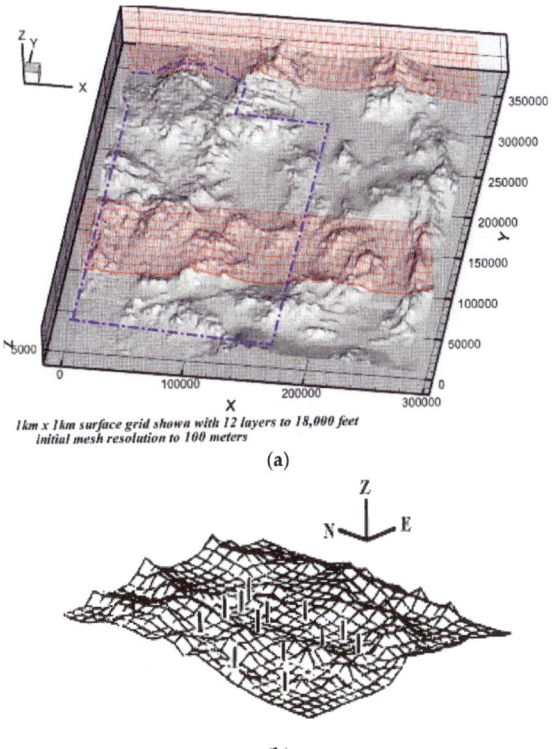

1km x 1km surface grid shown with 12 layers to 18,000 feet
initial mesh resolution to 100 meters

(a)

(b)

Figure 6. Nevada Test Site (**a**) topography and (**b**) meteorological tower system (NOAA).

Meteorological tower and upper air data from 1 January 1993, were used to initialize the wind field. The NTS meteorological towers (partially shown as dots in Figure 6b are scattered throughout the site. The 10 m level mesh is shown in Figure 7a,b for the h-adaptive FEM model. The additional velocity vectors in the FEM solution in Figure 8b occur from local refinement (h-adaptation). Results for the 50 m level are shown in Figure 9a,b. A power density map of the NTS is shown in Figure 10.

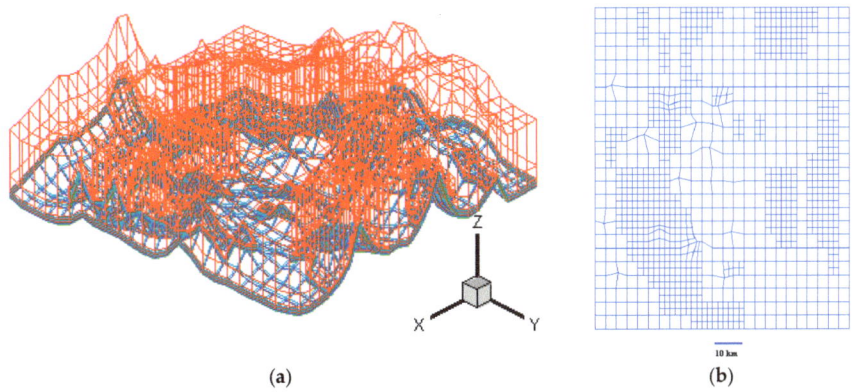

(a)

(b)

Figure 7. Adaptive mesh for Nevada Test Site (NTS) (**a**) 3-D view and (**b**) 2-D view.

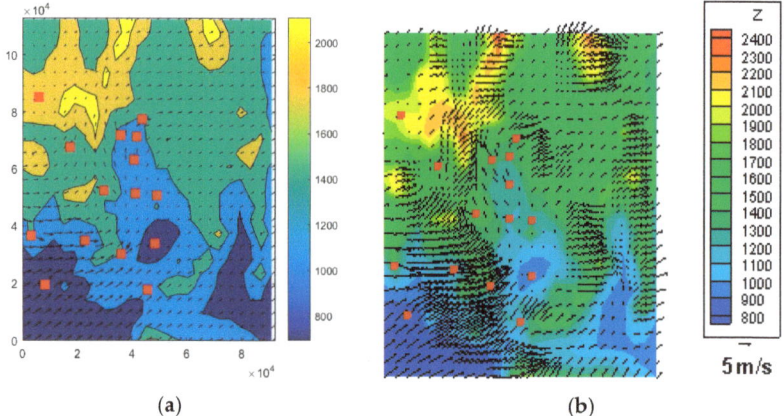

(a)   (b)

Figure 8. (**a**) Local Meshless results for 10 m level and (**b**) h-fem results. Figures indicate velocity vectors with tower locations indicated by the red markers on both figures (from Pepper, D.W., et al. [8]; ©American Meteorological Society, used with permission).

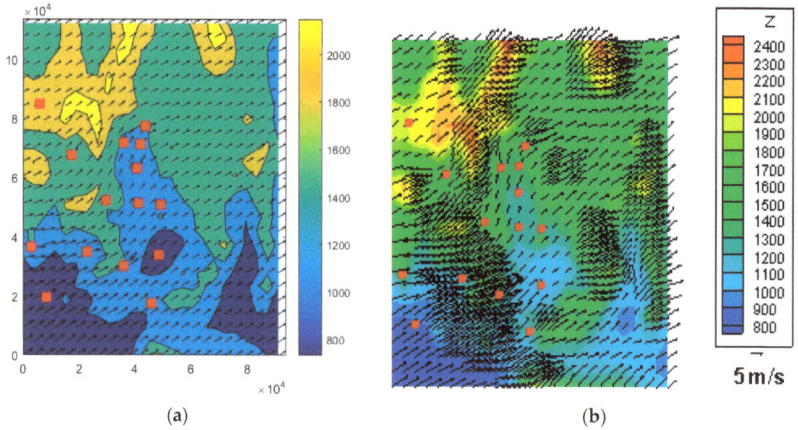

(a)   (b)

Figure 9. (**a**) Local Meshless results for 50 m level and (**b**) h-fem results. Figures indicate velocity vectors with tower locations indicated by the red markers on both figures (from Pepper, D.W., et al. [8]; ©American Meteorological Society, used with permission).

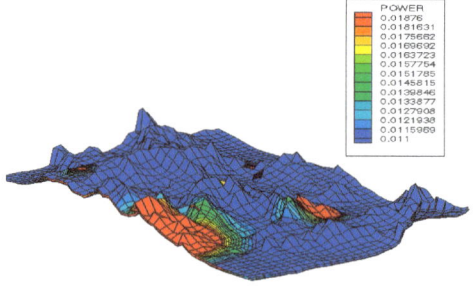

Figure 10. Power density map for 50 m height at NTS.

The meshless method employed only 240 nodes. The FEM model required over 12,500 nodes. While the meshless method utilized a coarse density of nodes, the velocities and patterns were generally close to the results obtained using the high-resolution finite element model. Furthermore, the meshless code was written in MATLAB, a widely popular and inexpensive software package used in many institutions than runs on PC platforms, while the h-adaptive FEM was written in FORTRAN, parallelized, and was run on a supercomputer.

A simple flow chart is listed in Figure 11 for generating the model output. The implementation of the coding is very simple, especially since the method is explicit and does not require matrix solvers.

Later efforts were undertaken to examine wind energy potential for central NV. The terrain surface plot, topographic contours, and tower locations are shown for the region near Whitney Mountain in central NV in Figure 12a,b [26].

The resulting power density contours per month for September 2001 to February 2002 are shown in Figure 13a–l.

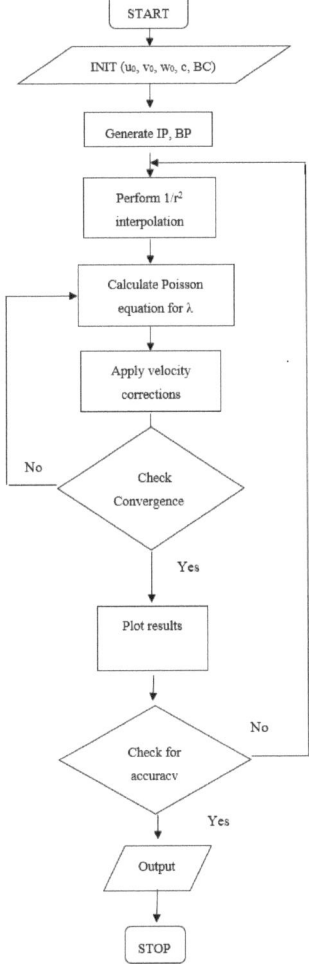

Figure 11. Modeling flow chart.

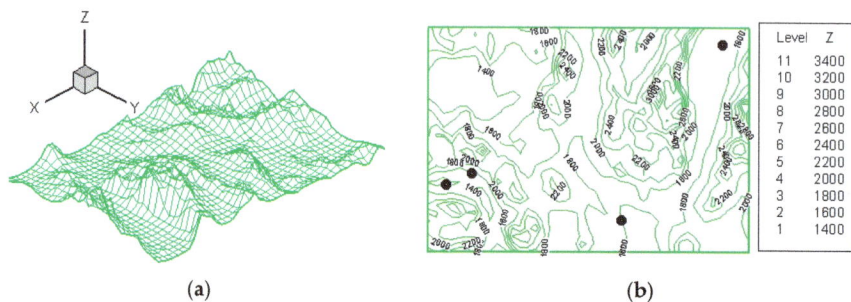

Figure 12. (**a**) Terrain surface plot, (**b**) topographic contours and tower placements.

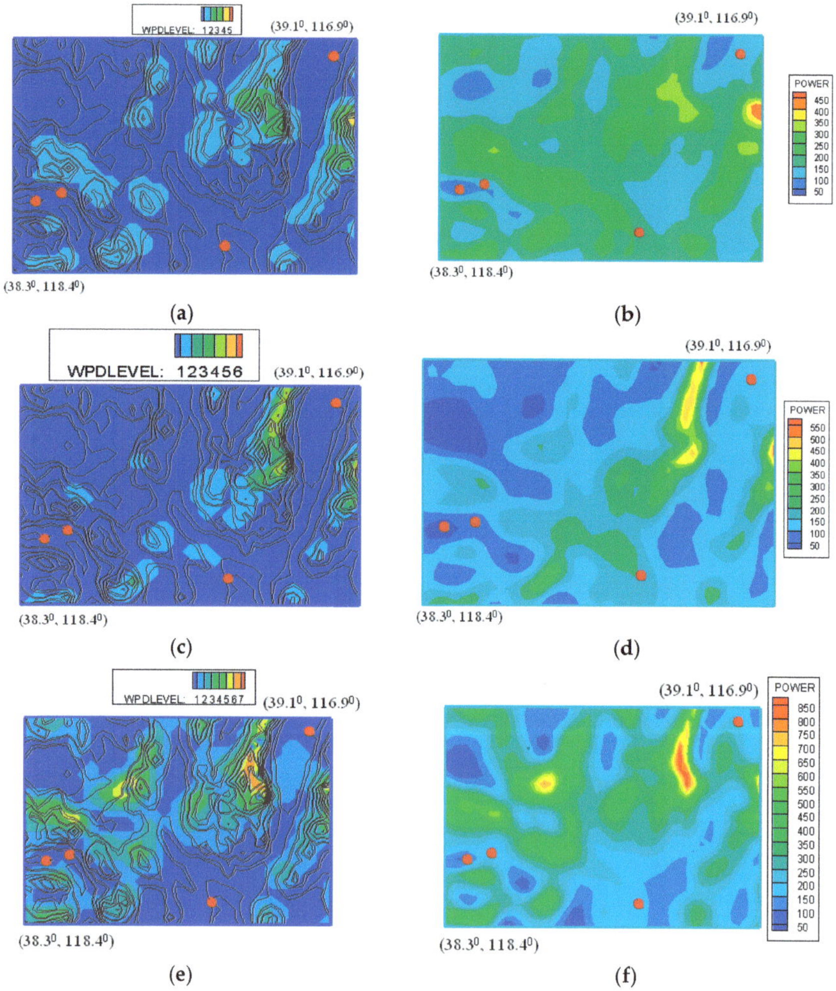

(a)

(b)

(c)

(d)

(e)

(f)

Figure 13. *Cont.*

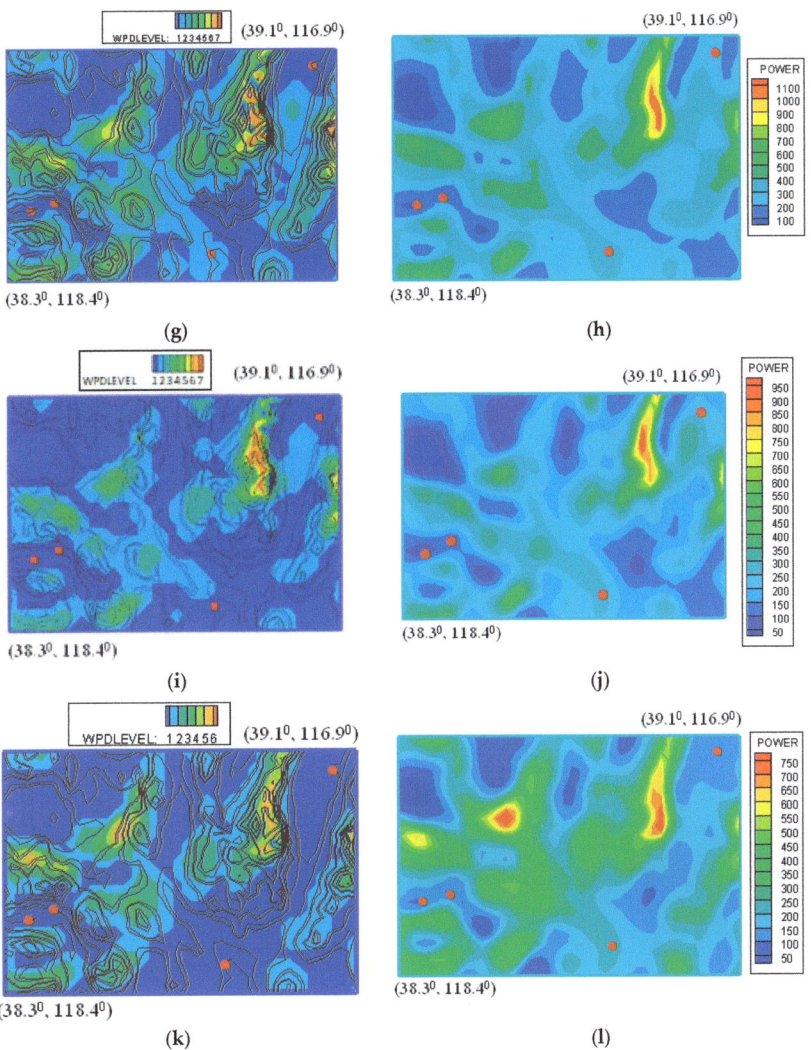

Figure 13. Power density contours for September 2001–February 2002. (**a**) 50 m and (**b**) 100 m (W/m²) (September 2001); (**c**) 50 m and (**d**) 100 m (W/m²) (October 2001); (**e**) 50 m and (**f**) 100 m (W/m²) (November 2001); (**g**) 50 m and (**h**) 100 m (W/m²) (December 2001); (**i**) 50 m and (**j**) 100 m (W/m²) (January 2002); (**k**) 50 m and (**l**) 100 m (W/m²) (February 2002).

6. Implementation of the Meshless Method for Mobile Applications

An advantage of the meshless method is its ability to run quickly and without the need for a supercomputer. This makes it an ideal method to run on a mobile application. A mobile application was developed to provide first responders with a 3-D wind field [27]. A local meshless technique obtains wind speeds, wind direction, and temperature data from various fire stations. The fire stations represent the nodes, which do not need to be meshed.

Figure 14 depicts fire stations across the Las Vegas Valley with their fire station numbers. Currently, the Clark County Department of Air Quality monitors resultant wind data in miles per hour and resultant wind direction measured in degrees compass. The monitoring stations information was used to collect initial wind speed and direction data closest to the fire stations. A hypothetical wind field was then developed showing information coming from each of the fire stations. Figure 15 illustrates the wind field.

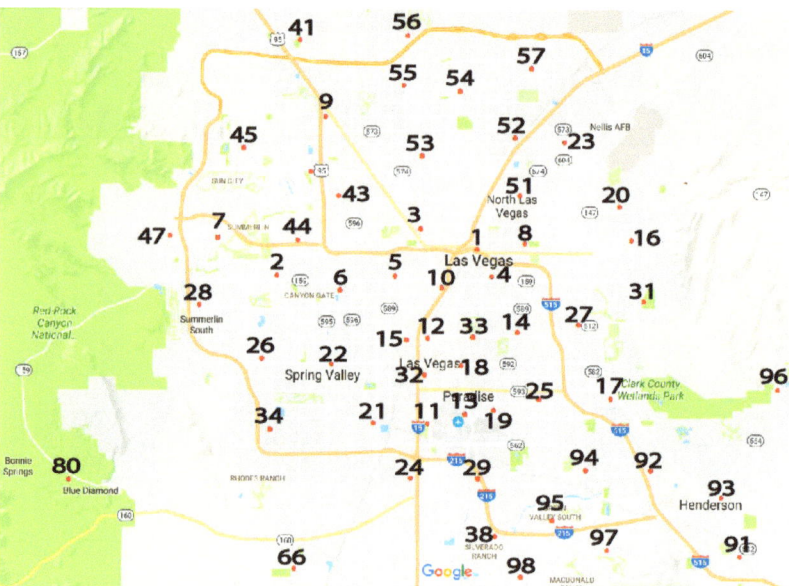

Figure 14. Las Vegas Valley Fire Station Numbers.

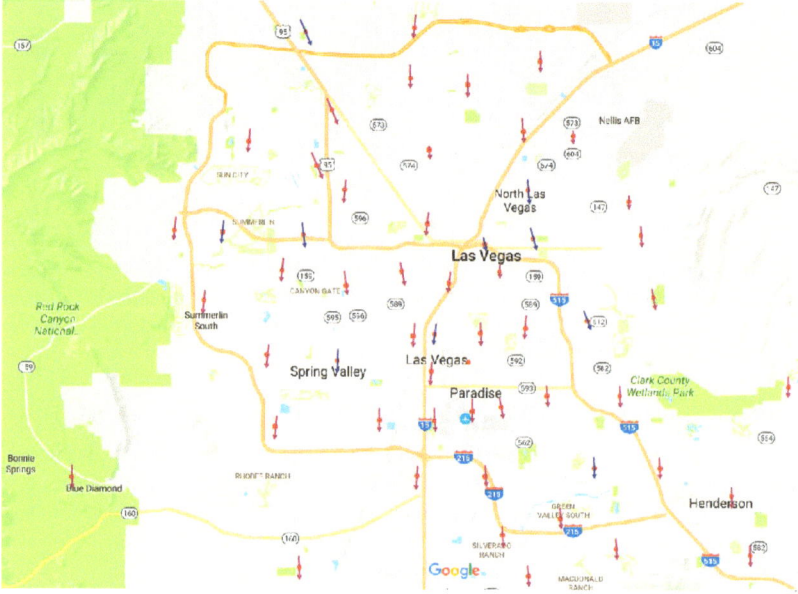

Figure 15. Hypothetical Wind Field with Fire Station Wind Data.

Currently, the Clark County Department of Air Quality monitoring stations provide data once an hour. The goal of the fire station monitoring stations would be to provide "real-time" updates. Depending on the equipment used, this can range from 10 min to as low as 1 min, depending on the accuracy of the data needed. The fire stations serve as the nodes for the meshless method. Once the intermediate wind vectors are populated, the updated image can be pushed to the mobile application. Figure 16 illustrates the image a first responder would observe of a populated 3-D wind field on a mobile device (Android version).

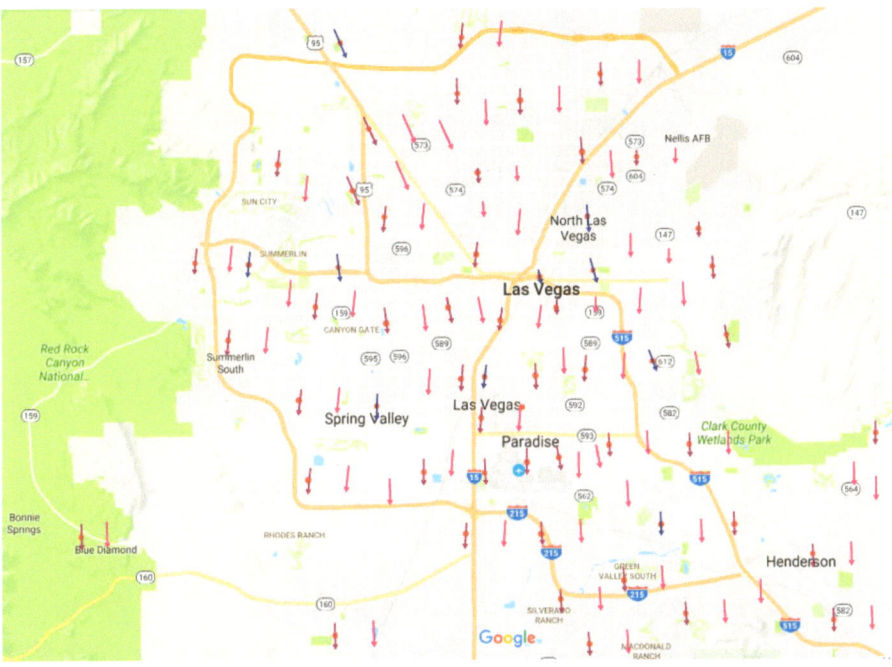

Figure 16. Populated 3-D Wind Field from Meshless Method.

An online connection is not always available for first responders in remote areas. The application can run independently of the server's information. A first responder would have the ability to call into a fire station of choice, collect u and v values for the wind data, and input them into the mobile application. The application would then run the meshless algorithm and update the map independently of the server. Once connection was established again, the server would push the latest information to the mobile device. Figure 17a,b depict the layout of the application and the various output maps and data inputs.

First responders have the flexibility of choosing what type of map to view through a drop-down menu. Options include fire station numbers only, fire station vectors, and populated vectors. A button enables them to update the map whenever they want, otherwise, the map will update every time data is available when a wireless connection is established. If there is no connection and a first responder would like update a specific node, the "change wind vector at location" button leads to a menu where the fire station number and u, v wind speed values can be input. This proof-of-concept mobile application has great potential and will be available for users in the future.

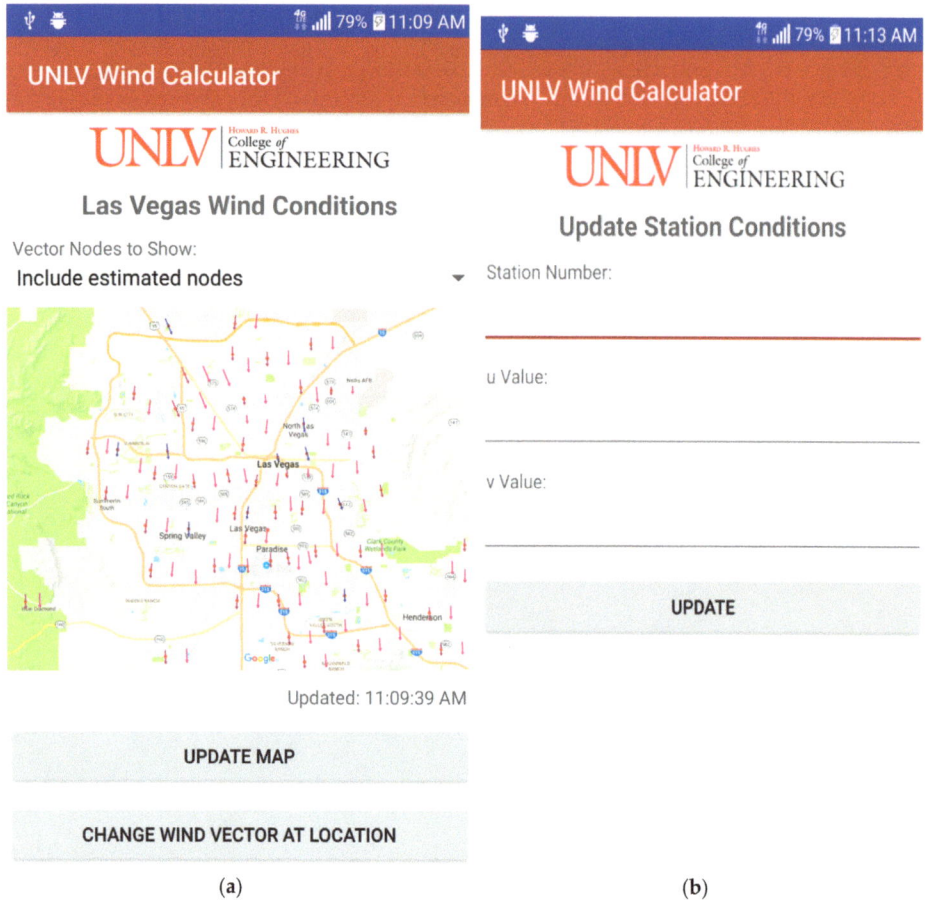

(a)   (b)

Figure 17. Mobile Application Layout. (**a**) Main page; (**b**) Manual input page.

7. Conclusions

A localized meshless method has been developed to calculate 3-D wind fields utilizing sparse data obtained from meteorological towers. Results were compared with field data obtained from a network of meteorological towers located at the Nevada Test Site (Nevada National Security Site) and an h-adaptive finite element model. The meshless method produced nearly identical wind velocity values and patterns as the h-adaptive finite element method, but with significantly less computational cost and difficulty.

The advantages of using localized meshless methods for meteorological simulations are significant when dealing with large, complex terrains, and completely eliminates the need for complicated and detailed meshes common to conventional numerical approaches. Additional node points can be easily added or removed from problem domains without having to re-mesh the entire system. The localized meshless technique is not only more computationally efficient but also yields equally accurate results compared with mesh-based methods. Current efforts are now underway to implement the method to display 3-D real-time wind data on mobile devices for use by the Las Vegas Fire Department in emergency response situations within the Las Vegas Valley.

Author Contributions: D.W.P. developed the original algorithm and conducted early tests of the meshless method, and wrote corresponding sections regarding the NTS and central NV wind energy studies. M.R.G. developed the mobile application, wrote the corresponding section covering the mobile application, and formatted the paper.

Conflicts of Interest: The authors declare no conflict of interest.

References

1.   Pepper, D.W. Utilization of Wind Energy in Nevada, Aerospace Sciences Meeting and Exhibit. In Proceedings of the 36th and 1998 ASME Wind Energy Symposium, Reno, NV, USA, 12–15 January 1998.

2.   AWS, Truewind, 2006. Available online: https://www.awstruepower.com/products/maps-and-resource-data/ (accessed on 3 February 2018).

3.   Cormier, C.K. *"Energy for Nevada"*, *Report to the Legislature on the Status of Energy in Nevada for the Year 1996*; Department of Business and Industry, Nevada, State Energy Office: Carson City, NV, USA, 1996; p. 36.

4.   Sherman, C.A. A Mass-consistent model for wind field over complex terrain. *J. Appl. Meteor.* **1978**, *17*, 312–319. [CrossRef]

5.   Pepper, D.W. *3-D Numerical Model for Predicting Mesoscale Wind Fields over Vandenberg Air Force Base, Final Report*; SBIR Contract F04701-89-C-0051; Advanced Project Research Inc.: Moorpark, CA, USA, 1990.

6.   Pielke, R.A. *Mesoscale Meteorological Modeling*; Academic Press: New York, NY, USA, 1984; p. 612.

7.   Sasaki, Y. An objective analysis based on the variational method. *J. Meteor. Soc. Jpn.* **1958**, *36*, 77–88. [CrossRef]

8.   Pepper, D.W.; Wang, X. An *h*-Adaptive Finite-Element Technique for Constructing 3-D Wind Fields. *J. Appl. Meteor. Clim.* **2009**, *48*, 580–599. [CrossRef]

9.   Dickerson, M.H. MASCON-A mass consistent atmospheric flux model for regions with complex terrain. *J. Appl. Meteor.* **1978**, *17*, 241–253. [CrossRef]

10. Renewable Resource Data Center: Wind Energy Resource Information-Wind Energy Resource Atlas of the United States, Chapter 1 Introduction-Map Descriptions. Available online: http://rredc.nrel.gov/wind/pubs/atlas/tables/1-1T.html (accessed on 3 February 2018).

11. Fasshauer, G.E. Newton iteration with multiquadrics for the solution of nonlinear pdes. *Comput. Math. Appl.* **2002**, *43*, 423–438. [CrossRef]

12. Fasshauer, G.E. Meshfree Approximation Methods with MATLAB. In *Interdisciplinary Mathematical Sciences*; World Scientific: Singapore, 2007; Volume 6, p. 500.

13. Atluri, S.N.; Zhu, T. A New Mesh-less Local Petrov-Galerkin Approach in Computational Mechanics. *Comput. Mech.* **1998**, *22*, 117–127. [CrossRef]

14. Balachandran, G.R.; Rajagopal, A.; Sivakumar, S.M. Mesh free Galerkin Method Based on Natural Neighbors and Conformal Mapping. *Comput. Mech.* **2009**, *42*, 885–905. [CrossRef]

15. Liu, G.R. *Mesh Free Methods, Moving Beyond the Finite Element Method*; CRC Press: Boca Raton, FL, USA, 2003; p. 692.

16. Li, H.; Mulay, S.S. *Meshless Methods and Their Numerical Properties*; CRC Press: Boca Raton, FL, USA, 2013; p. 429.

17. Choi, Y.; Kim, S.J. Node Generation Scheme for the Mesh-less Method by Voronoi Diagram and Weighted Bubble Packing. In Proceedings of the Fifth US National Congress on *Computational Mechanics*, Boulder, CO, USA, 4–6 August 1999.

18. Gewali, L.; Pepper, D.W. Adaptive Node Placement for Mesh-Free Methods. In Proceedings of the International Conference on Computational & Experimental Engineering and Sciences 2010 (*ICCES'10*), Las Vegas, NV, USA, 28 March–1 April 2010.

19. Franke, R. Scattered data interpolation tests of some methods. *Math Comput.* **1982**, *38*, 181–200.

20. Hardy, R.L. Multiquadric equations of topography and other irregular surfaces. *J. Geophys. Res.* **1971**, *76*, 1905–1915. [CrossRef]

21. Kansa, E.J. Highly accurate methods for solving elliptic and parabolic partial differential equations. *WIT Trans. Model. Simul.* **2005**, *39*, 5–15.

22. Roque, C.M.C.; Ferreira, A.J.M. Numerical Experiments on Optimal Shape Parameters for Radial Basis Functions. *Numer. Methods. Partial Differ. Equ.* **2009**, *26*, 675–689. [CrossRef]

23. Pepper, D.W.; Rasmussen, C.; Fyda, D. A Meshless Method for Creating 3-D Wind Fields using Sparse Meteorological Data. *CAMES* **2014**, *21*, 233–243.

24. Waters, J.; Pepper, D.W. Global versus Localized RBF Meshless Methods for Solving Incompressible Fluid Flow with Heat Transfer. *Numer. Heat Transf. B* **2015**, *68*, 185–203. [CrossRef]

25. Pepper, D.W.; Wang, X.; Carrington, D.B. A Meshless Method for Modeling Convective Heat Transfer. *ASME J. Heat Transf.* **2012**, *135*. [CrossRef]

26. Pepper, D.W.; Wang, X. Application of an h-adaptive finite element model for wind energy assessment in Nevada. *Renew. Energy* **2007**, *32*, 1705–1722. [CrossRef]

27. Ramos Gonzalez, M.; Pepper, D.W. A Cloud-based Method for Displaying 3-D Wind Fields on Mobile Devices. In Proceedings of the AMS 33rd Conference on Environmental Information Processing Technologies, Seattle, WA, USA, 22–26 January 2017.

Article

A Method of Accelerating the Convergence of Computational Fluid Dynamics for Micro-Siting Wind Mapping

Hyun-Goo Kim

New and Renewable Energy Resources & Policy Center, Korea Institute of Energy Research, Daejeon 34129, Korea; hyungoo@kier.re.kr; Tel.: +82-42-860-3376

Received: 13 February 2019; Accepted: 15 April 2019; Published: 24 April 2019

Abstract: To assess wind resources, a number of simulations should be performed by wind direction, wind speed, and atmospheric stability bins to conduct micro-siting using computational fluid dynamics (CFD). This study proposes a method of accelerating CFD convergence by generating initial conditions that are closer to the converged solution. In addition, the study proposes the 'mirrored initial condition' (IC) using the symmetry of wind direction and geography, the 'composed IC' using the vector composition principle, and the 'shifted IC' which assumes that the wind speed vectors are similar in conditions characterized by minute differences in wind direction as the well-posed initial conditions. They provided a significantly closer approximation to the converged flow field than did the conventional initial condition, which simply assumed a homogenous atmospheric boundary layer over the entire simulation domain. The results of this study show that the computation time taken for micro-siting can be shortened by around 35% when conducting CFD with 16 wind direction sectors by mixing the conventional and the proposed ICs properly.

Keywords: computational fluid dynamics; micro-siting; wind mapping; initial condition; convergence

---

1. Introduction

In a wind resource assessment (WRA) conducted to construct a wind farm, at least one or more meteorological towers should be installed at representative meteorological points within the candidate area, and the weather conditions, including seasonal changes, should be measured for at least one year. The measurement data should be converted to statistical data on wind resources at the hub height of the wind turbine at the installation points to be able to calculate the amount of wind power generated. However, the wind field is not homogeneous and varies according to the terrain. Thus, the meteorologically valid range of data measured with the meteorological tower is limited near the measurement point. Accordingly, wind flow modeling should be performed to identify the wind resources across a wide range of candidate areas for the construction of a wind farm. In other words, the wind speed distribution by wind direction should be mapped in the candidate area [1].

Wind flow modeling refers to a method of analyzing the Navier–Stokes equation, which is the governing equation of atmospheric wind flow. The modeling methods are divided into a linear method that is suitable for flat terrain, and a computational fluid dynamics (CFD) method that is suitable for complex terrain. As regards the representative software for each method, WAsP and WindSim can be used. Other methods, such as the interpolation method, continuity equation analysis method, and meso-scale numerical weather prediction (NWP) method, are also available, but the CFD method is now becoming the mainstream method [2,3].

The wind turbine layout that most effectively minimizes wake losses while maximizing energy production should be determined when the wind turbines are laid out in the candidate area. Then, the wind farm's annual energy production (AEP, MWh) can be calculated using the following equation [4,5]:

$$\text{AEP} = 8760 \times \sum_{i=1}^{nD} \sum_{j=1}^{nU} \sum_{k=1}^{nL} \sum_{l=1}^{nT} f_{ijkl} \cdot P_{ijkl} \tag{1}$$

In the above equation, nD, nU, nL, and nT refer to the number of wind direction sectors, the number of wind speed bins, the number of atmospheric stability intervals, and the number of wind turbines, respectively. For example, the wind speed range is divided into a series of intervals known as bins.

Here, f_{ijkl} refers to the probability density function that exhibits the frequency of occurrence of the j-th wind speed bin in the i-th wind direction sector and the k-th atmospheric stability interval in the l-th wind turbine location, while P_{ijkl} refers to the power output (kW). To calculate the AEP from Equation (1) after determining the wind turbine layout in the wind farm area, f_{ijkl} and P_{ijkl} should be identified first.

P_{ijkl} is given by the power curve of the wind turbine, and f_{ijkl} can be expressed by the Weibull distribution function, which is a probability distribution function of wind speed. f_{ijkm} can be evaluated by long-term correction after the measurement data have been extrapolated up to the wind turbine hub height at the installation location ($l = m$) of the meteorological tower. Either way, the results of a simulation of a mesoscale numerical weather prediction can be downscaled [6]. However, to determine f_{ijkl} at an arbitrary location within the wind farm area, the meteorological correlation between f_{ijkm} and f_{ijkl} should be evaluated by wind flow modeling, which process is called micro-siting.

f_{ijkl} at the arbitrary location can be calculated (as presented in the following equation) by applying the acceleration or deceleration ratio of the wind speed V predicted in the numerical modeling and f_{ijkm} at the meteorological tower's location.

$$f_{ijkl} = \frac{V_{ijkl}}{V_{ijkm}} f_{ijkm} \tag{2}$$

If a three-dimensional wind flow field that is changing in time should be predicted by transient simulation, an hourly numerical analysis of 8760 h is needed for one year, which requires a large amount of computation load and time. However, rather than conducting a numerical analysis for all 8760 h, if a typical case for each interval of wind direction, wind speed and atmospheric stability is analyzed by dynamical downscaling while assuming that the wind field at each hour is independent, and if the frequency of occurrence for each case is summed after multiplying it by the weighting factor, then the calculation load and time can be reduced significantly [7]. Thus, in such a case, wind flow modeling is performed with all of the wind condition sectors that can occur meteorologically and statistically, i.e., $nD \times nU \times nL$ cases, to reduce the calculation load and time.

If dynamical downscaling is set to 16 wind direction sectors, five wind speed bins, and five atmospheric stability intervals, a total of $16 \times 5 \times 5 = 400$ cases are to be simulated, which equals about 4.6% of the 8760 hourly cases. Nonetheless, 400 cases will still require a considerable calculation load and time for CFD. Here, $nD = 16$ means 16 wind direction sectors at 22.5° intervals, and $nU = 5$ means five wind speed bins from 0 m/s to 25 m/s, which is the cut-out wind speed that stops the operation of the wind turbine, at 5 m/s intervals. $nL = 5$ means that the Monin–Obukhov length is divided by five intervals from $-\infty$ to $+\infty$.

The CFD simulation of the atmospheric flow field means a process of iterative numerical analysis of the algebraic equations that satisfy the governing equation, i.e., the Reynolds-Averaged Navier–Stokes (RANS) equation, by all the flow field variables defined in each of the finite volume cells constituting the flow domain. To solve the partial differential RANS equation, boundary conditions should be imposed at the external surfaces of a three-dimensional physical space together with the initial conditions inside a three-dimensional physical space.

Since the RANS equation is an elliptic partial differential equation, there exists a unique solution regardless of the initial conditions in the case of a steady-state problem. However, an ill-posed initial condition would cause a divergence or deceleration of convergence in a numerical analysis [8]. Conversely, an acceleration of convergence can be expected when a good approximation of the initial conditions is imposed [9]. In particular, micro-siting wind mapping requires a considerable number of cases, such as the 400 described above. Thus, the assumption of the initial conditions can influence the overall computation time.

For an atmospheric flow field, a method that assumes the atmospheric boundary layer profiles of wind speed and turbulence, is slightly more effective in shortening the convergence speed than one that assumes a uniform flow field and turbulence field [10]. Either a potential or Euler flow field whose computation time is relatively shorter than the CFD is analyzed first to assume an accurate initial flow field, and its convergence solution may be used as the initial condition of the CFD [11,12].

This study proposes a novel method of accelerating the convergence speed in the CFD by assuming initial conditions that are closer to the real flow field, i.e., a solution that is converged as much as possible using the geometric characteristics in the atmospheric flow field according to the wind direction when producing the micro-siting wind map [13], and which proves the quantitative effect through real application cases.

2. Methods and Data

2.1. Method of Generating the Initial Conditions

To perform micro-siting wind mapping for a wind resource assessment, CFD simulations of a total number of $nD \times nU \times nL$ cases should be conducted with regard to the nD wind direction sectors, nU wind speed bins, and nL atmospheric stability intervals. In the wind energy industry, the Reynolds number invariance can be assumed in the case of a turbulent flow of a high Reynolds number without accompanying a flow separation [14,15]. Therefore, the number of CFD simulation cases can be reduced significantly using the $nU = 1$ assumption. If the neutral atmospheric stability is additionally assumed, then it satisfies $nL = 1$; thus the CFD can be performed with only the nD wind direction sectors [16]. Figure 1 shows the procedure for micro-siting wind mapping via a CFD simulation of the nD wind direction sectors.

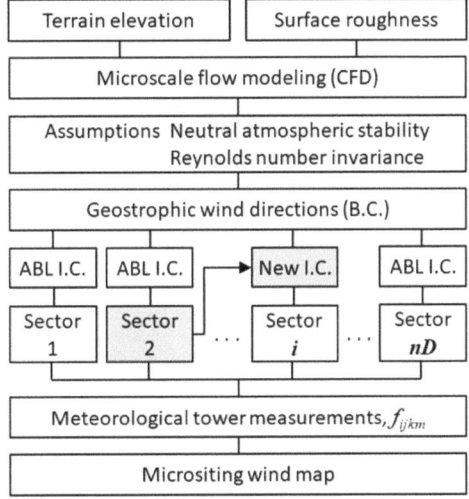

Figure 1. Flow chart of the micro-siting wind mapping procedure.

This study proposes a method of accelerating the convergence speed by assuming initial conditions that are very close to the converged solution, i.e., the real flow field, using the geometric characteristics of the atmospheric flow field and the topography when the CFD is conducted with regard to the nD wind direction sectors, as follows:

First, the geometric symmetry of the atmospheric flow field and the topography can be employed. For example, a northerly wind exhibits geometric symmetry with a southerly wind that has a 180° angular difference along the west–east axis. The initial condition that is reconfigured using this property is named the 'mirrored initial condition (IC)'.

This characteristic is expressed by the following equations:

$$\vec{V}(\theta) \cong -\vec{V}(\theta \pm 180) \tag{3}$$

$$VP(\theta) \cong -VP(\theta \pm 180) \tag{4}$$

where $\vec{V}(\theta)$ is the wind vector of the wind directional sector θ case, and VP is the pressure gradient in the wind vector direction.

Second, the wind vector of the wind direction sector θ case can be calculated mathematically by the vector composition of the wind vectors $\theta + d\theta$ and $\theta - d\theta$ when $d\theta$ is small enough. The initial condition that is reconfigured using this property is called the 'composed IC'.

This characteristic is expressed by the following equations:

$$\vec{V}(\theta) \cong \frac{\left|\vec{V}(\theta - d\theta)\right| + \left|\vec{V}(\theta + d\theta)\right|}{2} \cdot \frac{\vec{V}(\theta - d\theta) + \vec{V}(\theta + d\theta)}{\left|\vec{V}(\theta - d\theta) + \vec{V}(\theta + d\theta)\right|} \tag{5}$$

$$VP(\theta) \cong \frac{1}{2}\{VP(\theta - d\theta) + VP(\theta + d\theta)\} \tag{6}$$

Third, the wind vector of the wind direction sector θ case would be similar to the wind vector of the wind direction sector $\theta \pm d\theta$ case, which is rotated by as much as $d\theta$ with respect to the wind direction θ. The initial condition that is reconfigured using this property is called the 'shifted IC'.

This characteristic is expressed by the following equations:

$$\vec{V}(\theta + d\theta) \cong \left|\vec{V}(\theta)\right| \cdot \vec{i}(\theta + d\theta) \tag{7}$$

$$VP(\theta + d\theta) \cong VP(\theta) \tag{8}$$

In the above equation, $\vec{i}$ refers to the unit vector. That is, $\left|\vec{i}\right| = 1$.

2.2. Wind Mapping Steps for Convergence Acceleration

According to the international standard for wind energy, IEC 61400-1, the interval of the wind direction sectors shall be 30° or less [17]. Therefore, most wind resource assessments consider either 12 or 16 wind direction sectors. In case of $nD = 16$, convergence can be accelerated by conducting a CFD simulation using the following steps, by employing new initial conditions in Section 2.1 and Figure 1.

Step 1: CFD simulation is performed by applying a conventional initial condition for the four wind direction sectors, i.e., N, NE, E, and SE, thereby, obtaining the converged solution.

Step 2: The mirrored IC is applied with regard to the four wind direction sectors, i.e., S, SW, W, and SW, which have 180° symmetry with the above wind directions respectively, to perform the CFD simulation and thereby, obtain the convergence solution.

Step 3: Either the composed IC or the shifted IC is applied with regard to the other eight wind directions, i.e., NNE, ENE, ESE, SSE, SSW, SWS, NWN, and NNW, to conduct the CFD simulation and thereby, obtain the convergence solution.

As described above, the generated initial conditions can be applied to accelerate convergence for the 16 wind directions, except for the first four wind direction sectors out of the 16 wind directions.

2.3. Verification of the Convergence Acceleration Effect

To verify the effectiveness of this method of generating the initial conditions for convergence acceleration, WindSim, a representative CFD-based micro-siting software, was used. WindSim solves the RANS equations with the finite volume method and uses a meshed grid system of terrain [18]. A computer equipped with a Xeon CPU X5460 3.16 GHz with 32 GB RAM was used for testing, and the Hundhammerfjellet wind farm in Norway (which was included as a basic example in "WindSim: Getting Started") was used as the verification case. The grid system configured for the CFD simulation in the Hundhammerfjellet region was as follows: domain size = 15 km × 15 km, fine grid of 75 m × 75 m (200 × 200 × 25 = 1 million cells). For reference, this setting satisfies grid independency and is suitable for application to a wind farm design in terms of spatial resolution.

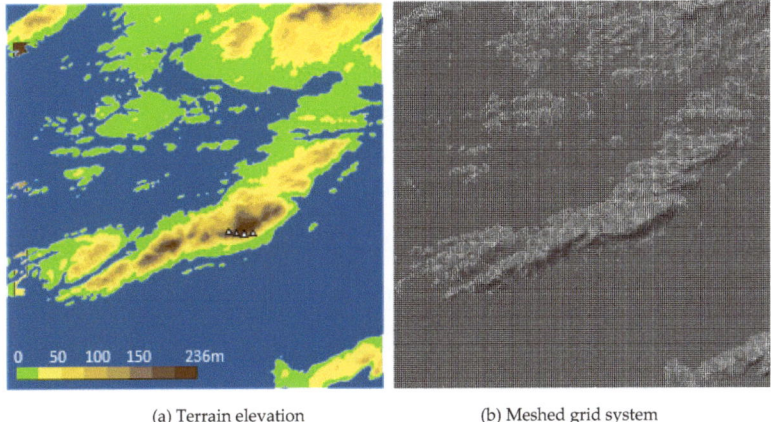

(a) Terrain elevation   (b) Meshed grid system

Figure 2. The computational domain around the Hundhammerfjellet wind farm (triangles: wind turbines, cobalt blue region: sea).

Since the atmospheric flow has a very large topographic scale generally, it has a high Reynolds number, and since the ground surface is rough, Reynolds number invariance can be assumed. To verify this assumption, the geostrophic wind speeds (V_{geo}) in the upper top part of the atmospheric boundary layer were set to 5 m/s, 10 m/s, and 15 m/s. As reference information, the Hundhammerfjellet wind farm is located along the ridge in the central part of the peninsula extending SSW to NNE in the center of the domain, as shown in Figure 2. Assuming that the maximum altitude above sea level (236 meters) of the Hundhammerfjellet ridge is set to a characteristic length, the corresponding Reynolds numbers become 0.8×10^8, 1.6×10^8, and 2.4×10^8, respectively.

3. Results and Discussion

3.1. Reynolds Number Invariance of the Wind Field

Figure 3a shows the wind speed contour in the northerly wind case, which is normalized with the geostrophic wind speed, meaning that $S = V/V_{geo}$. Furthermore, a low wind speed region was observed below the wind speed ratio $S < 0.2$ on the lee side due to the rapid downslope after a speed-up of more than $S > 1.0$ at the Hundhammerfjellet ridge in the central part of the computational domain. Figure 3b shows the difference between case S_{15} at a geostrophic wind speed of 15 m/s and case S_{05} at 5 m/s, that is, $dS = S_{15} - S_{05}$. The region which revealed the largest difference in the domain was the deceleration area of wind speed due to the downslope and this effect produced a long transport pattern along the downwind direction.

The minimum value of normalized wind speed difference dS in the deceleration area was –0.09, which meant that wind speed deceleration was predicted more on the ridge's lee side when the Reynolds number was smaller. The relative RMSE of dS in the overall computational domain was just 0.65%. In summary, it was verified that the atmospheric flow field had the characteristic of near invariability according to the Reynolds number overall, although there was a small variation when a rapid wind speed gradient was generated in local regions with a steep topography.

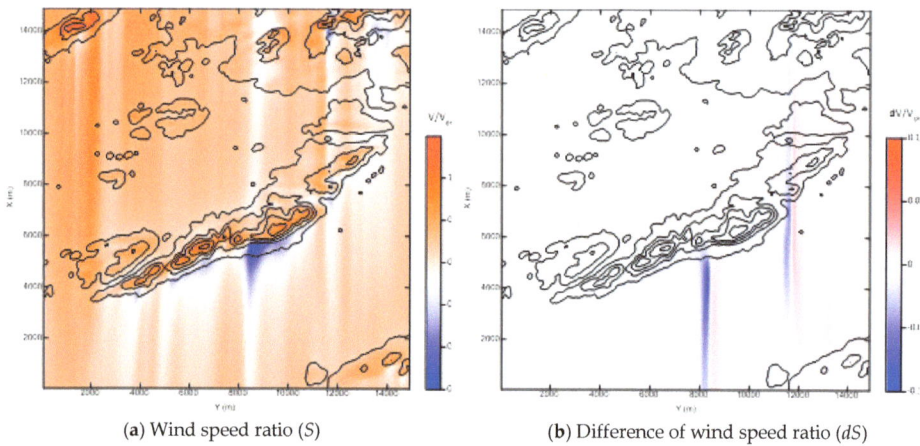

| (a) Wind speed ratio (S) | (b) Difference of wind speed ratio (dS) |

Figure 3. Contour plots of wind speed ratio for the northerly wind case (5 m above ground level).

3.2. Evaluation of New Initial Conditions

3.2.1. Error Analysis of New Initial Conditions

For the purposes of this study, an error analysis was performed to quantitatively evaluate the method of generating the new initial conditions. An approximation error wind field $d\vec{V}$ is defined as the difference between a converged wind field $\vec{V}_c$, which is assumed to be the true solution, and a guessed wind field $\vec{V}_i$, which is generated by the proposed method, i.e., Equations (3)~(8). If an initial condition is generated using the mirrored IC method, $d\vec{V}$ is as follows:

$$d\vec{V} = \vec{V}_c(\theta) - \vec{V}_i(\theta) = \vec{V}_c(\theta) - \left\{ -\vec{V}_c(\theta \pm 180) \right\} \tag{9}$$

where the subscripts c and i denote the 'converged solution' and the 'guessed initial condition', respectively.

Figure 4 shows the difference between the converged north-easterly wind field $\vec{V}_c(NE)$ and the guessed wind field $\vec{V}_i(NE) = -\vec{V}_c(SW)$ using the mirrored IC method with the converged south-westerly wind field $\vec{V}_c(SW)$. The largest error was found in the SW direction of the Hundhammerfjellet ridge, where the terrain slopes steeply, meaning that wind speed acceleration and deceleration occurred for the opposite wind directions, respectively.

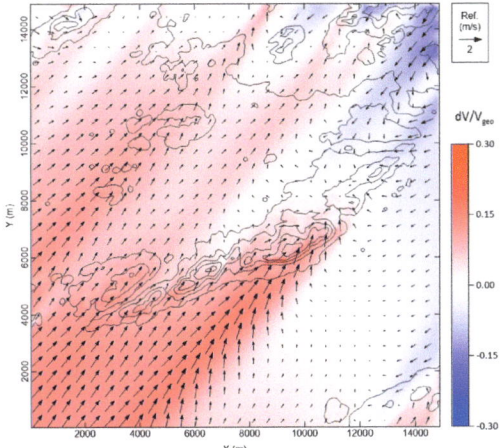

Figure 4. Error wind field of the mirrored initial condition for the north-easterly wind case (10 meters above ground level).

Table 1 summarizes the results of the evaluation of the approximation errors between the converged solutions and the guessed initial conditions. In the table, ABL IC stands for the atmospheric boundary layer assumption, which is generally used in micro-siting wind mapping. Note that the results were calculated on the layer at a height of 10 m above ground, where wind field deformation is significant. The proposed initial conditions showed a lower margin of error in all cases than those of the conventional initial condition (ABL) for wind speed and direction. Therefore, the proposed method of generating the initial condition provides a closer approximation to the real wind field than the conventional initial condition. Among them, the composed IC method showed the lowest approximation error.

Table 1. Comparison of approximation error of normalized wind speed difference and wind direction difference by the method of generating the initial condition.

Initial Condition	$dV/V_{geo} \times 100$ (%)			$d\theta$		
	MBE	MAE	RMSE	MBE	MAE	RMSE
Mirrored	3.3	6.4	8.0	−0.97	2.35	3.75
Composed	4.3	**4.9**	**5.9**	0.17	**2.12**	**3.17**
Shifted	**−1.9**	6.1	7.9	−0.49	2.90	6.29
ABL	−5.7	8.7	1.2	3.62	4.35	7.46

3.2.2. Sensitivity Analysis of Directional Interval

Because a directional interval is involved in the generation of the composed and shifted ICs (Equations (5) and (7)), it is necessary to check the sensitivity of the directional interval to approximation error. As expected, the mean absolute error (MAE) of the approximation errors of wind speed (the dashed lines with hollow circles) and direction (the solid lines with black squares) increased linearly in line with the increase of the directional intervals, as shown in Figure 5. The mean bias error (MBE) and root mean square error (RMSE) showed the same trends.

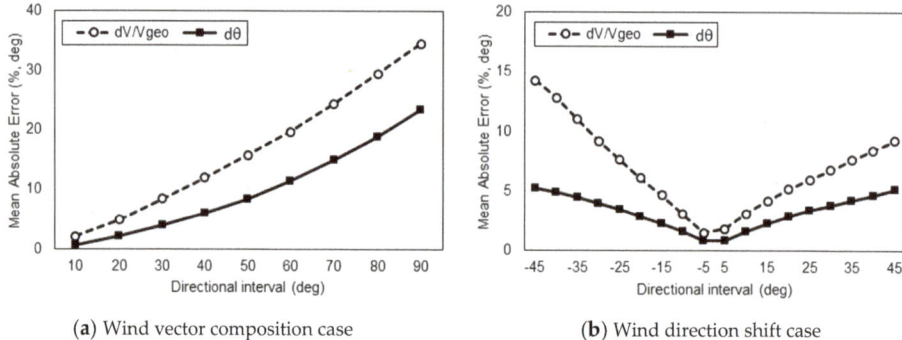

(**a**) Wind vector composition case (**b**) Wind direction shift case

Figure 5. Analysis of the sensitivity of directional intervals to approximation error.

If the maximum error is limited to the MAE of the mirrored IC (Table 1), then the maximum directional intervals for the composed and shifted ICs will be less than 25°, meaning that at least 16 wind directional sectors are needed to apply the new initial conditions.

3.3. Convergence Acceleration by the New Initial Conditions

3.3.1. Convergence Acceleration of the Individual CFD Simulation

Figure 6a,b show the improved results of the CFD's convergence speed as the initial conditions are changed from the ABL assumption to the mirrored IC, respectively. Figure 6 shows the history of the field variables at the monitoring point and residuals according to the iteration number. By applying the mirrored IC, the number of iterations that reached convergence was reduced from 100 (ABL IC) to 50 (mirrored IC), meaning an acceleration rate of 50%. In the case of the composed IC or the shifted IC, the acceleration effect of the convergence speed was similar to that of the mirrored IC.

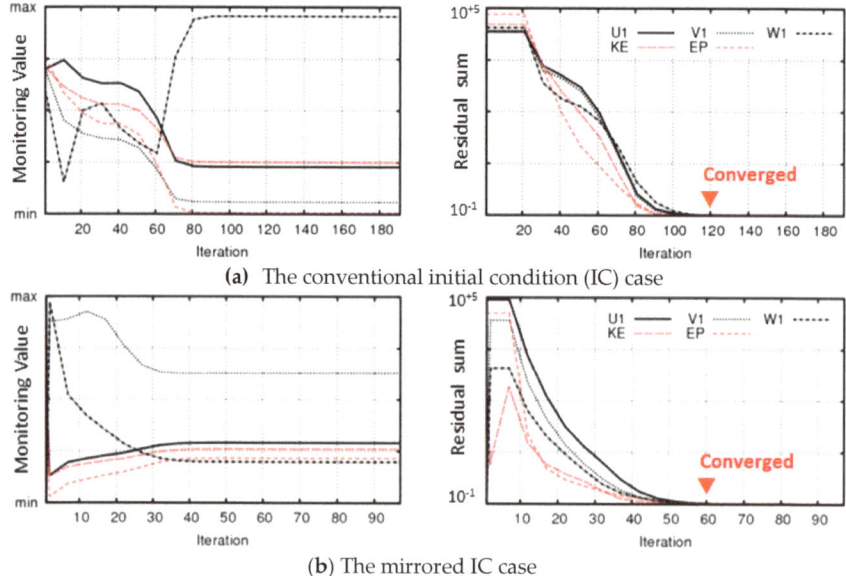

(**a**) The conventional initial condition (IC) case

(**b**) The mirrored IC case

Figure 6. Comparison of the convergence history of monitoring values of the field variables (normalized by maximum; left graphs) and the residual values of the field variables (right graphs).

3.3.2. Convergence Acceleration of the Overall CFD Simulations

Table 2 shows the quantitative improvements in the convergence speed obtained when the CFD simulation was conducted for the $nD = 16$, $nU = 1$, and $nL = 1$ cases. The overall computation time took 27,150 s when only the ABL was assumed homogeneously in the computation domain. In contrast, the computation time according to the proposed method combining the ABL, mirrored, composed, and shifted ICs (as proposed in Section 2.2) was as follows:

Step 1: For the four wind direction sectors, i.e., N, NE, E, and SE, the ABL IC took 7167 s until convergence.

Step 2: For the four symmetric wind direction sectors, i.e., S, SW, W, and NW, the converged solutions of the previous four sectors of N, NE, E, and SE were used to generate the mirrored IC, and took 3603 s until convergence.

Step 3: For the remaining eight wind direction sectors, i.e., NNE, ENE, ESE, SSE, SSW, SWS, NWN, and NNW, the converged solutions of the previous eight sectors were used to generate either the vector composed IC (e.g., NNE from N+NE) or the shifted IC (e.g., SSW from either S or SSW), and took 6719 s until convergence.

Thus, the overall computation time was 17,489 s, which was 36% shorter than in the conventional case (27,150 s).

Table 2. Comparison of the convergence times of the 16 wind direction cases between the conventional initial condition (IC) and the proposed ICs.

Wind Directional Sector	Conventional Method ABL IC	Proposed Method Using New ICs Step 1 ABL IC	Step 2 Mirrored IC	Step 3 Composed or Shifted IC
N	1740	1740		
NNE	1837			919
NE	1980	1980		
ENE	1855			927
E	1565	1565		
ESE	1591			795
SE	1883	1883		
SSE	1691			845
S	1770		885	
SSW	1688			844
SW	1674		1004	
SWS	1564			782
W	1471		735	
NWN	1583			791
NW	1631		979	
NNW	1632			816
Total	27,150	7167	3603	6719
			17,489	

3.3.3. Analysis of Sensitivity of the Computation Cell Numbers

In general, the convergence time does not increase linearly according to the number of computation cells. For the purposes of this study, a sensitivity analysis was conducted by increasing the computational cell numbers from half a million up to 4 million to figure out the effect on the convergence time. Figure 7 shows the graph of the empirical equation of the convergence time according to the number of computation cells, in which the convergence time increases as a quadratic function with regard to the number of computation cells (ABL IC was applied). Thus, if 160 min can be reduced when the number of computation cells is 1 million, as presented in Table 2, the shortening time of the convergence speed is estimated to be 50 hours, which is around 20 times of 160 min, if the number of computation cells is increased fourfold to 4 million.

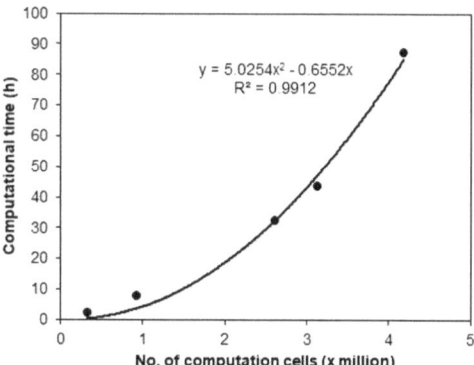

Figure 7. Computation time depending on a number of computational cells (for a single sector).

4. Conclusions

A large number of CFD simulations need to be performed by wind direction sector, wind speed bin, and atmospheric stability interval to conduct micro-siting in a wind resource assessment. As such, this study proposed a method of shortening the CFD convergence time by assuming initial conditions that are closer to the real flow field. The conclusions obtained in this study are as follows:

(1)   Mirrored, composed, and shifted ICs were generated from the converged solutions with regard to the different wind direction sectors by using the geometric similarity or vector composition principle. In the case of the CFD simulations of the 16 wind direction sectors in the Hundhammerfjellet wind farm case, the new ICs showed better convergence performance than that of the conventional ABL IC case, shortening the convergence time by 50%. Compared to the converged solution, the new ICs showed approximation errors of only 4.9%~6.4% of the wind speed ratio MAE and 2.10~2.90 of the wind direction MAE, which are about 34% and 44% lower than those of ABL IC, respectively.

(2)   When the method of generating the initial conditions proposed in this study and the conventional initial conditions were mixed appropriately by wind direction sector, the overall CFD convergence time was confirmed to have been reduced by around 36% when employing 1 million computation cells and 16 wind direction sectors. Therefore, the proposed method is expected to make a substantial contribution to shortening the micro-siting project period for the design of a wind farm.

(3)   The validity of the Reynolds number invariance of atmospheric wind flow over rough terrain was verified from the Hundhammerfjellet wind farm simulation with regard to the gradient wind speeds of 5 m/s, 10 m/s, and 15 m/s. The relative RMSE of the difference in wind speed between the Reynolds number 0.8×10^8 and 2.4×10^8 cases was only 0.65% and differences were found on the lee side of the steeply sloped, high terrain.

Funding: This work was conducted under the framework of the research and development program of the Korea Institute of Energy Research (B9-2414).

Conflicts of Interest: The authors declare no conflict of interest.

Patent: The main idea of this work has been registered to U.S. Patent 10,242,131 in March 2019.

References

1. Bower, M.C. *Wind Resource Assessment—A Practical Guide to Developing a Wind Project*; John Wiley & Sons, Inc.: Hoboken, NJ, USA, 2012.
2. Probst, O.; Cardenas, D. State of the Art and Trends in Wind Resource Assessment. *Energies* **2010**, *3*, 1087–1141. [CrossRef]
3. Calautit, K.; Aquino, A.; Calautit, J.K.; Nejat, P.; Jomehzadeh, F.; Hughes, B.R. A Review of Numerical Modelling of Multi-Scale Wind Turbines and Their Environment. *Computation* **2018**, *6*, 24. [CrossRef]
4. Zhang, M.H. *Wind Resource Assessment and Micro-siting*; John Wiley & Sons, Inc.: Singapore, 2015.
5. AWS Truepower. *Openwind—Theoretical Basis and Validation*; AWS Truepower: Albany, NY, USA, 2010.
6. Rodrigo, J.S.; Arroyo, R.A.C.; Moriarty, P.; Churchfield, M.; Kosovic, B.; Rethore, P.E.; Hansen, K.S.; Hahmann, A.; Mirocha, J.D.; Rife, D. Mesoscale to Microscale Wind Farm Flow Modeling and Evaluation. *WIREs Energy Environ.* **2017**, *6*, 1–30. [CrossRef]
7. Hay, L.E.; Clark, M.P. Use of Statistically and Dynamically Downscaled Atmospheric Model Output for Hydrologic Simulations in Three Mountainous Basins in the Western United States. *J. Hydrol.* **2003**, *282*, 56–75. [CrossRef]
8. Nordstrom, J. Well Posed Problems and Boundary Conditions in Computational Fluid Dynamics. In Proceedings of the 22nd AIAA Computational Fluid Dynamics Conference, Dallas, TX, USA, 22–26 June 2015.
9. Ferziger, J.H.; Peric, M. *Computational Methods for Fluid Dynamics*; Springer-Verlag: Berlin, Germany, 1996.
10. Beaucage, P.; Brower, M.C. *Wind Flow Model Performance—Do More Sophisticated Models Produce More Accurate Wind Resource Estimates?* AWS Truepower: Albany, NY, USA, 2012.
11. Tu, J.; Yeoh, G.H.; Liu, C. *Computational Fluid Dynamics—A Practical Approach*, 2nd ed.; Butterworth-Heinemann: Oxford, UK, 2013.
12. ANSYS. *ANSYS Fluent Theory Guide, Release 15.0*; ANSYS, Inc.: Canonsburg, PA, USA, 2013; Chapter 20.8 Hybrid Initialization.
13. Kim, H.-G. Numerical Simulation System and Numerical Simulation Method for Atmospheric Flow by Computational Fluid Dynamics, U.S. Patent 10,242,131, March 2019.
14. Kato, M.; Hanafusa, T. Wind Tunnel Simulation of Atmospheric Turbulent Flow Over a Flat Terrain. *Atmos. Environ.* **1996**, *30*, 2853–2858. [CrossRef]
15. Kilpatrick, R.; Hangan, H.; Siddiqui, K.; Parvu, D.; Lange, J.; Mann, J.; Berg, J. Effect of Reynolds Number and Inflow Parameters on Mean and Turbulent Flow over Complex Topography. *Wind Energy Science* **2016**, *1*, 237–254. [CrossRef]
16. Beaucage, P.; Brower, M.C.; Tensen, J. Evaluation of Four Numerical Wind Flow Models for Wind Resource Mapping. *Wind Energy* **2014**, *17*, 197–208. [CrossRef]
17. International Electrotechnical Commission. *IEC 61400-1:2019, Wind Energy Generation System—Part 1: Design Requirements*, 3rd ed.; International Electrotechnical Commission: Geneva, Switzerland, 2019.
18. WindSim AS. *WindSim v9 Getting Started*; WindSim AS: Tonsberg, Norway, 2017.

Article

Wind Pressure Distributions on Buildings Using the Coherent Structure Smagorinsky Model for LES

Pham Van Phuc [1,*], Tsuyoshi Nozu [1], Hirotoshi Kikuchi [1], Kazuki Hibi [2] and Yukio Tamura [3]

[1] Institute of Technology, Shimizu Corporation, Tokyo 1358530, Japan; nozu@shimz.co.jp (T.N.);
   h_kikuchi@shimz.co.jp (H.K.)
[2] Numerical Flow Designing Co., Ltd., Tokyo 1410022, Japan; hibi@nufd.jp
[3] School of Civil Engineering, Chongqing University, Chongqing 400045, China; yukio@arch.t-kougei.ac.jp
* Correspondence: p_phuc@shimz.co.jp; Tel.: +81-3-3820-8496

Received: 22 January 2018; Accepted: 10 April 2018; Published: 14 April 2018

Abstract: A subgrid-scale model based on coherent structures, called the Coherent Structure Smagorinsky Model (CSM), has been applied to a large eddy simulation to assess its performance in the prediction of wind pressure distributions on buildings. The study cases were carried out for the assessment of an isolated rectangular high-rise building and a building with a setback (both in a uniform flow) and an actual high-rise building in an urban city with turbulent boundary layer flow. For the isolated rectangular high-rise building in uniform flow, the CSM showed good agreement with both the traditional Smagorinsky Model (SM) and the experiments (values within 20%). For the building with a setback as well as the actual high-rise building in an urban city, both of which have a distinctive wind pressure distribution with large negative pressure caused by the complicated flow due to the strong influence of neighboring buildings, the CSM effectively gives more accurate results with less variation than the SM in comparison with the experimental results (within 20%). The CSM also yielded consistent peak pressure coefficients for all wind directions, within 20% of experimental values in a relatively high-pressure region of the case study of the actual high-rise building in an urban city.

Keywords: LES; SGS models; wind pressure; building; Coherent Structure Smagorinsky Model

---

1. Introduction

Large eddy simulation (LES) generally shows good performance for the prediction of any turbulent flows. As is well known, LES solves large eddies on a grid scale (GS) and has been shown to implicitly account for small eddies using a subgrid-scale model (SGS model). The most-used SGS model is the Smagorinsky model (SM) [1]. The SM is determined using a model parameter. However, its model parameter must be changed to represent different turbulent flows such as a homogeneous isotropic turbulence, a turbulent mixing layer, or a turbulent channel flow.

Some SGS models have also been proposed to improve the weaknesses of the SM. A well-known SGS model is the dynamic Smagorinsky model (DSM) proposed by Germano et al. [2] that self-adjusts the model parameter using a dynamic approach. However, its parameter model often becomes negative and highly fluctuates in space and time, causing numerical instability.

To overcome this drawback, several models have been proposed. Ghosal et al. [3] proposed a dynamic localization model with the clipping operation. Meneveau et al. [4] proposed a Lagrangian averaging along the path line for the dynamic model. They are applicable to complex geometrical applications [5]; however, it still takes more computational time [4].

A number of local SGS models have been developed to offer several advantages over the SM. Yoshizawa et al. [6] suggested a nonequilibrium fixed-parameter SGS model and showed that the model was more accurate than the SM for turbulent channel flow. Vreman [7] suggested a localized

Computation **2018**, *6*, 32; doi:10.3390/computation6020032   www.mdpi.com/journal/computation

filter SGS model and showed that it works better than the SM, as well as the DSM, for a turbulent mixing layer and turbulent channel flow. Park et al. [8] suggested a dynamic SGS model with a global coefficient model based on the global equilibrium between the SGS dissipation and the viscous dissipation, and showed that it works well for isotropic turbulence, turbulent channel flows, or the complex flow field over a circular cylinder or a sphere.

More recently, Kobayashi [9] proposed an SGS model based on coherent structures, called the Coherent Structure Smagorinsky model (CSM). Its model parameter is composed of a fixed model parameter and a coherent structure function, which is defined by the second invariant of the GS flow field normalized by the magnitude of a velocity gradient tensor, and it plays a role in wall-damping near the wall boundary. Some studies have indicated that the CSM produces better predictions than the DSM in a series of turbulent flow problems, such as turbulent channel flows [10], turbulent duct flows [11], or flows over complex geometries [12]. The CSM could run 15% faster in terms of the total CPU time than the DSM which gives it a significant advantage over the DSM [12]. In comparison with the SM, the model parameter that is used in the CSM does not need to change to model the different turbulent flows and is appropriate for large-scale computations [13].

For wind engineering problems, wind pressure is an important issue in building cladding design. Large negative wind pressures are commonly found on the roof and sidewall which are strongly related with the separation flow and vortex from the leading edges and corners of buildings [14–16]. The flow field is a distinctive and complex turbulent bluff body flow which differs from traditional turbulent flows such as turbulent channel flow. Some studies have indicated that LES could give sufficient accuracy for the prediction of the flow field around buildings, and of the wind load and wind pressure of isolated buildings or buildings in urban areas. However, it needs large-scale computation [17–22]. Several benchmark tests were done by the Architectural Institute of Japan [23] using LES with different Computational Fluid Dynamics (CFD) codes for an isolated high-rise building and for a complicatedly shaped building in an actual urban area with limited wind direction. It was indicated that LES could estimate the wind pressure with consistent accuracy within 20% in comparison with the target experimental results in these wind engineering problems [21–23]. However, most of these works used the SM model and did not provide an in-depth discussion of the SGS model details.

All SGS models are attractive for wind engineering problems. Among them is the CSM determined by the second invariant of the flow field which reflects the vortex structures. This makes it acceptable for strong vortex interference in the turbulent bluff body flow as well as for the building wind pressure problem. It is for this reason that we chose the CSM in the first stage. The other models remain to be explored in future study.

In this study, the applicability of the CSM is mainly assessed in the LES of wind pressure distributions acting on buildings. Two case studies are examined: isolated buildings in uniform flow and an actual high-rise building in an urban city with turbulent boundary layer flow. First, this paper briefly describes the SGS models. For each case study, the wind tunnel experiments and the target buildings are presented. Then, the numerical models and results are given and a discussion is presented on the performance of the CSM in comparison with the SM and experimental results.

2. SGS Models and Numerical Methods

2.1. SGS Models

In LES, the momentum equation is filtered with the grid filtering operator (-) as follows:

$$\frac{\partial \overline{u_i}}{\partial t} + \overline{u_j} \frac{\partial \overline{u_i}}{\partial x_j} = -\frac{1}{\rho} \frac{\partial \overline{p}}{\partial x_i} - \frac{\partial \tau_{ij}}{\partial x_j} + \nu \frac{\partial^2 \overline{u_i}}{\partial x_j^2} \tag{1}$$

$$\tau_{ij} = \overline{u_i u_j} - \overline{u_i}\,\overline{u_j} \tag{2}$$

$$\tau_{ij}^a = \tau_{ij} - \frac{1}{3} \tau_{aa} \delta_{ij} \tag{3}$$

where x, t, u, p, ρ, and ν are the spatial coordinate, time, velocity vector, pressure, density, and kinematic viscosity, respectively. δ_{ij} is the Kronecker delta, and τ_{ij} and τ_{ij}^a denote the SGS stress tensor and the traceless SGS stress tensor, respectively. The SM and CSM are examined in the present study.

In the SM [1], the traceless SGS stress tensor based on the eddy viscosity concept is defined by the following equation:

$$\tau_{ij}^a = -2C\overline{\Delta}^2 |\overline{S}|\overline{S}_{ij}, \ |\overline{S}| = \sqrt{2\overline{S}_{ij}\overline{S}_{ij}}, \ \overline{S}_{ij} = \frac{1}{2}\left(\frac{\partial \overline{u}_j}{\partial x_i} + \frac{\partial \overline{u}_i}{\partial x_j}\right) \tag{4}$$

where C is the model parameter, Δ is the filter width, and $\overline{S}_{ij}$ is the velocity strain tensor. The Smagorinsky constant C_S as $C_S = \sqrt{C}$ is used hereafter. Because the model parameter is always positive, the simulation of the SM can be stably carried out. However, the SM has some flaws [9–12]. The Smagorinsky constant must be changed depending on the flow field; for example, $C_S = 0.2$ for homogeneous turbulences and $C_S = 0.1$ for turbulent channel flows. The wall damping function is also required to modify the eddy viscosity both at the wall and near the wall. The explicit van Driest wall damping function $f = 1 - \exp(-y^+/25)$ is the most commonly used function. Within this function, the wall coordinate y^+ commonly results in high computational cost for large-scale models with unstructured meshes.

In the CSM, the traceless SGS stress tensor is determined by Equation (4). However, the model parameter C is locally determined based on the coherent structure as follows [9]:

$$C = C_{CSM}|F_{CS}|^{3/2}F_\Omega \tag{5}$$

with

$$C_{CSM} = \frac{1}{22} \tag{6}$$

$$F_{CS} = \frac{Q}{E}, \ F_\Omega = 1 - F_{CS} \tag{7}$$

$$Q = \frac{1}{2}\left(\overline{W_{ij}W_{ij}} - \overline{S_{ij}S_{ij}}\right) = -\frac{1}{2}\frac{\partial \overline{u}_j}{\partial x_i}\frac{\partial \overline{u}_i}{\partial x_j} \tag{8}$$

$$E = \frac{1}{2}\left(\overline{W_{ij}W_{ij}} + \overline{S_{ij}S_{ij}}\right) = \frac{1}{2}\left(\frac{\partial \overline{u}_j}{\partial x_i}\right)^2 \tag{9}$$

$$\overline{W}_{ij} = \frac{1}{2}\left(\frac{\partial \overline{u}_j}{\partial x_i} - \frac{\partial \overline{u}_i}{\partial x_j}\right) \tag{10}$$

where C_{CSM} is a fixed model constant, F_{CS} is the coherent structure function defined as the second invariant Q normalized by the magnitude of a velocity gradient tensor E in a GS flow field, and F_Ω is the energy decay suppression function. $\overline{W}_{ij}$ is the vorticity tensor in a GS flow field. The wall damping effect is introduced by the coherent structure function F_{CS}, which reflects the behavior of the second invariant Q [9].

Moreover, F_{CS} and F_Ω have definite upper and lower limits [12]. Therefore, the CSM has small variance in the model parameter and the simulations performed using the CSM are more stable than the simulations that use other SGS models.

In addition, it should be noted that the second invariant Q is a useful parameter usually used to visualize the vortex structures in a wind flow field. Hence, the CSM has a quality that effectively assimilates the distinctive vortex structures separately from the buildings that cause the dominant wind pressures acting on the building surfaces.

2.2. Numerical Methods

In the present study, we used the pisoFoam solver from the open-source software OpenFOAM-2.0.0 [24] to solve the filtered governing equations for the LES. The discretization of the solver is based on the finite volume method of a cell-centered unstructured mesh.

For the numerical schemes, the linear scheme was used as a default to calculate the interpolation of values typically from cell centers to face centers (specified by "interpolationSchemes {default linear;}" in OpenFOAM). An implicit second-order backward scheme was used for the time derivative term (specified as "ddtSchemes {backward;}"). A second-order central difference scheme was used for the convective term (specified as "divSchemes {Gauss linear;}"). A Gaussian integration with linear interpolation was used for the gradient terms (specified as the default by "gradSchemes {Gauss linear;}"). A Gaussian integration, in which the surface normal gradient was specified by a limiter for the nonorthogonal correction, was used for the diffusion term (specified as "laplacianSchemes {Gauss linear limited 0.333;}"). Although assessing the numerical schemes for the accuracy of the simulation is attractive, the numerical dissipation from the second-order central difference scheme for the convective term [25] is also a valuable topic, but it is to be explored in further studies.

The momentum equation for velocity and the Poisson equation for pressure were solved using the linear equation solvers of the Biconjugate Gradient (BiCG) method and the Algebraic Multigrid (AMG) method, respectively. The Pressure-Implicit with Splitting of Operators (PISO) method was adopted for the pressure–velocity coupling of the transient flow calculations. A nonorthogonality correction was also used to modify the accuracy and stability of the diffusion term on the nonorthogonal meshes.

For the SGS models of LES, we used the SM in OpenFOAM with the default parameter in which the estimated Smagorinsky constant Cs was 0.13, and the explicit wall damping function was of the van Driest type. The CSM was developed as new code based on Equation (5) and the SM implementation code.

Furthermore, we used the wall-resolved LES (without using any wall layer models). The wall boundaries of the computational domains were set as no-slip boundaries. The finest grid size was small enough to have two grids within the viscous sublayer (more details in Phuc et al. [26]). However, target buildings in this study had rectangular shapes with sharp edges. For the cases of the building shapes, the separation points are generally fixed at the sharp edges and corners. Practically, there is not much Reynolds number dependence, and it is not critical for predicting the flow in the separation area of these buildings in comparison with others—for example, a circular cylinder or an airfoil.

3. Numerical Simulation for Isolated Buildings in Uniform Flow

3.1. Experiments for Validation

Two types of experiments—wind pressure experiments and particle image velocimetry (PIV) experiments in a uniform flow—were carried out to measure the wind pressure distribution on the building models and the flow fields around them. The experiments were done in a 104 m long wind tunnel at the Shimizu Corporation, Tokyo, Japan. The measurement section is 3.5 m wide and 2.5 m in height. Figure 1 shows pictures of the experimental setups. The building models were set up on a flat plate (width: 1 m; length: 1.8 m), which acted as a virtual foundation with a leading edge that was processed into a streamlined shape. The wind profile on the flat plate was examined using a hot-wire anemometer. It had a uniform flow with a wind speed of $U_0 = 10$ m/s, and its turbulence intensity was less than 0.2%.

There were two target buildings: an isolated high-rise rectangular building called R01 ($B/D/H = 2{:}1{:}2$) with a height of 50 m, and a building with a setback, referred to as SBL. Herein, the building SBL constituted of a high-rise part based on the building R01, and a low-rise part which was packed closely featuring a building setback. The test models of the buildings were made of acrylic plastic at the scale of 1:250. Table 1 and Figure 2 describe the geometries of the building models.

Experiments were conducted with a wind direction normal to the building. The Reynolds number ($Re = U_0 B/\nu$, $B = 0.2$ m) was about 112,000.

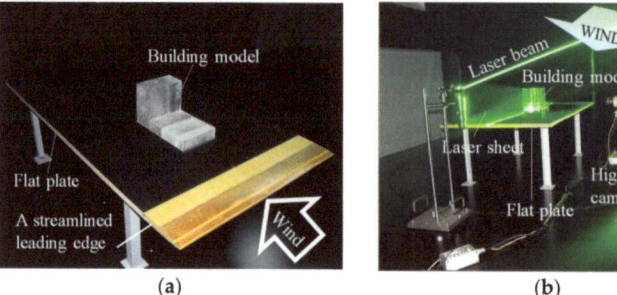

(a)   (b)

Figure 1. The experimental setup. (a) Pressure experiment; (b) particle image velocimetry (PIV) experiment.

Table 1. The dimensions of the building models in the scale of 1:250 (unit: m).

Type	B	D	H	H_1	H_2	D_1
R01	0.20	0.10	0.20			
SBL	0.20	0.10	0.20	0.15	0.05	0.35

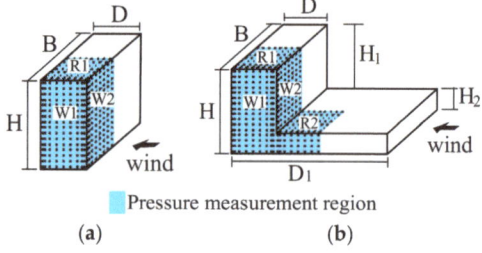

Pressure measurement region

(a)   (b)

Figure 2. The definition of the building models and pressure measurement regions. (a) The building referred to as R01; (b) the building referred to as SBL.

For the pressure experiments, 412 pressure taps were concentrated at one side of the roofs and the walls (roof surfaces: R1 and R2; wall surfaces: W1 and W2) to measure the external wind pressure acting on the models. It was adequate to measure only one side due to their structural symmetries as shown in Figure 2. Experimental data were recorded for 8 s at a sampling frequency of 1000 Hz, and the variation of both the mean and peak pressures during the recorded time was less than 5%. The wind pressures of the roof and wall surfaces were statistically summarized: the peak pressure coefficients were estimated using a moving average with a window of one second of real time.

For the PIV experiments, the system consisted of a high-speed digital video camera (Plantom V7, maximum frame rate: 4800 frames/s, effective pixels: 800 × 600, sensor type: SR-CMOS), a double-pulse Nd:YAG laser (Lee Laser Inc., Orlando, FL, USA, average power 50 W, the power of the laser pulse is 19 mJ), a laser pulse synchronizer, and a tracer particle generator (PivPar40, oil mist with particle diameter: 1 μm). The tracer particles were discharged downstream of the building model and circulated inside the wind tunnel to create a uniform particle distribution. In order to manage the experimental conditions to be consistent with the pressure experiments, the laser sheet was precisely adjusted with high-intensity power. The video camera recorded for 3 s at a frame rate of 4000 frames/s due to PIV system limitations. The 4000 images taken each second were grouped into 2000 consecutive pairs, and each pair was used to calculate the flow field information. Figure 3 shows the planes that were chosen for the PIV experiments. The regions A1, A2, and A3 were used to examine the flow field at the central cross section of the models. The region B1 was 5 mm away from the wall surface W1 in order to examine the flow field near its corner.

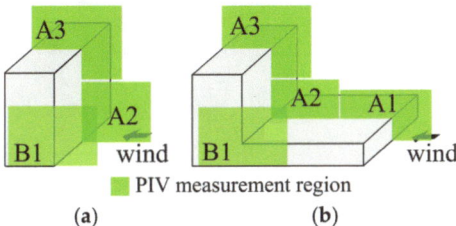

Figure 3. The definition of the building models and PIV measurement regions. (a) The building R01; (b) the building SBL.

3.2. Computational Model and Calculation Conditions

Figure 4 shows the computational domain which was 3 m wide, 6 m long, and 2.5 m high, including the flat plate and building model. The inflow condition was set as a uniform flow of $U_0 = 10$ m/s. The outlet boundary was an open boundary with an inletOutlet condition [24]. The walls of the building model and the flat plate were no-slip boundaries. The other boundaries were slip boundaries.

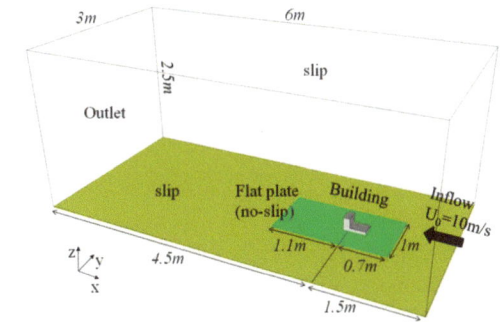

Figure 4. The computational model and boundary conditions.

Meshes were generated using the snappyHexMesh system from OpenFOAM [24]. Figure 5 depicts the entire mesh in the plane view, the surface meshes of the building model R01 and SBL in the vicinity, and a close-up of their corners. A fundamental mesh was constructed with a mesh size of 2 mm near the building model, then stretched out with factors of 1.005 in the upstream and 1.03 in the downstream x directions, 1.07 in the y direction, and 1.07 in the z direction. Then, the mesh cells were refined for two further levels to achieve a high resolution around the building model in which the nearest mesh size Δ was 0.5 mm. The total mesh cells for each model numbered about 570 million.

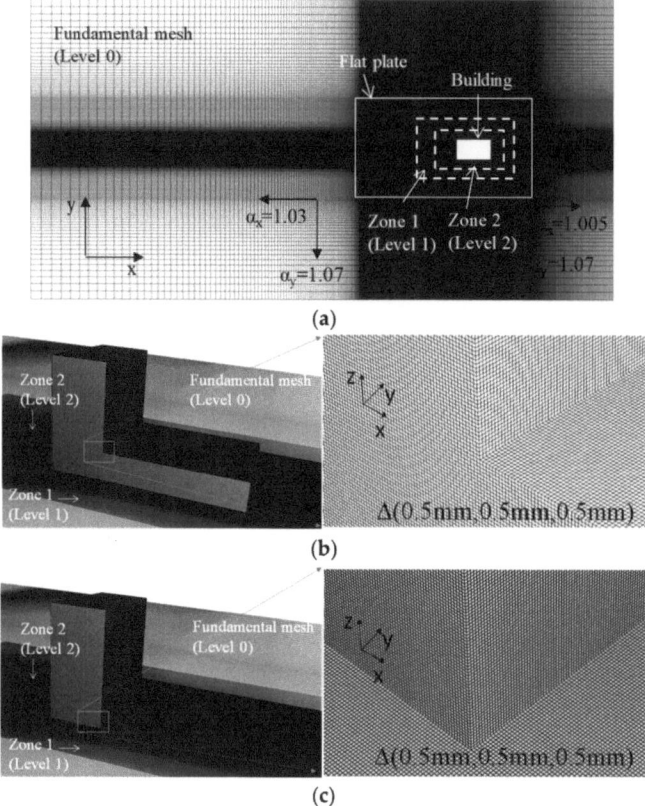

Figure 5. The computational mesh and its close-up with refinement levels. (**a**) The entire mesh in plane view; (**b**) mesh of building R01; (**c**) mesh of building SBL.

Table 2 describes the calculation conditions. LESs with the SM and the CSM were carried out. The results obtained from these SGS models were verified by comparison with experimental results, mainly to clarify the performance of the CSM. Time steps Δt were 1×10^{-4}, 5×10^{-5}, and 2.5×10^{-5} (s), corresponding to the approximated Courant numbers ($Cr = U_0 \Delta t / \Delta$) of 2.0, 1.0, and 0.5, respectively. The simulations were conducted using the 6144 parallel CPUs in "The K Computer", which was the world's first-ranked supercomputer of the TOP500 Supercomputers in 2012. Peak pressure coefficients of the building models were calculated from the results of a real-time 1.0 s moving average—the same as the average calculated in the experiment.

Table 2. The calculation conditions.

Subgrid-Scale (SGS) Model	Smagorinsky Model (SM)	Coherent Structure Smagorinsky Model (CSM)
Mesh cells (millions)	570	570
Time increment Δt (s)	10^{-4}	$10^{-4}, 5 \times 10^{-5}, 2.5 \times 10^{-5}$
Courant number Cr	2.0	2.0, 1.0, 0.5
Initial run-up time (s)	3	3
Evaluation time (s)	8	8
Number of parallel CPUs	6144	6144

3.3. Results and Discussion

3.3.1. Pressure Coefficients of Buildings

This section discusses the mean and negative peak pressure coefficients, which are important parameters for the assessment of building cladding design. Here, the wind pressure coefficient C_p is calculated as follows:

$$C_p = \frac{p - p_0}{0.5\rho U_H^2} \tag{11}$$

where p_0 and U_H are the reference pressure at a 1.4 m height above the building and the wind speed at the eave height of the building, respectively. In this case, the inflow condition was set as the uniform flow, so the wind speed U_H is equal to $U_0 = 10$ m/s.

Figure 6 shows the distributions of these coefficients for the buildings R01 and SBL in uniform flow. In comparison with the building R01, the building SBL has a specific pressure distribution on the sidewall surface with an unexpectedly large mean pressure coefficient of -1.3 and a negative peak pressure coefficient of -3.0 at its corner.

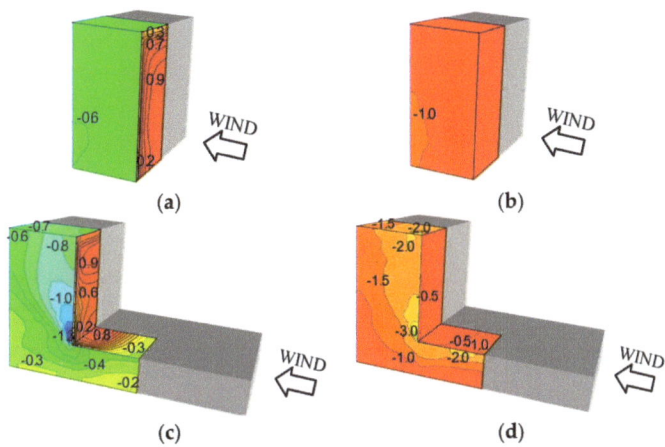

Figure 6. The pressure distribution on buildings obtained from the pressure experiments. (a) Mean pressure coefficient of R01; (b) negative peak pressure coefficient of R01; (c) mean pressure coefficient of SBL; (d) negative peak pressure coefficient of SBL.

Figure 7 shows the mean and negative peak pressure coefficients obtained from LES using the SM and the CSM for the buildings R01 and SBL in comparison with the experimental results. For the building R01, the pressure coefficients of the SM and CSM are very similar and consistent with the experimental results (values within 20%). For the building SBL with a specific pressure distribution and large pressure coefficients, the SM results show quite a large difference from the experimental data in both positive and negative wind pressure regions. However, the CSM shows good agreement with the experimental results (within 20%).

Figure 8 shows the mean and negative peak pressure coefficients obtained from both the experiments and LES using the CSM with a Courant number, Cr, of 2.0, 1.0, or 0.5, respectively, for the buildings R01 and SBL. The pressure coefficients calculated using the CSM are consistent with the experimental results for both buildings. Decreasing the Cr caused the simulated mean and negative peak pressure coefficients to more closely match the experimental results. In particular, the mean pressure coefficient of -1 or less, and negative peak values of -2 or less, agreed well with the experimental values.

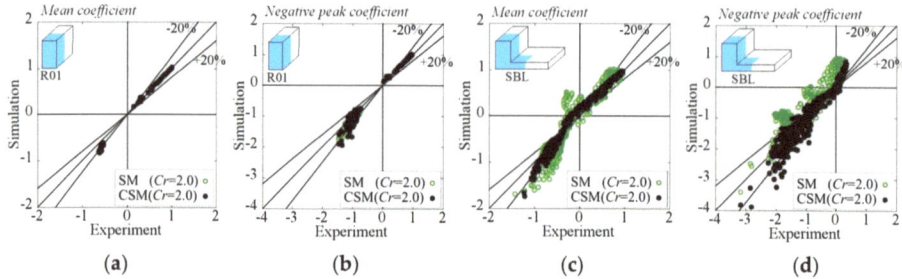

Figure 7. The pressure coefficients obtained from the SM and CSM with *Cr* = 2.0 in comparison with experimental results. (**a**) Mean pressure coefficient of R01; (**b**) negative peak pressure coefficient of R01; (**c**) mean pressure coefficient of SBL; (**d**) negative peak pressure coefficient of SBL.

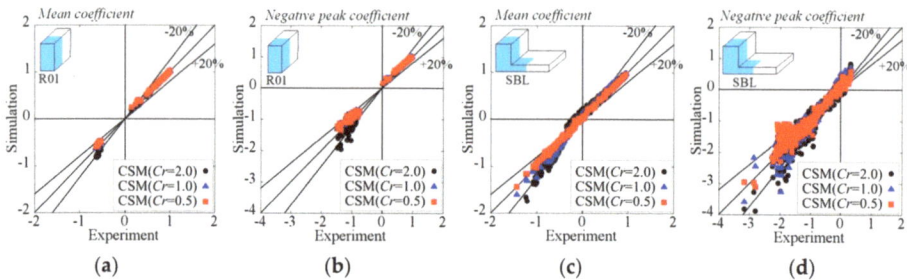

Figure 8. Pressure coefficients obtained from the CSM with different *Cr* values. (**a**) Mean pressure coefficient of R01; (**b**) negative peak pressure coefficient of R01; (**c**) mean pressure coefficient of SBL; (**d**) negative peak pressure coefficient of SBL.

3.3.2. Flow Fields around Buildings

In order to understand the characteristics of the flow field around the buildings, the PIV results are considered. Figure 9a,b show the mean velocity vector and average vorticity contour in the planes A1, A2, and A3 of the central cross section of the buildings R01 and SBL as obtained by the PIV experiments. Figure 9c,d show these results in the plane 5 mm away from the sidewall surface near the corner where the unexpected, large negative peak coefficient occurred, as shown in Figure 6c,d. A three-dimensional visualization was also done to clarify the flow field structure around the buildings. The mean streamline estimated from the results of the CSM is shown in Figure 10.

For the building R01 (Figures 9a and 10a), a well-known horseshoe vortex is found in the vicinity of the lower part of the front of the building. A strong flow separation is generated from the leading edge of the roof surface, and they seem to behave independently. In the building SBL (Figures 9b and 10b), two vortices formed in front of the lower and upper parts of the building. The former vortex is a horseshoe vortex. The latter vortex is generated by the complex interaction of the flow field separated from the leading edge of the lower roof, and the downward flow at the windward wall of the upper part of the building. As a result, this vortex becomes larger than the other ones. In addition, the flow separation at the upper part of the leading edge of the roof (Figure 9b) is slightly weaker than the flow separation from the building R01 (Figure 9a). In the plane 5 mm from the sidewall (Figure 9d), an upward flow with strong vorticity is also found near the corner of the sidewall W1 that generated a distinctively complex flow. Furthermore, these vortices and the flow separations of the building SBL (Figure 10b) seemingly interfere with each other more than do those from building R01 (Figure 10a).

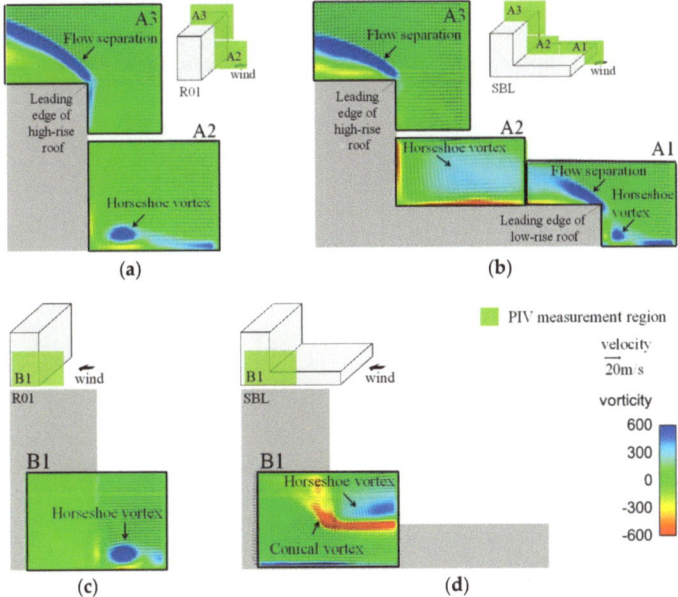

Figure 9. The mean velocity vector and average vorticity contour obtained by the PIV experiments. (a) The results of building R01 at the central cross section; (b) results of building SBL at the central cross section; (c) results of building R01 at the plane 5 mm away from the sidewall; (d) results of building SBL at the plane 5 mm away from the sidewall.

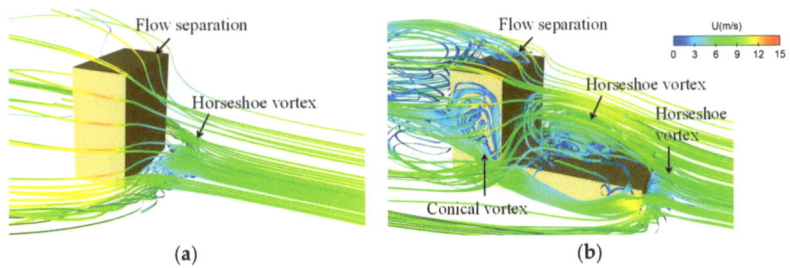

Figure 10. The mean streamline around buildings as obtained using the CSM. (a) Building R01; (b) building SBL.

Figure 11 shows the profiles of the mean velocities and partial enlarged views calculated using the SM and CSM (Cr = 2.0) in comparison with the PIV results across the planes A1, A2, and A3 in both buildings R01 and SBL. For building R01, as shown in Figure 11a,b, a boundary layer is developed on the flat plate in the region x/D = 1.0–3.5. The behavior of the horseshoe vortex in the lower part of the front of the building is in the region x/D = 0–1.0. The region after x/D = 0 corresponds to the flow separation at the leading edge of the roof. The overall profiles calculated using the SM and the CSM are almost the same in these regions. For the building SBL, the region of x/D = 0.0–3.5 (Figure 11c,d) is the interference region of the vortices and the flow separation. The SM under-predicts this region, but the CSM shows good agreement with the PIV experiments. In particular, the CSM gives a profile with a level of accuracy similar to the PIV results in the region of the large vortex. As discussed in Section 2, the model parameter of the CSM is defined by the second invariant Q which is a quantity to describe the vortex structures. It appears that the CSM might reflect the vortex behaviors and simulate well the interference between the vortex and the flow separation in the complex flow field. Even at high computational model resolutions, the SGS model could affect the results of the velocity profiles.

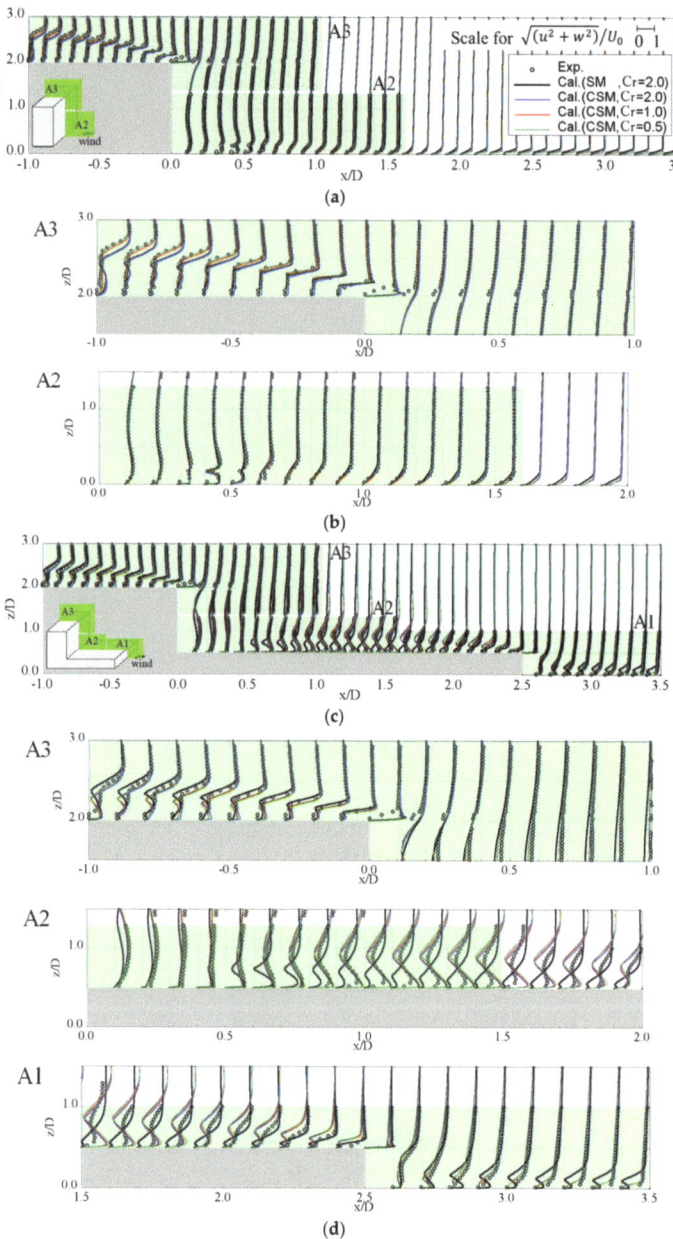

Figure 11. The mean velocity profile in the planes A1, A2, and A3 as obtained by the SM and the CSM in comparison with the PIV experiments. (a) Results of building R01; (b) partially enlarged view of results of building R01; (c) results of building SBL; (d) partially enlarged view of results of building SBL.

Figure 12 shows the profiles and partially enlarged views of mean velocities in the plane 5 mm away from the sidewall of these buildings. Again, the SM and CSM are in good agreement with the PIV results for the building R01 (Figure 12a,b). For the building SBL, the SM results are under-predicted, but the CSM predictions more closely match the results of the PIV experiments in the region of $x/D = -1$ to 1 as shown in Figure 12c,d.

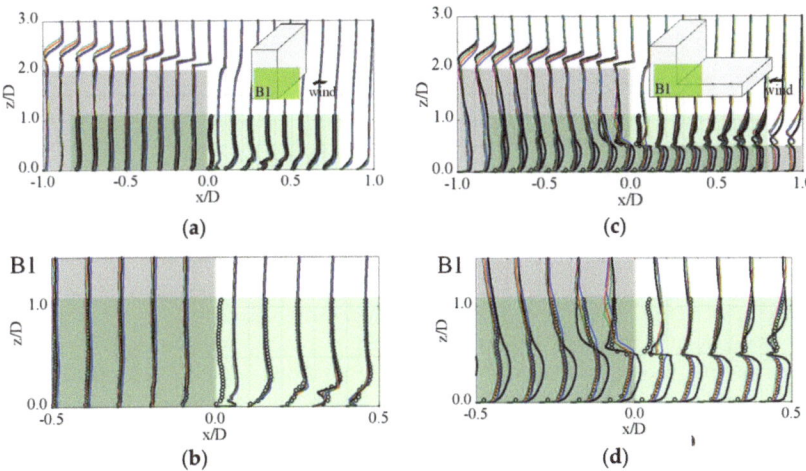

Figure 12. The mean velocity profile in the plane B1, 5 mm away from surface W1, obtained using the SM and the CSM in comparison with the PIV experiments. (**a**) Results of building R01; (**b**) partially enlarged view of results of building R01; (**c**) results of building SBL; (**d**) partially enlarged view of results of building SBL.

Furthermore, the results of the CSM for both buildings R01 and SBL, for Courant numbers of 2.0, 1.0, and 0.5, are also plotted in Figures 11 and 12. When the Cr is reduced, the predictions for the planes A3 and B1 are slightly closer to the PIV results.

4. Numerical Simulation for a High-Rise Building in an Urban City with Turbulent Flow

4.1. Validation Experiments

In this section, an actual high-rise building with a height of 100 m ($D/B/H = 1:2:3$) with uneven surfaces is investigated. Herein, the building is constructed in a dense urban area in which medium-rise buildings are packed closely together. The pressure experiment was carried out at a scale of 1:400. Figure 13 shows the experimental setup and the test model inside the 104 m long circuit boundary layer wind tunnel at the Shimizu Corporation, Tokyo, Japan. The test section is 3.5 m wide and 2.5 m high.

The approaching flow field was generated using spires and roughness blocks to satisfy the flat suburban terrain with few medium-rise buildings, of Category III according to the Architectural Institute of Japan [27]. During the experiment, the wind tunnel fan's rotation was constantly controlled to maintain an approximate mean wind speed, U_H, of 11 m/s at the test model eaves height ($H = 0.25$ m), which corresponds to a basic wind speed of 36 m/s in terms of real-time conversion. The vertical wind profile at the center of the turntable was measured using a hot-wire anemometer. The mean wind profile was examined using a power law of exponent, α, of 0.2 and longitudinal wind turbulence intensity, I_u, of 15% at the eaves height, H, of the building. The Reynolds number ($Re = U_H D/v$, $D = 0.085$ m) of the experiment was about 52,000.

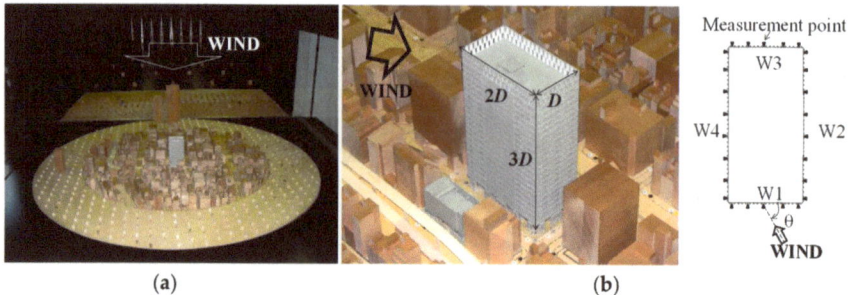

Figure 13. Wind tunnel experiment. (**a**) Wind tunnel model setup; (**b**) target building and pressure measurement point layers.

Data logging equipment was used to measure the external pressures acting on the target building at 234 different points on the wall surfaces, arranged in 9 layers at different heights. The measurements were carried out for 36 wind directions at 10 degree intervals. Experimental data were recorded for about 30 s at a sampling rate of 1000 Hz, corresponding to five data samples in each ten-minute record in terms of real-time conversion (one sample for each ten-minute record is 6 s in experimental time). The external wind pressures measured on the wall surfaces were used to estimate the mean, standard deviation, and largest positive and negative peak pressure coefficients of the target building. The peak pressure coefficients, which are required for building wall cladding assessment, were moving-averaged using five samples, corresponding to a real-time moving average window of 0.5 s. The results for the 60 degree wind direction are discussed in detail in this paper due to the strong influence of neighboring buildings on this wind direction.

4.2. Computational Models and Calculation Conditions

A 30 m long computational domain was constructed to conscientiously model the wind tunnel measurement section including spires, block roughness, and buildings as shown in Figure 14. Two meshes with different resolutions (Meshes A and B) were generated using the snappyHexMesh system [24]. Figures 15 and 16 show the surface mesh of the spire and roughness blocks, the building model in the vicinity, and an enlarged view of the top corner for a wind direction of 60 degree. The fundamental meshes of the snappyHexMesh system (Level 0) were generated at a mesh size with dimensions 64 mm × 64 mm × 32 mm for Mesh A, and 32 mm × 32 mm × 16 mm for Mesh B. Then, the mesh cells around the target building were refined to achieve a high resolution (Level 7) in which the smallest mesh cell size was 0.5 mm for Mesh A, and 0.25 mm for Mesh B. The total numbers of cells in Meshes A and B were about 140 million and 1.1 billion, respectively.

The boundary conditions are shown in Figure 14. The inflow condition is a uniform velocity U = 15 m/s in order to obtain a wind velocity at the eaves height, U_H, of 11 m/s—the same as in the wind tunnel experiment. The outlet boundary is an open boundary with an inletOutlet condition [24]. The walls of the building model and wind tunnel are no-slip boundaries.

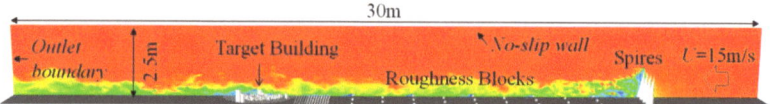

Figure 14. The computational model and boundary conditions.

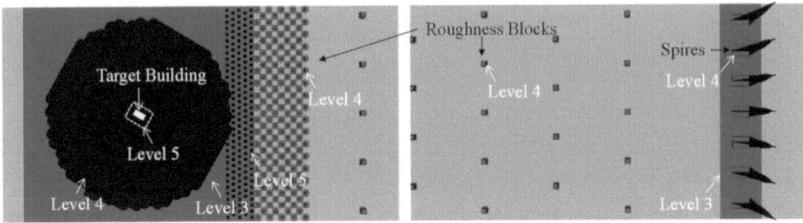

Figure 15. The computational mesh of the spire and roughness blocks with the refinement levels.

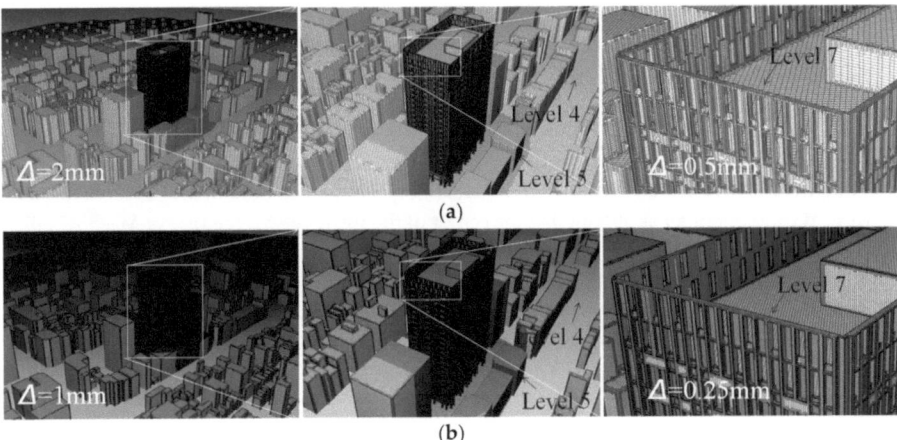

Figure 16. The computational mesh of the building model, its vicinity, and an enlarged view. (**a**) Mesh A (140 million cells); (**b**) Mesh B (1.1 billion cells).

Table 3 describes the calculation conditions. Firstly, LES was performed with two SGS models: the SM and the CSM were carried out for Meshes A and B for a wind direction of 60 degree. The results obtained from these SGS models were verified by comparison with the experimental results. Next, the simulations for all wind directions (36 wind directions at 10 degree intervals) were conducted for one sample corresponding to a ten-minute record when converted to real time. Statistical data such as the largest peak pressure coefficients for all wind directions were evaluated. Hence, the peak pressure coefficients were estimated from the samples of a real-time 0.5 s moving average, as was the case in the experiment. By using OpenFOAM, a simulation of 6 s (corresponding to one sample in each ten-minute record when converted to real time) with Mesh A for each wind direction took about 20 days for the CSM and 40 days for the SM in terms of computational time using 768 parallel CPUs of "The K Computer". It was found that the calculation of the wall coordinate y^+ for the SM in OpenFOAM using the wave propagation method resulted in a significantly higher computational cost due to the complex geometry of the unstructured mesh and the large-scale computational domain of several hundred million mesh cells.

Table 3. The calculation conditions.

SGS Model Use in Large Eddy Simulation (LES)	SM	CSM	CSM
Mesh type	A	A	B
Mesh cells (millions)	140	140	1100
Wind direction θ (degree)	60	60 (0, .., 350)	60
Time increment Δt (s)	2.5×10^{-5}	2.5×10^{-5}	1.25×10^{-5}
Courant number Cr	1	1	1
Initial run-up time (s)	3	3	3
Evaluation time (s)	18	30 (6)	6
Number of samples in ten-minute record in real-time conversion for evaluation	3	5 (1)	1
Number of parallel CPUs	768	768	6144
Computational time for one sample (days)	40	20	20

4.3. Results and Discussion

4.3.1. Wind Flow Characteristics

Figure 17 illustrates the vertical profiles of the mean wind speed, turbulence intensity, and power spectrum densities of the three wind components (longitudinal component u, lateral component v, and vertical component w) as obtained at the center of the turntable for the case of Mesh A without buildings. Because of the precise modeling of the wind tunnel measurement section, the mean wind profile and turbulence intensities calculated using both the SM and the CSM show very good agreement with the experimental values and also agree with the profiles of the Architectural Institute of Japan [27]. The experimental and calculated power spectral densities are compared with the Karman spectrum. Although the experimental power spectrum densities of the wind components are consistent with the Karman spectrum, the calculated results are significantly lower in the high-frequency region, where the normalized frequencies are less than 2 on account of the fineness of the computational mesh.

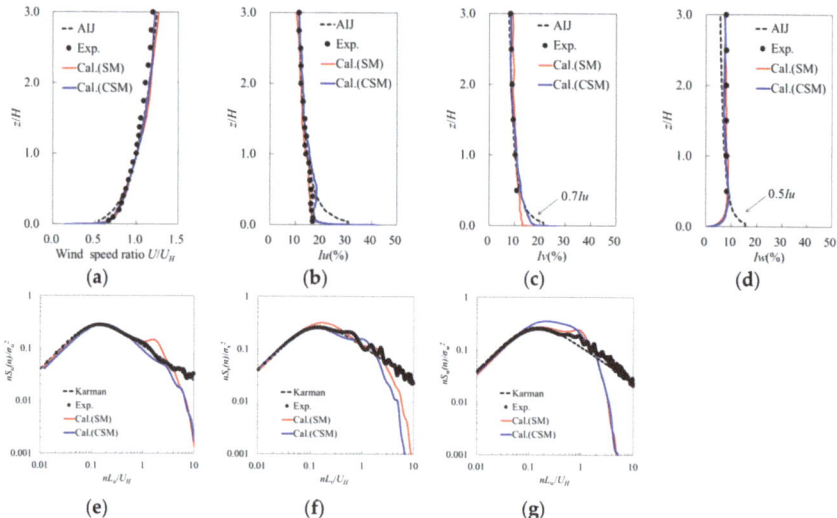

Figure 17. The wind flow characteristics as obtained by the experiments and LES (Mesh A without buildings). (**a**) Mean wind speed; (**b**) longitudinal turbulence intensity, Iu; (**c**) lateral turbulence intensity, Iv; (**d**) vertical turbulence intensity, Iw; (**e**) power spectrum density, Su; (**f**) power spectrum density, Sv; (**g**) power spectrum density, Sw.

4.3.2. Flow Fields around the Target Building

In order to understand the flow fields around the target building, the contours of the mean wind speed around the target building at heights $z = 0.2H$, $0.5H$, and $0.9H$ for the 60 degree wind direction, as obtained from LES using the SM and the CSM with Mesh A, are shown in Figure 18. Moreover, Figure 19 shows the mean streamline and instantaneous Q-criterion isosurface ($Q = 300,000$) obtained from the three-dimensional visualization. The flow field around the target building is greatly deformed in the vertical direction. At height $z = 0.2H$, the flow field substantially follows the street due to the influence of the densely packed surrounding buildings. However, the influences of the upstream and downstream adjacent medium-rise buildings are remarkable at the height $z = 0.5H$. Separated shear layers generated from the target building and adjacent buildings are strongly coupled and greatly deformed. At height $z = 0.9H$, which exceeds the height of the adjacent medium-rise buildings, the flow field is the same as the typical flow field around an isolated building. As a result, a complex three-dimensional flow with strong vortices separated from the leading edges is formed due to the strong influence of the windward neighboring buildings.

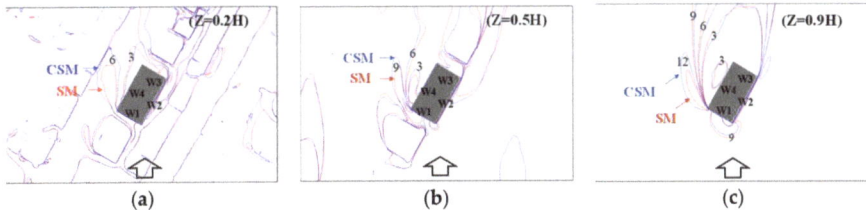

Figure 18. The mean wind speed contours. (**a**) Section $z = 0.2H$; (**b**) section $z = 0.5H$; (**c**) section $z = 0.9H$.

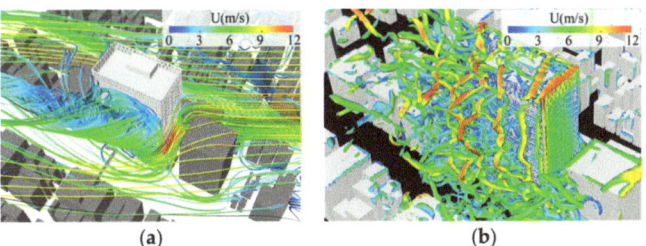

Figure 19. The flow field around the target building as obtained by the CSM with Mesh A. (**a**) Mean streamline; (**b**) instantaneous Q-criterion isosurface ($Q = 300,000$).

We compared the results of the SM and CSM models as shown in Figure 18 and found a difference in the separated shear layers generated from the target building and its adjacent buildings. The CSM gives a larger flow separation than the SM in the situation. It seems that the SM underestimated the flow field in the separation area. Related to Figure 19, this separation area has a strong effect from the vortex separated from the leading edges. The CSM, whose model parameter is defined from the Q-criterion as a quantity for description of the vortex structure, takes into account the effect of the vortex behavior. Therefore, it may simulate the situation well.

4.3.3. Pressure Coefficients of the Target Building for a Specific Wind Direction

Figure 20 shows the mean pressure coefficients of the target building as estimated from the experiments. The figure also shows the coefficients estimated from one sample obtained using LES with the SM and the CSM with different meshes. A distinctive pressure distribution is found on the front wall, W1, in which a strong positive pressure coefficient occurs at the upper right portion, while a negative pressure coefficient occurs at the lower left portion. This can be understood from the flow field around the target building due to the strong influence of the adjacent buildings mentioned above. Generally, the CSM gives a better pressure distribution than does the SM in comparison with experimental data.

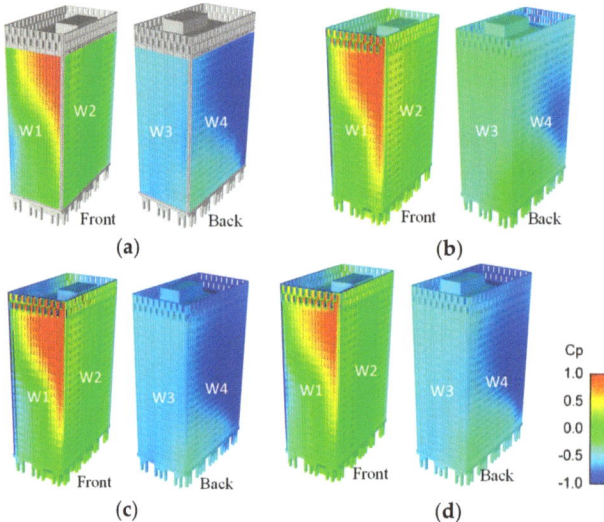

Figure 20. The mean pressure coefficient. (**a**) Experimental values; (**b**) result of the SM with Mesh A; (**c**) result of the CSM with Mesh A; (**d**) result of the CSM with Mesh B.

Figures 21 and 22 show a comparison of the mean and largest negative peak pressure coefficients between the experimental results (values within 20%) and LES for the first sample, averaged from three samples or five samples. We found that the variation of the SM is large, and that the CSM gives more accurate results and less variation than does the SM. Using a finer mesh (Mesh B) yields better results, which are especially consistent with experimental results (discrepancy of less than 20%) in the relatively high-wind-pressure region that is important in building cladding assessments.

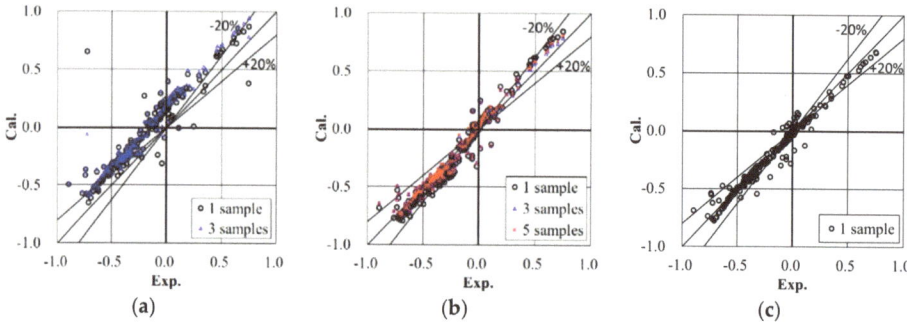

Figure 21. The comparisons of the mean pressure coefficients between the experiments and LES. (**a**) Result of the SM with Mesh A; (**b**) result of the CSM with Mesh A; (**c**) results of the CSM with Mesh B.

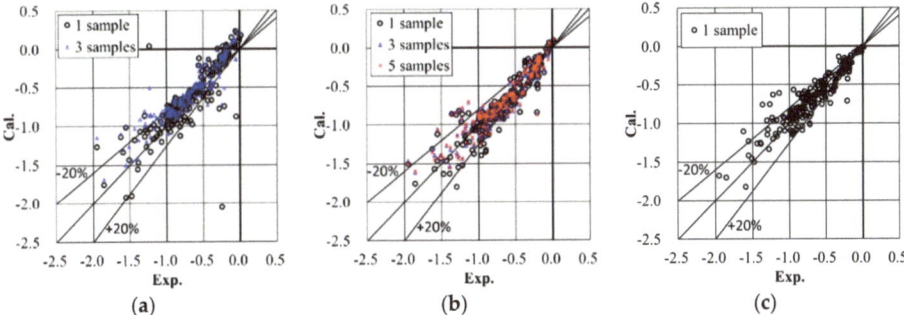

Figure 22. The comparisons between experiments and LES of the largest negative peak pressure coefficients. (**a**) SM with Mesh A; (**b**) results of the CSM with Mesh A; (**c**) results of the CSM with Mesh B.

Moreover, it is interesting to compare the average results from all samples with the first sample's results for the SM and CSM predictions. When using the SM as shown in Figures 21a and 22a, it is evident that the variation of the first sample is more scattered than the variation in the value averaged from the three samples. When using the CSM, as shown in Figures 21b and 22b, the variations averaged from three samples or five samples are quite similar to the variation of the first results. As a result, we suggest that the CSM is an effective method for understanding coherent structures within a flow field.

Figure 23 shows the mean, standard deviation, and largest positive and negative peaks of the pressure coefficients averaged from five samples, obtained from the experiments and LES using the CSM with Mesh A at heights $z = 0.2H$, $0.5H$, and $0.9H$. Whereas the coefficients of the walls W2 and W3 are almost the same, the values for wall W1 differ in the vertical direction. A large negative peak value is found on the medium-rise section ($z = 0.5H$) on wall W4. The simulation results show good agreement with the experimental results.

4.3.4. Pressure Coefficients of the Target Building for All Wind Directions

The previous section discussed the CSM results for a specific wind direction. Commonly, the wind pressure distributions on a building in an urban area change according to the wind direction and depend on the influence of different neighboring buildings. To assess the universality of the CSM for predicting wind pressure distributions on a building, similar mesh generations and simulations for all 36 wind directions at 10 degree intervals were conducted.

Figure 24 shows the largest positive and negative peak pressure coefficients estimated from all 36 wind directions, as estimated from the experiments and LES using the CSM (Mesh A) for the first sample. The calculated peak pressure coefficients are consistently within 20% of the experimental values in the relatively high-pressure region—the same as the results for the specific wind direction as shown in the previous section. Furthermore, the consistent accuracy of these results is found to be at least similar to or less than the wind tunnel coefficients of variation (COVs) as discussed by Tamura and Phuc [20] in their assessment of the variation in a series of wind tunnel test results.

In addition, Figure 25 shows these peak pressure coefficients at the heights $z = 0.2H$, $0.5H$, and $0.9H$. The numerical simulation results show quite a good agreement with the experimental results.

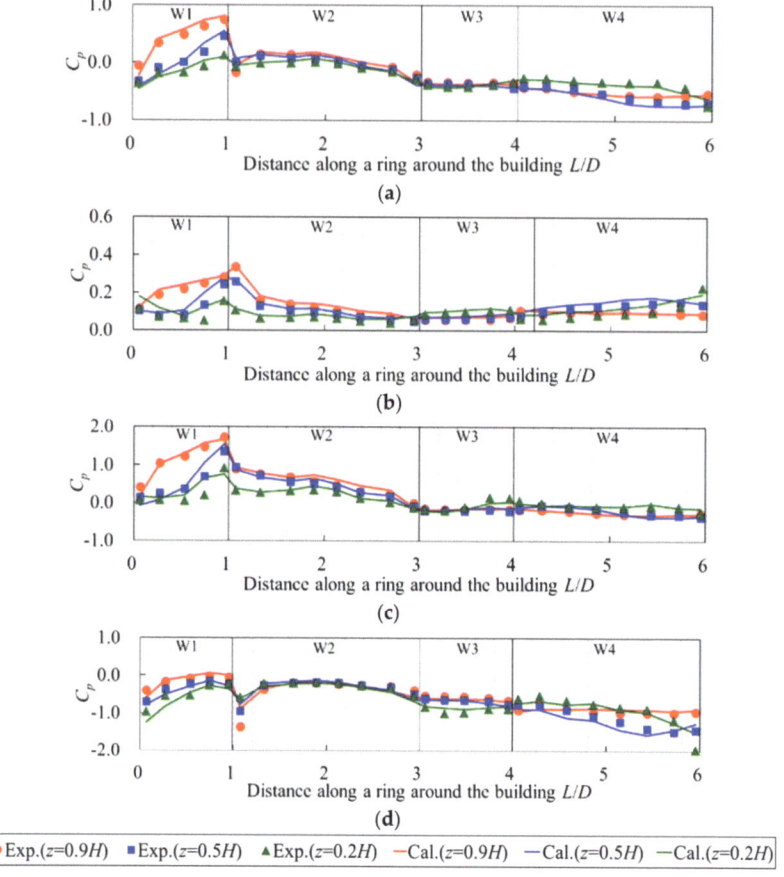

Figure 23. The pressure coefficients as obtained by the experiments and LES using CSM (Mesh A, five samples). (**a**) Mean coefficient; (**b**) standard deviation coefficient; (**c**) largest positive peak pressure coefficient; (**d**) largest negative peak pressure coefficient.

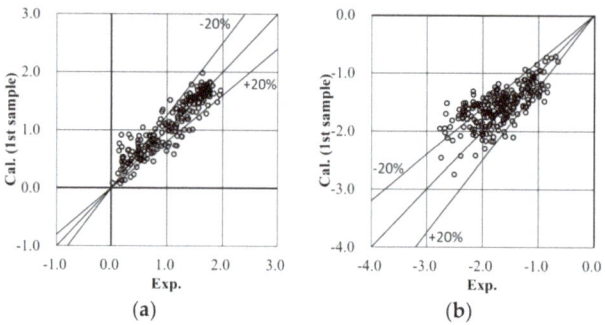

Figure 24. The comparison of the peak pressure coefficients estimated for all wind directions (CSM, Mesh A). (**a**) Largest positive peak pressure coefficient; (**b**) largest negative peak pressure coefficient.

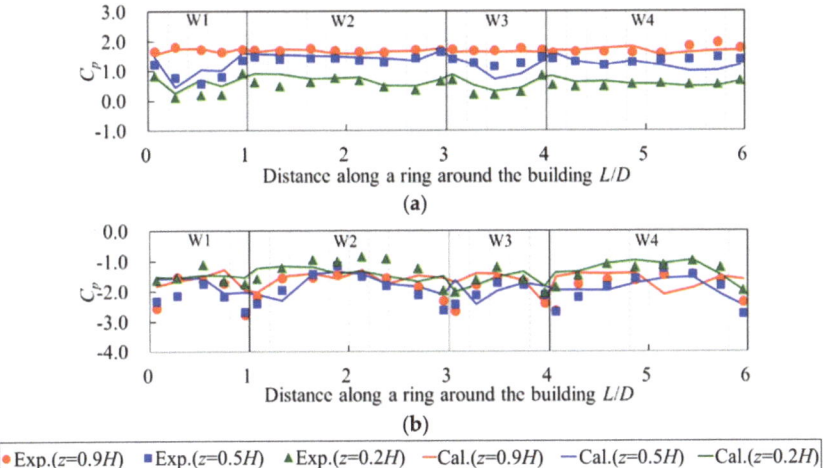

Figure 25. The pressure coefficients for all wind directions calculated from experiments and LES using the CSM. (**a**) Largest positive peak pressure coefficient; (**b**) largest negative peak pressure coefficient.

5. Conclusions

Case studies using LES have been carried out to investigate the performance of the CSM in predicting the wind pressure distributions on buildings in various flow fields. Comparison between the SM results and experimental results led to the following conclusions:

1. For an isolated rectangular building in uniform flow, the flow field around the building is generated by the horseshoe vortex and separated flow. Both SM and CSM show good agreement with the PIV results in the flow separation region as well as in the horseshoe vortex regions. The wind pressure coefficients calculated using both SM and CSM consistently agree with the experimental results (values within 20%).

2. For an isolated building with a setback in uniform flow, a complex flow field is generated by a distinctive large horseshoe vortex interfering with the separated flow from the lower roof. A large negative pressure coefficient is found at the corner of the sidewall, near the interfered-with area. Although using the SM results in under-prediction, the predictions made using the CSM show good agreement with the PIV results for the flow field. This means that the CSM with the model parameter based on the coherent structure reflects the vortex behaviors and simulates well the complex flow fields due to the strong interference of the vorticities and flow separations. The CSM results also showed much better performance than the SM results for the wind pressure distribution on this building, being within 20% of the experimental results.

3. For a high-rise building in an actual urban city with a turbulent boundary layer flow, we found that a strong three-dimensional complex wind flow occurs due to the strong influence of neighboring buildings, including interference of vortices and separated flows. We also found a distinctive wind pressure distribution that had strong positive and negative pressures simultaneously occurring on the front wall of the target building. The CSM also gives more accurate results with less variation than the SM, being within 20% of experimental results. In addition, LES with the CSM was conducted for all wind directions. The calculated largest positive and negative peak pressure coefficients were consistently in good agreement with experimental results (within 20%) in the relatively high-pressure region, at least similar to or less than the COVs of the wind tunnel test results [20].

Furthermore, it should be mentioned again that LES solves large eddies/vortices on a grid scale (GS), and takes account of small eddies on a sub-grid scale (SGS) using an SGS model. The difference between the SM and the CSM is only a model parameter of an SGS model. This model parameter is determined by a Smagorinsky constant for the SM, but is specifically determined by a second invariant parameter for the CSM which could describe the effect of the vortex structures from the GS.

From the results of the case of an isolated rectangular building, it is found that the SGS models are not sensitive to the flow field around the building (including the horseshoe vortex and separated flow). The grid size is seemingly small enough for LES to resolve the flow field in the GS, or the effect from the small eddies in the SGS is not so dominant. From the results of the case of an isolated building with a setback as well as the case of a high-rise building in an actual urban city, the CSM showed better performance than the SM. This implies that the small eddies become more activated in the flow fields of the interference of the vortices and separated flows. The activation is found to be related to the vortex structures from the GS.

It could be useful to investigate the contribution of the CSM parameters to understand these flow fields, or to develop a much more appropriate SGS model. However, this remains for future studies.

Acknowledgments: This research used the computational resources of the K computer provided by the RIKEN Advanced Institute for Computational Science through the HPCI System Research project (Project ID: hp150031, hp160054).

Author Contributions: P.V.P. performed the experiments and simulations, analyzed the data and wrote the paper; T.N. and H.K. performed some experiments and discussions; K.H. and Y.T. participated in the discussions.

Conflicts of Interest: The authors declare no conflict of interest.

References

1. Smagorinsky, J. General circulation experiments with the primitive equations I, The basic experiment. *Mon. Weather Rev.* **1963**, *91*, 99–164. [CrossRef]
2. Germano, M.; Piomelli, U.; Moin, P.; Cabot, W.H. A dynamic subgrid-scale eddy viscosity model. *Phys. Fluids* **1991**, *3*, 1760–1765. [CrossRef]
3. Ghosal, S.; Lund, T.S.; Moin, P.; Akselvoll, K. A dynamic localization model for large-eddy simulation of turbulent flows. *J. Fluid Mech.* **1995**, *286*, 229–255. [CrossRef]
4. Meneveau, C.; Lund, T.S.; Cabot, W.H. A lagrangian dynamic subgrid-scale model of turbulence. *J. Fluid Mech.* **1996**, *319*, 353–385. [CrossRef]
5. Murakami, S. Current status and future trends in computational wind engineering. *J. Wind Eng. Ind. Aerodyn.* **1997**, *67–68*, 3–34. [CrossRef]
6. Yoshizawa, A.; Kobayashi, K.; Kobayashi, T.; Taniguchi, N. A nonequilibrium fixed-parameter subgrid-scale model obeying the near-wall asymptotic constraint. *Phys. Fluids* **2000**, *12*, 2338–2344. [CrossRef]
7. Vreman, A.W. An eddy-viscosity subgrid-scale model for turbulent shear flow: Algebraic theory and applications. *Phys. Fluids* **2004**, *16*, 3670–3681. [CrossRef]
8. Park, N.; Lee, S.; Lee, J.; Choi, H. A dynamic subgrid-scale eddy viscosity model with a global model coefficient. *Phys. Fluids* **2006**, *18*, 125109. [CrossRef]
9. Kobayashi, H. The subgrid-scale models based on coherent structures for rotating homogeneous turbulence and turbulent channel flow. *Phys. Fluids* **2005**, *17*, 045104. [CrossRef]
10. Kobayashi, H. Large eddy simulation of magnetohydrodynamic turbulent channel flows with local subgrid-scale model based on coherent structures. *Phys. Fluids* **2006**, *18*, 045107. [CrossRef]
11. Kobayashi, H. Large eddy simulation of magnetohydrodynamic turbulent duct flows turbulent duct flows. *Phys. Fluids* **2008**, *20*, 015102. [CrossRef]
12. Kobayashi, H.; Ham, F.; Wu, X. Application of a local SGS model based on coherent structures to complex geometries. *Int. J. Heat Fluid Flow* **2008**, *29*, 640–653. [CrossRef]
13. Onodera, N.; Aoki, T.; Shimokawabe, T.; Kobayashi, H. Large-scale LES Wind Simulation using Lattice Boltzmann Method for a 10 km × 10 km Area in Metropolitan Tokyo. *Tsubame ESJ* **2013**, *9*, 2–8.
14. Melbourne, W.H. Turbulence and the leading edge phenomenon. *J. Wind Eng. Ind. Aerodyn.* **1993**, *49*, 45–63. [CrossRef]

15. Okuda, Y.; Taniike, Y. Conical vortices over side face of a three dimensional square prism. *J. Wind Eng. Ind. Aerodyn.* **1993**, *50*, 163–172. [CrossRef]

16. Kawai, H. Local peak pressure and conical vortex on building. *J. Wind Eng. Ind. Aerodyn.* **2002**, *90*, 251–263. [CrossRef]

17. Tominaga, Y.; Mochida, A.; Yoshie, R.; Kataoka, H.; Nozu, T.; Yoshikawa, M.; Shirasawa, T. AIJ guidelines for practical applications of CFD to pedestrian wind environment around buildings. *J. Wind Eng. Ind. Aerodyn.* **2008**, *96*, 1749–1761. [CrossRef]

18. Tamura, T.; Miyagi, T.; Kitagishi, T. Numerical prediction of unsteady pressures on a square cylinder with various corner shapes. *J. Wind Eng. Ind. Aerodyn.* **1998**, *74–76*, 531–542. [CrossRef]

19. Tamura, T.; Nozawa, K.; Kondo, K. AIJ guide for numerical prediction of wind loads on buildings. *J. Wind Eng. Ind. Aerodyn.* **2008**, *96*, 1974–1984. [CrossRef]

20. Tamura, Y.; Phuc, P.V. Development of CFD and applications: Monologue by a non-CFD-expert. *J. Wind Eng. Ind. Aerodyn.* **2015**, *144*, 3–13. [CrossRef]

21. Yoshikawa, M. Wind load for cladding. In *Material of Panel Discussion of Steering Committee for Loads on Buildings at Annual Meeting of AIJ in Tokai*; Architectural Institute of Japan: Nagoya, Japan, 2012; pp. 21–24. (In Japanese)

22. Nozu, T.; Tamura, T.; Takeshi, K.; Akira, K. Mesh-adaptive LES for wind load estimation of a high-rise building in a city. *J. Wind Eng. Ind. Aerodyn.* **2015**, *144*, 62–69. [CrossRef]

23. Architectural Institute of Japan. *Guidebook of Recommendations for Loads on Buildings 2*; Wind-Induce Response and Load Estimation/Practical Guide of CFD for Wind Resistant Design; Architectural Institute of Japan: Tokyo, Japan, 2017; pp. 381–434. (In Japanese)

24. OpenFOAM. User Guide. Available online: https://www.openfoam.com/documentation/user-guide/ (accessed on 22 January 2018).

25. Rafei, M.E.; Könözsy, L.; Rana, Z. Investigation of Numerical Dissipation in Classical and Implicit Large Eddy Simulations. *Aerospace* **2017**, *4*, 59. [CrossRef]

26. Phuc, V.P.; Nozu, T.; Kikuchi, H.; Hibi, K.; Tamura, Y. Wind pressure distributions on a high-rise building in the actual urban area using Coherent-structure Smagorinsky model for LES. In Proceedings of the 24th National Symposium on Wind Engineering, Tokyo, Japan, 6 December 2016; pp. 241–246. (In Japanese)

27. Architectural Institute of Japan. *Recommendations for Loads on Buildings*; Architectural Institute of Japan: Tokyo, Japan, 2015.

Article

LES and Wind Tunnel Test of Flow around Two Tall Buildings in Staggered Arrangement

Gongbo Zu [1],* and Kit Ming Lam [2]

1   Department of Civil Engineering, The University of Hong Kong, Pokfulam Road, Hong Kong, China
2   Department of Civil and Environmental Engineering, The Hong Kong University of Science and Technology, Clear Water Bay, Hong Kong, China; kitminglam@ust.hk
*   Correspondence: gbzu@hku.hk; Tel.: +852-2358-1534

Received: 30 January 2018; Accepted: 20 March 2018; Published: 23 March 2018

Abstract: Wind flow structures and their consequent wind loads on two high-rise buildings in staggered arrangement are investigated by Large Eddy Simulation (LES). Synchronized pressure and flow field measurements by particle image velocimetry (PIV) are conducted in a boundary layer wind tunnel to validate the numerical simulations. The instantaneous and time-averaged flow fields are analyzed and discussed in detail. The coherent flow structures in the building gap are clearly observed and the upstream building wake is found to oscillate sideways and meander down to the downstream building in a coherent manner. The disruptive effect on the downstream building wake induced by the upstream building is also observed. Furthermore, the connection between the upstream building wake and the wind loads on the downstream building is explored by the simultaneous data of wind pressures and wind flow fields.

Keywords: LES; high-rise buildings; wake; interference effect; PIV

1. Introduction

Interference effect has been found to cause significant modifications to wind loading of a building being surrounded by neighboring buildings. Interference effects on wind forces have been thoroughly studied by wind tunnel experiments [1–5]. In the last few years, local wind pressure modifications have also attracted some attention due to the importance in cladding design [6–8]. Through numerous previous studies, large amounts of useful data have been obtained to enrich the database of interference effect and some empirical formulas have been proposed to estimate interference effects on local and overall wind loads for certain building geometries and arrangements.

Many parameters can modify wind loads induced by interference from surrounding buildings, such as geometry and arrangement of buildings, terrain type and turbulence intensity of approaching flow. Possible combinations of these parameters are extremely large and, thus, are impossible to be covered exhaustively. Therefore, a more physically-based approach, such as investigating the underlying mechanisms of interference effect, would be worth adopting to solve the problem.

Some efforts have been made to understand various interference mechanisms. Bailey and Kwok [1] measured the velocity spectrum in the wake of a tall building model with and without an identical upstream building in tandem arrangement and found that the periodic vortex shedding was obvious for the isolated building but totally disappeared for the building with an upstream building. They concluded that the upstream building had a disruptive effect on the vortex shedding of the downstream building. Under this situation, the across-wind fluctuating energy on the downstream building mainly came from the approaching flow. This finding was confirmed by flow visualization experiments conducted by Taniike [9] which also found that fluctuating drag on a downstream building increased as the size of the upstream building increased because the larger building width increases the scale of the shed vortices. Sakamoto and Haniu [10] observed the reattachment of shear layer of an upstream building onto the side surface of the downstream building in several different staggered arrangements by smoke visualization technique. Gowda and Sitheeq [11] visualized the flow pattern between two tandem twin buildings and found that the downstream building experienced three stages, namely, submergence in the shear layers, being attacked by the shear layer directly on the windward surface and insusceptibility to the interference, as the spacing between two buildings changed from small to large values. Hui et al. [12] observed the flow pattern between two rectangular-section high-rise buildings and found that peak pressure on the downstream building were usually caused by the shear layer from the upstream building. Findings in many of the above-described studies are made from flow visualizations in which wind flow pattern between two tall buildings and its possible connection with resulted wind load were qualitatively observed and analyzed. However, the exact interference mechanisms between two high-rise buildings remain unclear. More detailed investigation of the wind flow field around buildings and its relationship with the wind forces may provide more understandings of the interference mechanism.

With the development of computers, since the 1990s, researchers began to employ Large Eddy Simulation (LES) to study the highly time-dependent wind flow and wind loads of building structures. Various benchmark study of LES on buildings has been carried out to validate numerical results with wind tunnel experiments [13–15] with satisfactory agreement. However, in a real urban environment, tall buildings are usually built in proximity rather than being alone. For such complex situations, there has not been a systematic study validating the accuracy of LES. When two tall buildings are closely built, the strongest interference on across-wind force on the downstream building is reported to occur when the streamwise distance of two buildings is $5D$ and the transverse distance is $2.5D$, where D is the width of the building [16]. Figure 1 reproduces the results of [16] on the contour map of interference factors (IF) of Root-Mean-Square (RMS) across-wind force on the downstream building with the upstream building at various relative locations (X, Y). The IF is defined as the ratio between the RMS across-wind force on the building under interference and the same force on the building in the isolated single building situation. Very similar contours of IF have also been measured by the present authors in the wind tunnel [17], and the results are reproduced in Figure 1. The wind flow behavior and excitation mechanism for the largely magnified RMS across-wind force have not been studied in detail. This is partly due to the difficulties in obtaining simultaneous data on the fluctuating wind pressures on the buildings and turbulent wind fields past the building. While the present authors have attempted to use advanced measurement techniques to investigate the problem in the wind tunnel [17], unsteady CFD computation with LES is a promising tool to explore the flow-structure interaction. The present study chooses the critical arrangement of peak across-wind interference between of the two buildings in staggered arrangement for LES prediction to investigate the flow structures around two tall buildings and the excitation mechanism of building interference.

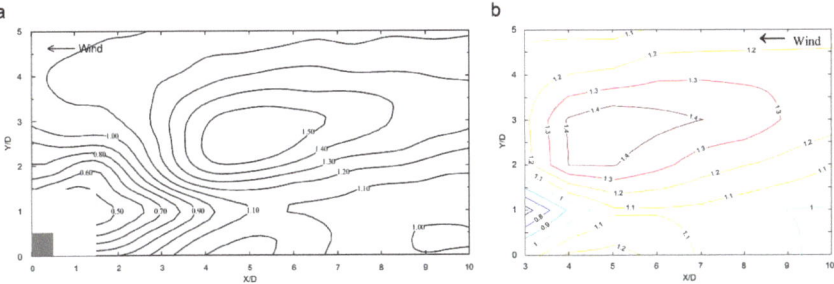

Figure 1. IF contours of RMS across-wind moment: (**a**) present study; (**b**) Mara et al. (with permission from [16]).

In this study, firstly, the LES method was applied to study the dynamic wind flow field around two staggered tall buildings in the critical arrangement for across-wind interference ($X/D = 5$, $Y/D = 2.5$). Then, the flow field around two staggered tall buildings is measured by time-resolved particle image velocimetry (TR-PIV) with synchronized pressure measurement on the downstream building. The flow characteristics between the simulated results from the LES method and those obtained from the wind tunnel test were compared to validate the simulated numerical results. Finally, the flow structures around the two buildings are further investigated aiming to bring about a better understanding of the interference effect.

2. Simulation on Shear Stress/Friction Velocity on Roofs

2.1. Governing Equations

The numerical simulations in the present study were performed using commercial CFD software Ansys Fluent [18]. In the LES turbulence model, large-scale eddies are explicitly resolved by solving the filtered Navier–Stokes equations whereas only small eddies are modelled. The governing equations of LES are obtained by filtering the time-dependent Navier–Stokes equations as follows:

$$\frac{\partial \rho \tilde{u}_i}{\partial x_i} = 0 \tag{1}$$

$$\frac{\partial}{\partial t}(\rho \tilde{u}_i) + \frac{\partial}{\partial X_j}(\rho \tilde{u}_i \tilde{u}_j) = \frac{\partial}{\partial X_j}(\mu \frac{\partial \tilde{u}_i}{\partial X_j}) - \frac{\partial \tilde{p}}{\partial X_i} - \frac{\partial \tau_{ij}}{\partial X_j} \tag{2}$$

where $\tilde{u}_i$ and $\tilde{p}$ are the filtered mean velocity and the filtered pressure respectively, ρ and v are the air density and the dynamic viscosity, respectively, and τ_{ij} is the subgrid-scale stress which is modeled as follows:

$$\tau_{ij} = -2\mu_t \tilde{S}_{ij} + \frac{1}{3}\tau_{kk}\delta_{ij} \tag{3}$$

$$\tilde{S}_{ij} \equiv \frac{1}{2}(\frac{\partial \tilde{u}_i}{\partial X_j} + \frac{\partial \tilde{u}_j}{\partial X_i}) \tag{4}$$

where μ_t is the subgrid-scale turbulent viscosity, and $\tilde{S}_{ij}$ is the rate-of-strain tensor for the resolved scale.

The Smagorinsky-Lilly model [19] is used for the subgrid-scale turbulent viscosity, where the eddy viscosity is modeled as follows:

$$\mu_t = \rho L_s^2 |\tilde{S}| = \rho L_s \sqrt{2\tilde{S}_{ij}\tilde{S}_{ij}} \tag{5}$$

$$L_s = \min(\kappa \delta, C_s V^{1/3}) \tag{6}$$

where L_s is the mixing length for subgrid-scales, κ is the von Karman constant, δ is the distance to the closest wall and V is the volume of a computational cell. The dynamic version of the Smagorinsky model [20] was employed in the present study, and C_s is computed at each time step with a test-filter and clipped to the range of 0 to 0.23 to avoid numerical instabilities. This imposed maximum value of 0.23 for C_s follows the default value in Ansys Fluent and is found to be appropriate for flow around an isolated bluff body [21].

2.2. Computational Domain and Boundary Conditions

The numerical simulations were conducted on two identical tall building models to compare the simulated wind flow around two tall buildings with that obtained from the wind tunnel experiment, which will be described in later sections. Both building models had a square-plan form of breadth $D = 30$ mm. The height-to-breadth ratio was $H/D = 6$. At the target geometric scale 1:1000, the models represented full-scale buildings of height 180 m and width 30 m. Figure 2 shows the computational domain and the study model. The length, breadth and depth of the computational domain were 16.7H, 34.5D and 3H, respectively, which follow the recommendation by Franke [22] and COST [23]. The distance between the windward face of the upstream building and the inlet was 5H. The outlet boundary was 10H away from the leeward face of the downstream building to allow flow re-development behind the wake region. This computational domain was discretized into 4.8×10^6 hexahedral meshes, which is refined near the target building and ground surface. The height of the first layer of cells around the building models was small enough ($y+ < 1$) to solve the viscous sublayer. Stretching ratios between neighboring cells were kept below 1.3 in accordance with the best practice guidelines [23,24].

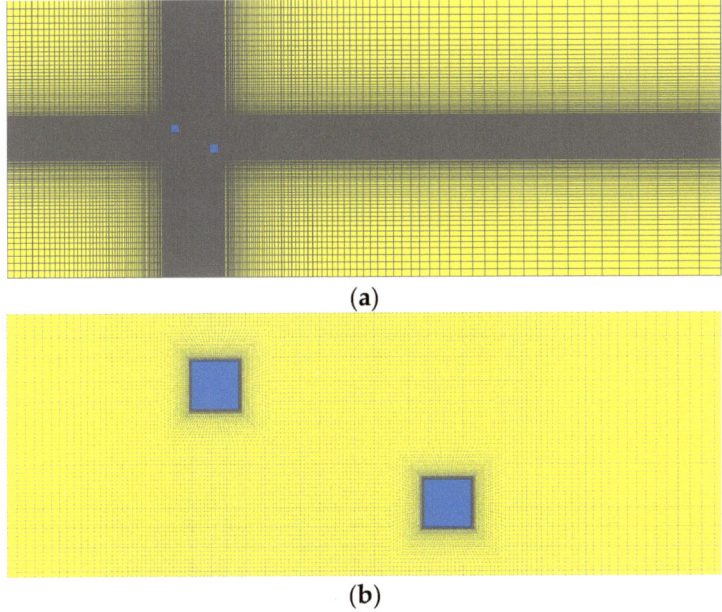

(a)

(b)

Figure 2. (a) Computational domain; (b) local grid around building models.

A time-dependent velocity profile was imposed at the inlet boundary targeting at that obtained from the wind tunnel test. The inflow turbulence was generated by FLUENT inherent vortex method and the kinetic energy of turbulence and the dissipation rate at the inlet section were calculated by

$$k(z) = \frac{3}{2}[u(z)I_u(z)]^2 \tag{7}$$

$$\varepsilon(z) = C_\mu^{3/4}\frac{k(z)^{3/2}}{\kappa z} \tag{8}$$

where $u(z)$ is time-averaged wind velocity at height z; $k(z)$ is turbulent kinetic energy; $\varepsilon(z)$ is dissipation rate; C_μ is a model constant of 0.09. The amount of vorticity was set to 50.

Symmetric boundary conditions were imposed at the sides and the top boundary of the domain, thereby implying zero normal velocity and zero gradients of all variables at the boundaries. Zero static pressure was imposed at the outlet of the domain. The building and ground surfaces were defined as non-slip wall boundary condition.

All the discretized equations were solved in a segregated manner with the pressure implicit with splitting of operators (PISO) algorithm. A second-order accurate bounded central-differencing scheme was used to discretize the convection term in the filtered momentum equation. Second order discretization schemes were adopted for time and spatial discretization. The simulation was initialized with the solution of a preceding RANS (Reynolds-averaged Navier–Stokes) simulation which allows fast convergence of computation. After an initialization period T_{init} = 3.0 s, the statistics were sampled for 20 s, corresponding to 38.7 flow-through times ($T_{ft} = L_x/U_H$, where L_x is the length of the computational domain), which are longer than the sampling duration suggested by Gousseau [21] who found that 21.8 flow-through times are sufficiently long to achieve statistical convergence.

3. Description of Wind Tunnel Test

The simulated wind flow field by LES is validated by comparison between the wind tunnel experiments that were carried out in the boundary layer wind tunnel in the Department of Civil Engineering at the University of Hong Kong. The working section of the tunnel was 3.0 m wide, 1.8 m tall and 12 m long. Wind tunnel tests were carried out under simulated wind flow of the open land terrain, where the mean wind profile followed the power law with a power exponent of 0.11 [25]. The mean wind speed and turbulence intensity at the height of the building model during the test were U_H = 5.8 m/s and 0.089, respectively. The measured mean wind velocity and the turbulence intensity profiles in the wind tunnel test and the simulated profiles in the numerical simulation are presented in Figure 3. The longitudinal integral scale of turbulence was about 0.39 m at the roof height in the wind tunnel. This corresponds to a full-scale integral scale of 390 m at 180 m height.

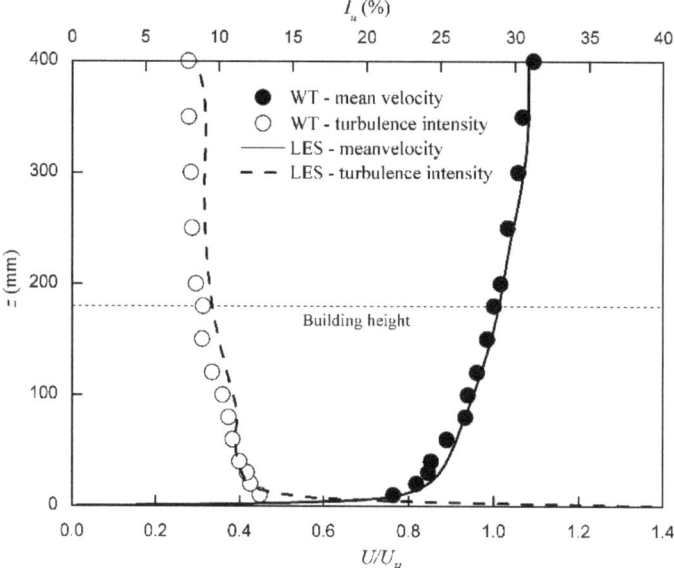

Figure 3. Inflow boundary condition of wind tunnel test and numerical simulation.

A total of 120 pressure taps, 20 on each of its six layers (Level 1 to 6 from the roof to the bottom), were installed on the walls of the test building as shown in Figure 4. A time-resolved PIV system measured the instantaneous velocity fields on a horizontal plane through the two buildings. The measurement plane was illuminated by a thin laser sheet generated from the laser beam of a double-cavity Q-switched Nd:YAG laser (Nano 50–100, Litron). The laser sheet generator and the laser steering arm were placed inside the working section of the wind tunnel and downstream of the building model. A 1:1 mixture of DEHS liquid and sunflower seed oil was used to produce seeding particles using a high-volume liquid seeding generator (10F03, Dantec Dynamics). The particles had diameters at about 2 to 5 μm and could satisfactorily scattered the laser light in the air flow when viewed as a small region of interest. Flow images were captured with a high-speed CMOS camera (SpeedSense, Dantec Dynamics). The camera had a high sensitivity for the weak scattered light signals in air flow with resolution at 1920 × 1200 pixels. The camera framing speed was set at 100 double-image/s to capture a time sequence of particle images of 1825-image length. A time interval 0.12 ms was used between the double laser pulses to fix the initial and final positions of seeding particles in the double image. The PIV analysis software was based on the adaptive PIV algorithm [26,27]. In the final iteration, PIV vectors were obtained on interrogation areas of size 16 × 16 pixels. The number of velocity vectors were 120 × 75 and the physical resolution of each vector was about 3.2 × 3.2 mm². With this configuration, the measurement uncertainty of individual velocity vector was estimated at about $\pm 0.02 U_H$ [28,29].

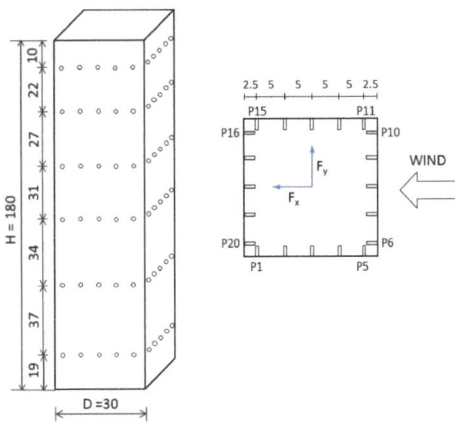

Figure 4. Layout of pressure taps on principal building model (unit: mm).

To synchronize the pressure measurement and flow field acquisition by PIV, pressure measurement was triggered by the framing signals of the PIV camera. This synchronization ensured that the pressure scanning was made at the same instants when the PIV camera captured the double-images of the flow and that both sampling was made at 100 Hz. Figure 5 shows the PIV set-up in the wind tunnel.

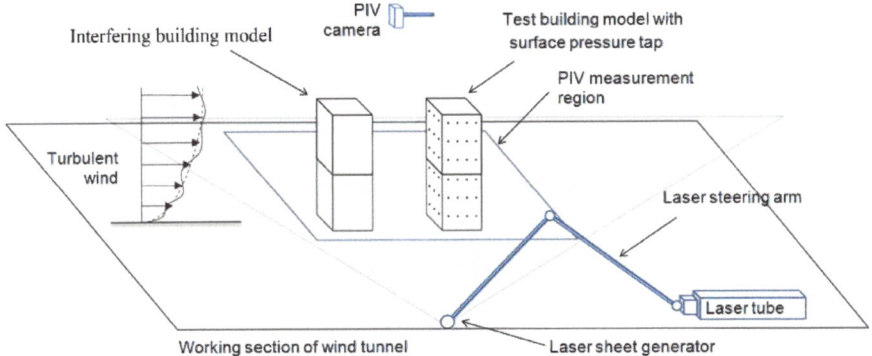

Figure 5. PIV set-up in wind tunnel.

4. Result Analysis and Discussion

4.1. Time-Averaged Wind Flow Characteristics

Time-averaged mean and RMS horizontal flow fields at half building height by LES are shown in Figure 6. Two antisymmetric building wakes are observed behind the two buildings. The upstream building wake slightly swings upward due to the presence of the downstream building. In addition, the upper separating shear layer of the downstream building is found to be weaker than its counterpart in both mean and fluctuating contours.

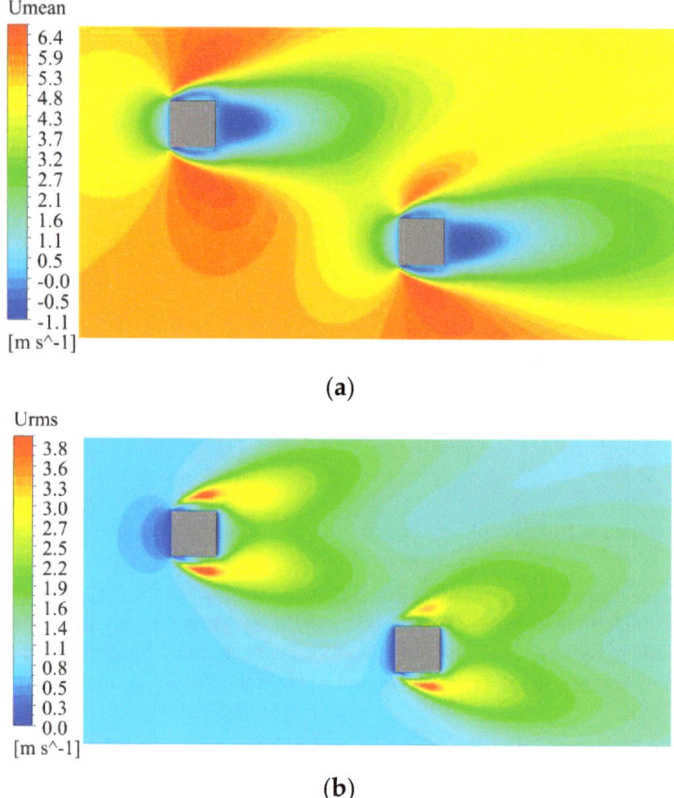

Figure 6. Wind velocity field for normal wind incidence. (**a**) Time-averaged mean flow field; (**b**) RMS flow field.

Figure 7 presents time-averaged streamlines by LES and wind tunnel test. The LES flow pattern agrees well with that obtained from wind tunnel test. A distinctively different wake pattern is observed on the downstream building. The mean flow approaching the building is shifted in a slightly sideway direction (or downward direction in the figure). As a result, the clockwise vortex at the upper side wall is suppressed largely by the downwards-shifted shear layer, while, the anti-clockwise vortex, which is supposed to appear near the lower side, is impaired dramatically in the time averaged sense. The recirculating region of the wake now occupies a smaller space up to a length of 1.7D from the center of the building, comparing with an isolated building wake of which the recirculation area is supposed to be extended to 2.2D [29]. As for the upstream building, the building wake pattern remains largely unchanged except for the slight upward bifurcation line.

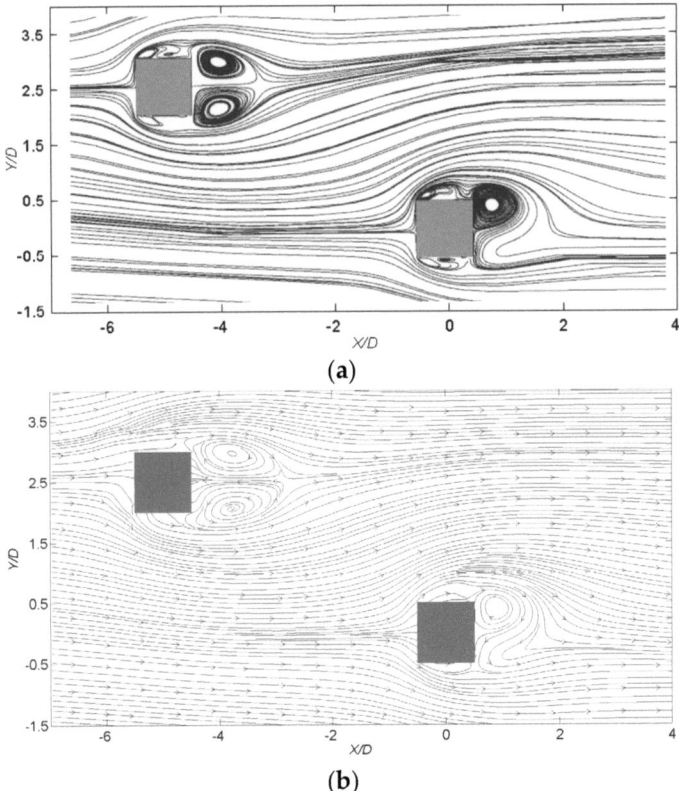

Figure 7. Time-averaged streamlines at mid-height: (**a**) LES result and (**b**) wind tunnel result.

4.2. LES Validation by Wind Tunnel Result

To validate the results of LES, the simulated values of the wind velocity around two building models are compared with those measured in the wind tunnel test by PIV. Figure 8 presents the profiles of the mean along-wind wind velocity $\bar{u}$ at the planes of half building height and near the building roof ($h/H = 0.82$). In this and the following figures, measurements of wind velocity in the wind tunnel by PIV at $X/D = -6, -5, -4, -3, -2, -1, 0, 1, 2, 3, 4$, and 5 are selected to validate the LES results. For each location, the axis is denoted by a longitudinal dotted axis, which is also acting as the origin for wind velocity plotted transversely with positive values on the right side of the axis and negative on the left. Generally, a good agreement is found between the LES and the wind tunnel test.

The time-averaged mean transverse velocity $\bar{v}$ in building wakes is plotted in Figure 9. A relatively larger difference between the numerical and the experiment results is observed for the transverse velocity than that of the streamwise velocity. The transverse component $\bar{v}$ of the flow approaching the downstream building is mainly negative, indicating a downward sideway direction, which coincides well with the time-averaged streamlines in Figure 7. Because of the flow separation, the vertical component of wind velocity $\bar{v}$ is positive near the upper side walls of the two buildings and negative near the opposite sides. It can be observed that the transverse velocity of the upper separating shear layer of the downstream building is larger than that of the upstream building, which means the flow separation from the side wall close to the upstream building is enhanced by the upstream building.

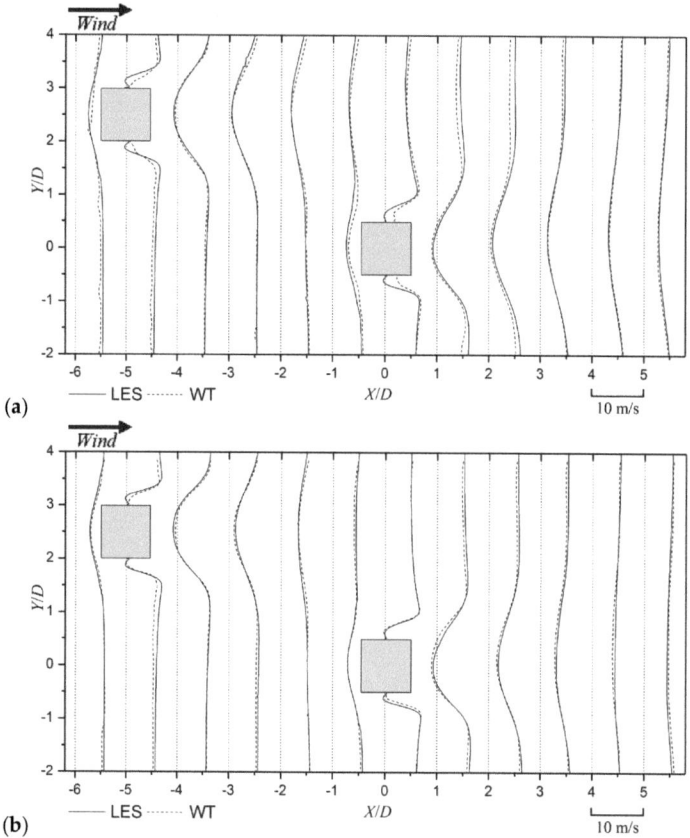

Figure 8. Comparison of wind tunnel (WT) measurements and LES results of mean streamwise velocity $\bar{u}$ in horizontal plane: (**a**) Level 3 (*h* = 0.5*H*) and (**b**) Level 5 (*h* = 0.82*H*). Wind velocity plots transversely with positive value on right side of the dotted axis and negative on left side.

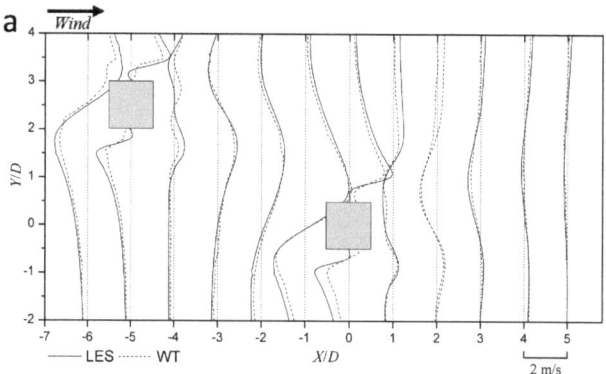

Figure 9. *Cont.*

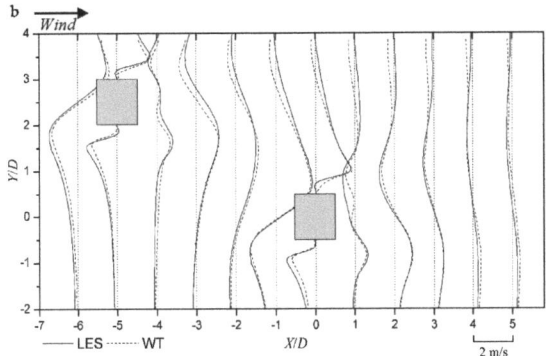

Figure 9. Comparison of wind tunnel (WT) measurements and LES results of mean transverse velocity in horizontal plane: (**a**) Level 3 ($h = 0.5H$) and (**b**) Level 5 ($h = 0.82H$). Wind velocity plots transversely with positive value on right side of the dotted axis and negative on left side.

The distributions of RMS wind velocity components u' are presented in Figure 10. The distributions of u' at two horizontal planes are quite similar. The strong fluctuations of separating shear layers result in large RMS values around both sides of the buildings. The main discrepancy between the numerical and experiment approaches lies in the prediction of the near wakes. LES tends to overestimate the streamwise fluctuating velocity in both building wakes.

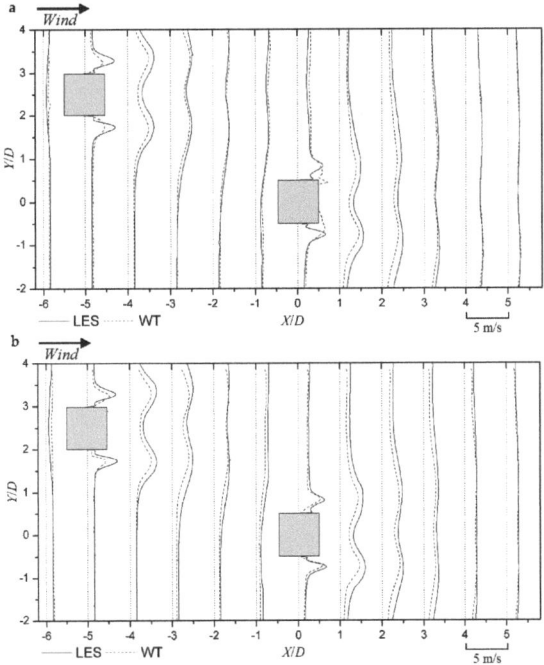

Figure 10. Comparison of wind tunnel (WT) measurements and LES results of fluctuating streamwise velocity u' in horizontal plane: (**a**) Level 3 ($h = 0.5H$) and (**b**) Level 5 ($h = 0.82H$). Wind velocity plots transversely with positive value on right side of the dotted axis and negative on left side.

Figure 11 shows results of fluctuating transverse velocity v' by two methods. Similar with streamwise component u', the LES results are slightly larger than the wind tunnel results in the near wakes of the two buildings. In these near wake regions, peak values of component v' are achieved due to the strong direction shift induced by the building wake oscillation.

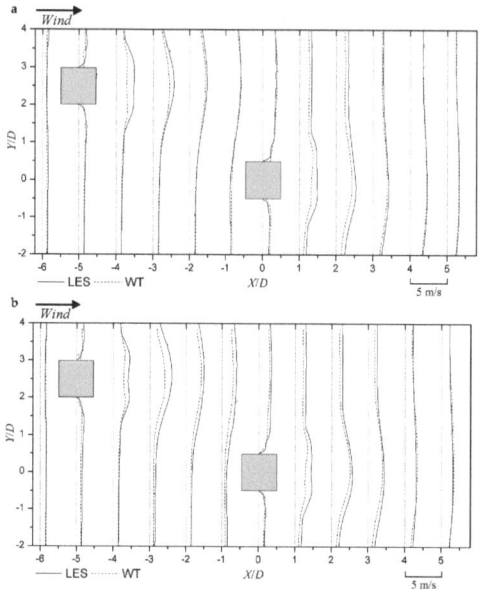

Figure 11. Comparison of wind tunnel (WT) measurements and LES results of fluctuating transverse velocity v' in horizontal plane: (**a**) Level 3 ($h = 0.5H$) and (**b**) Level 5 ($h = 0.82H$). Wind velocity plots transversely with positive value on right side of the dotted axis and negative on left side.

Generally, there is a very good agreement between the LES predictions and the wind tunnel measurements, especially for the time-averaged mean velocities. Wind velocity distributions at different heights are observed to be quite similar. In addition, the differences between two methods are similar at different heights.

4.3. Vortex Structures of Tall Buildings under Interference

It is known that, for an isolated square cylinder, spanwise vortices shed alternatively from both sides of the cylinder and dominates the near wake region [30]. Although the wind loads on buildings in group are thoroughly investigated, the vortex structures of buildings under interference are still unclear. This section intends to investigate flow structures of two tall buildings in proximity.

The normalized spectra of across-wind force acting on different heights along the building by LES are presented in Figure 12. Generally, these force spectra of each elevation have quite similar shapes. An obvious peak can be observed for the across-wind forces for all heights around the $St = 0.105$. This observation is same as wind tunnel results of which the local Strouhal number is 0.0995. Similar values of Strouhal number are found for the across-wind excitation on an isolated building [4,31]. The presence of the upstream building does not change the vortex shedding frequency of the downstream building. The local Strouhal numbers at different heights are approximately the same, and thus the vortices formed from the two sides of the building are shed periodically at a single frequency along the building height.

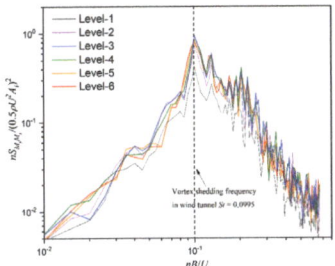

Figure 12. Normalized spectrum of across-wind forces on different levels along building height.

An attempt to reveal the dominant large-scale coherent characteristics of the LES flow field during the occurrence of peak across-wind forces on the downstream building is made using the conditional sampling method [32]. A peak across-wind force event on level i was determined by a peak in the force time history with magnitude above a trigger level. The trigger level was set using a "peak factor" g and the root-mean-square value of across-wind force coefficient σ_{C_F}:

$$\hat{C}_{F_{across,i}} = g\sigma_{C_F} \tag{9}$$

with zero mean across-wind forces and by using $g > 0$ or $g < 0$, both the peak across-wind force events in either of the two sideway directions could be identified and used as triggers for the conditional sampling. The value of g affects the stringency of peak event selection. For a signal with a Gaussian distribution, a peak factor of magnitude between 2 and 3 has been shown to be appropriate [32]. In this study, a less stringent value of $g > 2$ or $g < -2$ was chosen to increase the ensemble size of peak load events.

Figure 13 shows the conditionally sampled wind velocity fields and wind pressures on the horizontal plane at mid-height ($h/H = 0.5$) corresponding to the instants of peak maximum and minimum across-wind forces. An interesting in-phase synchronization phenomenon is observed for two building wakes. At peak maximum event, a clockwise rotating vortex is about to be shed from the upper side of the downstream building. At the same time, a similar large vortex is observed at the rear side of the upstream building at almost the same phase of shedding.

In Figure 13b, two counter-clockwise vortices dominate the near wake regions. The two in-phase vortices at peak minimum event together with those at maximum event recommend a highly synchronized relation between vortex shedding processes of the two buildings. It is worth noting that the developed vortex on the upper side of the downstream building is farther from the building as compared with the alternating vortex developed from the upper side (Figure 13a). This may contribute to the asymmetric mean flow pattern of the downstream building as observed in Figure 7.

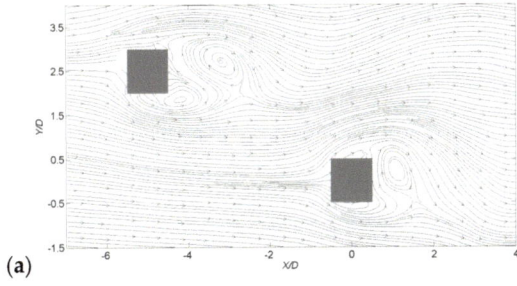

(a)

Figure 13. *Cont.*

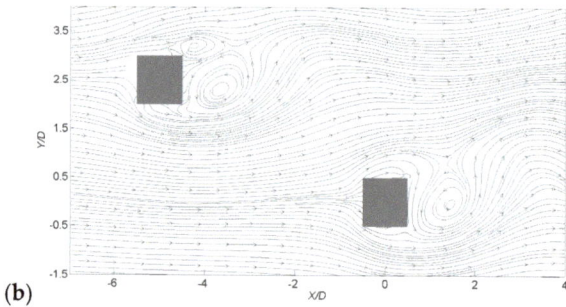

(b)

Figure 13. Conditionally sampled wind velocity field at: (**a**) peak maximum across-wind forces (g = 2) and (**b**) peak minimum across-wind forces (g = −2).

Figure 14 presents the instantaneous three-dimensional flow fields at two typical events corresponding to positive across-wind forces on the downstream building (Figure 14a–c), which is upward in Figure 14c and negative across-wind forces on the downstream building (Figure 14d–f), which is downward in Figure 14f.

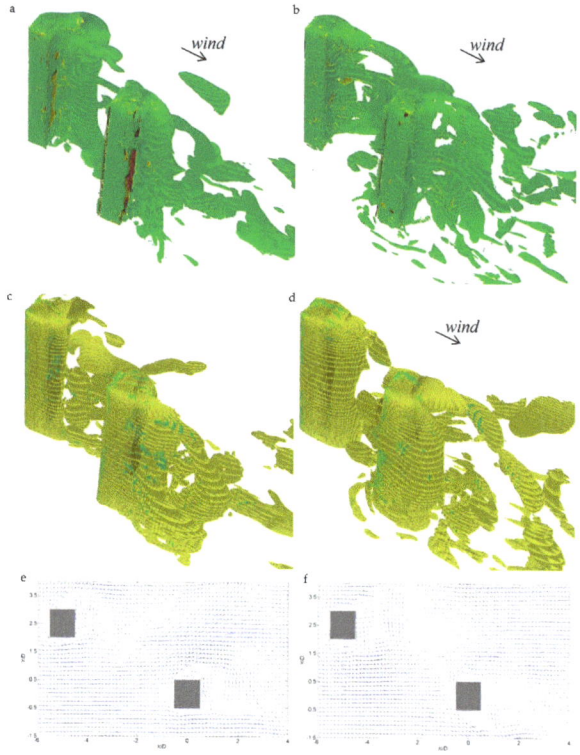

Figure 14. Three-dimensional view of Instantaneous vortex structures represented by spanwise vorticity $\omega^* = \omega D/U$: (**a–c**) positive across-wind force (upward) event and (**d–f**) negative across-wind force (downward) event; (**a,d**) Iso-surfaces of $\omega^* = -2\sim-5$; (**b,e**) Iso-surfaces of $\omega^* = 2\sim5$; (**c,f**) Vector field at mid-height.

For the positive force event, the flow pattern in Figure 14a is similar with that of the peak maximum event (Figure 13a), where two clock-wise vortices are observed to start to shed from the upper side walls of the both buildings. It can be seen that, although the buildings are wholly immersed in the boundary layer where streamwise velocity varies with height, for the both buildings the vortices at different heights develop and shed as a whole. Similar situations are also observed for the negative force event, where counter-clockwise vortices from the both buildings occupy the near-wake regions. For both events, in-phase synchronization phenomenon is also observed, resembling the conditional sampling results (Figure 13).

4.4. Excitation of Across-Wind Forces on Buildings

Vortex excitation described in the preceding section causes fluctuating across-wind forces on the tall buildings. Figure 15 shows the local RMS across-wind force coefficients at each level of the buildings which is integrated from the wind pressures on the corresponding level. Data are shown for the LES computations and wind tunnel tests. The simulated across-wind forces on the upstream and downstream buildings are denoted as "LES-upstream building" and "LES-downstream building", respectively. The across-wind forces measured on the downstream building in the wind tunnel are marked "WT-downstream building". For the reference case of the tall building without any surrounding buildings, the local across-wind forces are shown as "WT-isolated building".

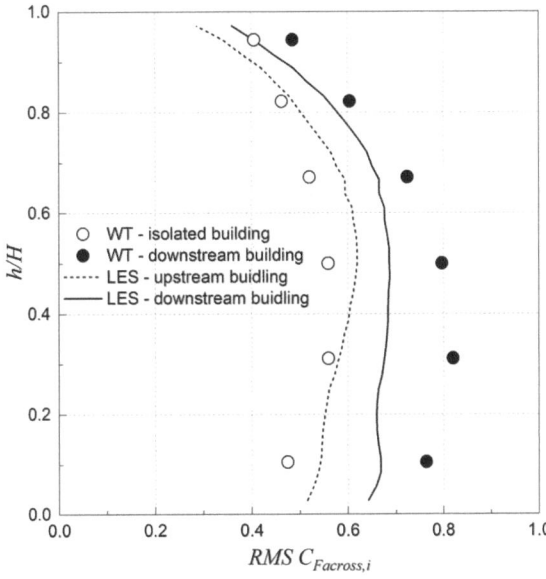

Figure 15. Local across-wind force coefficients obtained from LES and wind tunnel tests.

For the upstream building, the across-wind forces from LES are close to those measured on an isolated building in the wind tunnel. The local wind forces have the largest value at about mid-height of the building and decrease gradually towards both the roof and the bottom of the building. As for the downstream building, the smallest local across-wind force also occurs near the roof and then increases gradually with decreased height. This trend is also observed in the wind tunnel results. Both the LES and wind tunnel results show that the across-wind forces on the downstream building are largely magnified due to interference. The across-wind forces from LES, however, are obviously smaller than those from the experiment, especially for the lower half part of the building under interference. The reason for this disagreement is not known and needs future investigation.

Figure 16 shows some instantaneous across-wind forces on the two buildings from the LES results. It is evident that both force signals are characterized by obvious quasi-periodic fluctuations. This feature is also observed on the force signals obtained from the wind tunnel tests, but the data are not shown for brevity. For the across-wind force signal on the downstream building, the positive peaks have evidently larger magnitudes than the negative peaks, while the across-wind force signal on the upstream building fluctuates very symmetrically around the zero value. This indicates that the suction pressures acting on the upper side face of the downstream building (on the side facing the upstream building) are stronger than those acting on the lower side face. Moreover, the across-wind forces on the both buildings are found to fluctuate together in a largely synchronized manner over most periods, although small phase shifts in the in-phase relationship occur occasionally.

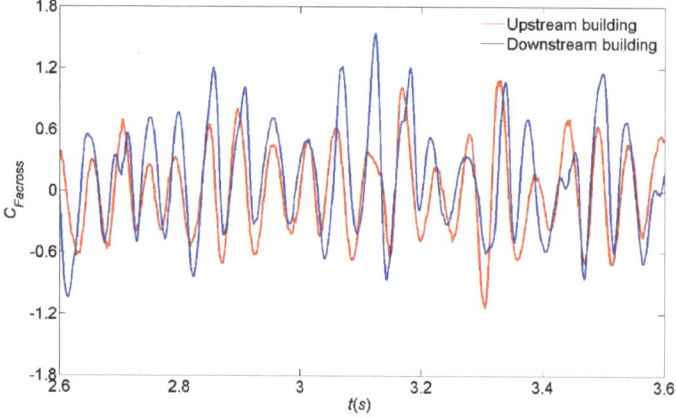

Figure 16. Simultaneous fluctuating overall across-wind force coefficients on upstream building and downstream building.

This near in-phase synchronization of the across-wind forces on the two buildings is further confirmed by correlation analysis. Figure 17 shows the time-lagged cross correlation curve $R(\tau)$ between the across-wind forces on the upstream and downstream buildings. One peak in the correlation coefficient curve occurs at time lag near $\tau = 0$ with $R = 0.40$. This indicates that the across-wind forces on the two buildings are positive correlated in time, which agrees well with the flow field results in Figures 13 and 14. The largest peak correlation is found to occur at $\tau = -1/f_{peak}$, where f_{peak} is the averaged dominant frequency of the quasi-periodic components in the across-wind force signal (Figure 16). This means that a quasi-cycle of the across-wind force on the downstream building has the strongest correlation with that on the upstream building happened one period earlier. The reason for this becomes evident from the flow excitation mechanism revealed in Figure 13. When a vortex is shed from the upstream building and subsequently convects downstream, the vortex dynamics causes flow oscillations in the building wake. When these oscillations reach the downstream building, they act to enhance flow separations on the building which is then responsible for the magnification of the across-wind force on it. As a result, the across-wind force signal on the downstream building relates to vortex shedding activities occurring earlier from the upstream building. In other works, the characteristics of the upstream building wake such as strength and regularity of vortex shedding strongly affect the generation of a peak across-wind force acting on the downstream building later.

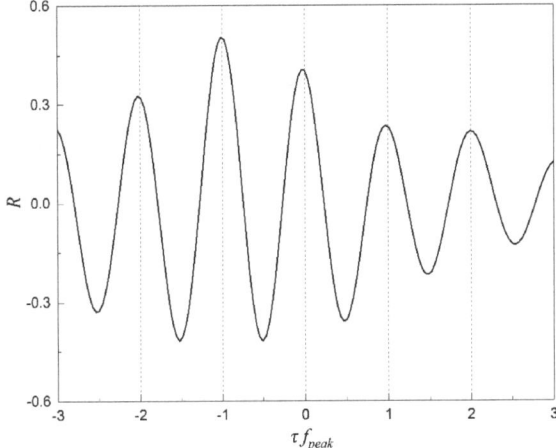

Figure 17. Simultaneous fluctuating surface pressure coefficient Cross correlation curves between across-wind forces on upstream building and downstream building.

5. Conclusions

LES of wind flow around two tall buildings in a critical staggered arrangement has been conducted in the present study. The characteristics of the flow field and the across-wind wind forces of the two buildings have been investigated and compared with wind tunnel tests. The results obtained are summarized as follows:

i.   The results of wind flow around two buildings, including time-averaged mean and fluctuating streamwise and transverse velocity distributions obtained by LES agree well with the wind tunnel measurements. A better agreement is found for time-averaged mean flow field than the fluctuating velocity distributions.

ii.   The large scale coherent patterns are successfully revealed by numerical simulation and wind tunnel test. A distinct relationship between the across-wind peak forces and the phases of alternating vortex shedding is observed. Three-dimensional flow structures are further observed by LES.

iii.   An in-phase synchronization of the vortex shedding from both buildings is observed and confirmed by the wind forces analysis. This would be the cause of largely amplified across-wind excitation of the downstream building.

Acknowledgments: The study is supported by a research grant awarded by the Research Grants Council of Hong Kong (HKU 713813E).

Author Contributions: G.B. Zu and K.M. Lam conceived and designed the experiments; G.B. Zu performed the simulation; G.B. Zu and K.M. Lam analyzed the data; G.B. Zu and K.M. Lam wrote the paper.

Conflicts of Interest: The authors declare no conflict of interest

References

1. Bailey, P.A.; Kwok, K.C.S. Interference excitation of twin tall buildings. *J. Wind Eng. Ind. Aerodyn.* **1985**, *21*, 323–338. [CrossRef]
2. Taniike, Y.; Inaoka, H. Aeroelastic behavior of tall buildings in wakes. *J. Wind Eng. Ind. Aerodyn.* **1988**, *28*, 317–327. [CrossRef]
3. Xie, Z.N.; Gu, M. Simplified formulas for evaluation of wind-induced interference effects among three tall buildings. *J. Wind Eng. Ind. Aerodyn.* **2007**, *95*, 31–52. [CrossRef]

4. Lam, K.M.; Zhao, J.G.; Leung, M.Y.H. Wind-induced loading and dynamic responses of a row of tall buildings under strong interference. *J. Wind Eng. Ind. Aerodyn.* **2011**, *99*, 573–583. [CrossRef]
5. Khanduri, A.C.; Stathopoulos, T.; Bedard, C. Wind-induced interference effects on buildings—A review of the state-of-the-art. *Eng. Struct.* **1998**, *20*, 617–630. [CrossRef]
6. English, E.C.; Fricke, F.R. The interference index and its prediction using a neural network analysis of wind-tunnel data. *J. Wind Eng. Ind. Aerodyn.* **1999**, *83*, 567–575. [CrossRef]
7. Kim, W.; Tamura, Y.; Yoshida, A. Interference effects on local peak pressures between two buildings. *J. Wind Eng. Ind. Aerodyn.* **2011**, *99*, 584–600. [CrossRef]
8. Yu, X.F.; Xie, Z.N.; Zhu, J.B.; Gu, M. Interference effects on wind pressure distribution between two high-rise buildings. *J. Wind Eng. Ind. Aerodyn.* **2015**, *142*, 188–197. [CrossRef]
9. Taniike, Y. Interference mechanism for enhanced wind forces on neighboring tall buildings. *J. Wind Eng. Ind. Aerodyn.* **1992**, *42*, 1073–1083. [CrossRef]
10. Sakamoto, H.; Haniu, H. Aerodynamic forces acting on two square prisms placed vertically in a turbulent boundary-layer. *J. Wind Eng. Ind. Aerodyn.* **1988**, *31*, 41–66. [CrossRef]
11. Gowda, B.H.L.; Sitheeq, M.M. Interference effects on the wind pressure distribution on prismatic bodies in tandem arrangement. *Indian J. Technol.* **1993**, *31*, 485–495.
12. Hui, Y.; Tamura, Y.; Yoshida, A.; Kikuchi, H. Pressure and flow field investigation of interference effects on external pressures between high-rise buildings. *J. Wind Eng. Ind. Aerodyn.* **2013**, *115*, 150–161. [CrossRef]
13. Blocken, B.; Stathopoulos, T. CFD simulation of pedestrian-level wind conditions around buildings: Past achievements and prospects. *J. Wind Eng. Ind. Aerodyn.* **2013**, *121*, 138–145. [CrossRef]
14. Sohankar, A. A LES study of the flow interference between tandem square cylinder pairs. *Theor. Comp. Fluid Dyn.* **2014**, *28*, 531–548. [CrossRef]
15. Tamura, T. Towards practical use of LES in wind engineering. *J. Wind Eng. Ind. Aerodyn.* **2008**, *96*, 1451–1471. [CrossRef]
16. Mara, T.G.; Terry, B.K.; Ho, T.C.E.; Isyumov, N. Aerodynamic and peak response interference factors for an upstream square building of identical height. *J. Wind Eng. Ind. Aerodyn.* **2014**, *133*, 200–210. [CrossRef]
17. Zu, G.B.; Lam, K.M. Interference mechanism of two tall buildings in staggered arrangement. In Proceedings of the 9th Asia-Pacific Conference on Wind Engineering, Auckland, New Zealand, 3–8 December 2017.
18. Ansys Inc. *Ansys Fluent 13.0, User's Guide*; Ansys Inc.: Canonsburg, PA, USA, 2010.
19. Lilly, D.K. A proposed modification of the Germano subgrid-scale closure model. *Phys. Fluids* **1992**, *4*, 633–635. [CrossRef]
20. Germano, M.; Piomelli, U.; Moin, P.; Cabot, W.H. A dynamic subgrid scale eddy viscosity model. *Phys. Fluids* **1991**, *A3*, 1760–1765. [CrossRef]
21. Gousseau, P.; Blocken, B.; Vanheijst, G.J.F. Quality assessment of large-eddy simulation of wind flow around a high-rise building: Validation and solution verification. *Comput. Fluids* **2013**, *79*, 120–133. [CrossRef]
22. Franke, J. Recommendations of the COST action C14 on the use of CFD in predicting pedestrian wind environment. In Proceedings of the Fourth International Symposium on Computational Wind Engineering, Yokohama, Japan, 16–19 July 2006.
23. Franke, J.; Hellsten, A.; Schlünzen, H.; Carissimo, B. *COST 732. Best Practice Guideline for the CFD Simulation of Flows in the Urban Environment*; University of Hamburg, Meteorological Inst.: Hamburg, Germany, 2007.
24. Tominaga, Y.; Mochida, A.; Yoshie, R.; Kataoka, H.; Nozu, T.; Yoshikawa, M.; Shirasawa, T. AIJ guidelines for practical applications of CFD to pedestrian wind environment around buildings. *J. Wind Eng. Ind. Aerodyn.* **2008**, *96*, 1749–1761. [CrossRef]
25. Lam, K.M.; Leung, M.Y.H.; Zhao, J.G. Interference effects on wind loading of a row of closely spaced tall buildings. *J. Wind Eng. Ind. Aerodyn.* **2008**, *96*, 562–583. [CrossRef]
26. Theunissen, R.; Scarano, F.; Riethmuller, M.L. Spatially adaptive PIV interrogation based on data ensemble. *Exp. Fluids* **2010**, *48*, 875–887. [CrossRef]
27. Willert, C.E.; Gharib, M. Digital particle image velocimetry. *Exp. Fluids* **1991**, *10*, 181–193. [CrossRef]
28. Adrian, R.J. Multi-point optical measurements of simultaneous vectors in unsteady flow—A review. *Int. J. Heat Fluid Flow* **1986**, *7*, 127–145. [CrossRef]
29. Adrian, R.J.; Westerweel, J. *Particle Image Velocimetry*; Cambridge University Press: Cambridge, UK, 2011.
30. Wang, H.F.; Zhou, Y. The finite-length square cylinder near wake. *J. Fluid Mech.* **2009**, *638*, 453–490. [CrossRef]

31. To, A.P.; Lam, K.M.; Xie, Z.N. Effect of a through-building gap on wind-induced loading and dynamic responses of a tall building. *Wind Struct.* **2012**, *15*, 531–553. [CrossRef]

32. Lam, K.M.; Zhao, J.G. Occurrence of peak lifting actions on a large horizontal cantilevered roof. *J. Wind Eng. Ind. Aerodyn.* **2002**, *90*, 897–940. [CrossRef]

 *computation*

Article

Temporal Variation of the Pressure from a Steady Impinging Jet Model of Dry Microburst-Like Wind Using URANS

Martin Skote [1],*, Tze Siang Sim [1] and Narasimalu Srikanth [2]

[1]   School of Mechanical and Aerospace Engineering, Nanyang Technological University, 50 Nanyang Avenue, Singapore 639798, Singapore; tssim1@e.ntu.edu.sg

[2]   Energy Research Institute (ERI@N), 1 CleanTech Loop, #06-04, CleanTech One, Singapore 637141, Singapore; nsrikanth@ntu.edu.sg

*   Correspondence: MSKOTE@ntu.edu.sg; Tel.: +65-6790-4271

Received: 16 November 2017; Accepted: 28 December 2017; Published: 5 January 2018

Abstract: The objective of this study is to investigate the temporal behavior of the pressure field of a stationary dry microburst-like wind phenomenon utilizing Unsteady Reynolds-averaged Navier-Stokes (URANS) numerical simulations. Using an axisymmetric steady impinging jet model, the dry microburst-like wind is simulated from the initial release of a steady downdraft flow, till the time after the primary vortices have fully convected out of the stagnation region. The validated URANS results presented herein shed light on the temporal variation of the pressure field which is in agreement with the qualitative description obtained from field measurements. The results have an impact on understanding the wind load on structures from the initial touch-down phase of the downdraft from a microburst. The investigation is based on CFD techniques, together with a simple impinging jet model that does not include any microphysical processes. Unlike previous investigations, this study focuses on the transient pressure field from a downdraft without obstacles.

Keywords: microburst; impinging jet; unsteady reynolds-averaged navier-stokes; pressure field

---

1. Introduction

A thunderstorm downburst is an intense transient downdraft of air that induces an outburst of damaging wind on or near the surface of the Earth. Fujita [1] classified a downburst as "microburst" when the outflow extends less than 4 km along the Earth's surface, and "macroburst" when the outflow reaches more than 4 km. Microbursts are also further classified as of dry or wet type. Dry microbursts are formed in deep, dry, and well-mixed atmospheric boundary layers, while wet microbursts are formed together with thunderstorm clouds with shallow, well-mixed boundary layers and large vertical gradients of potential energy [2]. The formation of downbursts begins with convection driving updrafts, which transport warm, moist, and more buoyant air to great height. The onset of downdrafts occurs when there is cooling of air by the evaporation of rain and melting of ice, causing the air density in the evaporation and melting regions to increase. The colder and denser air accelerates vertically downward from the cloud base. Difference in density between the downdraft and the surrounding atmosphere subsequently leads to the entrainment of the surrounding atmospheric air into the downdraft core, resulting in ring vortices due to Kelvin-Helmholtz instability (KHI). The behaviour of KHI is governed by Taylor-Goldstein equation. The KHI occurs when Richardson (Ri) number is below 0.25. Ri is a dimensionless number measuring the buoyancy effect to the inertia force effect. Fujita [1] reported that the scales of the full-scale downbursts are such that the diameter of the inlet of a full-scale downburst at the cloud base level is between 400 m and 4000 m, and the extreme wind event typically lasts from 5 to 30 min. The range of height (H) of the downburst cloud measured from the cloud base to the surface of the Earth usually falls within $0.75 < H/D < 7.5$, where D is the diameter of the downdraft at the level of the cloud base [3]. In passing, it is noted that the term micro in this context refers to very different scales when compared to those in microfluidics where downburst due to temperature gradients has also been studied [4].

Early studies of downburst wind shear were motivated by aviation accidents. There were numerous field studies conducted to capture the downburst wind in nature. Examples of field studies are: Northern Illinois Meteorological Research on Downbursts (NIMROD) [5], Joint Airport Weather Studies (JAWS) [6], the Federal Aviation Administrative Lincoln Laboratory Operational Weather Studies (FLOWS) [7], the Thunderstorm Wind Project in Singapore [8], the European Project "Wind and Ports" [9–11], project SCOUT [12], and the "forensic study of the Lubbock-Reese downdraft of 2002" [13].

The downburst wind shear near the Earth's surface is of great interest to wind engineers as the outflow exerts wind forces that may pose catastrophic failure risk to structures and buildings, which are typically designed according to wind-loading industry codes (International Electrotechnical Commission 2005). This is highlighted by many recent investigations during the last few decades [14–22]. The dry microburst-like wind near the ground surface is the scope of the present study. Hjelmfelt [3] and Choi [8] have proven in laboratories that the round impinging jets can be used to emulate the outflow near the ground surface because the mean radial field of the flow near the ground agreed reasonably well with one of the field measurements, particularly the time-averaged peak radial velocity. Apart from the impinging jet, other models, such as the 'cooling source' approach, as proposed by Anderson et al. [23] and meteorological full or sub-cloud modelling techniques, as demonstrated by Orf et al. [24–26] and Vermeire et al. [27], have been used previously to emulate downburst wind shear in laboratories, or in numerical simulations. The benefits of the impinging jet modelling approach, when compared to the other approaches, is a much lower computational cost and its ability to model the macro dynamics of downburst [28]. Note that a steady impinging jet model does not have the same meteorological processes (i.e., density stratification of the atmosphere and buoyancy-induced turbulence), transient behaviour and Reynolds number observed in a real full-scale microburst. However, it has been observed by Hjelmfelt [3] that the characteristics of a steady impinging-jet flow are akin to the major features in a 10-min transient microburst event at its maximum strength at the near-surface region. Moreover, the impinging jet has been widely utilized by many researchers to model the microburst's outburst-flow profiles. Even though there is a significant scale difference between an impinging jet model and a real microburst, the impinging jet flow is able to reveal the flow characteristics of a microburst-like wind and wind load acting on structures if the Reynolds number is above the order of 10^4, as demonstrated by Xu and Hangan [29]. The open literature has reported many researchers who have conducted numerical, experimental, and semi-empirical studies of a downburst using the impinging jet model. Below, we list past investigations categorized by their methodology rather than chronologically.

For numerical Computational Fluid Dynamics (CFD) studies, both unsteady and steady numerical Reynolds-averaged Navier-Stokes (URANS and RANS) simulations have been conducted by Chay et al. [30], Kim and Hangan [28], Li et al. [31] and Zhang et al. [22]. A combination of numerical and experimental work of steady impinging jet flow can be found in the work of Wood et al. [32], Sengupta and Sarkar [33], Xu and Hangan [29], and Das et al. [34]. Experimental results have been reported by Landreth and Adrian [35], Chay and Letchford [15], Choi [8], and Zhang et al. [36,37]. In addition, semi-empirical models by Oseguera and Bowles [38], Vicroy [39], Wood et al. [32], and Li et al. [40] were created to provide estimations of the microburst-like wind shear near the ground. Both the experimental results and semi-empirical models have been compared with the field measurements and they yielded reasonably good agreement.

To the authors' knowledge, there is no literature documenting the temporal variation of the pressure field for a microburst-like wind simulated with steady impinging jet model by Unsteady Reynolds Averaged Navier-Stokes (URANS) approach. The objective is to investigate the temporal variation of the pressure field along the radial direction of the steady impinging jet model, starting from the initial release of the jet to the time when the primary vortices have exited the computational domain. Even with a stationary impinging jet, the resulting flow field is unsteady. One of the goals with the present work is to demonstrate that the standard tool for simulating unsteady flow (URANS) is able to capture the transient effects reasonably well. In addition, we show that the unsteady solution approaches the same values of the pressure, as obtained from steady simulations (RANS), which is the most utilized method in past investigations.

The RANS results that are presented here are validated with the published laboratory impinging jet data, while the URANS results are compared qualitatively with the temporal variation of the pressure observed in nature. In addition, the RANS and URANS results are shown to be consistent. The aim of the study is to improve the understanding of the wind load from the initial touch-down phase of the downdraft from a microburst. The investigation, using CFD, is dealing with an impinging jet model, which does not include any microphysical processes. This simplification of the real physics shortens the duration of simulation. Microphysical processes are usually simulated with cloud models or numerical weather prediction to provide an even higher resolution estimation of the surface wind. However, the substantial increase in the duration of simulation might not be well justified.

2. Computational Method

The commercial CFD code ANSYS Fluent 13 [41] is used to model the steady impinging jet model in the present study.

2.1. Governing Equations

For the axisymmetric steady impinging jet model used herein, the Coriolis force is not modelled due to the minor influences on the mean wind direction and height, according to Holmes [42]. The highest wind speed of downburst is about 75 m/s, as observed in field measurements [43] (Mach number Ma < 0.3), which would infer that the flow is essentially incompressible [21]. The wind flow satisfies the Reynolds-averaged mass and momentum conservation equations:

$$\frac{\partial U_i}{\partial x_i} = 0 \tag{1}$$

$$\frac{\partial U_i}{\partial t} + U_j \frac{\partial U_i}{\partial x_j} = g_i - \frac{1}{\rho}\frac{\partial p}{\partial x_i} + \nu \frac{\partial^2 U_i}{\partial x_j^2} - \frac{\langle u_i u_j \rangle}{\partial x_j} \tag{2}$$

where ρ is the density of the fluid, p is the pressure, U is the mean velocity, x denotes the spatial co-ordinates, g_3 is the gravitational term and t is the time quantity. The term for Reynolds stress component corresponds to $\langle u_i u_j \rangle$, where u is the fluctuating velocity component. For RANS, the first term in Equation (2) is zero.

Note that the full governing equations (Navier-Stokes) cannot be solved directly as in the turbulence investigations using much smaller geometries (see further references in, for example, the recent work by Skote [44]). Hence, the equations have been averaged, with the penalty of the unknown Reynolds stress term that needs to be modelled in terms of mean flow variables in order to close to system of equations.

The RANS approach has the flow quantities time-averaged from the start of the simulation. On the other hand, URANS is based on a smaller averaging time frame, and can capture the developing flow structures, though the smaller turbulence time-scales are not resolved.

2.2. Computational Domain, Boundary Conditions and Numerical Schemes

The computational domain is presented in Figure 1. There are two possible outlets (E'F' and D'E') in the two-dimensional (2D) axisymmetric domain shown in the figure, and each outlet should be placed at a certain distance where the outflow has attained steady-state, fully developed boundary layer with mean gauge pressure of 0 Pa approximately. It is also expected that there might be some backflow re-entering at these outflow boundaries as the primary vortex ring convects out of the domain. Pressure outlets are placed far away from axis (A'B'), and wall (A'F') boundaries, respectively, to give sufficient length for flow development and to ensure that the outlets have minimal influence on the flow near the stagnation point (i.e., r/D less than 3). Boundary C'D' is specified as 'symmetry' boundary, such that the flux normal to the boundary is zero. The wall (A'F') boundary is specified as a smooth, no-slip wall, with length L = 10D.

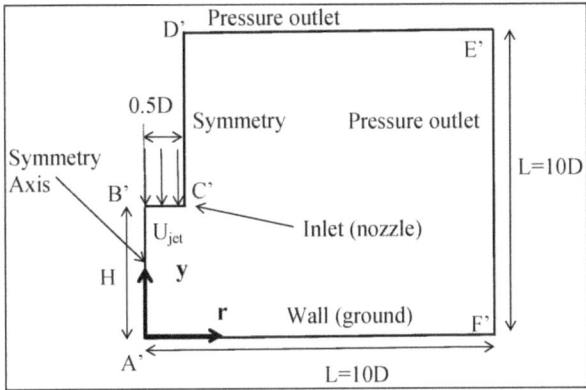

Figure 1. Two-dimensional (2D) axisymmetric computational domain.

The computational domain is packed with the uniformly distributed structured quadrilateral grids. The mesh at the wall (ground) region is strenuously refined in order to resolve the viscous laminar sub-layer and the log-law region at non-dimensionless wall distance: $\delta^+ = (\delta U_\tau)/\nu_T$ of order unity, because the enhanced wall treatment option in FLUENT is employed, where the U_τ is friction velocity, ν_T is the turbulent viscosity and δ is the wall-adjacent grid distance. The enhanced wall treatment in FLUENT is a near-wall modelling method that combines a two-layer model with enhanced wall functions and it is suitable for complex boundary layer seen in the impinging wall jet. The whole domain is subdivided into a viscosity-affected region and a fully-turbulent region. In the viscosity-affected near-wall region, the one-equation model of Wolfstein [45] is employed. In the fully turbulent outer region, the realizable k-ε turbulence [46] model is used. The turbulent viscosity is smoothly combined by a two-layer formulation approach. The law of the wall is constructed by utilizing a mathematical function proposed by Kader [47]. For the inlet (nozzle), a turbulent intensity of 1% is imposed and D is taken to be hydraulic diameter required to compute turbulence quantities: turbulent kinetic energy k and turbulent dissipation rate ε. The realizable k-ε turbulence model is tested to ensure that it is able to model the radial velocity in the impingement zone (r/D less than 3). Prior to any validation study, the selection of this turbulence model is solely based on the fact that it contains mathematical constraints that restrict the solution to be always physical, making it advantageous for calculating the flow around the stagnation center.

The spatial discretization schemes for k, ε, ω, and $\langle u_i u_j \rangle$ employ higher-order scheme Quadratic Upstream Interpolation for Convective Kinematics (QUICK) [48], which is 3rd-order accurate on structured uniform mesh. The pressure and momentum terms are discretized using 2nd-order upwind scheme. The 1st order discretization scheme is used only in the first 200 iterations in order to increase the rate of convergence, but the scheme is converted to QUICK and continued iterating from the intermediate solutions to final solutions. The 1st order scheme was not used to iterate to the final solution directly, due to false diffusion that gives rise to physically unrealistic final solutions [49]. For the pressure-velocity coupling, the Semi-Implicit Method for Pressure Linked Equations (SIMPLE) algorithm [50] is applied. The convergence criteria have been limited to 1×10^{-5}.

An evaluation of the time step sizes for the URANS simulation was conducted and a time step size of dt $= 1 \times 10^{-6}$ s was selected. Time is non-dimensionalised with U_{jet} and D, and is denoted T in the following. With this scaling, the time step becomes dT $= 3.48 \times 10^{-4}$. The selected time step size has passed a time sensitivity test to ensure that it will not have any significant influence on the CFD results.

2.3. Scaling Factors of the Impinging Jet Model

The spatial scale of the full-scale downburst is derived from the field measurements of dry microburst, as observed by Hjelmfelt [3]. The diameter of a full-scale dry microburst in nature is 1.8 km while the smaller diameter of the impinging jet nozzle used in the present study is D = 28.7 mm. Based on this field measurement, the geometric scaling factor in the present study is of the order of 1×10^{-5}.

The dry microburst observed by Fujita had a maximum velocity magnitude of about 60 m/s. The smaller inlet velocity magnitude at the impinging jet nozzle is about 10 m/s. Thus, the velocity scaling factor is about 1/6. Scaling factors calculation has also been performed previously by authors working on scale models, Mason et al. [51] and Das et al. [52], to reduce the total number of cells required when using impinging jet for downburst simulation.

The height of the downburst cloud has a base (H/D) between 0.75 and 7.5 (dimensionless) in nature, while the present impinging jet model has a nozzle height (H/D) varying between 1 and 5.

2.4. Grid Convergence

Four sets of meshes are constructed for the grid convergence study. The number of elements of a set has at least 35% more than any of the other sets. Grid resolution for all the meshes used for the present mesh convergence study are higher than any of the previously published numerical simulations [22,28,34]. Details of the meshes are summarized in Table 1.

The radial velocity profiles at r/D = 1.0, produced by the realizable k-ε RANS turbulence model, are compared for the different meshes in Figure 2. All of the meshes from M1 and M4 showed that the solutions are already grid-independent. The non-dimensional wall distance δ^+ varies from 0.4 to 0.6, depending on the local skin friction, and this is within the required $\delta^+ \leq 1$ for employing the enhanced wall function in FLUENT. M4 uses the least number of cells and is chosen for subsequent simulations.

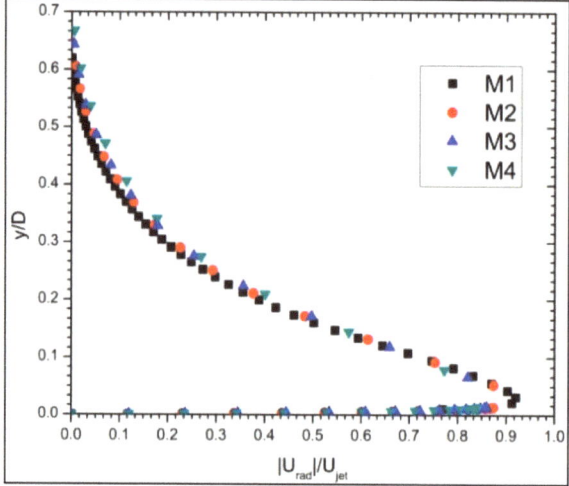

Figure 2. Normalised radial velocity | Urad | /Ujet at r/D = 1 (grid convergence).

Table 1. Mesh sizes for the purpose of grid convergence.

Mesh Case Notations	M1	M2	M3	M4
Number of Elements	565,566	66,861	38,412	25,144

2.5. Validation of RANS Results

The RANS CFD simulation of the round impinging jet flow will be validated with two published experimental data: Xu and Hangan [29] and Zhang [21], which we denote XH and ZG in the following. The impinging jet model used is a scale model of the full-scale downburst. The uniform velocity magnitude U_{jet} = 10 m/s and 100 m/s are applied at the inlet of the CFD domain, which correspond to the values in XH and ZG, respectively. Even though the inlet velocity magnitude are not the same as those that are prescribed in the two published experiments, the Reynolds numbers (Re) of the two simulations will be the same as those in the experiments (i.e., Re = 20,000 for XH, and Re = 288,046 for ZG). The diameter (D) of the jet is taken to be D = 28.7 mm and D = 41.3 mm at the inlet (nozzle), and the ratios of the height-to-ground wall surface are H/D = 2 and 4 for ZG and XH experiments, respectively (where H is the height of the nozzle).

From Figure 3, the RANS results at four radial locations r/D = 1, 1.4, 2, and 2.5 show good agreement with the experimental results from XH (H/D = 4 and Re = 20,000). The slight over-prediction of the peak normalized radial velocity at respective radial locations indicates that the realizable k-ε turbulence model gives a more 'conservative' prediction of the peak value. The term 'conservative' in the present study refers to the predicted peak value being slightly higher than the experimental results. Based on the studies by Lim et al. [53], it can be inferred that an accurate prediction of the mean velocity also will produce an accurate prediction of the mean pressure.

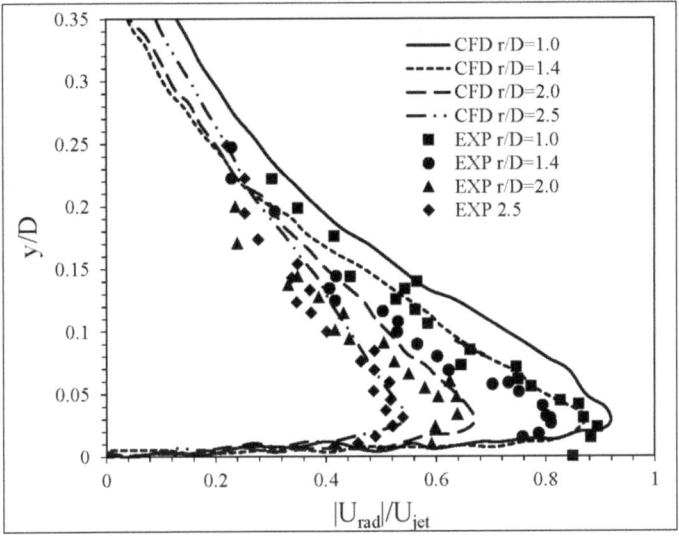

Figure 3. Comparison of Computational Fluid Dynamics (CFD) results (RANS with the realizable k-ε turbulence model) using mesh M4 with Xu and Hangan [29] experimental (EXP) data (Re = 20,000) at radial locations r/D = 1, 1.4, 2.0 and 2.5.

Furthermore, drawing experiences from the previous turbulent Atmospheric Boundary Layer (ABL) studies [54,55], when the flow is Re independent, the pressure force is much more significant than the skin friction force, and the pressure force would dominate the total resultant force. As the impinging jet flow in the present study becomes Re-independent from Re $\sim 10^4$ onwards, more emphasis will be placed on the pressure force from an engineering perspective. Apart from validating with the experimental data from XH, a further validation with the experimental data from ZG was performed. By validating with two experiments, it is ensured that the results of impinging jet model can be applied to a range of Re and H/D. The values were H/D = 2 and Re = 288,046 in the experiment of ZG. The validation of the CFD results with ZG published experimental results (Figure 4) shows reasonably good agreement. The maximum deviation between our CFD and ZG is around 10%. Furthermore, the present CFD results are also compared with the results that were obtained from the steady-state analytical models for the mean speed, as proposed by Oseguera and Bowles [38], Vicroy [39], and Wood et al. [32], and the field observed data by Fujita [5] and Hjelmfelt [3]. It can be concluded that the current numerical results are within the limits of all existing prediction methods and field measurement found in the open literature. Moreover, it also confirms that the CFD results near the wall boundary constitute an accurate and physical prediction of the mean wind profile of the downburst wind shear.

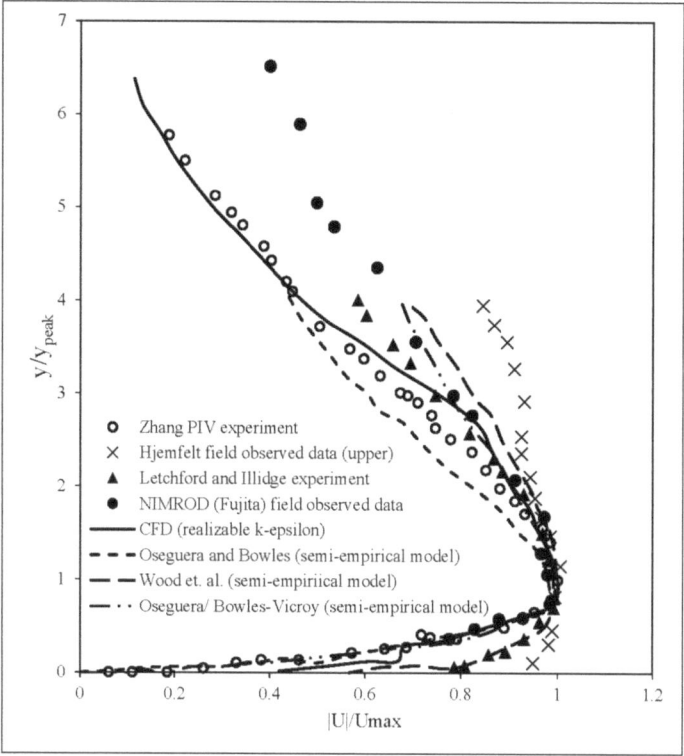

Figure 4. CFD results (RANS) validated with published particle image velocimetry (PIV) experimental data of Zhang. [21] The present result using the realizable k-ε turbulence model at Re = 288,046, H/D = 2 at r/D = 1.0 is shown as the solid line. U_{max} is the maximum speed of the outflow near the ground, and y_{peak} is the corresponding height where the maximum speed occurs.

3. Results and Discussion

The mean pressure field is measured in terms of the pressure coefficient (C_p):

$$C_p = (P - P_\infty)/0.5\rho U_{jet}^2 \tag{3}$$

where P, P_∞, ρ and U_{jet} are taken to be mean static gauge pressure, atmospheric gauge pressure, density of air, and inlet jet velocity, respectively. The Reynolds number chosen for the study in this section is fixed at Re = 20,000.

The radial distribution of C_p obtained from URANS and steady RANS simulation are extracted at y_{peak}, which is the height from the ground where the peak velocity is found at each radial location.

The values of y_{peak} from the RANS simulations are illustrated in Figure 5, where y_{peak}/D is shown for different values of H/D and r/D. Across all of the radial locations (from $r/D = 1$ to 2.5), $y_{peak}/D \approx 0.03$ is approximately constant for the cases of $H/D = 2, 3$, and 4. The exact value is determined to be 0.032 for the case of $H/D = 4$.

The evolution of the C_p with time is now investigated at $y_{peak}/D = 0.032$ for the case of $H/D = 4$. The C_p of the URANS simulation is extracted at flow-times, given in Table 2. These instances are between the release of the steady jet from the inlet T = 0 to the complete convection of the primary ring vortices out of the computational domain T = 348. The first value of T = 15.7 corresponds to the instance when the downdraft reaches the surface.

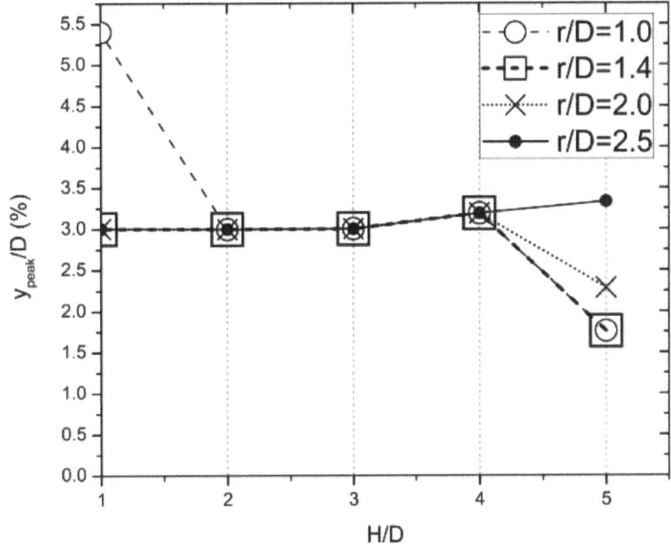

Figure 5. Effects of H/D on the normalized position where the peak velocity is found. From RANS at Re = 20,000.

Table 2. Flow time monitored. t is the dimensional time in seconds (s). T is the non-dimensionalised time.

t (s)	0.045	0.060	0.090	0.220	1.00
T	15.7	20.9	31.3	76.6	348

According to Fujita [1] and Mason et al. [50], the location of maximum velocity (r_{max}) would also be the location of the minimum in the radial distribution of the pressure. From Figure 6, the r_{max} can be deduced when C_p is first reduced to zero from a high positive value (at $r = 0$). Hence, r_{max} deduced from the pressure data is determined to be one diameter ($r_{max} = D$). This value of r_{max} that is reported here is relatively accurate and it is close to the earlier prediction [28] of maximum velocity location of $r_{max}/D = 1.1$ obtained from RANS simulation, and $r_{max}/D = 1.5$ in URANS simulation. Both types of the simulations had the same $Re = 20,000$, as in the present study.

The variation of C_p in Figure 6 from URANS simulation matches the qualitative account of [1] for the pressure variation along the radial direction. As the flow-time reaches the non-dimensional value of $T = 348$, which is considered to be long enough after the initial touchdown of the downburst at $T = 15.7$, the value of C_p coincides with the result from the steady RANS simulation, which has already been validated with published models and data. Therefore, at flow-time of $T = 348$, the impinging jet is at a quasi-steady state. The reason why there is no increase in C_p at $r/r_{max} > 1$ at $T = 348$ in Figure 6 for URANS simulation could be that the primary vortex rings have already convected away at that time, which was also the explanation made by Chay and Letchford [15]. A similar plot of radial distribution of C_p was published by Chay and Letchford [15] who reported the "sharp decrease" of static pressure and restoration of the static pressure back to atmospheric pressure at maximum velocity location $r/D = 1.5$, as well as no "negative static pressure region" in their RANS simulation. These reported features can be observed from the present URANS simulation results, including that the C_p is restored back to the atmospheric pressure at the maximum velocity location at $r/r_{max} = 1$. A high positive pressure at $r/r_{max} = 0$ is observed in both the RANS simulation results and URANS simulation results in Figure 6. This flow feature was reported by Cui and Chen [18] when they studied the spatial distribution of C_p across a curved-roof placed at $r/D = 0$ using RANS simulation. The high positive pressure dome at stagnation region around $r/D = 0$ was also found in the observed field data by Fujita [1].

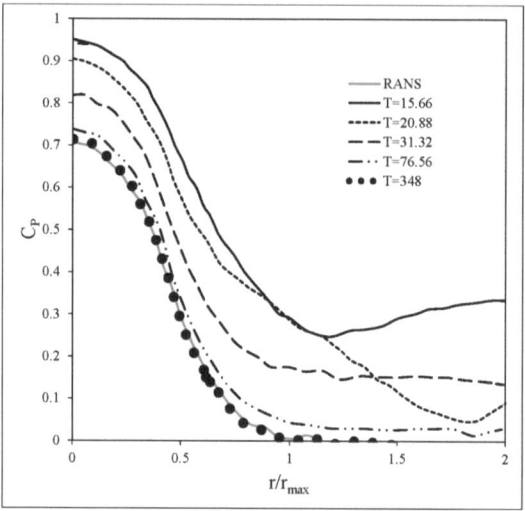

Figure 6. Radial distribution of the mean pressure coefficient obtained from present steady and transient simulations. Radial distribution of the mean pressure coefficient obtained from the steady and transient simulations. The pressure is taken from $y_{peak}/D = 0.032$ for the case of $H/D = 4$ at $Re = 20,000$.

4. Conclusions

The evolution of the pressure coefficient with time derived from the URANS simulation of a steady impinging jet flow has been shown to approach the RANS results after a sufficiently long time period ($T = 348$). The RANS results have been validated with existing field observed data [1,3,6], published experiments [21,29], and the semi-empirical velocity models [32,39]. The results have been validated with published literature to ensure that it is representative of the major feature in the dry microburst-like wind. The development of the pressure field from the initial release of the downdraft to a quasi-steady state is also consistent with the data from published field observations. Present study shows encouraging results that the methodology assures an accurate evaluation of the wind load impact, specifically for the mean pressure coefficient, which is caused by dry microburst-like wind on engineering structures and buildings. The height where the peak velocity occur for $r/D = 1$ to 2.5 and $H/D = 2$ to 4 is found to be consistently around $y_{peak}/D = 0.03$. The C_P distribution has been compared qualitatively with the field observed data and published experimental data. The results have an impact on understanding the variation of the mean wind load effect over engineering structures and buildings during the initial landing of the dry microburst-like wind on the ground, which is a major concern to the wind engineering community.

Acknowledgments: The research described in this paper is supported by the National Research Foundation (NRF) of Singapore and Joint Industry Programme (JIP)—Energy Research Institute (ERI@N) at Nanyang Technological University, Singapore.

Author Contributions: T.S.S., M.S. and N.S. conceived the computational study; T.S.S. performed the simulations; T.S.S. and M.S. analyzed the data; N.S. contributed analysis tools; T.S.S. and M.S. wrote the paper with valuable input from N.S.

Conflicts of Interest: The authors declare no conflict of interest.

References

1. Fujita, T.T. *The Downburst: Microburst and Macroburst: Report of Projects NIMROD and JAWS, Satellite and Mesometeorology Research Project*; Dept. of the Geophysical Sciences, University of Chicago Press: Chicago, IL, USA, 1985.
2. Atkins, N.T.; Wakimoto, R.M. Wet Microburst Activity over the Southeastern United States: Implications for Forecasting. *Weather Forecast.* **1991**, *6*, 470–482. [CrossRef]
3. Hjelmfelt, M.R. Structure and Life Cycle of Microburst Outflows Observed in Colorado. *J. Appl. Meteorol.* **1988**, *27*, 900–927. [CrossRef]
4. Mårtensson, G.; Skote, M.; Malmqvist, M.; Falk, M.; Asp, A.; Svanvik, N.; Johansson, A.V. Rapid PCR amplification of DNA utilizing Coriolis effects. *Eur. Biophys. J.* **2006**, *35*, 453–458. [CrossRef] [PubMed]
5. Fujita, T.T. Objectives, operation, and results of Project NIMROD. In Proceedings of the 11th Conference on Severe Local Storms, Kansas City, MO, USA, 2–5 October 1979; American Meteorological Society: Boston, MA, USA, 1979; pp. 259–266.
6. McCarthy, J.; Wilson, J.W.; Fujita, T.T. *The Joint Airport Weather Studies Project*; Bulletin of the American Meteorological Society; American Meteorological Society: Boston, MA, USA, 1982; Volume 63, p. 15.
7. Wolfson, M.M.; DiStafano, J.T.; Forman, B.E. *The FLOWS (FAA-Lincoln Laboratory Operational Weather Studies) Automatic Weather Station Network in Operation*; Defense Technical Information Center: Fort Belvoir, VA, USA, 1987.
8. Choi, E.C.C. Field measurement and experimental study of wind speed profile during thunderstorms. *J. Wind Eng. Ind. Aerodyn.* **2004**, *92*, 275–290. [CrossRef]
9. Burlando, M.; Romanić, D.; Solari, G.; Hangan, H.; Zhang, S. Field data analysis and weather scenario of a downburst event in Livorno, Italy, on 1 October 2012. *Mon. Weather Rev.* **2017**, *145*, 3507–3527. [CrossRef]
10. De Gaetano, P.; Repetto, M.P.; Repetto, T.; Solari, G. Separation and classification of extreme wind events from anemometric records. *J. Wind Eng. Ind. Aerodyn.* **2014**, *126*, 132–143. [CrossRef]
11. Solari, G.; Repetto, M.P.; Burlando, M.; De Gaetano, P.; Pizzo, M.; Tizzi, M.; Parodi, M. The wind forecast for safety management of port areas. *J. Wind Eng. Ind. Aerodyn.* **2012**, *104–106*, 266–277. [CrossRef]
12. Gunter, W.S.; Schroeder, J.L. High-resolution full-scale measurements of thunderstorm outflow winds. *J. Wind Eng. Ind. Aerodyn.* **2015**, *138*, 13–26. [CrossRef]
13. Holmes, J.D.; Hangan, H.M.; Schroeder, J.L.; Letchford, C.W.; Orwig, K.D. A forensic study of the Lubbock-Reese downdraft of 2002. *Wind Struct.* **2008**, *11*, 137–152. [CrossRef]

14. Holmes, J.D. Modelling of extreme thunderstorm winds for wind loading of structures and risk assessment. In Proceedings of the Tenth International Conference on Wind Engineering, Copenhagen, Denmark, 21–24 June 1999; Volume 2, pp. 1409–1416.

15. Chay, M.T.; Letchford, C.W. Pressure distributions on a cube in a simulated thunderstorm downburst—Part A: Stationary downburst observations. *J. Wind Eng. Ind. Aerodyn.* **2002**, *90*, 711–732. [CrossRef]

16. Letchford, C.W.; Chay, M.T. Pressure distributions on a cube in a simulated thunderstorm downburst. Part B: Moving downburst observations. *J. Wind Eng. Ind. Aerodyn.* **2002**, *90*, 733–753. [CrossRef]

17. Kim, J.; Hangan, H.; Ho, T.C.E. Downburst versus boundary layer induced wind loads for tall buildings. *Wind Struct.* **2007**, *10*, 481–494. [CrossRef]

18. Cui, B.; Chen, Y. CFD Simulation of Curved-roof subjected to Thunderstorm Downburst. In *Key Engineering Materials*; Trans Tech Publications: Zürich, Switzerland, 2017; Volume 474, pp. 1243–1248.

19. Nguyen, H.H.; Manuel, L.; Veers, P.S. Wind turbine loads during simulated thunderstorm microbursts. *J. Renew. Sustain. Energy* **2011**, *3*, 053104–053119. [CrossRef]

20. Nguyen, H.H.; Manuel, L. Thunderstorm downburst risks to wind farms. *J. Renew. Sustain. Energy* **2013**, *5*, 013120. [CrossRef]

21. Zhang, Y. *Study of Microburst-Like Wind and Its Loading Effects on Structures Using Impinging Jet and Cooling Source Approach*; Iowa State University: Ames, IA, USA, 2013.

22. Zhang, Y.; Hu, H.; Sarkar, P.P. Modeling of microburst outflows using impinging jet and cooling source approaches and their comparison. *Eng. Struct.* **2013**, *56*, 779–793. [CrossRef]

23. Anderson, J.R.; Orf, L.G.; Straka, J.M. A 3-D model system for simulating thunderstorm microburst outflows. *Meteorl. Atmos. Phys.* **1992**, *49*, 125–131. [CrossRef]

24. Orf, L.G.; Anderson, J.R.; Straka, J.M. A Three-Dimensional Numerical Analysis of Colliding Microburst Outflow Dynamics. *J. Atmos. Sci.* **1996**, *53*, 2490–2511. [CrossRef]

25. Orf, L.G.; Anderson, J.R. A Numerical Study of Traveling Microbursts. *Mon. Weather Rev.* **1999**, *127*, 1244–1258. [CrossRef]

26. Orf, L.G.; Kantor, E.; Savory, E. Simulation of a downburst-producing thunderstorm using a very high-resolution three-dimensional cloud model. *J. Wind Eng. Ind. Aerodyn.* **2012**, *104–106*, 547–557. [CrossRef]

27. Vermeire, B.C.; Orf, L.G.; Savory, E. A parametric study of downburst line near-surface outflows. *J. Wind Eng. Ind. Aerodyn.* **2011**, *99*, 226–238. [CrossRef]

28. Kim, J.; Hangan, H. Numerical simulations of impinging jets with application to downbursts. *J. Wind Eng. Ind. Aerodyn.* **2007**, *95*, 279–298. [CrossRef]

29. Xu, Z.; Hangan, H. Scale, boundary and inlet condition effects on impinging jets. *J. Wind Eng. Ind. Aerodyn.* **2008**, *96*, 2383–2402. [CrossRef]

30. Chay, M.T.; Albermani, F.; Wilson, R. Numerical and analytical simulation of downburst wind loads. *Eng. Struct.* **2006**, *28*, 240–254. [CrossRef]

31. Li, C.; Li, Q.S.; Xiao, Y.Q.; Ou, J.P. Simulations of moving downbursts using CFD. In Proceedings of the Seventh Asia-Pacific Conference on Wind Engineering, Taiwan, 8–12 November 2009.

32. Wood, G.S.; Kwok, K.C.S.; Motteram, N.A.; Fletcher, D.F. Physical and numerical modelling of thunderstorm downbursts. *J. Wind Eng. Ind. Aerodyn.* **2001**, *89*, 535–552. [CrossRef]

33. Sengupta, A.; Sarkar, P.P. Experimental measurement and numerical simulation of an impinging jet with application to thunderstorm microburst winds. *J. Wind Eng. Ind. Aerodyn.* **2008**, *96*, 345–365. [CrossRef]

34. Das, K.K.; Ghosh, A.K.; Sinhamahapatra, K.P. Experimental and Numerical simulation of the Translational Downburst using impinging jet model. *Int. J. Eng. Sci. Technol. (IJEST)* **2011**, *3*, 4656–4667.

35. Landreth, C.C.; Adrian, R.J. Impingement of a low Reynolds number turbulent circular jet onto a flat plate at normal incidence. *Exp. Fluids* **1990**, *9*, 74–84. [CrossRef]

36. Zhang, Y.; Hu, H.; Sarkar, P.P. Comparison of microburst-wind loads on low-rise structures of various geometric shapes. *J. Wind Eng. Ind. Aerodyn.* **2014**, *133*, 181–190. [CrossRef]

37. Zhang, Y.; Sarkar, P.; Hu, H. An experimental study on wind loads acting on a high-rise building model induced by microburst-like winds. *J. Fluids Struct.* **2014**, *50*, 547–564. [CrossRef]

38. Oseguera, R.M.; Bowles, R.L. *A Simple, Analytic 3-Dimensional Downburst Model Based on Boundary Layer Stagnation Flow*; National Aeronautics and Space Administration, Langley Research Center: Hampton, VA, USA, 1988.

39. Vicroy, D.D. *A Simple, Analytical, Axisymmetric Microburst Model for Downdraft Estimation*; National Aeronautics and Space Administration, Langley Research Center: Hampton, VA, USA, 1991.

40. Li, C.; Li, Q.S.; Xiao, Y.Q.; Ou, J.P. A revised empirical model and CFD simulations for 3D axisymmetric steady-state flows of downbursts and impinging jets. *J. Wind Eng. Ind. Aerodyn.* **2012**, *102*, 48–60. [CrossRef]

41. ANSYS Fluent User Manual by ANSYS Inc. Available online: www.ansys.com (accessed on 5 January 2018).

42. Holmes, J.D. Wind turbines-Part 1: Design Requirements. In *Wind Loading of Structures*; IEC 61400-1; Taylor & Francis International Electrotechnical Commission: Boca Raton, FL, USA, 2007.

43. Fujita, T.T. Tornadoes and Downbursts in the Context of Generalized Planetary Scales. *J. Atmos. Sci.* **1981**, *38*, 1511–1534. [CrossRef]

44. Skote, M. Scaling of the velocity profile in strongly drag reduced turbulent flows over an oscillating wall. *Int. J. Heat Fluid Flow* **2014**, *50*, 352–358. [CrossRef]

45. Wolfstein, M. The Velocity and Temperature Distribution of One-Dimensional Flow with Turbulence Augmentation and Pressure Gradient. *Int. J. Heat Mass Transf.* **1969**, *12*, 301–318. [CrossRef]

46. Shih, T.H.; Liou, W.; Shabbir, Z.Y.; Zhu, J. A New k-ε Eddy Viscosity Model for High Reynolds Number Turbulent Flows—Model Development and Validation. *Comput. Fluids* **1995**, *24*, 227–238. [CrossRef]

47. Kader, B. Temperature and Concentration Profiles in Fully Turbulent Boundary Layers. *Int. J. Heat Mass Transf.* **1981**, *24*, 1541–1544. [CrossRef]

48. Leonard, B.P. A stable and accurate convective modelling procedure based on quadratic upstream interpolation. *Comput. Methods Appl. Mech. Eng.* **1979**, *19*, 59–98. [CrossRef]

49. Versteeg, H.K.; Malalasekera, W. *An Introduction to Computational Fluid Dynamics: The Finite Volume Method*; Pearson Education Limited: London, UK, 2007.

50. Mangani, L.; Bianchini, C. Heat transfer applications in turbomachinery. In Proceedings of the OpenFOAM International Conference, London, UK, 26–27 November 2007.

51. Mason, M.S.; Letchford, C.W.; James, D.L. Pulsed wall jet simulation of a stationary thunderstorm downburst, Part A: Physical structure and flow field characterization. *J. Wind Eng. Ind. Aerodyn.* **2005**, *93*, 557–580. [CrossRef]

52. Das, K.K.; Ghosh, A.K.; Sinhamahapatra, K.P. Development of a numerical code for simulation of dry microburst using impinging jet model. *Int. J. Appl. Math. Mech.* **2011**, *7*, 56–71.

53. Lim, H.C.; Castro, I.P.; Hoxey, R.P. Bluff bodies in deep turbulent boundary layers: Reynolds-number issues. *J. Fluid Mech.* **2007**, *571*, 97–118. [CrossRef]

54. Claus, J.; Coceal, O.; Thomas, T.G.; Branford, S.; Belcher, S.E.; Castro, I. Wind-Direction Effects on Urban-Type Flows. *Bound. Layer Meteorol.* **2012**, *142*, 265–287. [CrossRef]

55. Claus, J.; Krogstad, P.Å.; Castro, I. Some Measurements of Surface Drag in Urban-Type Boundary Layers at Various Wind Angles. *Bound. Layer Meteorol.* **2002**, *145*, 407–442. [CrossRef]

 *computation*

Article

Application of Different Turbulence Models Simulating Wind Flow in Complex Terrain: A Case Study for the WindForS Test Site

Hermann Knaus [1,*], Martin Hofsäß [2], Alexander Rautenberg [3] and Jens Bange [3]

[1] Esslingen University of Applied Sciences, Faculty Building Services, Energy and Environment, Kanalstraße 33, D-73728 Esslingen, Germany

[2] University of Stuttgart, Stuttgart Wind Energy (SWE) at the Institute of Aircraft Design, Allmandring 5b, D-70569 Stuttgart, Germany; martin.hofsaess@ifb.uni-stuttgart.de

[3] Eberhard Karls University, Center for Applied Geoscience (ZAG), Hölderlinstraße 12, D-72074 Tübingen, Germany; alexander.rautenberg@uni-tuebingen.de (A.R.); jens.bange@uni-tuebingen.de (J.B.)

* Correspondence: hermann.knaus@hs-esslingen.de; Tel.: +49-711-397-49

Received: 4 July 2018; Accepted: 24 July 2018; Published: 27 July 2018

Abstract: A model for the simulation of wind flow in complex terrain is presented based on the Reynolds averaged Navier–Stokes (RANS) equations. For the description of turbulence, the standard k-ε, the renormalization group (RNG) k-ε, and a Reynolds stress turbulence model are applied. Additional terms are implemented in the momentum equations to describe stratification of the Earth's atmosphere and to account for the Coriolis forces driven by the Earth's rotation, as well as for the drag force due to forested canopy. Furthermore, turbulence production and dissipation terms are added to the turbulence equations for the two-equation, as well as for the Reynolds stress models, in order to capture different types of land use. The approaches for the turbulence models are verified by means of a homogeneous canopy test case with flat terrain and constant forest height. The validation of the models is performed by investigating the WindForS wind test site. The simulation results are compared with five-hole probe velocity measurements using multipurpose airborne sensor carrier (MASC) systems (unmanned small research aircraft)—UAV at different locations for the main wind regime. Additionally, Reynolds stresses measured with sonic anemometers at a meteorological wind mast at different heights are compared with simulation results using the Reynolds stress turbulence model.

Keywords: wind simulation; complex terrain; canopy; Reynolds averaged Navier–Stokes equations (RANS); second moment closure

1. Introduction

Most of the wind turbines in Germany are located on flat terrain or in coastal regions. Alternatively, wind energy production in southern Germany, with its widely hilly or even mountainous and forested landscape, has become more and more attractive. However, finding appropriate sites with sufficient wind potential and an acceptable orography-induced turbulence level, especially in this densely populated territory, is a challenging task. Therefore, stable, practice-oriented, and validated computational fluid dynamics (CFD) models enabling the detailed prediction of wind flow in complex terrain for the micro-siting of wind turbines are desirable for enabling the reliable prediction of the wind speed, wind direction, and turbulence intensity. An overview over the possibilities for flow modelling for wind turbine micro-siting in complex terrain is given by Palma et al. [1], where the need for nonlinear CFD models is highlighted.

One issue about the simulation of wind in complex terrain is the description of the anisotropic turbulence, which is driven by the inhomogeneous velocity distribution:

- The most generally applicable approach is to use is the large-eddy simulation (LES). However, the maximum grid resolution is still strongly limited because of the available computer resources. Possibilities, as well as limitations of this modelling approach are given in Chow et al. [2] and Churchfield et al. [3].
- Another option is the detached-eddy simulation (DES) using unsteady Reynolds averaged Navier-Stokes equations (URANS) in combination with two-equation turbulence models in the vicinity of the walls of the computational domain and LES elsewhere [4]. For DES, the computational time is significantly reduced in comparison with LES. As a result of the necessity of a transient simulation and subsequent time averaging for a significant period of time, the computational effort and storage requirements still tend to be too high for practical applications even using massively parallel computers.
- Two-equation turbulence models mostly in combination with wall models, for example, standard k-ε or RNG k-ε models, offer great numerical stability combined with a relatively low demand on computational resources. Their application for the computation of wind flow in complex terrain with strong velocity gradients has shown to give acceptable results despite the assumption of an isotropic turbulence [5–7]. However, for many applications, it is stated that the turbulence intensity is not accurately predicted for the k-ε turbulence model and that flow separation is under-predicted. Kim and Patel [8] found that the RNG k-ε model was superior for simulating wind flow in complex terrain, especially for separating flow conditions. The RNG k-ε model also had been successfully used in real complex terrain by Abdi and Bitsuamlak [9].
- A Reynolds stress model (RSM) promises a more accurate description of the anisotropic turbulence in wind flow. However, the computational effort is increased in comparison with the two equation turbulence models and it is numerically not as stable.

Another issue is that in forested areas, the model equations for momentum and turbulence have to be adjusted to get an adequate representation of additional drag forces as well as the generation and dissipation of turbulence. Two main approaches were developed and successfully applied in the past. One option is to introduce a roughness length z_0 in the logarithmic wall function [10]. Another possibility is the use of canopy models, introducing source terms in the momentum and turbulence equations as first suggested by Svensson and Häggkvist [11]. Similar approaches, all in combination with the standard k-ε model, have been adopted by Liu et al. [12] and Green [13]. Shaw and Schumann [14] set up a test case of a homogeneous forested area, which commonly is used for the verification of these canopy models. Lopes et al. [15] compared the different approaches using the data of Shaw and Schumann [14] and devised a further canopy model. The use of a RSM for canopy flow was first described by Wilson and Shaw [16]. Ayotte et al. [17] established a model aiming at the simulation of neutrally stratified flow in heterogeneous landscapes and compared the simulation results with a flat terrain dataset. Ayotte et al. [17] split the viscous dissipation into a contribution of the spectral eddy cascade, as well as a foliage contribution and the implementation of the RSM is based on the transport equation for the dissipation of the turbulence kinetic energy of the spectral eddy cascade. Dimitris and Panayotis [18] used a similar approach to Ayotte et al. [17]. However, the contribution of the vegetation is considered as source term directly in the transport equation for the total dissipation of turbulent kinetic energy. Dimitris and Panayotis [18] compared the simulation results with measurements from laboratory channels with aquatic vegetation. An application of these kinds of RSM capturing canopy effects for the micro-siting in complex terrain is not known to the authors, indicating that there is a strong need for validation.

In the following study, we describe a way to carry out flow modelling in complex, forested terrain that is accurate and fast enough for micro-siting and for planning of measurement campaigns. The turbulence model is one of the key factors to get an accurate prediction of the wind velocity and the turbulence intensity, which are the essential measures for the power generation and fatigue load of wind turbines. For this, the standard k-ε, RNG k-ε, and Reynolds stress turbulence models are compared. Additionally, canopy models for the description of forestry in the momentum equation and turbulence models are implemented to capture additional drag force as well as production and dissipation of turbulence. The problem of finding realistic boundary conditions for the simulation of wind fields in complex terrain is tackled using data from the weather model COSMO-DE of the German Meteorological Service (DWD) [19]. The models are verified for the homogeneous canopy test cases from Shaw and Schumann [14]. The validation of the models is carried out by means of an unmanned aerial vehicle (UAV) and 3D-ultrasonic anemometer measurement data for the WindForS test site.

2. Computational Model

The computational method is implemented in the commercial software ANSYS CFX Version 17.0 [20], based on the finite volume approach. The momentum equation in an inelastic formulation and the energy equation are solved. Turbulence is either described by the standard k-ε model, the RNG k-ε models, or the Reynolds stresses model. The pressure-weighted interpolation method (PWIN) [21] is used to prevent the decoupling of velocities and pressure on the non-staggered grid. The convective fluxes are approximated for all transport equations with a bounded second-order upwind scheme.

Additional source terms are implemented to incorporate stratification of the Earth's atmosphere and Coriolis force in the momentum equation. Furthermore, the capabilities of the software are extended to capture the influence of different land use on drag forces, as well as turbulence production and dissipation. The computational model is described in more detail in the following section.

2.1. Continuity and Momentum Equation

Fluid flow is described in a formulation of the continuity and momentum equations using the Boussinesq approximation [22], where density is only influenced by buoyancy forces.

Continuity equation:

$$\frac{\partial(\rho_h u_j)}{\partial x_j} = 0 \tag{1}$$

Momentum equation:

$$\frac{\partial(\rho_h u_j u_i)}{\partial x_j} = -\frac{\partial p'}{\partial x_i} + \frac{\partial}{\partial x_j}\left[\mu_{eff}\left(\frac{\partial u_i}{\partial x_j} + \frac{\partial u_j}{\partial x_i}\right) - \rho_h \frac{2}{3}k\right] - \rho_h\left(\frac{\Theta - \Theta_h}{\Theta_h}\right)g_i + F_{C,i} + F_{W,i} \tag{2}$$

Θ is the potential temperature and p' is the average perturbation of pressure to the hydrostatic reference state defined according as follows [23]:

$$P_h = P_0 \exp\left(-\frac{T_0}{\beta} + \sqrt{\left(\frac{T_0}{\beta}\right)^2 - \frac{2\,g\,z}{\beta\,R_d}}\right) \tag{3}$$

$$T_h = T_0\sqrt{1 - \frac{2\beta g z}{R_d T_0^2}} \tag{4}$$

with β = 42 K, T_0 = 288.15 K, p_0 = 100,000 Pa, R_d = 287.05 J/(kg K), and g = 9.81 m/s^2.

The forest canopy can be modelled as a porous media by means of an additional drag force $F_{W,i}$ in the momentum equation (Equation (2)):

$$F_{W,i} = -\frac{1}{2}\rho_h C_D a(z)|u|u_i \tag{5}$$

where a is the local foliage density in the dependency of forestry height, C_D is the constant drag coefficient set to 0.30, and $|u|$ is the magnitude of the velocity vector.

The Coriolis force terms $F_{C,i}$ in Equation (2) are defined as follows:

$$
\begin{aligned}
F_{C,1} &= 2\,\rho_h\,\Omega\,(\sin(\phi)u_2 - \cos(\phi)u_3) \\
F_{C,2} &= -2\,\rho_h\,\Omega\,(\sin(\phi)u_1) \\
F_{C,3} &= 2\,\rho_h\,\Omega\,(\cos(\phi)u_1)
\end{aligned}
\tag{6}
$$

with the average latitude ϕ depending on the area under consideration and the angular velocity of the earth $\Omega = 7.292 \times 10^{-5}\,\mathrm{s}^{-1}$.

The effective viscosity is a combination of the molecular viscosity μ and turbulent viscosity μ_t:

$$
\mu_{\text{eff}} = \mu + \mu_t
\tag{7}
$$

μ_t can be expressed by the turbulent kinetic energy k and the dissipation of the turbulent kinetic energy ε assuming isotropic turbulence:

$$
\mu_t = C_\mu \rho_h \frac{k^2}{\varepsilon}
\tag{8}
$$

2.2. Energy Equation

Energy transport is described by means of the potential temperature Θ:

$$
\frac{\partial(\rho_h u_j \Theta)}{\partial x_j} = \frac{\partial}{\partial x_j}\left[\left(\frac{\lambda}{c_p} + \frac{\mu_t}{\sigma_\Theta}\right)\frac{\partial \Theta}{\partial x_j}\right]
\tag{9}
$$

with the turbulent Prandtl number σ_Θ set to 1.0.

2.3. Two Equation Turbulence Models

Two equation turbulence models are commonly used for industrial applications because of their numerical stability and low demand on computer resources. In this study, the standard k-ε model and the RNG k-ε model are applied for the simulation of wind flow in complex terrain, solving transport equations for the turbulent kinetic energy k and the dissipation of turbulent kinetic energy ε.

2.3.1. Standard k-ε Turbulence Model

The turbulent kinetic energy k and dissipation of turbulent kinetic energy ε are described with the following transport equations:

$$
\frac{\partial(\rho_h u_j k)}{\partial x_j} = \frac{\partial}{\partial x_j}\left[\left(\mu + \frac{\mu_t}{\sigma_k}\right)\frac{\partial k}{\partial x_j}\right] + P_k - \rho_h \varepsilon + S_k
\tag{10}
$$

$$
\frac{\partial(\rho_h u_j \varepsilon)}{\partial x_j} = \frac{\partial}{\partial x_j}\left[\left(\mu + \frac{\mu_t}{\sigma_\varepsilon}\right)\frac{\partial \varepsilon}{\partial x_j}\right] + \frac{\varepsilon}{k}(C_{\varepsilon 1}P_k - C_{\varepsilon 2}\rho_h \varepsilon) + S_\varepsilon
\tag{11}
$$

The turbulence production due to turbulent eddy viscosity is calculated as follows:

$$
P_k = \mu_t\left(\frac{\partial u_i}{\partial x_j} + \frac{\partial u_j}{\partial x_i}\right)\frac{\partial u_i}{\partial x_j} - \frac{2}{3}\frac{\partial u_k}{\partial x_k}\left(3\mu_t\frac{\partial u_k}{\partial x_k} + \rho_h k\right)
\tag{12}
$$

The constants of Equations (10)–(12) are summarized in Table 1 and are chosen according to Launder and Spalding [24].

Table 1. Constants of the standard k-ε turbulence model.

$C_\mu = 0.09$	$C_{\varepsilon 1} = 1.44$	$C_{\varepsilon 2} = 1.92$	$\sigma_k = 1.0$	$\sigma_\varepsilon = 1.3$

2.3.2. RNG k-ε Turbulence Model

The RNG k-ε model of Yakhot et al. [25] includes a correction to the k-ε model by revaluating the constants. No adjustment of the constants is made, they are derived analytically from the RNG theory (renormalization group methods). Equations (10) and (13), as well as Equations (11) and (14), are identical except for the constants:

$$\frac{\partial(\rho_h u_j k)}{\partial x_j} = \frac{\partial}{\partial x_j}\left[\left(\mu + \frac{\mu_t}{\sigma_{kRNG}}\right)\frac{\partial k}{\partial x_j}\right] + P_k - \rho_h \varepsilon + S_k \tag{13}$$

$$\frac{\partial(\rho_h u_j \varepsilon)}{\partial x_j} = \frac{\partial}{\partial x_j}\left[\left(\mu + \frac{\mu_t}{\sigma_{\varepsilon RNG}}\right)\frac{\partial \varepsilon}{\partial x_j}\right] + \frac{\varepsilon}{k}(C_{\varepsilon 1RNG}P_k - C_{\varepsilon 2RNG}\rho_h \varepsilon) + S_\varepsilon \tag{14}$$

With

$$C_{\varepsilon 1RNG} = 1.42 - f_\eta \tag{15}$$

$$f_\eta = \frac{\eta\left(1 - \frac{\eta}{4.38}\right)}{(1 + \beta_{RNG}\eta^3)} \tag{16}$$

$$\eta = \sqrt{\frac{P_k}{\rho_h C_{\mu RNG}\varepsilon}} \tag{17}$$

The constants used for the RNG k-ε turbulence model are summarized in Table 2.

Table 2. Constants of the RNG k-ε turbulence model.

$C_{\mu RNG} = 0.085$	$C_{\varepsilon 2RNG} = 1.68$	$\sigma_{kRNG} = 0.7179$	$\sigma_{\varepsilon RNG} = 0.7179$	$\beta_{RNG} = 0.012$

2.3.3. Canopy Model Source Terms for Two Equation Turbulence Models

Additionally, terms for production and dissipation have to be added to the transport equations for turbulent kinetic energy (Equations (10) and (13), respectively) and dissipation of turbulent kinetic energy (Equations (11) and (14), respectively). Generally, these source terms are written according to Katul et al. [26]:

$$S_k = \frac{1}{2}\rho_h C_D a(z)(\beta_p|u|^3 - \beta_d|u|k) \tag{18}$$

$$S_\varepsilon = \frac{1}{2}\rho_h C_D a(z)(C_{\varepsilon 4}\beta_p|u|^3\frac{\varepsilon}{k} - C_{\varepsilon 5}\beta_d|u|\varepsilon) \tag{19}$$

In this study, the model of Liu et al. [12] is chosen, taking the dissipation and production terms with the constants summarized in Table 3 into consideration.

Table 3. Constants for the canopy model considered [12].

$\beta_p = 1.0$	$\beta_d = 4.0$	$C_{\varepsilon 4} = 1.5$	$C_{\varepsilon 5} = 0.6$

2.4. A Second-Order Turbulence Closure

The turbulence model is based on the formulation of Launder et al. [27] and its extension on vegetated canopy flows of Ayotte et al. [17] in combination with those of Dimitris and Panayotis [18].

Reynolds Stress Turbulence Model (RSM)

In case of the Reynolds stress model, six transport equations have to be solved for the computation of the Reynolds stress tensor:

$$\frac{\partial}{\partial x_k}\left(u_k\rho_h\overline{u_i'u_j'}\right) - \frac{\partial}{\partial x_k}\left[\left(\delta_{kl}\mu + \rho_hC_S\frac{k}{\varepsilon}\overline{u_k'u_l'}\right)\frac{\overline{\partial u_iu_j}}{\partial x_l}\right] = P_{ij} - \frac{2}{3}\delta_{ij}\rho_h\varepsilon - d_{ij} + \Phi_{ij,1} + \Phi_{ij,2} + p_{ij} \quad (20)$$

where P_{ij} is the production term:

$$P_{ij} = -\rho_h\left(\overline{u_i'u_k'}\frac{\partial u_j}{\partial x_k} + \overline{u_j'u_k'}\frac{\partial u_i}{\partial x_k}\right) \quad (21)$$

The pressure–strain correlations $\Phi_{ij,1}$ and $\Phi_{ij,2}$ are described according to Rotta [28] and Launder et al. [27], respectively:

$$\Phi_{ij,1} = -C_1\rho_h\frac{\varepsilon}{k}(\overline{u_i'u_j'} - \frac{2}{3}\delta_{ij}k) \quad (22)$$

$$\Phi_{ij,2} = \frac{-C_2+8}{11}\left(P_{ij} - \frac{2}{3}\delta_{ij}P\right) - \frac{30C_2-2}{55}\rho_hk\left(\frac{\partial u_i}{\partial x_j} + \frac{\partial u_j}{\partial x_i}\right) - \frac{8C_2-2}{11}\left(D_{ij} - \frac{2}{3}\delta_{ij}P\right) \quad (23)$$

With

$$P = \frac{1}{2}P_{ii} \quad (24)$$

and

$$D_{ij} = -\rho_h\left(\overline{u_i'u_k'}\frac{\partial u_k}{\partial x_j} + \overline{u_j'u_k'}\frac{\partial u_k}{\partial x_i}\right) \quad (25)$$

d_{ij} and p_{ij} are additional dissipation and production terms capturing the increase of dissipation and production within the canopy [17].

$$d_{ij} = \frac{1}{2}\rho_hC_Da(z)\left(|u|\overline{u_i'u_j'} + \frac{u_iu_k\overline{u_k'u_j'}}{|u|} + \frac{u_ju_k\overline{u_k'u_i'}}{|u|}\right) \quad (26)$$

Note the positive sign for the additional dissipation terms and the factor $\frac{1}{2}$ in Equation (26) [29].

$$P_{ij} = -\rho_h\left(\overline{u_j'u_k'}\frac{\partial u_i}{\partial x_k} + \overline{u_i'u_k'}\frac{\partial u_j}{\partial x_k}\right) = \frac{1}{2}\rho_hC_Da(z)|u|^3\frac{\delta_{ij}}{3} \quad (27)$$

The turbulent kinetic energy k is computed explicitly from the normal Reynolds stresses:

$$k = \frac{1}{2}\left(\overline{u_i'u_i'}\right) \quad (28)$$

The implementation of the Reynolds stress model is based on the transport equation for the turbulence eddy dissipation ε, mainly for the purpose of numerical stability. Dimitris and

Panayotis [18] suggested the following formulation using a transport equation for the total turbulence eddy dissipation including an additional source term S_ε for the canopy:

$$\frac{\partial(\rho_h u_j \varepsilon)}{\partial x_j} = \frac{\partial}{\partial x_j}\left[\left(\mu \delta_{ij} + \rho_h C_\varepsilon \frac{k}{\varepsilon}\overline{u_i' u_j'}\right)\frac{\partial \varepsilon}{\partial x_i}\right] + \frac{\varepsilon}{k}(C_{\varepsilon 1} P_k - C_{\varepsilon 2}\rho_h \varepsilon) + S_\varepsilon \tag{29}$$

In the canopy source term,

$$S_\varepsilon = \frac{1}{2}\frac{d_{ii}}{\tau_{eff}} \tag{30}$$

the internal time scale in the canopy according to Uittenbogaard [30] is included:

$$\tau_{eff} = f\frac{k}{\varepsilon} \tag{31}$$

Depending on the distance between the stems and their diameter, the length scale of the turbulent eddies is reduced in the canopy, decreasing their lifetime. For this reason, the internal canopy time scale τ_{eff} based on the total time scale $\frac{k}{\varepsilon}$ may be adapted using a multiplication coefficient f to fit the model results to measurements, as discussed in Lopez and Garcia [31].

All model constants used for the Reynolds stress model are summarized in Table 4.

Table 4. Constants of the Reynolds stress turbulence model.

$C_S = 0.22$	$C_1 = 1.8$	$C_2 = 0.6$	$C_\varepsilon = 0.18$	$C_{\varepsilon 1} = 1.45$	$C_\varepsilon = 1.90$

3. Model Verification Using a Homogeneous Canopy Test Case

The different turbulence models, including their extension for the description of flow within the canopy, are verified via the test case of Shaw & Schumann [14] representing flat terrain and constant canopy height of h = 20 m. The test case enables the comparison of different turbulence models in combination with the canopy models independently of the influence of the orography due to the homogeneous landscape. The computational domain has an extent of 9.6 h × 4.8 h × 3.0 h, spatially resolved with 96 × 48 × 30 grid lines in x-, y-, and z-directions in the original mesh. Additionally, a refined mesh with 192 × 96 × 120 grid lines is set up to increase the spatial resolution by a factor of two in the x- and y-directions, and by a factor of four in the z-direction. The flow is aligned along the x-axis, with the z-axis pointing upwards in the vertical direction. For the lateral and longitudinal boundaries, periodic boundary conditions are used. In the case of longitudinal boundaries, a pressure gradient along the test case is prescribed to reach an average axial velocity of 2 m/s. The leaf area index (LAI) can be computed with Equation (32) from the local leaf area density a(z) shown in Figure 1.

$$LAI = \int_0^h a(z)dz \tag{32}$$

LAI was set to five, which is an appropriate choice for a coniferous forest and deciduous forest in summer [14].

The distribution of the heat source was neglected, representing a neutral stratification of the atmosphere for the verification of the canopy models according to Lopes et al. [15]. Despite the reference solution of Shaw and Schumann [14] referring to a weakly unstable stratification, the comparison of the different canopy models seems to be appropriate when assuming a minor influence of the stratification on the flow in this test case with limited height.

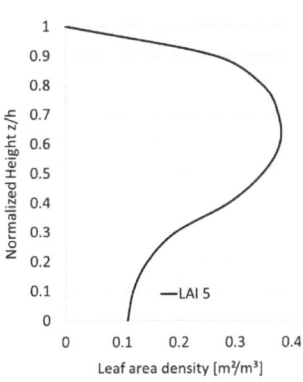

Figure 1. Distribution of leaf area density (LAD).

In Figure 2a, the profiles of the normalized longitudinal velocity are plotted versus the height for the standard k-ε, the RNG k-ε, and the Reynolds stress model, as well as for the LES reference solution of Shaw and Schumann [14]. For the RSM, the factor f of Equation (31) describing the turbulent time scale in the canopy is varied to get a more accurate fit with the reference solution. The velocity u is normalized by the vertically averaged longitudinal velocity. All turbulence models investigated can capture the maximum of the wind speed at a height of $z/h \approx 0.1$ and the minimum of the wind speed at a height of $z/h \approx 0.5$. Wiggles are observed for the RSM velocity profiles above the forest. This effect is the result of mesh resolution, which is too coarse in the z-direction. For this reason, the RANS simulations are rerun on the refined mesh and the results are depicted in Figure 2b–d. Additionally, a LES simulation with the Smagorinsky subgrid-scale model is set up to get a conformal comparison based on an identical mesh resolution for all models. On the refined mesh, smooth curves for the normalized velocities are obtained for the RSM (Figure 2b). However, the differences for the turbulent models become larger in and above the canopy than for the original mesh. It can be stated for the RSM that the velocities are getting smaller in and just above the canopy, but larger in the free flow by increasing factor f for the internal time scale from 1 to 4. An excellent agreement between the LES and RSM is reached by using a factor $f = 4$.

The spread of the turbulent kinetic energy normalized with the friction velocity u_* (Figure 2c) is larger than the spread of velocity within the canopy. The gradient of normalized kinetic energy becomes very high around $z/h \approx 0.7$ in case of the RSM with the factor $f = 4$, as well as for the standard k-ε and RNG k-ε models. For smaller factors ($f = 1, 2$), for the RSM as well as for the LES, the increase of the normalized turbulent kinetic energy over the height of the canopy is smaller. Looking at the maximum of the normalized kinetic energy above tree top, the values are over-predicted by the standard k-ε and RNG k-ε models. For the RSM, there is a good agreement with the LES solution independently of the factor f. However, this maximum is much broader for the LES than for the RSM.

Regarding the Reynolds stress $-\overline{u'w'}$ normalized by the Reynolds shear stress at the canopy top (u_*^2), the gradient towards the top of the canopy becomes larger with an increasing factor for the RSM model (Figure 2d). The LES solution lies in between the RSM solutions using a factor $f = 2$ and 4 for the forested area.

To judge the agreement between the RSM with the LES reference solution quantitatively, the root mean square deviation (RMSD) values are computed for the forested area ($0 \leq z/h \leq 1$) as well as for the whole computational domain (Table 5) regarding the normalized velocity, the normalized turbulent kinetic energy, and the normalized Reynolds stress. It is shown that for the evaluation of the whole domain, as well as particularly for the canopy area, the factor of 4 for the internal time scale in the canopy gives the lowest RMSD values for the three variables. It has to be considered that the diameters of the stems and the leaf area density vary with height of the forest, and therefore a constant factor f

over height is a further approximation. However, this is an indication that the time scale of the eddy dissipation is increased in the canopy because of the smaller eddy length scales and that this effect can be captured by a scale factor f.

Generally, the results for the RSM fit very well using the factor $f = 4$ with the LES reference and this setup is finally chosen for further simulations.

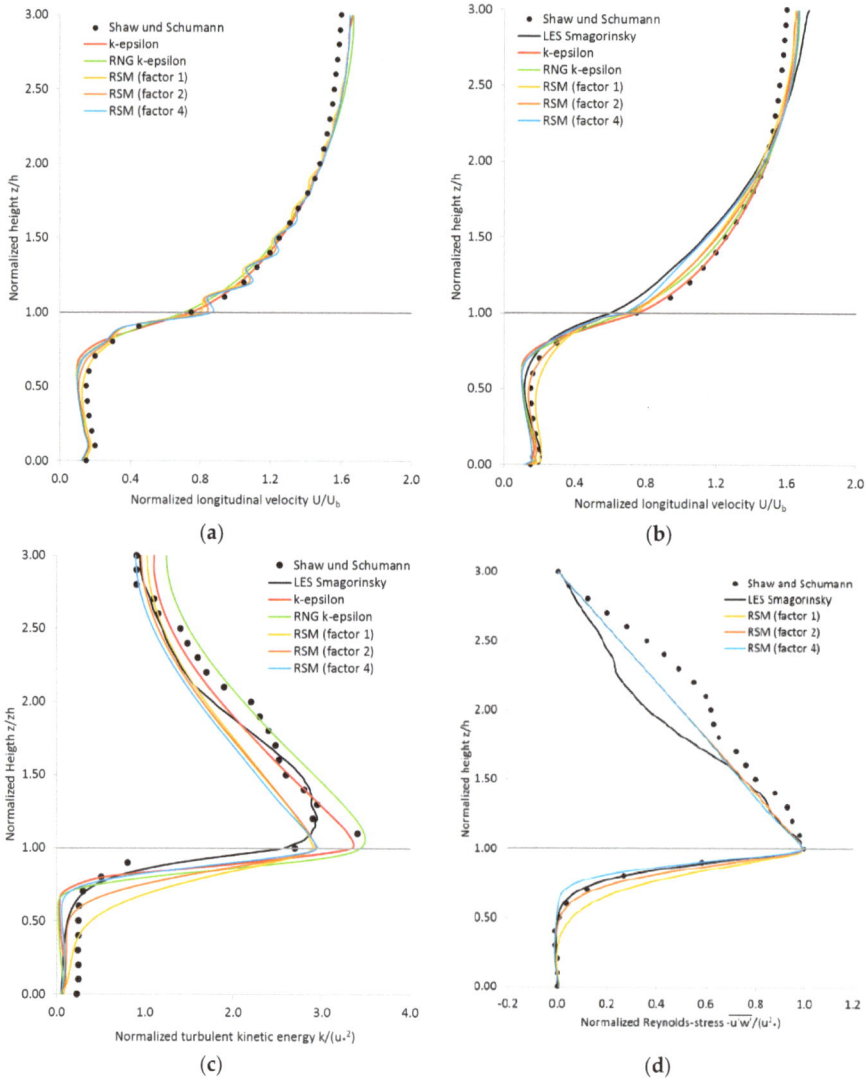

Figure 2. (**a**) Normalized longitudinal velocity, original mesh; (**b**) normalized longitudinal velocity, refined mesh; (**c**) normalized turbulent kinetic energy, refined mesh; (**d**) normalized Reynolds stress, refined mesh.

Table 5. Root mean square deviation (RMSD) between large-eddy simulation (LES) and Reynolds stress model (RSM) using different internal time scale factors f.

RMSD	RSM Factor $f = 1$		RSM Factor $f = 2$		RSM Factor $f = 4$	
	Comp. Domain	Canopy	Comp. Domain	Canopy	Comp. Domain	Canopy
Normalized velocity	0.0577	0.0617	0.0485	0.0377	0.0295	0.0316
Normalized turbulent kinetic energy	0.3566	0.5490	0.2810	0.3888	0.2423	0.2310
Normalized Reynolds stress	0.0841	0.1020	0.0645	0.0424	0.0636	0.0383

4. Model Setup for the WindForS Test Site

The computational domain includes the WindForS wind test site near Stötten (734 m a.s.l., 48.6654° latitude, 9.8655° longitude) in Baden-Württemberg, South Germany. In the past, various measuring campaigns using UAV (small unmanned research aircraft), sonic and cup anemometers, and Lidar were conducted to study the flow phenomena in complex terrain (Schulz et al. [4]; Anger et al. [32]; Hofsäß et al. [33]; Wildmann et al. [34]). The test site area is characterized by an escarpment located close to the towns of Geislingen an der Steige (464 m a.s.l.) and Donzdorf (407 m a.s.l.). The escarpment is completely forested, reaching a height of approximately 660 m a.s.l. at the upper ridge (Figure 3).

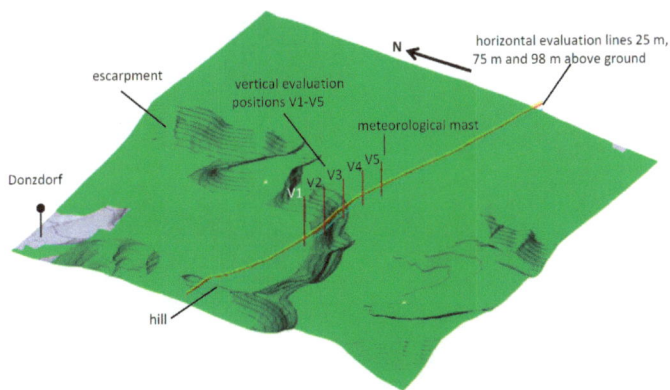

Figure 3. Nested domain 4 × 4 with vertical evaluation lines V1–V5 and horizontal evaluation lines 25 m (blue), 75 m (red), and 98 m (orange) above ground, as well as met mast position.

The main wind direction is north–west with an angle between 270° and 290°, as seen in the wind rose depicted in Figure 4a. Generally, the flow domain features various hills and valleys, as well as forested and un-forested areas, making it an ideal test case for the use of numerical flow models in complex terrain.

Nested domains with varying size and resolution were used for the simulations of the test site. First, a computational domain of 20 km × 20 km × 2.0 km (parent domain) is chosen. From this, two nested domains with spatial extensions of 10 km × 10 km × 1.5 km (nested domain 10 × 10) and 4.0 km × 4.0 km × 1.5 km (nested domain 4 × 4) are chosen, reducing the horizontal extensions by a factor of around two. The spatial resolution and the number of cells are summarised in Table 6.

Table 6. Mesh parameters for nested domains.

Case	Number of Cells	Horizontal Grid Resolution at the Ground	Vertical Grid Resolution at the Ground	Maximum Cell Size
Parent Model	57.6 Mio.	30 m	3.0 m	100 m
Nested Domain 10 × 10	18.5 Mio.	24 m	1.5 m	48.0 m
Nested Domain 4 × 4	6.86 Mio.	10 m	1.0 m	40.0 m

The parent domain and the nested domain 10 × 10 were centred in the area of interest (Figure 4c), whereas the nested domain 4 × 4 is shifted in a north–west direction to better capture the influence of the flow upstream depending on the flow direction (Figure 4d). In Figure 4c,d, the different land uses can also be seen (urban in grey, forest in dark green, agriculture in light green). All meshes are unstructured and mainly built of tetrahedral cells. On top of the ground, several prism layers are placed to get a constant spatial resolution in this area. For the nested domain 4 × 4, a resolution next to the ground of 1.0 m in the vertical direction and 10 m in the horizontal direction is reached. The nested domain 4 × 4 is depicted in Figure 3 together with the measurement positons and the positions for the evaluation of simulation results.

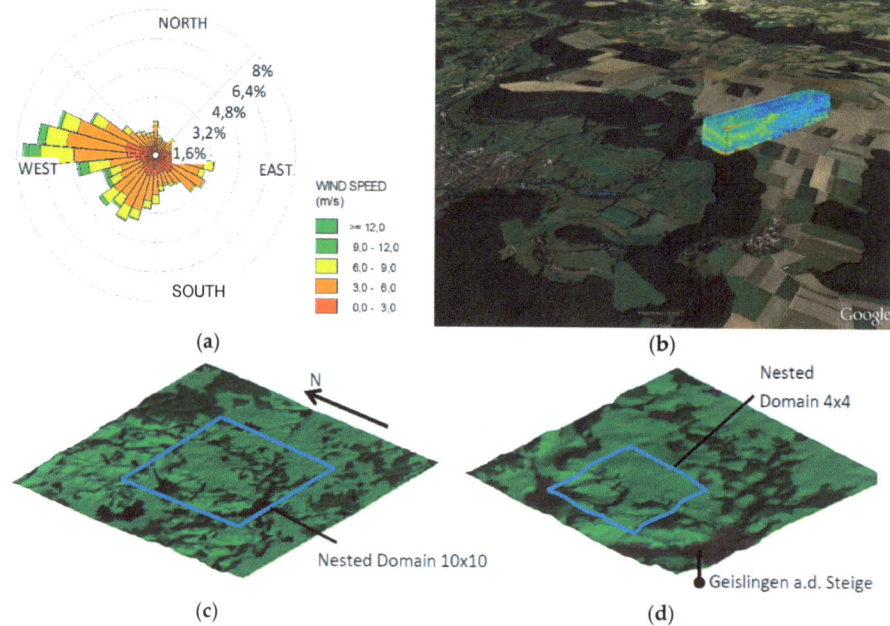

Figure 4. (**a**) Wind rose in the timeframe 2014–2015 at DWD measuring station Stötten (734 m a.s.l., 48.6654° latitude, 9.8655° longitude); (**b**) unmanned aerial vehicle (UAV) measurement race tracks (© 2009 GeoBasis-DE/BKG, © 2016 Google); (**c**) parent model; (**d**) nested domain 10 × 10.

The generation of the computational mesh, and therefore the reproduction of the Earth's surface for the computational domain, is realized using the digital height model (DGM) and digitized landscape model (DLM) from State Authorities for Spatial Information and Rural Development Baden-Württemberg (LGL).

In case of the domain measuring 20 km × 20 km (parent model), weather data from DWD is used for the generation of boundary conditions. In particular, data from 27 March 2015 at 3:00 p.m. were selected, which are linked to the most frequently occurring north–west wind and dry, near-neutral conditions. Wind speed and wind direction are measured at the nearby DWD measuring station Stötten (734 m a.s.l., 48.6654° latitude, 9.8655° longitude) for this period of time showing a stable wind speed of around 7 m/s and a north–west wind direction of 290°.

The weather data is derived from the COSMO-DE weather model of DWD with a spatial resolution in the horizontal direction of approximately 2.8 km. Perpendicular to the Earth's surface, a maximum vertical resolution of 20 m is reached close to the surface, rapidly increasing with the height above the surface. The weather data provides wind speed, pressure, density, air and surface temperature, as well as information about turbulence kinetic energy with a temporal resolution of one hour. Radiative heat transfer is neglected in the model.

The simulations were performed on a NEC LX-2400 cluster consisting of 180 blades equipped with Intel Nehalem Processors (2.27 GHz/2.80 GHz, 8 cores, 24 GB memory) and connected by an InfiBand network. The relative computational time per iteration on the nested domain 4 × 4 for the different turbulence models is summarized in Table 7.

Table 7. Computational time per iteration for different turbulence models and domains.

Computational Domain	k-ε Model	RNG k-ε Model	RSM
Nested domain 4 × 4	100%	118%	207%

4.1. Initial Conditions for the Parent Domain

For lateral and top boundaries, data from the weather model is linearly interpolated to define the Dirichlet boundary conditions for velocities and temperature. At the top boundary, a flow in and out of the domain is allowed, whereas the flow for lateral boundaries is limited to one direction. No correction of the mass flow was needed, reaching a conservative one-way coupling of the COSMO-DE and CFD model.

4.2. Boundary Conditions for Nested Domains

For all cases based on nested domains with dimensions of 10 km × 10 km, as well as 4.0 km × 4.0 km, the boundary conditions are imposed using the solution provided by CFD simulation with the domain size of 20 km × 20 km and 10 km × 10 km, respectively. The boundary values for velocities, temperature, and turbulent quantities are interpolated according to the second order accurate discretization scheme on the boundary surfaces. For the nested domains, Dirichlet boundary conditions are defined for the lateral, top, and bottom boundaries. Again, for the top boundary, a flow in and out the domain is allowed.

4.3. Boundary Conditions at the Ground for Parent and Nested Domains

A wall model is used for the bottom boundary (ground) to handle velocities and turbulence quantities. Temperatures on the ground, which are extracted from the weather model data, are used as Dirichlet boundary conditions. For the different land use, displacement length z_0 is set to 0.02 m and 2.67 m for un-forested and urban areas, respectively. For the forested areas, a z_0 value of 0.02 m in combination with the canopy models is applied. An LAI of five representing deciduous forest with the LAD distribution according to Figure 5 and a forest height of 20 m is used for the canopy model.

5. Results for the WindForS Test Site

In the following section, the results of simulations with the models described above for the test site Stötten are presented. They represent a general description of the wind flow on 27 March 2015 at 3:00 p.m., characterized by dry conditions and a thermally near-neutral stratification of the atmospheric boundary layer. The simulation results are compared with UAV and sonic anemometer measurements for the model validation.

5.1. Qualitative Comparison of Simulation Results

In Figure 5a–c, the two-dimensional spatial velocity distribution at a constant height of 75 m normal to the Earth's surface is depicted for the different turbulence models. For orientation, the position of the meterological mast as well as the escarpment and the hill are marked in Figure 5a–c. A very heterogeneous flow along the surface becomes visible for all turbulence models characterized by a flow separation downstream the hill and a strong acceleration of the flow along the escarpment. Furthermore, downstream the crest of the escarpment streaks with reduced velocities are staggered with areas of accelerated flow. In the case of using the RNG k-ε model (Figure 5b), this distribution is highly pronounced, whereas for the standard k-ε model (Figure 5a), the flow is predicted almost equally. Generally, the computed velocities are higher on this level in the case of using the standard k-ε model than for the RNG k-ε model and the RSM (Figure 5c). This becomes particularly obvious in the area, with downstream the hill and the escarpment showing the tendency of the standard k-ε model to under-predict flow separation zones. Looking at the main flow direction, it can be observed that the flow is directed more in easterly direction for the standard k-ε model than for the RNG k-ε model and the RSM model.

To get more detailed information, the results are contrasted in Figures 6–9 along the evaluation lines shown in Figure 3. The lines are located in a constant offset of 25 m, 75 m, and 98 m perpendicular to the Earth's surface. The boundaries of the forested areas are marked in Figures 6–9 with vertical black lines and the topography along the evaluation plane is depicted together with the evaluation line underneath the diagrams. In Figure 6a/b, the different turbulence models are compared for the 25 m distance above ground. Looking at horizontal velocity (Figure 6a), only minor differences are found upstream the crest of the escarpment. The flow is decelerated downstream the hill and tends to separate. Subsequently, it is accelerated again along the escarpment reaching the highest velocity at the crest in the case of using the standard k-ε turbulence model. Downstream the forest edge at the crest, the results differ from each other. With the RNG k-ε model, a flow separation with reverse flow is predicted in this area, whereas for the standard k-ε model and the RSM, the flow is decelerated but still directed in the main flow direction. With increasing distance from the crest, the results predicted from the different turbulence models are increasingly converging. Considering the turbulence intensity (Figure 6b), it is found that the increase is steeper upstream the hill as well as upstream the escarpment and it is decreasing much slower downstream for the RSM than in the case of the RNG k-ε and the standard k-ε models. This is an indication that turbulent kinetic energy is dissipated too rapidly in the case of the RNG k-ε and standard k-ε models.

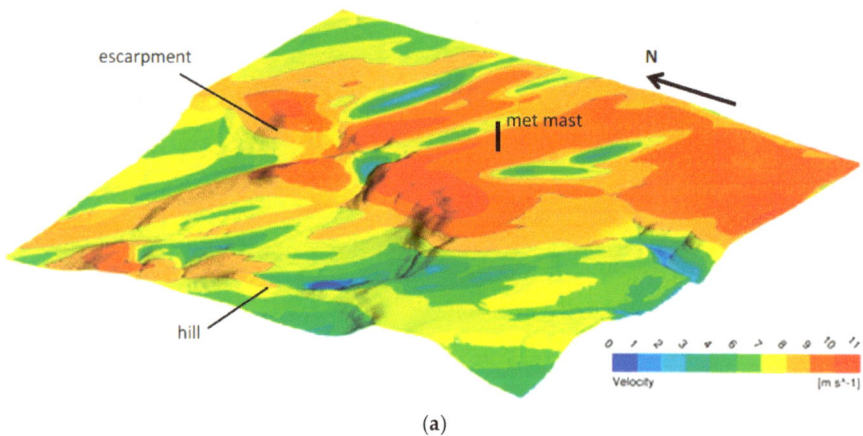

(a)

Figure 5. *Cont.*

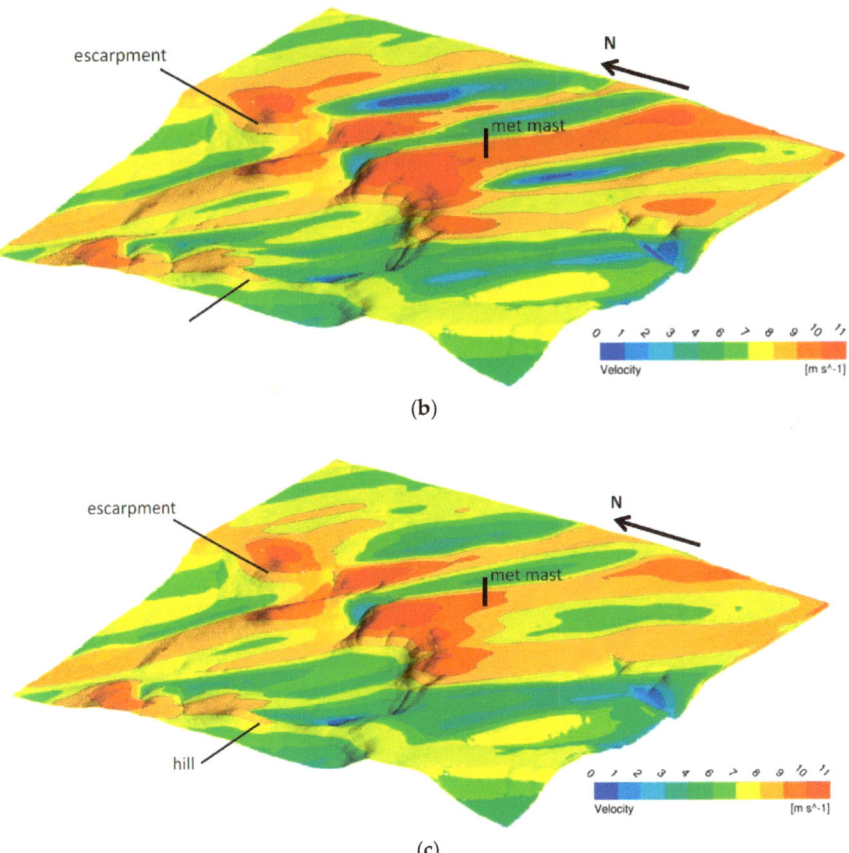

Figure 5. (a) Velocities computed with k-ε model on a height of 75 m above ground; (b) velocities computed with RNG k-ε model on a height of 75 m above ground; (c) velocities computed with RSM model on a height of 75 m above ground.

Along the evaluation lines 75 m and 98 m above the ground, the flow accelerations due to the hill and the escarpment can still be seen in Figures 7a and 8a, respectively. The two velocity maxima are on the same level for the two elevations. On both levels, the minima of the horizontal velocity between the hill and the escarpment, as well as downstream the crest, are visible accordingly. However, for the evaluation line 98 m, the deceleration of the flow is smaller than along the line at 75 m, indicating that the flow already becomes more equal in this higher elevation. Analogous to the line on 25 m, it can be observed that at the lines at 75 m and at 98 m (Figures 7b and 8b), the turbulence intensity is much stronger along the hill and along the escarpment, and that the decrease downstream to these obstacles is much lesser for the RSM than for the two equation turbulence models.

One major drawback of using the RNG k-ε and standard k-ε models for the simulation of wind flow in complex terrain is the assumption of an isotropic turbulence. To judge the differences of the Reynolds stresses in different directions, the principle Reynolds stresses computed with the RSM are depicted in Figure 9a. Therefore, the Reynolds stress tensor is rotated in the main flow direction, which is aligned with the velocity component u. It can be seen that the principle Reynolds stresses differ up to a factor of two and that the anisotropy is driven as a result of the orography. Along the upwind side of the hill and the escarpment, the differences strongly increase and diminish at downwind sides.

The Reynolds stress $\overline{u'u'}$ directing in the main flow direction is always the biggest component, whereas the Reynolds stress $\overline{w'w'}$ pointing in an upward direction is the smallest. Another interesting aspect for the wind energy production is the turbulent vertical momentum transport due to the shear stress $\overline{u'w'}$. In Figure 9b, the shear stress $\overline{u'w'}$ is evaluated at the levels 25 m, 75 m, and 98 m. Initially, at 25 m, the Reynolds shear stress is increased along the hill. As a result of the flow separation downstream the hill, the shear stress becomes negative, indicating turbulent momentum flow towards the Earth's surface. The maxima of the Reynolds shear stress at the levels 75 m and 98 m due to the hill are slightly shifted in a downwind direction. Along the escarpment, the Reynolds shear stress is even more increased than along the hill. The maxima again are located just downstream the crest, with highest values for the lowest level at 25 m. Figure 9b shows that along all evaluation lines, a constant shear layer is not reached.

5.2. Validation of the Model by Means of Measurement Data

In the following section, the different modelling approaches are validated against measurement data for the test site Stötten. Therefore, the results are compared with UAV measurements along vertical lines, particularly those placed at the escarpment within the computational domain. Additionally, sonic anemometer measurements from a meteorological mast are used.

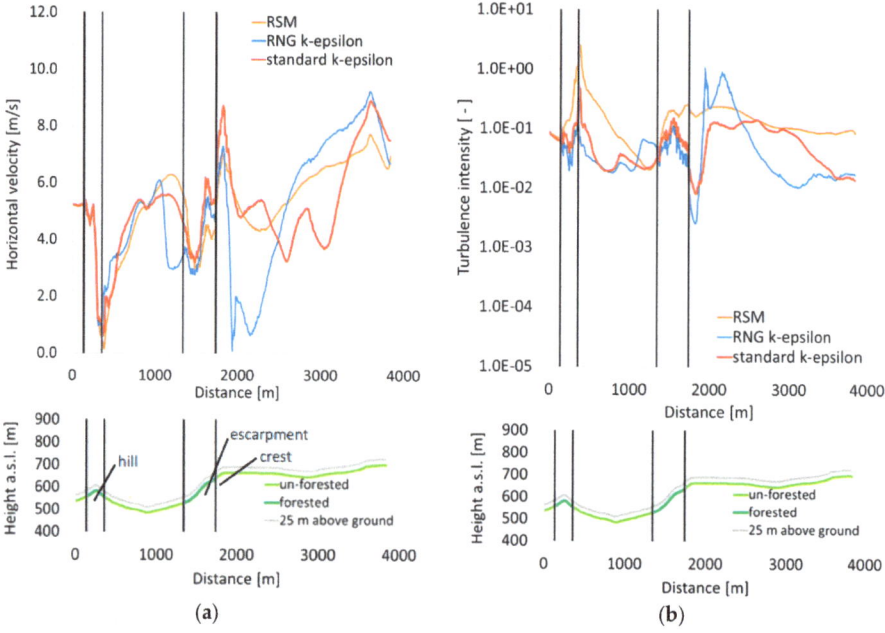

Figure 6. (**a**) Horizontal velocity at a constant distance of 25 m above the ground (grey line); (**b**) turbulence intensity at a constant distance of 25 m above the ground (grey line).

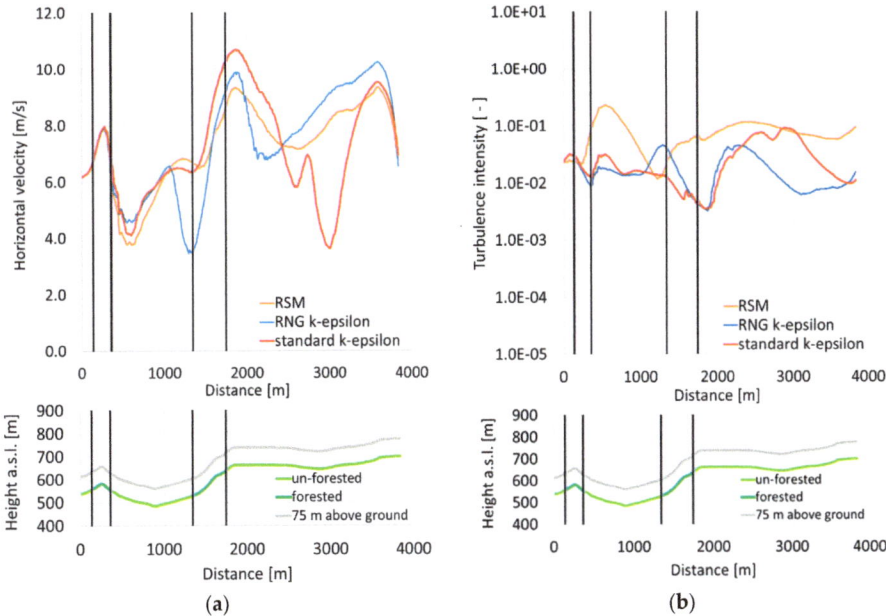

Figure 7. (**a**) Horizontal velocity at a constant distance of 75 m above the ground (grey line); (**b**) turbulence intensity at a constant distance of 75 m above the ground (grey line).

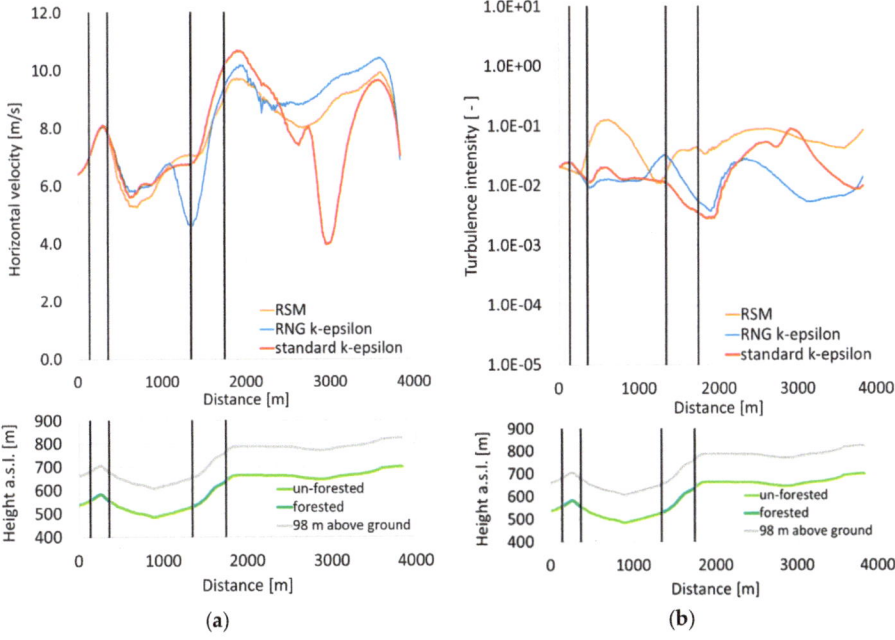

Figure 8. (**a**) Horizontal velocity at a constant distance of 98 m above the ground (grey line); (**b**) turbulence intensity at a constant distance of 98 m above the ground (grey line).

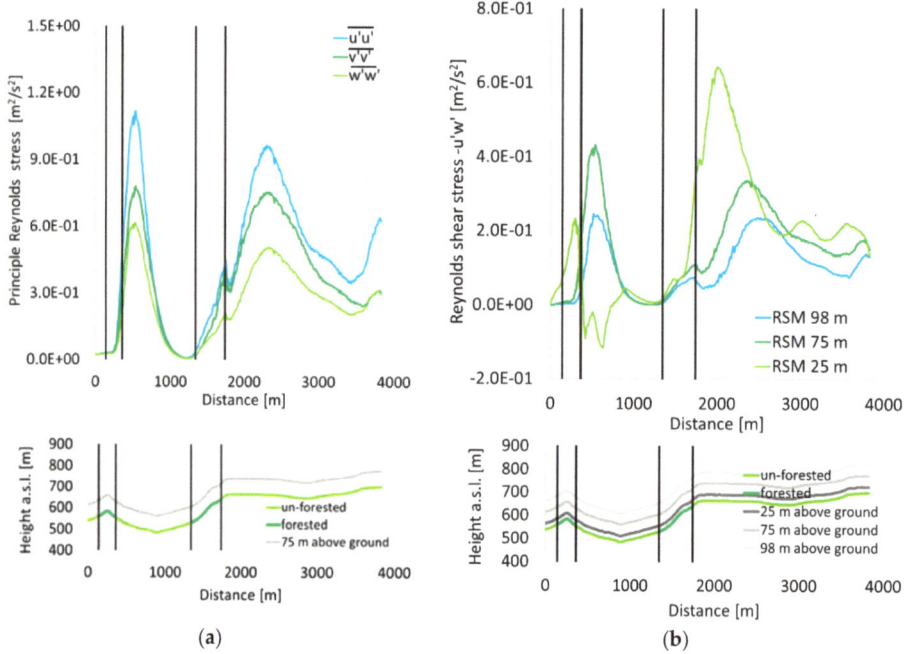

Figure 9. (a) Principal Reynolds stresses at a constant distance of 75 m above the ground; (b) shear stress $-\overline{u'w'}$ at constant distance of 25 m, 75 m, and 98 m above the ground.

5.2.1. Description of Measurements

Multipurpose Airborne Sensor Carrier (MASC)

MASC [34] is a propeller-driven, unmanned single-electric-engine aerial vehicle (UAV) of 2.7- to 3.5-m wing span, developed and operated by the University of Tübingen. The total weight of the aircraft is 5 to 8 kg, including up to 1.5 kg of measuring devices. The typical horizontal flight speed of the UAV is 22 m/s airspeed, giving the optimum trade-off between high spatial resolution of measured data and gathering of atmospheric data from a certain area in a short period of time. MASC operates fully automatically except for landing and take-off. Height, flight path, and all other parameters of flight guidance are controlled by the research onboard computer system (ROCS). The overall endurance achieved with MASC is up to 90 min, which is associated with a flight distance of 135 km. MASC is standardly equipped with several subsystems specifically to measure the wind vector in three dimensions with a five-hole probe [35], air temperature with fast fine-wire probes [36], and humidity [37] with a capacitive sensor. The measurement equipment is able to resolve wind and temperature fluctuations up to 30 Hz and humidity fluctuations up to 3 Hz, all sampled with a rate of 100 Hz. Additionally, an inertial measurement unit (IMU) and a global navigation satellite system (GNSS) provide position, altitude, and velocity of the aircraft above ground.

Three flights with a duration of one hour each were carried out on 27 March 2015 between 1:00 p.m. and 4:00 p.m. UTC. An example of a flight path is shown in Figure 4b. Each flight is composed of several so-called racetracks, consisting of two legs (straight and level flight path) along the mean wind direction (west-east direction). Two racetracks were flown at each altitude. Legs where the UAV was flying into the wind were used for the analysis as this gives the lowest ground speed, and thus the greatest spatial resolution keeping the flight velocity with respect to the air constant at 22 m/s. This results in a varying ground speed, because the meteorological wind is fluctuating.

On each and every leg, the wind velocity was arithmetically averaged over subsections of 20 m length (block averages). Each block comprises of an average time between 1.37 and 1.81 s depending on the wind speed, equivalent to 137 and 181 data points, respectively. The block means were subsequently averaged over all legs measured, that is, six racetracks at the same height. These values are depicted as black dots in Figures 10a–e and 11a–e for the comparison of measurements with simulation results in Section 5.2.2 representing a constant spatial resolution of 20 m.

Meteorological Mast

The meteorological mast is located approximately 1.3 km to the east of the escarpment (48.6658° latitude, 9.8424° longitude). It has a height of 100 m and is built up in a triangular, steel lattice construction with additional tensioning. The booms, which are mounted in north–south direction, have a length of 5 m to reduce shadowing effects as far as possible. In order to obtain detailed information about the flow including turbulent quantities, three 3D-ultrasonic anemometers are installed at heights of 50 m, 75 m, and 98 m. Operating at a sampling frequency of 20 Hz, an accuracy with an RMSD < 1.5% at 12 m/s is reached according to the specification of the manufacturer. To characterize the flow further, four first class wind vanes (25 m, 50 m, 75 m, 92 m) are installed. Additionally, three first class cup anemometers and a hygrometer, as well as several temperature and pressure sensors, are mounted at different heights.

The data are automatically prepared in the post processing, where the measurements are checked for errors and filtered for plausibility. The ultrasonic sensors transmit an internal quality signal, which detects possible errors in the internal calculation. Furthermore, two statistical tests are performed, investigating whether or not the signal is a zero line and whether or not values are outside the interquartile range of 5% to 95%. Only data that is 100% available in this period is included in the evaluation. The operation of the three ultrasonic sensors is decoupled from each other. Subsequently, the statistical parameters mean value and variance are determined for different averaging intervals (1 min, 2 min, 10 min, and 1 h). Additionally, the components of the Reynolds stress tensor are determined. Mean values and variance of wind velocities and the Reynolds stress tensor are calculated in the global geographic, as well as in a local flow-oriented coordinate system. The local coordinate system is rotated in such a way that the main wind direction and the flow component u are facing in the wind direction in the averaging interval. The other components follow the right-hand rule accordingly, with w pointing perpendicularly off the Earth's surface. In this study, an averaging interval of 60 s is applied for the turbulence quantities and 10 min for velocities and wind direction.

5.2.2. Comparison of Simulation Results and UAV Measurements

To validate the results quantitatively, the simulations results are also compared with flight data, horizontally averaged at various altitudes. This enables a better understanding of the velocity profiles in the vicinity of the escarpment at the test site. Additionally, the inclination angle of the flow is investigated, providing information about the flow direction in reference to the horizontal plane. Therefore, the results are evaluated along five vertical lines V1–V5, which are arranged perpendicularly along the flight path of the UAV (Figures 3 and 10f). As reference, the height at the crest of 660 m a.s.l. is chosen and set to 0 m for the evaluation in Figures 10 and 11.

For the RNG k-ε model, the velocities close to the ground are found to be considerably lower along position V1 than for the standard k-ε model and the RSM because the flow separation on the lee side of the hill is predicted larger. This effect still is visible at position V2. In Figure 10b,c it can be seen that the flow is displaced along the forested escarpment. Therefore, the velocity at the ground is increased, and a strong velocity gradient is developed in the near-wall region. The acceleration is largest for the standard k-ε model. At a distance of 600 m at the crest at position V4, again, the maximum speed is predicted by the standard k-ε model. There, the topography becomes almost flat, which is why the flow tends to separate. The velocity up to a height of 20 m above the ground is already close to zero for the standard k-ε and RNG k-ε models, whereas the flow is still directed more forward for the

RSM. This effect is additionally driven because of the forest edge located directly at the crest. Further downstream at position V5, a separation zone with reverse flow is predicted by the RNG k-ε model up to a height of around 45 m. However, this is not the case for the standard k-ε model and the RSM.

From Figure 10c, the typical velocity distribution within the forest is developed for all turbulence models, as observed in in Section 3, for the canopy test case of Shaw and Schumann [14]. Therefore, a local velocity maximum close to the ground and a local minimum at the maximum LAD close to the treetop is observed. This flow distribution disappears for position V4 and position V5 because these positions are located downstream to the forested escarpment.

The simulation results for the horizontal velocities are generally in very good agreement with the measured data. The shape of the profiles and the velocity level can be captured with high accuracy. Unfortunately, there are no measurements available below 75 m above ground from the UAV at present, where the largest differences for the turbulence models are found. However, the interesting heights for the use of wind energy are covered by the UAV measurements. Overall, the most accurate prediction of the velocities is achieved by means of the standard k-ε model and the RSM, resulting in an RMSD value of 0.62 m/s and 0.63 m/s in total for all measuring positions, respectively. However, the agreement for the RNG k-ε model is also on a very good level, giving an RMSD for the horizontal velocity of 0.71 m/s.

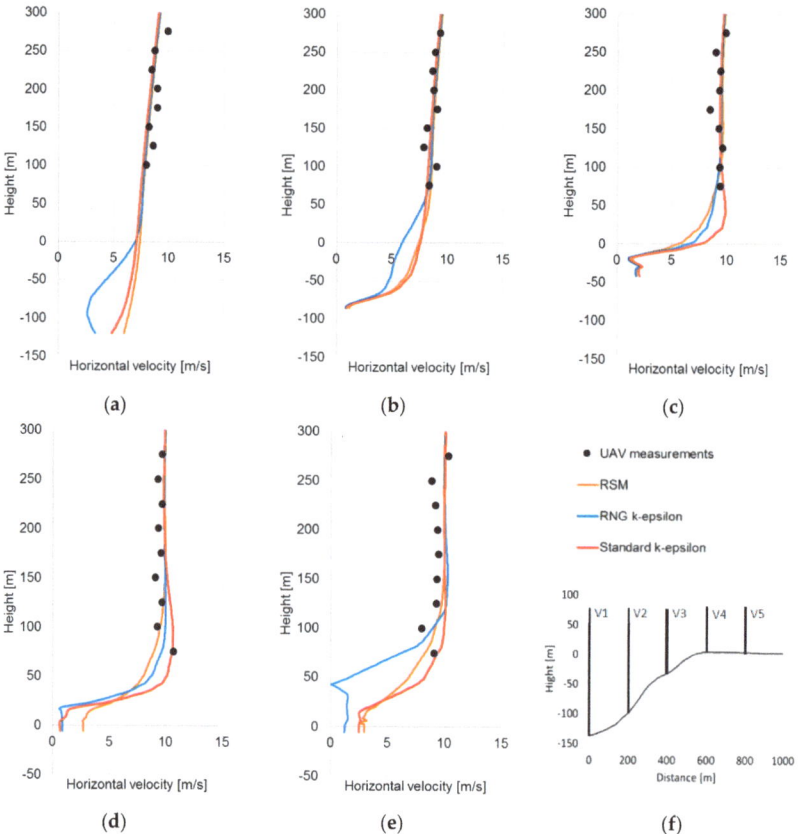

Figure 10. (a) Horizontal velocity profile at position V1; (b) horizontal velocity profile at position V2; (c) horizontal velocity profile at position V3; (d) horizontal velocity profile at position V4; (e) horizontal velocity profile at position V5; (f) legend and positions of vertical evaluation lines.

Regarding the inclination angle (Figure 11), the profile along V1 is determined by the wake downstream to the hill in front of the escarpment. The extension of the wake is largest for the RNG k-ε model. Therefore, the flow is directed upwards just upstream to the escarpment in a stronger manner than for the other turbulence models (Figure 11a). At position V2 depicted in Figure 11b, the differences when applying different turbulence models can be seen. The flow is displaced in the forested near-wall area, leading to high inclination angles. Again, the inclination becomes largest in the near-wall area for the RNG k-ε model followed by the standard k-ε model and the RSM. The differences diminish at elevations higher than 100 m above ground. For the positions V3 and V4, the differences are quite small for all models and can be observed only in the vicinity of the ground.

At position V5 (Figure 11e), it is shown that the inclination angle has mostly negative values for the standard k-ε model. Accordingly, the slope of the inclination angle over height is predicted by the RSM, showing slightly higher, positive inclination angles. However, the result for the RNG k-ε model displays high, positive inclination angles in the near-wall area. This difference is due to the reverse flow predicted by the RNG k-ε model at this position.

As for the horizontal velocities, the simulation results and measurements of the inclination angle are in very good agreement. For the standard k-ε model, the smallest RMSD value for the inclination angle is computed (3.12 deg). The RSMDs for the RSM and RNG k-ε model are slightly higher, giving values of 4.51 deg and 4.93 deg, respectively.

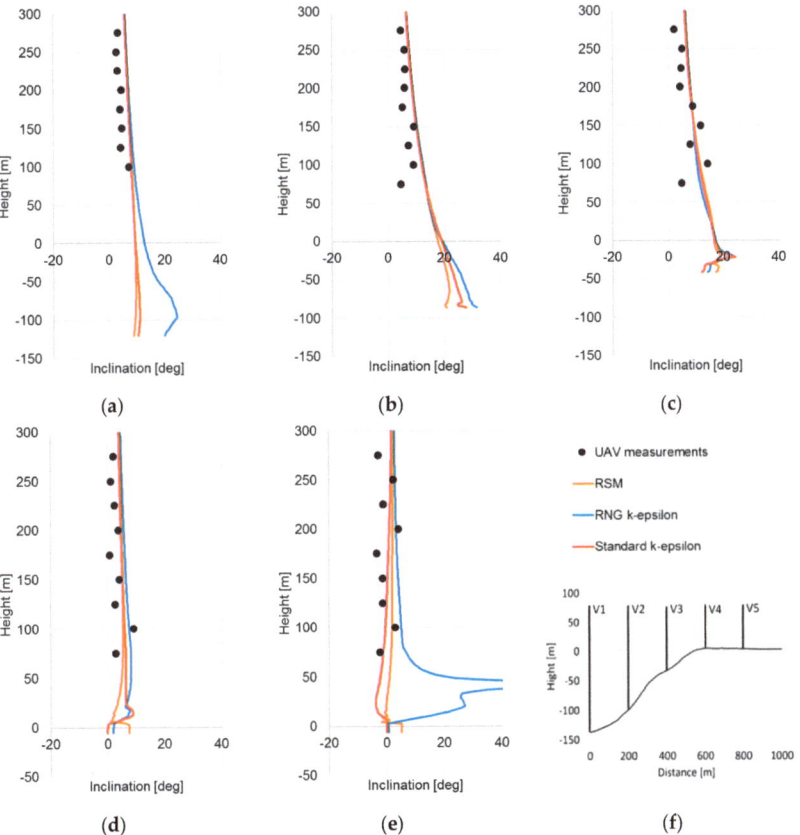

Figure 11. (a) Inclination position V1; (b) inclination position V2; (c) inclination position V3; (d) inclination position V4; (e) inclination position V5; (f) legend and location of measuring positions.

5.2.3. Comparison of Simulation Results and Measurements from a Meteorological Wind Mast

Sonic anemometer measurements enable the evaluation of Reynolds stresses by means of high frequency velocity measurements. In the following section, these from measurement devised Reynolds stresses are compared with the Reynolds stresses predicted by the RSM at the position of the meteorological mast. For the comparison, the different time and length scales in the atmospheric flow phenomena are an important issue. Using a single time slice from the weather model COSMO-DE as boundary conditions for the simulations, only turbulence effects of the topography and thermal stratification are captured by the CFD model. The length and time scales of these phenomena are within 1 km and a few minutes, respectively. All other phenomena—for example, convection and diurnal cycle, among others—have much larger time scales (10 min to hours). As long as the difference of these time scales is big, it can be assumed that the quasi stationary time slice approach works relatively well, according to Schlünzen [38].

The measurement values are depicted in Figure 12a–c for the 27 March 2015 at 3:00 p.m., which is the time used for the simulations. As described above, the boundary conditions for the simulations are based on one specific time slice from the COSMO-DE weather model and, therefore, flow phenomena with time scales larger than a few minutes are not captured in the models. To eliminate the phenomena with larger time scales from the measurements, a time averaging of 2 min is applied for the Reynolds stresses, the turbulence intensity, and the wind direction. For the comparison, the co-ordinate system is rotated with the x-axis pointing in flow direction and the z-axis perpendicular to the Earth's surface.

In Figure 12a, the Reynolds stresses $\overline{u'u'}$, $\overline{w'w'}$, and $\overline{v'w'}$ are opposed for the measurements (2 min averages) and simulation results. For all measurements, the mean value and its variance are depicted. The largest deviations occur for the Reynolds stress $\overline{u'u'}$ at the measurement height of 75 m. Looking at the sonic measurements at the height of 75 m, the variance for the Reynolds stress $\overline{u'u'}$ accordingly becomes large as well. Despite this, the agreement between simulation results and the sonic anemometer measurements are in good accordance on both measurement levels at constant heights of 75 m and 98 m above ground. Further validation for the Reynolds stresses below 75 m would be desirable. Unfortunately, no measurement data is available at 50 m for this particular date.

The principle Reynolds stresses are used for the computation of the turbulent kinetic energy. From this quantity, the turbulence intensity, which is the measure for the fatigue load of wind energy turbines, is derived for all turbulence models (Figure 12b). The RNG and standard k-ε models show a higher turbulence intensity close to the ground than the RSM. However, the turbulence intensity decreases rapidly with height. In connection to the measurements, this is a clear indication that the dissipation of turbulence is over-predicted by the two-equation models. Comparing the turbulence intensity, again, a good agreement is found for both measuring levels in the case of using the RSM, showing its potential. However, the turbulence intensity still is under-predicted, especially at the height of 75 m.

In Figure 12c, the wind direction is depicted for the different turbulence models in combination with the values measured with the sonic at heights of 75 m and 98 m, and a wind vane at a height of 92 m. Only a minor change of the angle over the height between 20 m and 150 m above ground can be observed. This is because of the fact that viscous forces are much bigger in the laminar and Prandtl boundary layers than the Coriolis force. In the immediate vicinity to the ground below 20 m, the results of the RNG and standard k-ε models show a slight increase of the angle. For the RSM and RNG k-ε models, slightly higher values are generally predicted than those for the standard k-ε model. The simulation results are in very good accordance with the measurements for all turbulence models. The standard k-ε model gives the best agreement, whereas the RNG k-ε model and RSM show slightly larger deviations.

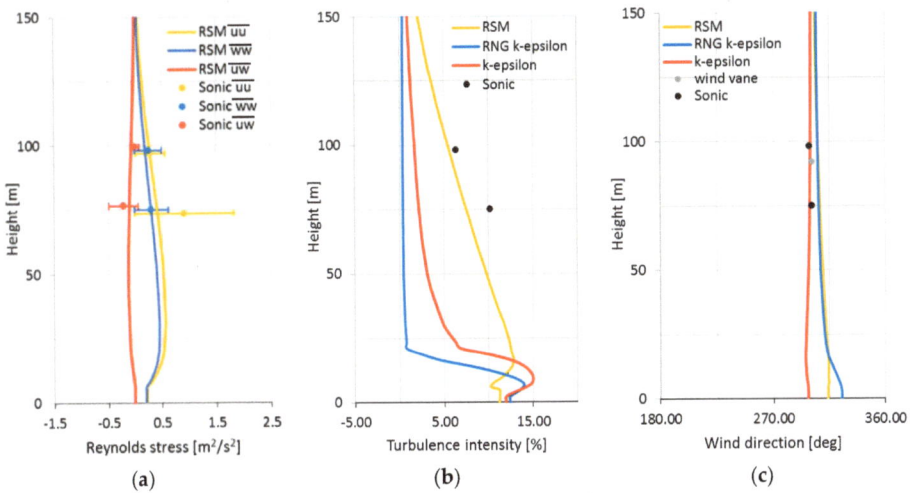

Figure 12. (a) Reynolds stresses; (b) turbulence intensity; (c) wind direction.

6. Conclusions

An formulation of the Navier–Stokes equations based on the Boussinesq approximation was used, considering the stratification of the Earth's atmosphere and Coriolis force. The Reynolds stress model (RSM) as well as the RNG k-ε and the standard k-ε turbulence models were applied, including additional dissipation and production terms to capture the influence on turbulence in forested areas.

The implementation of the additional capabilities was verified by means of a homogeneous canopy test case. Additionally, the internal canopy time scale was adapted using a coefficient f to fit the results of the RSM to the reference solution achieved by LES simulations. A factor of $f = 4$ was found to be most appropriate, giving the lowest RMSDs for the normalized horizontal velocity, the normalized turbulent kinetic energy, and the normalized Reynolds stresses with respect to the reference solution. Generally, a very good agreement for all turbulence models was achieved regarding the predicting of the wind velocity. Differences in the turbulent kinetic energy are more apparent, and show that the best agreement occurs when the RSM is used. Most striking is that the maximum of the turbulent kinetic energy just above tree top is well in accordance with the reference solution for the RSM, whereas for the RNG k-ε model and standard k-ε models, the turbulent kinetic energy is over-predicted.

In a second step, the wind flow for the WindForS wind energy test site with partly forested complex terrain in Stötten near Geislingen an der Steige, southern Germany, was simulated, with the goal of model validation for this specific location. In particular, data from the 27 March 2015 at 3:00 p.m. were selected, linked to the most frequently occurring north–west wind and dry, near-neutral conditions. The orography and flora were described using digital height and digital landscape models. For the computations, boundary conditions were derived from the COSMO-DE weather model. The simulation results were compared with measurements from an unmanned aerial vehicle (UAV) and from a meteorological mast using sonic anemometer.

Generally, for the RSM, the RNG k-ε model, and the standard k-ε model, a very good agreement was achieved for predicting horizontal wind velocities and inclination angles in comparison to the UAV measurements. The very good agreement was confirmed by the RMSDs for the horizontal velocities of 0.71 m/s, 0.63 m/s, and 0.62 m/s along vertical measurement locations, respectively. The smallest RMSD value of 3.12 deg was computed using the standard k-ε model. The RSMDs for the RSM and RNG k-ε model are slightly higher, giving values of 4.51 deg and 4.93 deg, respectively.

Sonic anemometer measurements were used to validate the turbulent quantities. It was shown that only the RSM managed to predict the turbulence intensity with high accuracy. Using the RNG k-ε and standard k-ε models, the turbulence intensity prediction was far too low. It was found that the turbulent kinetic energy downwind of obstacles like hills or the escarpment dissipates much faster for the RNG k-ε and standard k-ε models than for the RSM connected to an under-prediction of the turbulence intensity. Furthermore, it was confirmed by the RSM model that turbulence becomes anisotropic in the complex terrain, mainly driven by the orography. For these reasons, the RSM is the best choice for RANS models to predict fatigue load on wind turbines in complex terrain.

It was shown that by means of one-way coupling of the CFD code with the weather model COSMO-DE from German Meteorological Service, appropriate boundary conditions for the simulations can be initialized, enabling the prediction of the inhomogeneous flow situation with high velocity gradients along and perpendicular to the main flow direction in complex terrain with high accuracy. For this reason, different nested domains with increasing spatial resolutions were devised to capture influences on the flow in the far field of the test site in an appropriate manner.

For the model validation, a homogeneous forest canopy was assumed. The LAD was used according to Shaw and Schumann [14] in combination with a mean forest height. However, the canopy morphology may also have an impact on the wind flow [39]. Unfortunately, as often this data is not available for the WindForS test site at present and, therefore, this aspect could be part of future investigations. Because this validation took place under thermally near-neutral conditions and only uses a short period of data, it is essential to investigate the accuracy of the model chain under thermally stable or unstable conditions, as this can impact the generation and dissipation of turbulence in the atmosphere both locally and further afield. Finally, transient effects due to diurnal changes in the atmosphere have to be studied. Therefore, further UAV measurements at lower heights above the Earth's surface are planned within the BMWi-funded project WINSENT, further validating the simulation code for the prediction of wind flow at the WindForS test site and in complex terrain in general. Additionally, Lidar measurements as well as 3D-ultrasonic and cup anemometer measurements from four meteorological masts are going to be provided. This will enable further, more detailed investigations of the wind flow, and particularly the turbulence, especially in the Prandtl layer of the atmosphere. However, for the understanding of the main flow phenomena and the characterization of the test site for the use of wind energy, the approaches investigated so far are already valuable tools, which are going to be operationally utilized for the planning of the following measuring campaigns and the layout and construction of the wind test site.

Author Contributions: All the authors have contributed substantially to the publication.

Funding: The authors acknowledge the State of Baden-Württemberg through bwHPC for providing computational resources and the German Federal Ministry for Economic Affairs and Energy for funding measurement campaigns in the framework of the German joint research projects Lidar complex (No. 0325519) and KonTest (No. 0325665), as well of the simulations within WINSENT (No. 0324129).

Acknowledgments: This publication was made possible through the collaboration in the WindForS wind energy research cluster.

Conflicts of Interest: The authors declare no conflict of interest.

References

1. Palma, J.; Castro, F.; Ribeiro, L.; Rodrigues, A.; Pinto, A. Linear and nonlinear models in wind resource assessment and wind turbine micro-siting in complex terrain. *J. Wind Eng. Ind. Aerodyn.* **2008**, *96*, 2308–2326. [CrossRef]

2. Chow, F.K.; Weigel, A.P.; Street, R.L.; Rotach, M.W.; Xue, M. High-resolution large-eddy simulations of flow in a steep alpine valley. Part I: Methodology, verification and sensitivity experiments. *J. Appl. Meteorol. Climatol.* **2006**, *45*, 63–86. [CrossRef]

3. Churchfield, M.J.; Lee, S.; Michalakes, J.; Moriarty, P.J. A numerical study of the effects of atmospheric and wake turbulence on wind turbine dynamics. *J. Turbul.* **2012**, *13*. [CrossRef]

4. Schulz, C.; Hofsäß, M.; Anger, J.; Rautenberg, A.; Lutz, T.; Cheng, P.W.; Bange, J. Comparison of different measurement techniques and a CFD simulation in complex terrain. In *Science of Making Torque from Wind (TORQUE 2016)*; IOP Publishing: Munich, Germany, 2016.

5. Rodrigues, C.V.; Palma, J.M.L.M.; Rodrigues, Á.H. Atmospheric flow over a mountainous region by a one-way coupled approach based on Reynolds-averaged turbulence modelling. *Bound. Layer Meteorol.* **2016**, *159*, 407–437. [CrossRef]

6. Knaus, H.; Rautenberg, A.; Bange, J. Model comparison of two different non-hydrostatic formulations for the Navier-Stokes equations simulating wind flow in complex terrain. *J. Wind Eng. Ind. Aerodyn.* **2017**, *169*, 290–307. [CrossRef]

7. Knaus, H.; Dürr, B. Numerical simulation including model validation of wind flow in alpine terrain in eastern Switzerland. *Prog. Comput. Fluid Dyn.* **2015**, *15*, 168–176. [CrossRef]

8. Kim, H.G.; Patel, V.C. Test of turbulence models for wind flow over terrain with separation and recirculation. *Bound. Layer Meteorol.* **2000**, *94*, 5–21. [CrossRef]

9. Abdi, D.S.; Bitsuamlak, T.G. Wind flow simulations on idealized and real complex terrain using various turbulence models. *Adv. Eng. Softw.* **2014**, *75*, 30–41. [CrossRef]

10. Brutsaert, W.H. *Evaporation into the Atmosphere: Theory, History and Applications*; D. Reidel Publishing Company: Boston, MA, USA, 1982.

11. Svensson, U.; Häggkvist, K. A two-equation turbulence model for canopy flows. *J. Wind Eng. Ind. Aerodyn.* **1990**, *25*, 201–211. [CrossRef]

12. Liu, J.; Chen, J.M.; Black, T.A.; Novak, M.D. Modelling of turbulent air flow downwind of a model forest edge. *Bound. Layer Meteorol.* **1996**, *77*, 21–44. [CrossRef]

13. Green, S.R. Modelling turbulent air flow in a stand of widely-spaced trees. *Phoenics J.* **1992**, *5*, 294–312.

14. Shaw, R.H.; Schumann, U. Large eddy simulation of turbulent flow above and within a forest. *Bound. Layer Meteorol.* **1992**, *61*, 47–64. [CrossRef]

15. Lopes, A.S.; Palma, J.M.L.M.; Lopes, J.V. Improving a two-equation turbulence model for canopy flows using large-eddy simulation. *Bound. Layer Meteorol.* **2013**, *149*, 231–257. [CrossRef]

16. Wilson, N.R.; Shaw, R.H. A higher order closure model for canopy flow. *J. Appl. Meteorol.* **1977**, *16*, 1197–1205. [CrossRef]

17. Ayotte, K.W.; Finnigan, J.J.; Raupach, M.R. A second-order closure for neutrally stratified vegetative canopy flows. *Bound. Layer Meteorol.* **1999**, *90*, 189–216. [CrossRef]

18. Dimitris, S.; Panayotis, P. Macroscopic turbulence models and their application in turbulent vegetated flows. *J. Hydraul. Eng.* **2011**, *137*, 315–332. [CrossRef]

19. Baldauf, M.; Förstner, S.; Klink, S.; Reinhardt, T.; Schraff, C.; Seifert, A.; Stephan, K. *Kurze Beschreibung des Lokal-Modells Kürzestfrist COSMO-DE (LMK) und Seiner Datenbanken auf dem Datenserver des DWD*; Version 2.4; Deutscher Wetterdienst: Offenbach, Germany, 2016.

20. ANSYS, Inc. *ANSYS CFX-Theory Guide, Release 17.0*; ANSYS, Inc.: Canonsburg, PA, USA, 2016.

21. Rhie, C.M.; Chow, W.L. Numerical study of the turbulent flow past an airfoil with trailing edge separation. *AIAA J.* **1983**, *21*, 1525–1532. [CrossRef]

22. Etling, D. *Theoretische Meteorologie: Eine Einführung*; 3. Auflage; Springer: Berlin, Germany, 2008.

23. Doms, G.; Baldauf, M. *Consortium for Small Scale Modelling: A Description of the Nonhydrostatic Regional COSMO-Model, Part I: Dynamics and Numerics*; Deutscher Wetterdienst: Offenbach, Germany, 2015.

24. Launder, B.E.; Spalding, D.B. The numerical computation of turbulent flows. *Comput. Methods Appl. Mech. Eng.* **1974**, *3*, 269–289. [CrossRef]

25. Yakhot, V.; Orszag, S.A.; Thangam, S.; Gatski, T.B.; Speziale, C.G. Development of turbulence models for shear flows by a double expansion technique. *Phys. Fluids* **1992**, *4*, 1510–1520. [CrossRef]

26. Katul, G.; Mahrt, L.; Poggi, D.; Sanz, C. One- and two-Equation models for canopy turbulence. *Bound. Layer Meteorol.* **2004**, *113*, 81–109. [CrossRef]

27. Launder, B.E.; Reece, G.C.; Rodi, W. Progress in the development of a Reynolds-Stress turbulence closure. *J. Fluid Mech.* **1975**, *68*, 537–566. [CrossRef]

28. Rotta, J.C. Statistische Theorie nichthomogener Turbulenz. *Z. Phys.* **1951**, *129*, 547–572. [CrossRef]

29. Ayotte, K.W. Personal conversation on 5 September 2017.

30. Uittenbogaard, R. Modelling turbulence in vegetation aquatic flows. In *International Workshop on Riparian Forest Vegetated Channels*; International Workshop: Trento, Italy, 2003.

31. López, F.; Garcia, M.H. Open-channel flow through simulated vegetation: Suspended sediment transport modelling. *Water Resour. Res.* **1998**, *34*, 2341–2352. [CrossRef]

32. Anger, J.; Bange, J.; Blick, C.; Brosz, F.; Emeis, S.; Fallmann, J. *Erstellung einer Konzeption eines Windenergie-Testgeländes in Bergig Komplexem Terrain: Abschlussbericht des Förderprojektes KonTest*; WindForS: Tbilisi, Georgia, 2015.

33. Hofsäß, M.; Bergmann, D.; Bischoff, O.; Denzel, J.; Cheng, P.W.; Lutz, T.; Peters, B.; Schulz, C. *Entwicklung von Lidar-Technologien zur Erfassung von Windfeldstrukturen Hinsichtlich der Optimierung der Windenergienutzung im Bergigen, Komplexen Gelände: Abschlussbericht des Förderprojekts Lidar Complex*; WindForS: Tbilisi, Georgia, 2017.

34. Wildmann, N.; Hofsäß, M.; Weimer, F.; Joos, A.; Bange, J. MASC—A small remotely piloted aircraft (RPA) for wind energy research. *Adv. Sci. Res.* **2014**, *11*, 55–61. [CrossRef]

35. Van den Kroonenberg, A.; Martin, T.; Buschmann, M.; Bange, J.; Vörsmann, P. Measuring the wind vector using the autonomous Mini Aerial Vehicle M2AV. *J. Atmos. Ocean. Technol.* **2008**, *25*, 1969–1982. [CrossRef]

36. Wildmann, N.; Mauz, M.; Bange, J. Two fast temperature sensors for probing of the atmospheric boundary layer using small remotely piloted aircraft (RPA). *Atmos. Meas. Tech.* **2013**, *6*, 2101–2113. [CrossRef]

37. Wildmann, N.; Kaufmann, F.; Bange, J. An inverse-modelling approach for frequency response correction of capacitive humidity sensors in ABL research with small remotely piloted aircraft (RPA). *Atmos. Meas. Tech.* **2014**, *7*, 3059–3069. [CrossRef]

38. Schlünzen, K.H.; Grawe, D.; Bohnenstengel, S.I.; Schlüter, I.; Koppmann, R. Joint modelling of obstacle induced and mesoscale changes—Current limits and challenges. *J. Wind Eng. Ind. Aerodyn.* **2011**, *99*, 217–225. [CrossRef]

39. Desmond, C.J.; Watson, S.J.; Aubrun, S.; Ávila, S.; Hancock, P.; Sayer, A. A study on the inclusion of forest canopy morphology data in numerical simulations for the purpose of wind resource assessment. *J. Wind Eng. Ind. Aerodyn.* **2014**, *126*, 24–37. [CrossRef]

Article

Mode Pressure Coefficient Maps as an Alternative to Mean Pressure Coefficient Maps for Non-Gaussian Processes: Hyperbolic Paraboloid Roofs as Cases of Study

Alberto Viskovic

Department of Engineering and Geology, G. D'Annunzio University, viale Pindaro 42, 65127 Pescara, Italy;
alberto.viskovic.unich@gmail.com

Received: 9 November 2018; Accepted: 10 December 2018; Published: 12 December 2018

Abstract: Wind tunnel experiments are necessary for geometries that are not investigated by codes or that are not generally and parametrically investigated by literature. One example is the hyperbolic parabolic shape mostly used for cable net roofs, for which codes do not provide pressure coefficients and literature only gives mean, maxima, and minima pressure coefficient maps. However, most of pressure series acquired in wind tunnels on the roof are not Gaussian processes and, for this reason, the mean values are not precisely representative of the process. The paper investigates the ratio between mean and mode of pressure coefficient series acquired in wind tunnels on buildings covered with hyperbolic paraboloid roofs with square plans. Mode pressure coefficient maps are given as an addition to traditional pressure coefficient maps.

Keywords: wind tunnel tests; non-Gaussian processes; pressure coefficient; mode; hyperbolic paraboloid roofs

---

1. Introduction

Wind tunnel tests are necessary for structure sensitivity to wind action regarding shapes not discussed in technical codes or literature. This is the case of the structures with hyperbolic paraboloid shapes mostly used for roofs made of cable nets and concrete shells, widely used, for example, in sport arenas, meeting rooms, or music halls [1–4]. The shortcoming relates the generalization and parametrization of aerodynamic coefficients to the widest number of geometries derived from the hyperbolic paraboloid.

Codes of practice, such as those found in the literature [5–14], for example, do not give values of pressure coefficients for buildings covered with hyperbolic paraboloid roofs.

The literature discusses a great number of examples of wind tunnel test campaigns [11,15–32]. However, all references regard particular cases that are not generalizable for different geometries.

There are some exceptions [26,27] that have followed a parametric approach in order to give generalizable values. In addition, the authors of [33,34] have synthetized experimental results in order to give simplified pressure coefficient maps.

The simplified pressure coefficient maps are used by designers to calculate the structure and evaluate the cost–benefit convenience in advance.

All publications and codes give mean or maxima and minima pressure coefficient maps. The maxima and minima pressure coefficients are usually considered to estimate the local extreme values of wind action, whereas the mean values are used to investigate the global wind action distribution on the surface.

However, some information about the processes that have been used to generate the maps should be given too.

Computation **2018**, *6*, 64; doi:10.3390/computation6040064   www.mdpi.com/journal/computation

In fact, if the processes are non-Gaussian, the mean value is not precise enough to represent them. The non-Gaussianity generally depends on very big flow fluctuation because of, for example, flow separation near edges or vortex shedding caused by a complex geometry [27,35]. Recently, the authors of [35,36] illustrated the peak factor distributions on a hyperbolic paraboloid roof and showed that many processes acquired by pressure taps, particularly near the roof borders and corners, are non-Gaussian processes. For these reasons, the mean values of the pressure coefficient series are representative as much as the mode, for example.

In cases where the difference between mean and mode values is significant, if the mean is lower than the mode (i.e., which is the most frequent value), the use of mean pressure coefficients can affect structure reliability. In particular, this variation can affect the structural reliability for flexible structures and in general for cables structures. In fact, analyses of instability on tensile structures, in particular on suspended bridges under flutter (i.e., [37–39]), have shown that smaller variations of wind action can also give global instability, contrary to the case of concrete bridges, which are more sensitive to seismic action [40]. In addition, the cable net tensile structures' sensitivity to wind action is well-known from many studies [1,2,23,41–52].

This paper investigates this aspect on four geometries of buildings covered with hyperbolic paraboloid roofs with square plans. This shape was chosen because it is frequently used for tensile structures that are very sensitive to wind action. For this reason, the paper proposes to optimize the structural design of these structures using mode instead of mean values from wind tunnel experiments. In total, two different heights and hyperbolic paraboloid surface curvatures are considered. The paper aims to show the differences between pressure coefficient maps obtained by mean and mode values in order to propose also taking into account this value for non-Gaussian processes. The paper does not aim to propose a prediction method of pressure coefficient distribution on the roof and, consequently, peak factors of pressure coefficients are not investigated in this phase. The differences between mean and mode values are shown in terms of wind loads on the roof too.

Section 2 discusses the geometrical sample and the experimental data set given by [40], used to investigate the mean and mode pressure coefficient ratio, while Section 3 discusses the main results of the research. It is important to note that in this study, the author used the same experimental data set discussed in the work of [27], made available by authors. Finally, some maps contain asymmetries because experimental results are affected by inaccuracies in the experimental set-up given by models.

2. Geometrical Sample and Experimental Setup

Wind tunnel tests were carried out by [27] and [34] on 12 plan shapes, 2 different heights, and 2 different curvatures of buildings covered with hyperbolic paraboloid roofs.

This paper is focused on four of these samples and, in particular, on buildings that have a square plan, two different curvatures, and two different heights, described in [27,34,46], respectively.

Figure 1 shows the geometrical parameters listed in Table 1 for the geometries investigated. Parameters $l_1, f_1, l_2,$ and f_2 are the upward and downward parabolas' sags and spans, respectively. For the square plan, l_1 is equal to l_2; H is the sum of $f_1 + f_2$ and in this research, it was equal to $1/10\, l_1$ (for model 1 and 2) and $1/6\, l_1$ (for model 3 and 4 of l_1 [27]); and H_B is the distance between the ground and the lower point of the roof.

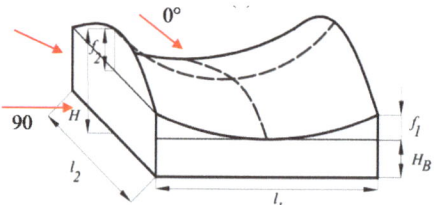

Figure 1. Geometrical parameters.

Table 1. Wind tunnel model sizes.

Model	l_1 [cm]	l_2 [cm]	f_1 [cm]	f_2 [cm]	H [cm]	H_B [cm]
1	80.00	80.00	2.67	5.33	8.00	13.33
2	80.00	80.00	2.67	5.33	8.00	26.66
3	80.00	80.00	4.44	8.89	13.33	13.33
4	80.00	80.00	4.44	8.89	13.33	26.66

Aerodynamic tests were carried out in the open circuit CRIACIV (Interuniversity Research Center on Building Aerodynamics and Wind Engineering, city, country) wind tunnel with a developed boundary layer. The CRIACIV test chamber sizes are 2.4 × 1.6 m. The pressure series were acquired at a frequency equal to approximately 252 Hz for about 30 s [27,35]. The scaled models were made in wood and 1.5 mm Teflon diameter tubes instrumented the pressure taps. The pressure tap distribution on the square plan roofs is illustrated in Figure 2, which shows the Thiessen polygon shape for each pressure tap. In total, 89 pressure taps were located on the roof and 16 wind angles were acquired. The mean wind speed profile measured before placement of the model and its logarithmic approximation were estimated with $z_0 = 0.247$ cm, model scale. This value was calculated by fitting the experimental points in the range of heights of interest, that is, from the ground level to the highest point of the roof. In a geometric scale of 1:100, this corresponds to a roughness length of 0.247 m, which is slightly lower than that of exposure category III of EN-1991 ($z_0 = 0.3$ m), described as "area with regular cover of vegetation or buildings or with isolated obstacles with separations of maximum 20 obstacle heights (such as villages, suburban terrain, permanent forest)".

The turbulence intensity profile at the roof level, ranges between 11% and 12%. The tests were performed at a mean wind speed of 16.7 m/s at a height of 10 cm, which, in a 1:100 scale, would be the standard reference height. Assuming that the prototype mean wind speed at 10 m of height is $U = 27$ m/s (design value for most of the Italian territory), then there is a velocity scale $\lambda v = 0.62$, which corresponds to a time scale $\lambda t = 0.0162$. Therefore, the 30 s model scale acquisition time corresponds to a full scale time of approximately 1800 s, well located within the interval of 600 s to 3600 s. The Reynolds number at model scale is about 9.4×10^5, and 1.7×10^8 at real scale. Turbulence intensity is about 10%. It is known that the Reynolds scale effect can affect results. However, it is expected that no Reynolds effects take place, because of the sharpness of the roof edges [33]. The longitudinal integral length scale at the roof height is about 30 cm at model scale, which would bring a full scale value lower than actual ones. This mismatch, common in most wind tunnel tests, is assumed to have minimal consequences on the results.

For the sake of brevity, the paper discusses only 0°, 45°, and 90° wind angles. More details about wind velocity, turbulence in wind tunnel, and wind tunnel setup were given in the work of [27].

The pressure coefficient c_p was estimated according to Equation (1).

$$c_p(P,t) = \frac{p(P,t) - p_0}{\frac{1}{2}\rho V_m^2} \tag{1}$$

where $p(P,t)$ is the measured pressure at point P of the roof surface, p_0 is the static pressure in the bare tunnel, and $\frac{1}{2} r V^2$ m is the dynamic pressure measured by pressure taps.

Figure 3 shows an example of pressure coefficient time history (i.e., model 1, pressure tap #50, wind angle 0°); its maximum, minimum, mean, and mode values are overlapped on the time history. Figure 3 shows that the difference between mean and mode values is relevant for the pressure tap acquisition, taken as an example. However, the following results show that this trend is generalizable.

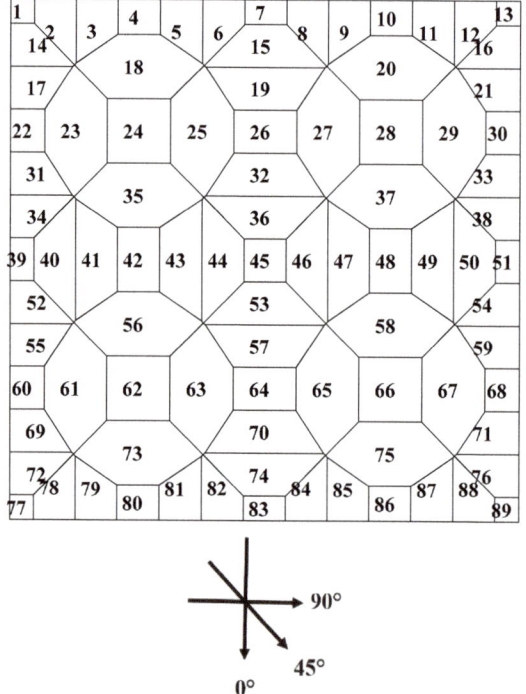

Figure 2. Thiessen polygons distribution.

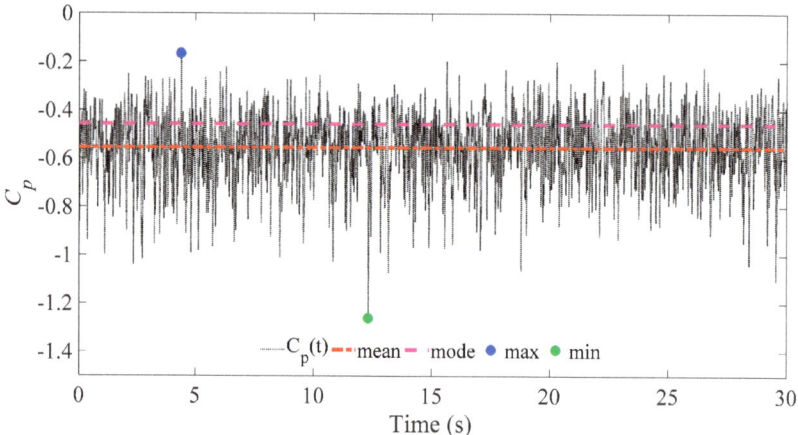

Figure 3. Examples of pressure coefficients time history: model 1, pressure tap #50, wind angle 0°.

The pressure tap distribution chosen by the researchers closely affected the results. In fact, the processes acquired near the borders of the roof were statistically very different from others located in the middle of the roof [35].

3. Experimental Data

Pressure coefficient time histories (i.e., in the following processes) were evaluated from pressure series acquired in wind tunnels. The statistical analyses of the pressure coefficient processes showed that some processes were Gaussian and others were non-Gaussian. The difference is crucial. As it is known, Gaussian processes are represented by mean and standard deviation, while for non-Gaussian processes, the mean value does not represent the process. Figure 4 shows the *pdf* (i.e., probability density function) of two examples of Gaussian (i.e., Figure 4a) and non-Gaussian (i.e., Figure 4b) processes. The two processes are estimated from series acquired on the same roof (i.e., model 1).

Figure 4a shows that mode is equal to the mean value, while on the contrary, Figure 4b shows that mode and mean are very different, with a ratio equal to 1.21. This trend suggests that the mean pressure coefficient maps may not adequately represent all processes on the roof. Similarly, the maxima and minima value maps are not representative because the extreme values are not simultaneous for all pressure taps.

It would desirable to put the pressure taps near borders because the vortex shedding caused by the 103 corners and the borders closely affected the pressure coefficient values

In order to investigate the Gaussian and non-Gaussian process distributions on the geometrical sample considered, Figure 5 represents the pressure taps that have non-Gaussian processes in red. This Gaussian characteristic was investigated both using the one-sided Kolmogorov–Smirnov test on the *cdf* (i.e., cumulative density function) of the processes compared with the normal *cdf* distribution, and following the work of [53]. According to the authors of [53], if the trend is Gaussian, the skewness γ_3 and the excess kurtosis γ_4 (i.e., kurtosis-3) should be less than or equal to 0.5.

Figure 5 shows the Gaussian (i.e., in white) and non-Gaussian (i.e., in red) processes for $0°$, $45°$, and $90°$ wind angles and for models 1 to 4.

For the geometry investigated (i.e., buildings covered with hyperbolic paraboloid roofs), the results show that the Gaussian process is closely affected by the building height, the curvature, and the wind angles.

On comparing different curvatures (i.e., model 1 and 2 with model 3 and 4), the results showed that for $\alpha = 0°$ (i.e., Figure 5a,d,g,j), the values were more affected by height and wind angles than by curvature. In fact, the number of Gaussian processes were similar between model 1 and 3 (i.e., the same height, but different curvature) and between model 2 and 4. The difference increased for $\alpha = 45°$ (i.e., Figure 5b,e,h,k) and $\alpha = 90°$ (Figure 5c,f,i,l). The number of Gaussian processes decreased when the height increased and when the radius of the curvature decreased (i.e., from model 1 and 2 surface to model 3 and 4 surface). Table 2 gives the percentage of Gaussian processes for all geometries and wind angles discussed in this paper.

Table 2. Percentage of Gaussian processes.

Model	$\alpha = 0°$	$\alpha = 45°$	$\alpha = 90°$
1	44.9	27.0	32.6
2	29.2	40.4	28.1
3	41.6	41.6	21.3
4	34.8	46.1	16.9

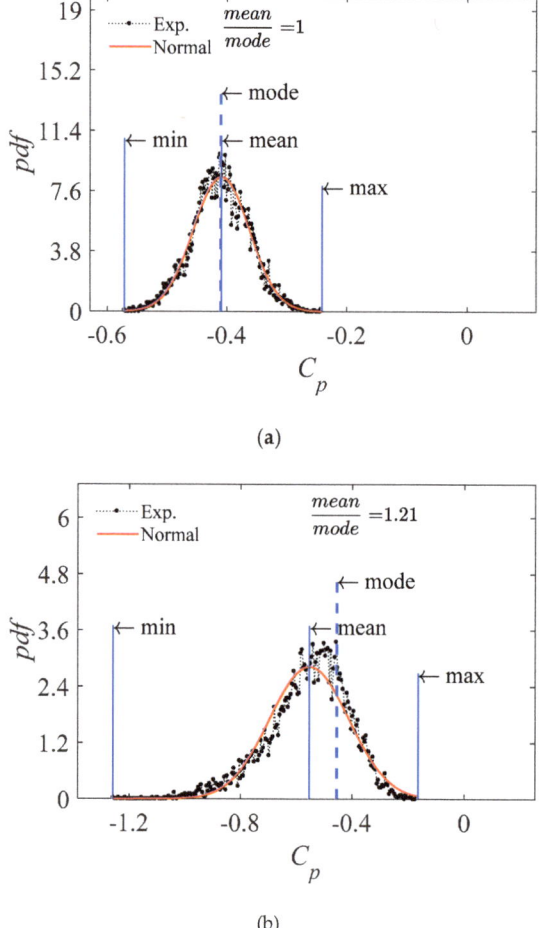

(a)

(b)

Figure 4. Gaussian process, model 1, #19 = 0° *pdf* (probability density function) (**a**); non-Gaussian process #2 = 0° (**b**).

Globally, the wind angles closely affected the number of Gaussian processes. α = 90° had the smallest number of Gaussian processes (Figure 5c,f,i,l) and all values were smaller than 50%.

Considering the results shown in Figure 5, the mean pressure coefficient maps do not seem to be representative of most of the processes acquired. In Figure 5, white means Gaussian process and red means non-Gaussian process.

On this basis, the ratio between the mean value and the mode value, $\frac{\mu_{cp}}{v_{cp}}$, was calculated in order to measure the difference between them.

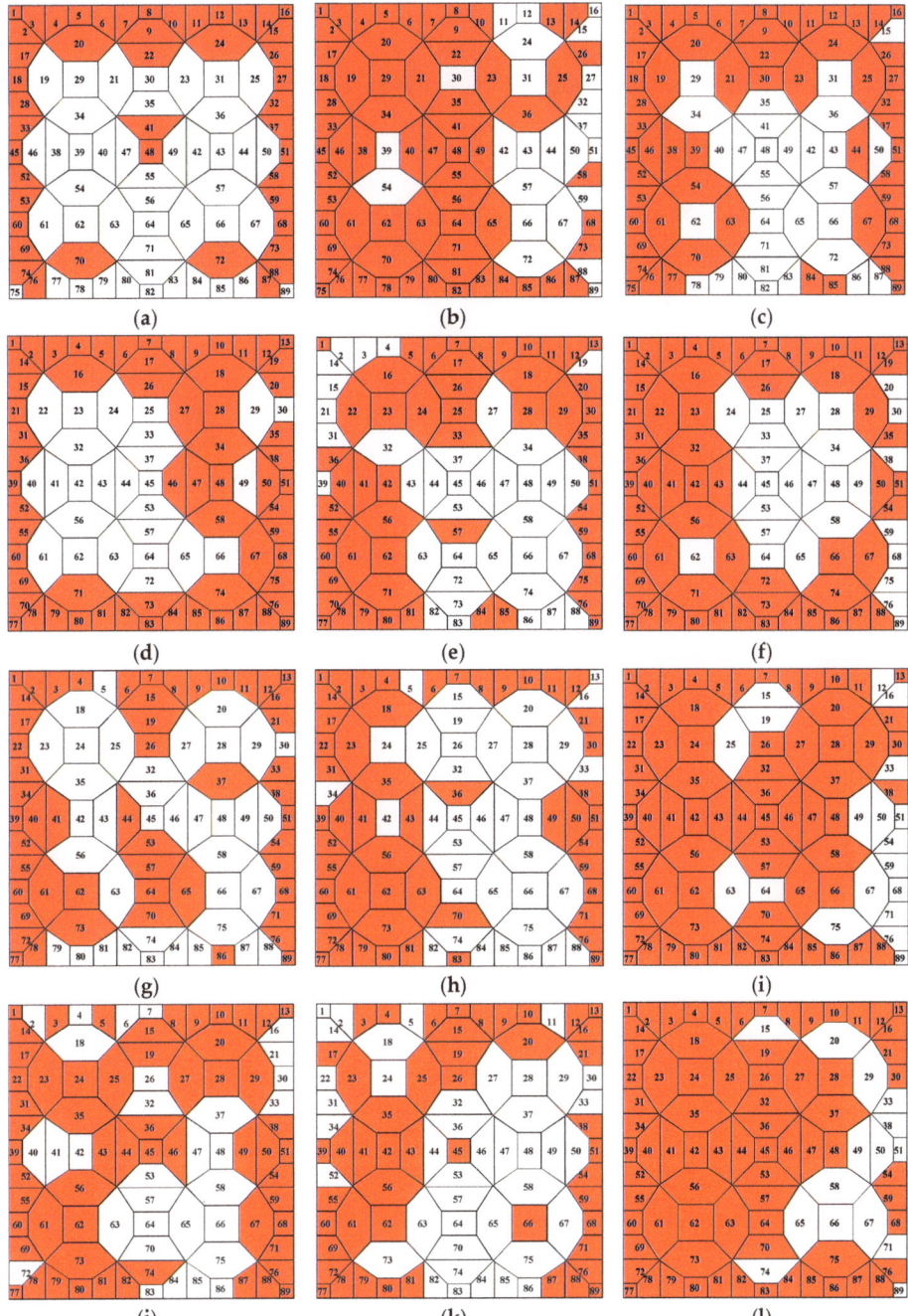

Figure 5. Gaussian process distribution on the roofs, model 1 α = 0° (**a**), α = 45° (**b**), and α = 90° (**c**); model 2 α = 0° (**d**), α = 45° (**e**), and α = 90° (**f**); model 3 α = 0° (**g**), α = 45° (**h**), and α = 90° (**i**); model 4 α = 0° (**j**), α = 45° (**k**), and α = 90° (**l**).

Figure 6 shows the $\frac{\mu_{Cp}}{v_{Cp}}$ for each pressure tap and all the geometries and wind angles considered. In Figure 6, yellow means $\frac{\mu_{Cp}}{v_{Cp}} > 1$; purple means $\frac{\mu_{Cp}}{v_{Cp}} < 1$; and finally, white means $\frac{\mu_{Cp}}{v_{Cp}} = 1$. Table 3 synthetizes the results. In particular, Table 3 gives the mean of $\frac{\mu_{Cp}}{v_{Cp}}$ for all models (i.e., 1 to 4) and wind angles (i.e., $\alpha = 0°$, $45°$, and $90°$), the percentage of $\frac{\mu_{Cp}}{v_{Cp}} < 1$ and $\frac{\mu_{Cp}}{v_{Cp}} > 1$, and the mean of $\frac{\mu_{Cp}}{v_{Cp}}$ for both (in brackets).

Table 3. Mean value of $\frac{\mu_{Cp}}{v_{Cp}}$ and percentage of cases where $\frac{\mu_{Cp}}{v_{Cp}} < 1$ and $\frac{\mu_{Cp}}{v_{Cp}} > 1$.

Model	$\alpha = 0°$	$\alpha = 45°$	$\alpha = 90°$
	Mean of $\left(\frac{\mu_{Cp}}{v_{Cp}}\right)$ ratio		
1	1.03	1.01	1.05
2	1.03	1.01	1.05
3	1.02	1.02	1.01
4	1.00	1.01	1.02
	Percentage of cases where $\left(\frac{\mu_{Cp}}{v_{Cp}}\right) < 1$ (%) Value in parenthesis is the mean value of the ratio restricted to cases where ratio <1		
1	30.3 (0.98)	41.6 (0.97)	32.6 (0.94)
2	36.0 (0.99)	46.1 (0.98)	28.1 (0.95)
3	34.8 (0.98)	28.1 (0.97)	38.2 (0.87)
4	56.2 (0.97)	41.6 (0.98)	38.2 (0.92)
	Percentage of cases where $\left(\frac{\mu_{Cp}}{v_{Cp}}\right) > 1$ (%) Value in parenthesis is the mean value of the ratio restricted to cases where ratio >1		
1	69.7 (1.05)	58.4 (1.04)	67.4 (1.10)
2	64.0 (1.05)	53.9 (1.03)	71.9 (1.09)
3	65.2 (1.04)	71.9 (1.04)	61.8 (1.10)
4	43.8 (1.03)	58.4 (1.03)	61.8 (1.08)

For $\alpha = 0°$ (Figure 6a,d,g,j), model 1 has 30.3% of processes for which the mean pressure coefficients underestimate the mode on average by 2%–3%. The percentage increases from model 2 to 4, with the maximum values equal to 56.2% for model 4.

For $\alpha = 45°$ (Figure 6b,e,h,k), model 1 has 41.6% of processes for which the mean pressure coefficients are lower than the mode on average by 2%–3%. The percentage increases in model 2, with maximum values equal to 46.1%. However, the percentage of processes with $\frac{\mu_{Cp}}{v_{Cp}} < 1$ is quite constant for all models, except for model 3, which has the smallest percentage, equal to about 28%.

For $\alpha = 90°$, (Figure 6c,f,i,l), the percentage of $\frac{\mu_{Cp}}{v_{Cp}} < 1$ varies from 28.1% (i.e., model 2) to 38.2% (i.e., model 3 and 4). However, the mean of $\frac{\mu_{Cp}}{v_{Cp}}$, for $\frac{\mu_{Cp}}{v_{Cp}} < 1$, increases from 2% to 3% for $\alpha = 0°$ and 45° from 5% to 8% for $\alpha = 90°$.

The percentage of $\frac{\mu_{Cp}}{v_{Cp}} > 1$ is between 43.8% (i.e., model 4, $\alpha = 0°$) and 71.9% (i.e., model 3, $\alpha = 45°$).

The mean of $\frac{\mu_{Cp}}{v_{Cp}}$, for $\frac{\mu_{Cp}}{v_{Cp}} > 1$, ranges from 1.03 (i.e., model 4, $\alpha = 0°$) to 1.10 (i.e., model 1, $\alpha = 90°$).

Regarding wind action estimation, if designers previously used mean pressure coefficients maps to design structures, the most dangerous situation was $\frac{\mu_{cp}}{v_{cp}} < 1$, because the most frequent values of pressure coefficients did not correspond to the mean values used for its design. This means that the roof may be loaded differently. In order to take into account this aspect, using both the mean and mode pressure coefficient maps is suggested. These last maps, for Gaussian processes, correspond to mean pressure coefficient maps, while for non-Gaussian processes, the designer can choose the biggest value between mean and mode. This approach increases the reliability of the calculations.

Figures 7–10 show a comparison between the mean pressure coefficient maps given by the authors of [27] (i.e., Figure 7a,c,e; Figure 8a,c,e; Figure 9a,c,e; and Figure 10a,c,e) and the mode pressure coefficient maps (i.e., Figure 7b,d,f; Figure 8b,d,f; Figure 9b,d,f; and Figure 10b,d,f).

Figures 7–10 show that the trend is the same and that values vary slightly but, in many cases, significantly in term (i.e., 0–5%). However, as was previously discussed, this difference cannot be neglected for wind action on big surfaces varying up to 5% of wind loads.

It is reasonable to think that the wind load increase of 5% is negligible. This is true for many kinds of structures for which the dead and permanent loads are better than wind action (i.e., concrete, steel trusses, etc.). This cannot be true for flexible cables structures. It is important to specify that this value was obtained for this particular experiment's campaign and shape. However, the paper aims to suggest an approach that is not taken into account, and the purpose is to suggest using both maps. The reason is that these structures are generally designed using equivalent static wind loads. When the shape is powered by codes, the static loads are generally estimated by equations that take into account mean values for the serviceability limit state, or maxima and minima for the ultimate limit state. Anyway, commonly, the Gaussianity is not discussed and so the representative role of the mean is not discussed either. In addition, the hyperbolic paraboloid net has two orders of cables—the first is upward and is load bearing for gravitational loads, while the second is downward and is load bearing for suction loads. If the sags of these two orders of cables are not equal (as is in the case of study investigated), the cables areas are different. This means that cables work differently under wind or under gravitational loads. Finally, in order to have a measure of this, take a practical example. Pressure taps are generally representative of roof areas. Each pressure tap, depending on the geometrical scale, corresponds to a specific zone in which the pressure coefficient is considered constant (i.e., experimental approximation due to the scaled model). In the case of study considered, each pressure tap represents at least 1/89 of the roof surface. If the geometrical scale of prototype is 1/100, it represents at least 72 m^2 of the roof (about 8.5 m × 8.5 m). Considering a pressure in suction equal to 0.45 kN/m^2 (0.5 × 1.25 × 27^2), and considering pressure coefficients equal to 1.5, cables are loaded by wind with forces equal to about 49 kN. Finally, considering that the dead and permanent loads are about 0.2 kN/m^2, in the pressure tap area, there is a gravitational force equal to at least 14 kN (i.e., 0.9 kN for each node). The gravitational force is about 1/3 of the wind action. In this case, it corresponds to a uniformly distributed load on cables with a spacing equal to 2 m equal to (49 kN − 14 kN)/2 m = 17.5 kN/m or (49 kN × 1.05 − 14 kN)/2 m = 18.7 kN/m [27]. The difference is bigger than 7%. The cables traction load supports structures that are generally made of steel. It is important to consider that for steel structures, safety coefficients for material (i.e., material factors) given by Eurocode for the ultimate limit state are between 1 and 1.33. In particular, the safety coefficient for yielding of a metal face, shear failure of a profiled face, and support reaction capacity of a profiled face is equal to 1.1 (i.e., 10%). This value is dangerously close to 7%.

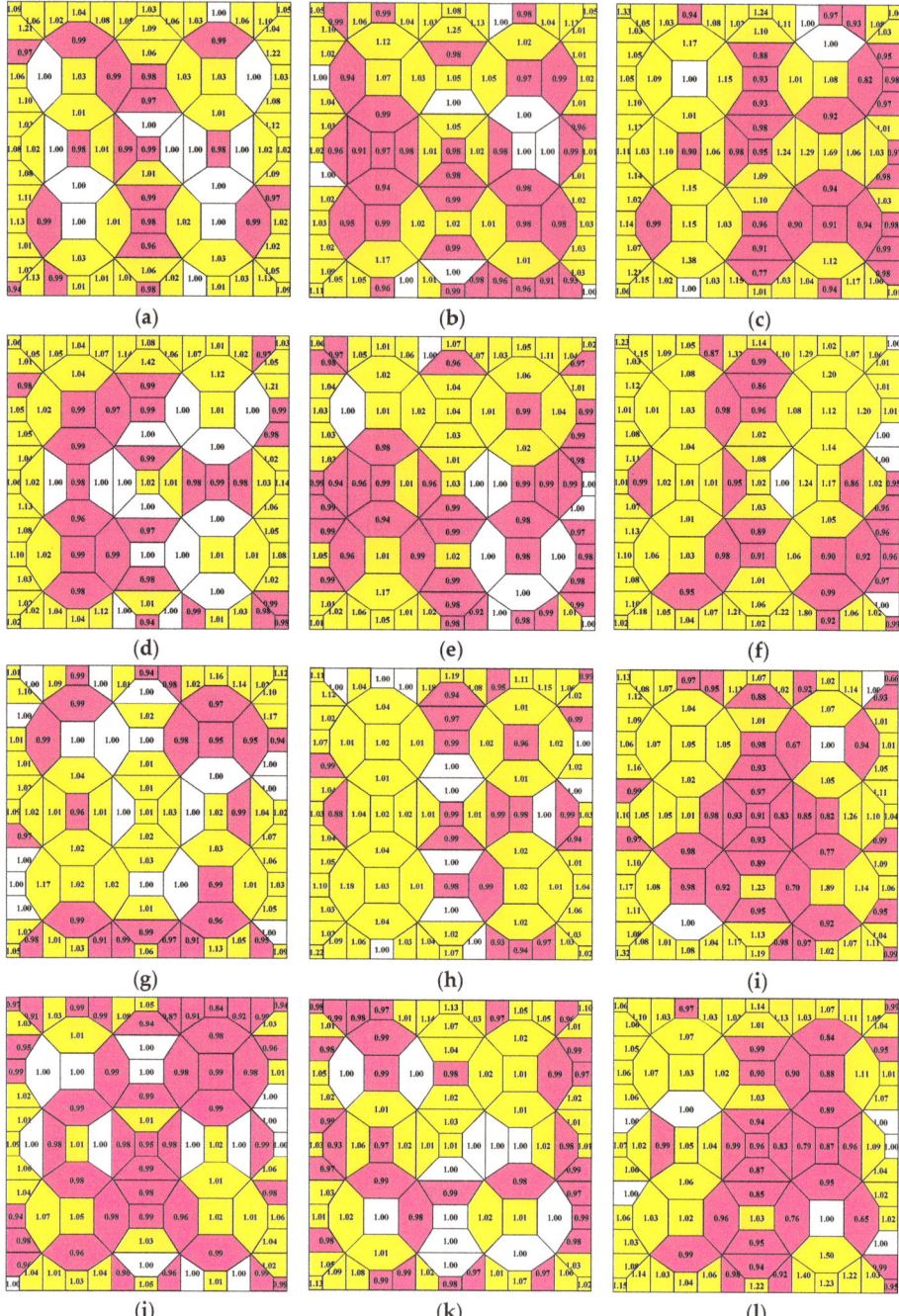

Figure 6. Ratio $\frac{\mu_{cp}}{v_{cp}}$ distribution on the roofs, model 1 $\alpha = 0°$ (**a**), $\alpha = 45°$ (**b**), and $\alpha = 90°$ (**c**); model 2 $\alpha = 0°$ (**d**), $\alpha = 45°$ (**e**), and $\alpha = 90°$ (**f**); model 3 $\alpha = 0°$ (**g**), $\alpha = 45°$ (**h**), and $\alpha = 90°$ (**i**); model 4 $\alpha = 0°$ (**j**), $\alpha = 45°$ (**k**), and $\alpha = 90°$ (**l**).

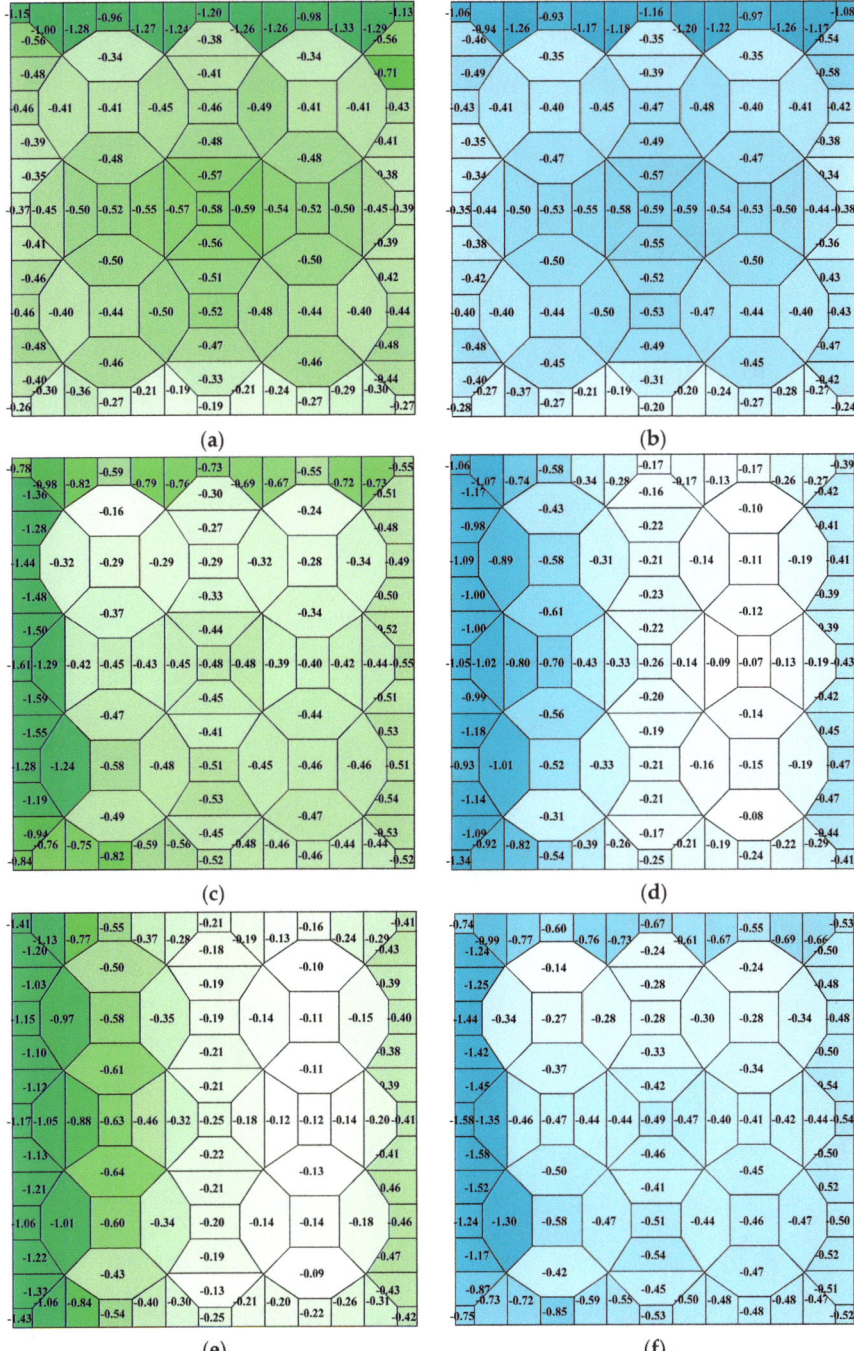

Figure 7. Model 1, mean pressure coefficient maps for α = 0° (**a**), α = 45° (**c**), and α = 90° (**e**); maps using mode of pressure coefficients for α = 0° (**b**), α = 45° (**d**), and α = 90° (**f**).

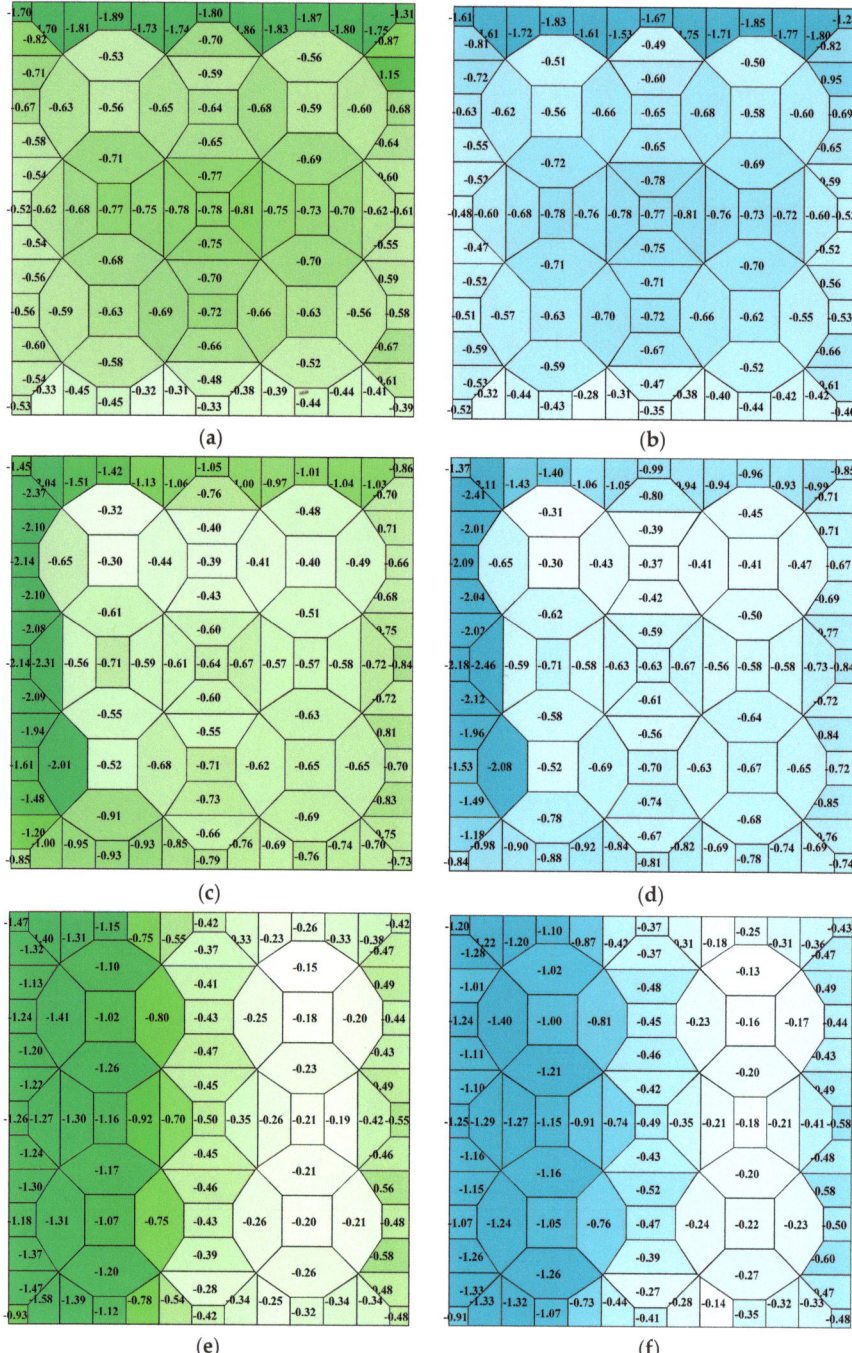

Figure 8. Model 2, mean pressure coefficient maps for α = 0° (**a**), α = 45° (**c**), and α = 90° (**e**); maps using mode of pressure coefficients for α = 0° (**b**), α = 45° (**d**), and α = 90° (**f**).

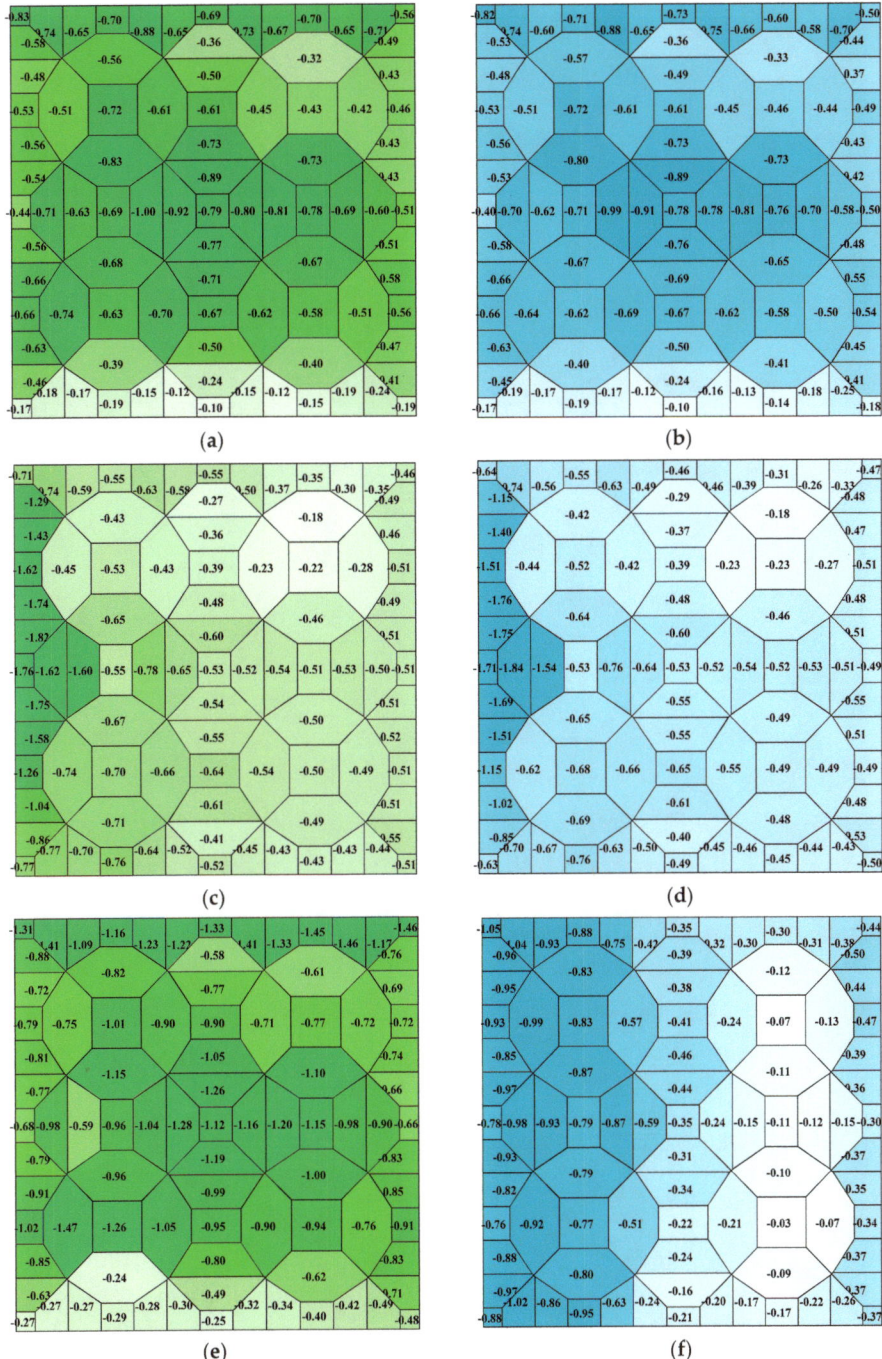

Figure 9. Model 3, mean pressure coefficient maps for $\alpha = 0°$ (**a**), $\alpha = 45°$ (**c**), and $\alpha = 90°$ (**e**); maps using mode of pressure coefficients for $\alpha = 0°$ (**b**), $\alpha = 45°$ (**d**), and $\alpha = 90°$ (**f**).

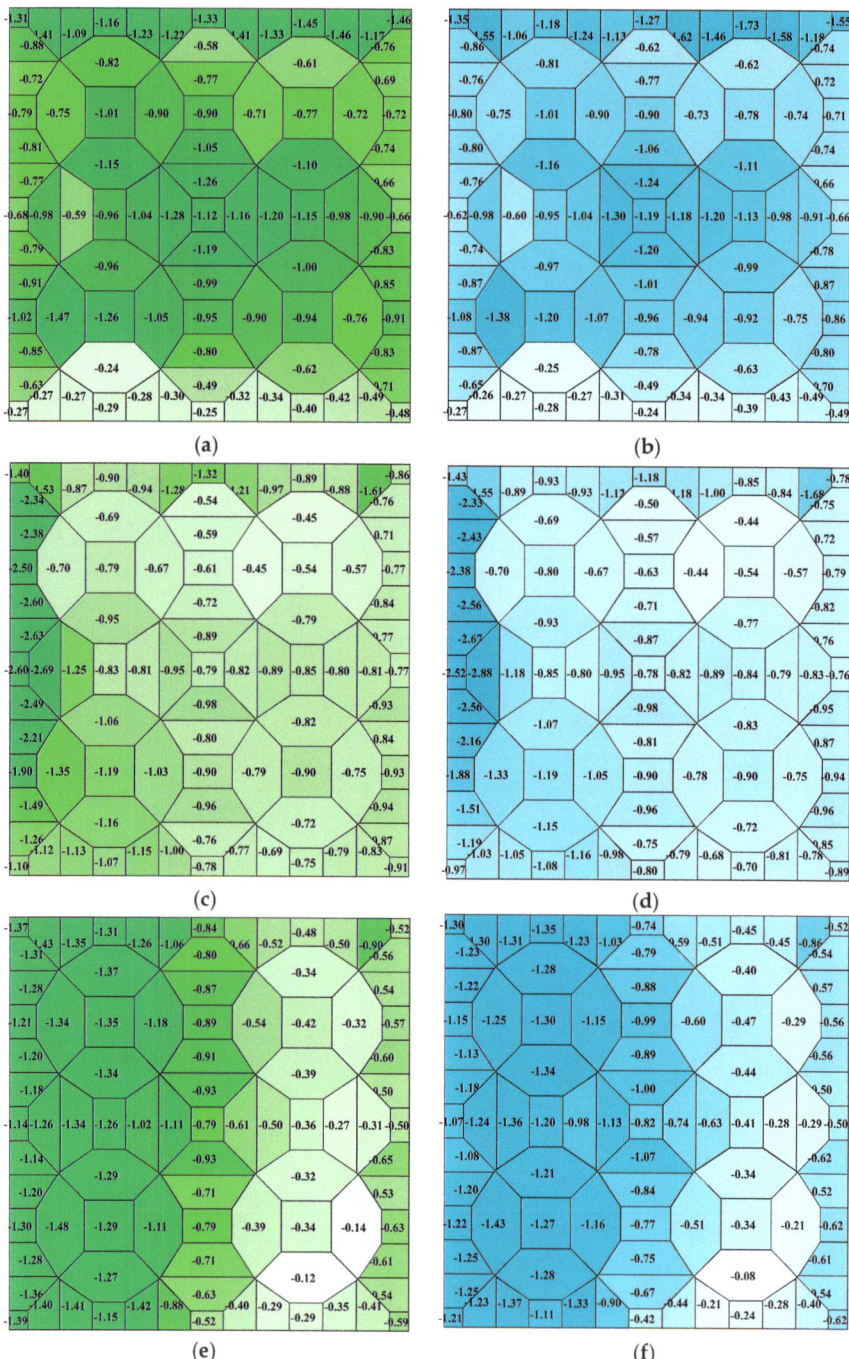

Figure 10. Model 4, mean pressure coefficient maps for α = 0° (**a**), α = 45° (**c**), and α = 90° (**e**); maps using mode of pressure coefficients for α = 0° (**b**), α = 45° (**d**), and α = 90° (**f**).

Computation **2018**, *6*, 64

4. Conclusions

Experimental wind tunnel tests on roofs usually give pressure coefficient maps of mean, maxima, and minima values of the pressure series acquired. However, the measured processes are not all Gaussian along the entire roof, and most of these are considerably non-Gaussian. For these, the mean values are not as significant as the mode. This paper compares the mode and mean values of pressure coefficient time histories acquired in a wind tunnel on hyperbolic paraboloid roofs with square plans. In total, four different geometries were investigated, varying the building height and the hyperbolic paraboloid surface curvature. Three wind angles were taken into account, namely, $0°$, $45°$, and $90°$. Mode pressure coefficients are given for all geometries and wind angles investigated.

The results showed that less than 50% of the processes were Gaussian and that the difference between the mean and mode values is up to 5%. Moreover, for 50% of the non-Gaussian processes, the mean is lower than the mode value. Regarding the investigated geometry (i.e., hyperbolic paraboloid roofs), the percentage of non-Gaussian processes was closely affected by height and mostly by wind angles.

Using both mean and mode pressure coefficient maps is suggested. These last maps, for Gaussian processes, correspond to mean pressure coefficient maps, while for non-Gaussian processes, the designer can choose the biggest value between mean and mode. This approach increases the reliability of the calculations.

Funding: This research received no external funding.

Conflicts of Interest: The author declares no conflict of interest.

References

1. Lewis, W.J. *Tension Structures: Form and Behavior*; Thomas Telford: London, UK, 2003.
2. Majowiecki, M. *Tensostrutture: Progetto e Verifica*; Edizioni Crea: Massa, Italy, 1994.
3. Rizzo, F.; Zazzini, P. Improving the acoustical properties of an elliptical plan space with a cable net membrane roof. *J. Acoust. Aust.* **2016**, *44*, 449–456. [CrossRef]
4. Rizzo, F.; Zazzini, P. Shape dependence of acoustic performances in buildings with a Hyperbolic Paraboloid cable net membrane roof. *J. Acoust. Aust.* **2017**, *45*, 421–443. [CrossRef]
5. AIJ (Architectural Institute of Japan). *Recommendations for Loads on Buildings*; AIJ: Tokyo, Japan, 2004; Chapter 6: Wind Loads.
6. ASCE (American Society of Civil Engineering). *Wind Tunnel Studies of Buildings and Structures*; Manuals of Practice (MOP); Isyumov, N., Ed.; ASCE: Reston, VA, USA, 1999; Volume 67.
7. ASCE (American Society of Civil Engineering). *Minimum Design Loads for Buildings and Other Structures*; ASCE: Reston, VA, USA, 2010; Volume 7.
8. AS/NZS (Standards Australia/Standards New Zealand). *Structural Design Actions*; Part 2: Wind Actions; AS/NZS 1170.2:2002; AS/NZS: Sydney, Australia, 2011.
9. CEN (Comité Européen de Normalization). *Eurocode 1: Actions on Structures—Part 1–4: General actions—Wind Actions*; EN-1991-1-4; CEN: European Union, 2005.
10. CNR (National Research Council of Italy). *Guide for the Assessment of Wind Actions and Effects on Structures*; CNR-DT 207/2008; CNR: Rome, Italy, 2008.
11. Krishna, P.; Kumar, K.; Bhandari, N.M. *Wind Loads on Buildings and Structures*; Indian Standard IS:875, Part 3, Proposed Draft & Commentary; Wiley: New York, NY, USA, 2012.
12. ISO (International Standards Organization). *Wind Action on Structures—D.3 Wind Tunnel Testing Procedures*; 4354:2012(E); ISO: Geneva, Switzerland, 2012.
13. NRC/CNRC (National Research Council/Conseil National de Recherches Canada). *Commentary to the National Building Code of Canada, Commentary I: Wind Load and Effects*; NRC/CNRC: Ottawa, ON, Canada, 2010.
14. SIA (Swiss Society of Engineers and Architects). *Action on Structures—Appendix C: Force and Pressure Factors for Wind*; SIA 261:2003; SIA: Zurich, Switzerland, 2003.
15. Biagini, P.; Borri, C.; Facchini, L. Wind response of large roofs of stadiums and arena. *J. Wind Eng. Ind. Aerodyn.* **2007**, *95*, 9–11. [CrossRef]

16. Dong, X.; Ye, J.H. Development and verification of a flow model of conical vortices on saddle roofs. *J. Eng. Mech.* **2015**, *141*, 04014127. [CrossRef]
17. Elashkar, I.; Novak, M. Wind tunnel studies of cable roofs. *J. Wind Eng. Ind. Aerodyn.* **1983**, *13*, 407–419. [CrossRef]
18. Kawai, H.; Yoshie, R. Wind-induced response of a large cantilevered roof. *J. Wind Eng. Ind. Aerodyn.* **1999**, *83*, 263–275. [CrossRef]
19. Kawakita, S.; Bienkiewicz, B.; Cermak, J.E. *Aeroelastic Model Study of Suspended Cable Roof*; Fluid Mechanics and Wind Engineering Program, Department of Civil Engineering, Colorado State University: Fort Collins, CO, USA, 1992.
20. Killen, G.P.; Letchford, C.W. A parametric study of wind loads on grandstand roofs. *Eng. Struct.* **2001**, *23*, 725–735. [CrossRef]
21. Kimoto, E.; Kawamura, S. Aerodynamic criteria of hanging roofs for structural Design. In Proceedings of the IASS Symposium on Membrane Structures and Space Frames, Osaka, Japan, 15–19 September 1986.
22. Irwin, H.P.A.H.; Wardlaw, R.L.A. Wind tunnel investigation of a retractable fabric roof for the Montreal Olympic stadium. In Proceedings of the 5th International Conference on Wind Engineering, Fort Collins, CO, USA, 8–14 July 1979; pp. 925–938.
23. Letchford, C.W.; Killen, G.P. Equivalent static wind loads for cantilevered grandstand roofs. *Eng. Struct.* **2002**, *24*, 207–217. [CrossRef]
24. Vitale, A.; Letchford, C.W. Full-scale wind loads on a porous canopy roof. In Proceedings of the Australasian Structural Engineering Conference, Auckland, New Zealand, 30 September–2 October 1998.
25. Letchford, C.W.; Denoon, R.O.; Johnson, G.; Mallam, A. Dynamic characteristics of cantilever grandstand roofs. *Eng. Struct.* **2002**, *24*, 1085–1090. [CrossRef]
26. Rizzo, F.; Sepe, V.; Vasta, V. Correlation structure of wind-tunnel pressure fields for a hyperbolic paraboloid roof. In *Proceedings of the Italian Association of Theoretical and Applied Mechanics (AIMETA 2017), Salerno, Italy, 4–7 September 2017*; Gechi Edizioni: Salerno, Italy, 2017; ISBN 978-889-42484-7-0.
27. Rizzo, F. Wind tunnel tests on hyperbolic paraboloid roofs with elliptical plane shapes. *Eng. Struct.* **2012**, *45*, 536–558. [CrossRef]
28. Rizzo, F.; D'Asdia, P.; Lazzari, M.; Procino, L. Wind action evaluation on tension roofs of hyperbolic paraboloid shape. *Eng. Struct.* **2011**, *33*, 445–461. [CrossRef]
29. Rizzo, F.; D'Asdia, P.; Procino, L.; Lazzari, M.; Olivato, G. Aerodynamic behavior of hyperbolic parabolic shaped roofs: Wind tunnel test, POD and CFD analysis. In Proceedings of the 12th International Conference on Civil, Structural and Environmental Engineering Computing (CC 2009), Madeira, Portugal, 1–4 September 2009.
30. Rizzo, F.; D'Asdia, P.; Lazzari, M.; Olivato, G. Aerodynamic behavior of hyperbolic paraboloid shaped roofs: POD and CFD analysis. In Proceedings of the 5th European & African Conference on Wind Engineering (EACWE 5 2009), Florence, Italy, 19–23 July 2009.
31. Rizzo, F.; D'Asdia, P.; Lazzari, M. Aerodynamic behavior of hyperbolic paraboloid shaped roofs: Wind tunnel tests. In Proceedings of the 5th European & African Conference on Wind Engineering (EACWE 5 2009), Florence, Italy, 19–23 July 2009.
32. Sykes, D.M. Wind loading tests on models of two tension structures for EXPO'92, Seville. *J. Wind Eng. Ind. Aerodyn.* **1994**, *52*, 371–383. [CrossRef]
33. Sun, X.; Wu, Y.; Yang, Q.; Shen, S. Wind tunnel tests on the aeroelastic behaviors of tension structures. In Proceedings of the VI International Colloquium on Bluff Bodies Aerodynamics & Applications, BBAA VI, Milan, Italy, 20–24 July 2008.
34. Rizzo, F.; Ricciardelli, F. Design pressure coefficients for circular and elliptical plan structures with hyperbolic paraboloid roof. *J. Eng. Struct.* **2017**, *139*, 153–169. [CrossRef]
35. Rizzo, F.; D'Asdia, P.; Ricciardelli, F.; Bartoli, G. Characterization of pressure coefficients on hyperbolic paraboloid roofs. *J. Wind Eng. Ind. Aerodyn.* **2012**, *102*, 61–71. [CrossRef]
36. Rizzo, F.; Barbato, M.; Sepe, V. Peak factor statistics of wind effects for hyperbolic paraboloid roofs. *Eng. Struct.* **2018**, *173*, 313–330. [CrossRef]
37. Liu, M.; Chen, X.; Yang, Q. Characteristics of dynamic pressures on a saddle type roof in various boundary layer flows. *J. Wind Eng. Ind. Aerodyn.* **2016**, *150*, 1–14. [CrossRef]

38. Brito, R.; Caracoglia, L. Extraction of flutter derivatives from small scale wind tunnel experiments. In Proceedings of the 11th Americas Conference on Wind Engineering, American Association for Wind Engineering (AAWE), San Juan, Puerto Rico, 22–26 June 2009.

39. Rizzo, F.; Caracoglia, L.; Montelpare, S. Predicting the flutter speed of a pedestrian suspension bridge through examination of laboratory experimental errors. *Eng. Struct.* **2018**, *172*, 589–613. [CrossRef]

40. Rizzo, F.; Caracoglia, L. Examining wind tunnel errors in Scanlan derivatives and flutter speed of a closed-box. *J. Wind Struct.* **2018**, *26*, 231–251.

41. Avossa, A.M.; Di Giacinto, D.; Malangone, P.; Rizzo, F. Seismic Retrofit of a Multi-Span Prestressed Concrete Girder Bridge with Friction Pendulum Devices. *Shock Vib.* **2018**. [CrossRef]

42. Daw, D.J.; Davenport, A.G. Aerodynamic damping and stiffness of a semi-circular roof in turbulent wind. *J. Wind Eng. Ind. Aerodyn.* **1989**, *32*, 83–92. [CrossRef]

43. Forster, B. Cable and membrane roofs, a historical survey. *Struct. Eng. Rev.* **1994**, *6*, 3–5.

44. Kassem, M.; Novak, M. Wind-Induced response of hemispherical air-supported Structures. *J. Wind Eng. Ind. Aerodyn.* **1992**, *41*, 177–178. [CrossRef]

45. Knudson, W.C. Recent advances in the field of long span tension structures. *Eng. Struct.* **1991**, *13*, 174–193. [CrossRef]

46. Pun, P.K.F.; Letchford, C.W. Analysis of a tension membrane HYPAR roof subjected to fluctuating wind loads. In Proceedings of the 3rd Asia-Pacific Symposium on Wind Engineering, Hong Kong, 13–15 December 1993; pp. 741–746.

47. Rizzo, F.; Sepe, V. Static loads to simulate dynamic effects of wind on hyperbolic paraboloid roofs with square plan. *J. Wind Eng. Ind. Aerodyn.* **2015**, *137*, 46–57. [CrossRef]

48. Shen, S.; Yang, Q. Wind-induced response analysis and wind-resistant design of hyperbolic paraboloid cable net structures. *Int. J. Space Struct.* **1999**, *14*, 57–65. [CrossRef]

49. Vassilopoulou, I.; Gantes, C.J. Nonlinear dynamic behavior of saddle form cable nets under uniform harmonic load. *Eng. Struct.* **2011**, *33*, 2762–2771. [CrossRef]

50. Vassilopoulou, I.; Gantes, C.J. Vibration modes and natural frequencies of saddle form cable nets. *Comput. Struct.* **2012**, *88*, 105–119. [CrossRef]

51. Vassilopoulou, I.; Petrini, F.; Gantes, C.J. Nonlinear dynamic behavior of cable nets subjected to wind loading. *Structures* **2017**, *10*, 170–183. [CrossRef]

52. Yang, Q.; Liu, R. On Aerodynamic Stability of Membrane Structures. *Int. J. Space Struct.* **2005**, *20*, 181–188. [CrossRef]

53. Suresh Kumar, K.; Stathopoulos, T. Wind loads on low building roofs: A stochastic perspective. *J. Struct. Eng.* **2000**, *126*, 944–956. [CrossRef]

Article

Optimization of Airfoils Using the Adjoint Approach and the Influence of Adjoint Turbulent Viscosity

Matthias Schramm [1,2,*], Bernhard Stoevesandt [2] and Joachim Peinke [1,2]

[1] ForWind, University of Oldenburg, Ammerländer Heerstr. 114-118, 26129 Oldenburg, Germany;
    peinke@uni-oldenburg.de

[2] Fraunhofer Institute for Wind Energy Systems, Küpkersweg 70, 26129 Oldenburg, Germany;
    bernhard.stoevesandt@iwes.fraunhofer.de

*   Correspondence: matthias.schramm@uni-oldenburg.de; Tel.: +49-441-798-5015

Received: 29 September 2017; Accepted: 17 January 2018; Published: date

Abstract: The adjoint approach in gradient-based optimization combined with computational fluid dynamics is commonly applied in various engineering fields. In this work, the gradients are used for the design of a two-dimensional airfoil shape, where the aim is a change in lift and drag coefficient, respectively, to a given target value. The optimizations use the unconstrained quasi-Newton method with an approximation of the Hessian. The flow field is computed with a finite-volume solver where the continuous adjoint approach is implemented. A common assumption in this approach is the use of the same turbulent viscosity in the adjoint diffusion term as for the primal flow field. The effect of this so-called "frozen turbulence" assumption is compared to the results using adjoints to the Spalart–Allmaras turbulence model. The comparison is done at a Reynolds number of $Re = 2 \times 10^6$ for two different airfoils at different angles of attack.

Keywords: airfoil optimization; gradient-based; adjoint approach; frozen turbulence; adjoint turbulence; OpenFOAM

---

1. Introduction

The design of aerodynamic shapes is increasingly based on Computational Fluid Dynamics (CFD). Since CFD is computationally more expensive than the coupling of potential flow theory with boundary layer corrections, a computationally inexpensive optimization technique is preferable. Stochastic search optimization methods require a large number of function evaluations [1], but gradient-based optimizations can be used in order to have fewer function calls. Gradients can be computed via finite differencing, however, the computational cost scales linearly with the number of design parameters [2]. In the adjoint approach, the influence of the primal flow field is decoupled from the gradients depending on the design parameters. This results in another set of Partial Differential Equations (PDEs), the adjoint equations, in which each adjoint variable refers to a variable of the flow field. Solving the adjoint equations has a comparable cost to solving the primal state equations [3] and the gradients can be computed from primal and adjoint fields with minor additional calculations compared to the CFD iterations. Practically, the gradient evaluation cost does not scale with the number of design parameters, in contrast to traditional finite differencing. Thus, the adjoint approach is often combined when using gradient-based optimization with many design parameters and CFD.

Two types of adjoint methods are known from the literature: the discrete method and the continuous method [4–6]. In the discrete approach, the adjoint equations are generated from the discretized flow equations, often via an automatic differentiation tool. This method is strongly connected to the selected flow solver and the discretization schemes of the primal state equations. If no approximations are used, the discrete approach leads to the exact gradients of the original discretized flow equations, but tend to have higher memory requirements [5].

In the continuous approach, the adjoint equations are derived analytically from the flow equations and are subsequently discretized. The discretization schemes can be different than the schemes of the primal flow equations and the continuous adjoints may need less memory as well as less computational effort [4,7]. The "physical significance of the adjoint variables is much clearer" [4] than in the discrete approach. It can be seen from the analytical adjoint equations that the adjoint field develops backwards in time and upstream to the primal flow. A known disadvantage of the continuous adjoint approach is that it can produce inaccurate gradients in turbulent flows [8], because the adjoints to the turbulence parameters are often neglected. This is the so-called "frozen turbulence" assumption [9]: The same turbulent viscosity from the primal Navier–Stokes equations is used in the adjoint equations.

In the first publications, discrete adjoints with "differentiated" turbulence models were implemented without an investigation of the effect on the optimization compared to frozen turbulence [10,11]. Lyu et al. [12] used discrete adjoints and the Spalart–Allmaras turbulence model for compressible flows. For the flow over a bump as simple verification case, they found clear differences between the gradients by frozen and adjoint turbulence. The main focus of their work was on the optimization of the ONERA M6 wing and the results of the optimizations were slightly better with adjoint turbulence, but there were also 70% higher computational costs. Osusky et al. [13] used discrete adjoints for drag reduction of wings in compressible flows. They compared the results by optimizations based on Euler and Reynolds-averaged Navier–Stokes (RANS) equations using the Spalart–Allmaras model and obtained inferior designs by the inviscid flow analysis. Besides other approximations, Dwight and Brezillon [14] investigated the effect of frozen turbulence, there called the "constant eddy-viscosity assumption". They used discrete adjoints in compressible flows and optimized airfoils at small angles of attack without any separation. In an optimization of a transonic airfoil, the frozen turbulence led to poorer optimization behavior compared to the exact adjoint gradients. In an optimization of a subsonic high-lift configuration, the gradients via frozen turbulence were as good as the exact gradients, but it is not clear if these results also hold for continuous adjoints in incompressible flows.

Zymaris et al. [15] derived a continuous adjoint approach to the Spalart–Allmaras turbulence model [16] in incompressible flows. They focused on the verification of the adjoint gradients for duct flows and investigated the effect of different terms in the adjoint turbulence model as well as in its boundary conditions. The resulting effect of frozen turbulence in external flows was not described. Bueno-Orovio et al. [17] derived a continuous adjoint approach to the Spalart–Allmaras model in compressible flows. For a transonic airfoil as well as a transonic wing at a small angle of attack, they showed that the frozen turbulence assumption leads to poorer optimization results compared to the shapes resulting from the inclusion of the adjoint turbulent viscosity. Papoutsis-Kiachagias and Giannakoglou [5] provided a good survey of the adjoints for turbulent flows, where they derived and extended various theoretical aspects. They also verified gradients at two-dimensional airfoils and computed sensitivities for different aerodynamic shapes. Several industrial examples are shown, but an airfoil optimization using the presented approaches is not discussed. Kavvadias et al. [18] derived the continuous adjoints approach to the k-ω-SST turbulence model and verified the resulting gradients. Optimization results of ducts using frozen and adjoint turbulence are shown. Also, an optimization of an airfoil with thickness constraint is presented, where the gradients of both approaches are compared as well. However, a detailed comparison of the optimization results using frozen and adjoint turbulence for airfoil shapes is missing.

Since the effect of adjoint turbulence in the continuous approach on the resulting shapes in incompressible, subsonic flows around airfoils have been rarely investigated, it is the aim of our work to compare these results to frozen turbulence in airfoil optimization. Besides, a complete procedure for shape optimization is presented, which may inspire interested readers to develop their own frameworks. The continuous adjoints are used and the adjoints to the turbulence model are implemented following the derivation by Zymaris et al. [15]. The incompressible, steady-state Reynolds-averaged Navier–Stokes equations (RANS) are closed by the Spalart–Allmaras turbulence model [16] without transition. The flow is computed with the open-source code OpenFOAM-2.3.0 [19] based on the Finite Volume Method (FVM). The code is written in C++ and strongly uses the capabilities of object-oriented programming. Although Towara and Naumann [20] use discrete adjoints with OpenFOAM, more often the continuous approach is followed when using this flow solver [21,22]. As this code is very suitable for the implementation of analytical equations, as well as the expected lower memory costs, continuous adjoints are used in our work. The basic equations of this approach have already been implemented by Othmer et al. [23], but their implementation has been made for ducted flows. There, the flow is optimized via a change of the cell porosity, modeling "walls" by obstacles with high porosity blocking. In our work, the shape of the airfoil is changed by the motion of the mesh and the solver is extended to external aerodynamics. The comparison is done for two airfoils and at different angles of attack in order to change the flow complexity.

As an outline for this work, firstly the implementation of a precise and stable mesh motion, which is essential for the later processes, is described in Section 2. Then, a short description of the general adjoint approach follows in Section 3 with the details and simplifications made in the presented implementation. The gradients by the adjoint method are verified and the projection of the gradients to a spline parametrization is described. Finally in Section 4, the effects of frozen and adjoint turbulence on shape optimization of airfoils in incompressible flows are compared.

2. Mesh Motion

During the optimization process, the flow around the changed shape has to be re-computed, which means that the mesh has either to be "re-meshed" completely or the mesh points have to be moved from their previous or initial position. The former approach is more suitable for large geometry changes, but requires more time. The latter method is more suitable for small changes in the shape and requires less time. In any case, it is essential for the optimization that the generated mesh delivers smooth results of the objective function in order to have low noise in the gradients. The flow simulations have to be independent from the mesh deformation.

Since the expected changes in the airfoil shapes are small, the mesh is moved during the optimization in this work. The mesh motion techniques in OpenFOAM are made for general purposes and are not necessarily suitable for airfoil design. Internal tests led to deformed or even overlapping cells, which are obstructive for the computation of the flow around airfoils, in particular in the boundary layer. In order to accurately resolve the boundary layer flow, the meshes at high Reynolds numbers (Re) have a small off-wall distance. Any inaccuracies in mesh deformation such as overlapping cells, increased skewness, or higher non-orthogonality can disrupt the whole optimization process. This is why a robust mesh motion technique is implemented based on the principle from Jameson and Reuther [24]. In a hexahedral mesh, the points in the near and far field are moved according to the movement of the surface points x_S. For this purpose, each surface point is considered as the starting point of a spline reaching from the airfoil to the end of the domain. This is shown in an example in Figure 1 for a single spline.

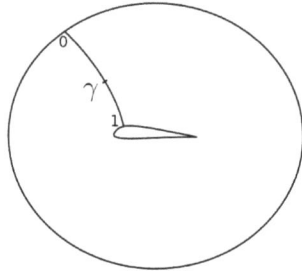

Figure 1. Example spline from the airfoil to the far field with interpolation factor γ.

In order to keep the far-field borders of the domain constant, the motion is linearly interpolated with a factor $\gamma = 0, ..., 1$ ($\gamma = 1$ at the airfoil and $\gamma = 0$ at the far field):

$$x^{new} = x^{old} + \gamma(x_S^{new} - x_S^{old}) \,, \tag{1}$$

where x represents the point positions of the numerical grid and the index S stands for the airfoil surface. In order to show the capabilities of this mesh motion, an example is shown in Figure 2 as a close-up view of the suction side of an airfoil.

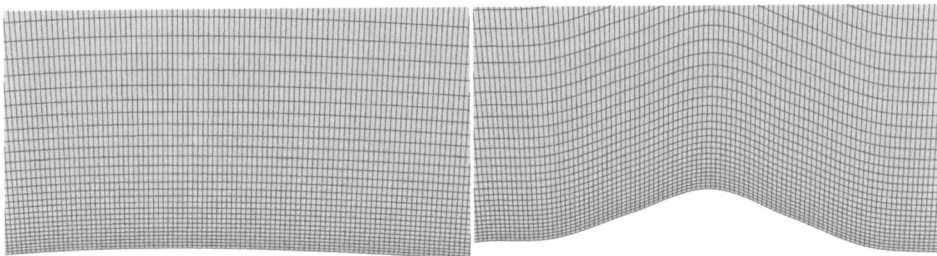

Figure 2. Mesh deformation of the suction side of an airfoil.

The initial mesh is deformed via different spline coordinates of the airfoil and the produced bump on the airfoil is smoothly transferred into the internal mesh with a linear relaxation as in Equation (1). The deformations of the following sections are much smaller and this example is only used in order to show the capabilities of this technique.

As implemented here, the motion technique works only for hexahedral meshes, but for small and smooth shape changes it ensures the same quality of the boundary layer close to the geometry, which is an essential requirement for a successful optimization.

3. The Adjoint Approach

3.1. The General Principle

The derivation of the adjoint approach can be found in the literature [3,4,9,10,15,25,26] and for the sake of brevity only the basic principles are described here according to the notation of Soto and Löhner [27]. Let I be the objective function, which shall be optimized with respect to the design parameters β, and R be the steady-state incompressible Navier–Stokes equations. Then, the optimization problem can be written as:

$$\text{minimize } I(u, p, \beta) \text{ with respect to } \beta \tag{2}$$
$$\text{subject to } R(u, p, \beta) = 0 \text{ in } \Omega \,,$$

where (u, p) are flow variables in the flow domain Ω. Objective function and equality constraints can be combined via a Lagrange function L:

$$L = I + \int_{\Omega} \Psi^T \cdot R \, d\Omega \,, \tag{3}$$

where Ψ are the Lagrangian multipliers or as they are often called, the adjoint variables. A variation of the Lagrangian leads to:

$$\delta L = \left(\frac{\partial I}{\partial \beta} + \int_{\Omega} (\mathbf{\Psi}_u^T, \mathbf{\Psi}_p) \cdot \frac{\partial \mathbf{R}}{\partial \beta} \, d\Omega \right) \delta \beta$$
$$+ \left(\frac{\partial I}{\partial \mathbf{u}} + \int_{\Omega} \mathbf{\Psi}_u^T \cdot \frac{\partial \mathbf{R}^u}{\partial \mathbf{u}} \, d\Omega \right) \delta \mathbf{u} \qquad (4)$$
$$+ \left(\frac{\partial I}{\partial p} + \int_{\Omega} \mathbf{\Psi}_p \cdot \frac{\partial R^p}{\partial p} \, d\Omega \right) \delta p \; ,$$

where $\mathbf{\Psi}^T = (\mathbf{\Psi}_u^T, \mathbf{\Psi}_p)$ denote the adjoints to velocity and pressure.

The adjoint variables $\mathbf{\Psi}$ can now be defined in such a way that the last two brackets become zero, which leads to a new set of PDEs for the adjoint variables, making δL independent of any variation $(\delta \mathbf{u}, \delta p)$ of the flow field. Equation (4) then simplifies to the following gradient expression:

$$\frac{\delta L}{\delta \beta} = \frac{\partial I}{\partial \beta} + \int_{\Omega} (\mathbf{\Psi}_u^T, \mathbf{\Psi}_p) \cdot \frac{\partial \mathbf{R}}{\partial \beta} \, d\Omega \; . \qquad (5)$$

Since the flow field does not have to be computed for each design variable again as with finite differences, this basically means that the gradient computation becomes independent from the amount of design parameters. As a matter of fact, some extra computations have to be done, which scale with the number of design parameters, but these are insignificant compared with the effort of the remaining CFD iterations. Finally, the geometry can be parametrized by every surface grid point without an increase in the computational costs, which is the strength of the adjoint approach.

3.2. Adjoint Equations and Gradient Calculation

The general adjoint equations are derived via integration by parts from the Navier–Stokes equations. Further details can be found in common literature [15,23,25,27], where the following form is often found for steady-state and incompressible flows:

$$-\nabla \mathbf{\Psi}_u \cdot \mathbf{u} - (\mathbf{u} \cdot \nabla) \mathbf{\Psi}_u = \nabla \mathbf{\Psi}_p + \nabla \cdot \left[\nu \left(\nabla \mathbf{\Psi}_u + (\nabla \mathbf{\Psi}_u)^T \right) \right] \; , \qquad (6)$$

$$-\nabla \cdot \mathbf{\Psi}_u = 0 \; , \qquad (7)$$

with the kinematic viscosity ν. The first term on the left-hand side of Equation (6), the so-called "adjoint transpose convection", can lead to diverging simulations. Following the suggestions from Önder [21] and Choi et al. [28], the integration by parts is not necessary in the derivation of the adjoint transpose convection. This leads to the following more stable adjoint momentum equation, which is used in this work:

$$(\nabla \mathbf{u})^T \cdot \mathbf{\Psi}_u - (\mathbf{u} \cdot \nabla) \mathbf{\Psi}_u = \nabla \mathbf{\Psi}_p + \nabla \cdot \left[\nu \left(\nabla \mathbf{\Psi}_u + (\nabla \mathbf{\Psi}_u)^T \right) \right] \; . \qquad (8)$$

Soto and Löhner [27] derived the gradients for the optimization of total forces (pressure-based and viscous) leading to the following expression:

$$\frac{\delta L}{\delta \beta} = \frac{\partial I}{\partial \beta} - \int_S (\nabla p \cdot \mathbf{n}) (\mathbf{\Psi}_u \cdot \mathbf{n}) \, dS$$
$$- \int_S \mathbf{\Psi}_p \, \mathbf{n} \, (\mathbf{n} \cdot \nabla \mathbf{u}) \, dS$$
$$- \int_S \nu \, \mathbf{n} \left[\nabla \mathbf{\Psi}_u + (\nabla \mathbf{\Psi}_u)^T \right] \cdot (\mathbf{n} \cdot \nabla \mathbf{u}) \, dS$$
$$+ \int_S \nu \left[\nabla (\mathbf{n} \cdot \nabla \mathbf{u}) + (\nabla (\mathbf{n} \cdot \nabla \mathbf{u}))^T \right] \cdot \mathbf{n} \, dS \; , \qquad (9)$$

where S is the domain boundary at the airfoil. Due to a zero Neumann boundary condition of the pressure at the geometry, the first integral vanishes and omitting the second order term leads to an expression similar to the one of other authors [9,15,25,29]. Castro et al. [25] showed that the so-called "geometric term" $\frac{\partial I}{\partial \beta}$ in Equation (9) vanishes in the case of force optimization (for fully converged solutions of the incompressible or compressible Navier–Stokes equations). This was also shown by others [29,30] in different ways and thus, Equation (9) is further simplified to the final expression used in this work:

$$
\begin{aligned}
\frac{\delta L}{\delta \beta} = & - \int_S \Psi_p\, n\, (n \cdot \nabla u)\ dS \\
& - \int_S \nu\, n \left(\nabla \Psi_u + (\nabla \Psi_u)^T \right) \cdot (n \cdot \nabla u)\ dS\ ,
\end{aligned}
\tag{10}
$$

where from the authors' experience the last term is the most dominant one, independent of the Reynolds number.

Since there is no effect of the objective function in Equation (10), the boundary conditions (BCs) have to include a connection to the objectives of the optimization. Zymaris et al. [15] derive the mathematically correct boundary conditions for the far field and walls. From the authors' experience at small, laminar Reynolds numbers, the correct boundary conditions at the far field do not affect the gradient at the airfoil (unless the domain is too small), but can easily lead to unstable convergence behavior. This is why here, standard Dirichlet and Neumann boundary conditions are used at the far field, where the adjoint BCs are opposite to the primal BCs, as was also done by Soto and Löhner [27]. The condition for the adjoint pressure Ψ_p at the wall is a zero Neumann condition, and the condition for the adjoint velocity is the negative force direction [27]:

$$
\Psi_u = -d \quad \text{at } S\ ,
\tag{11}
$$

where d is the direction vector of the force to be optimized, here the direction of lift or drag, respectively.

3.3. Details of the Present Implementation

OpenFOAM-2.3.0 comes with a solver using the adjoint approach for the optimization of ducted flows [23], which are optimized by inserting cells with high porosity blocking in the domain. This solver is extended to external aerodynamics by the authors, so the approach of porous cells is replaced by walls and the complete gradient calculation is redefined according to Equation (10). Note, the objective function for airfoil optimization is different than in most duct optimizations, which has to be considered in the gradient calculation.

Besides the use of the stable adjoint transpose convection in Equation (8), it is reasonable to use a finer mesh and a better convergence than for standard airfoil simulations with RANS, because the adjoints are based on the flow variables and any error of the primal field is amplified in the adjoint variables. A high convergence of the RANS equations improves the accuracy of the gradients and thus the convergence and the results of the optimization.

Instead of using the SIMPLE algorithm (Semi-Implicit Method for Pressure Linked Equations [31]), which is implemented in the standard adjoint solver of OpenFOAM, the SIMPLEC algorithm (SIMPLE-consistent [32]) is used in this work for the solution of primal and adjoint fields. The algorithm needs nearly no under-relaxation and thus, it is faster than the initial implementation. Internal tests showed that the time for convergence is reduced by half, which is particularly beneficial for the adjoint approach, since two sets of PDEs have to be solved.

The "adjoint turbulence model", i.e., the adjoints to the Spalart–Allmaras turbulence model [16], is implemented based on the derivation by Zymaris et al. [15]. For the sake of brevity, the final equations are shown in Appendix C only. A simplification in our implementation is the use of standard Neumann and Dirichlet boundary conditions for the adjoint eddy-viscosity at the far field. Zymaris showed an insignificant effect of the exact far-field BCs on the gradient and Bueno-Orovio et al. [17] used "characteristic" boundary conditions. The authors' experience with far-field BCs on airfoils at low Reynolds numbers showed that Neumann and Dirichlet conditions do not negatively affect the gradient computation on the airfoil (unless the domain is clearly too small). As a matter of fact, standard BCs increase the stability when solving the adjoint equations.

The inclusion of the adjoint turbulence model can be beneficial for the solution and optimization process, which will be shown later. However, the solution of an additional PDE, the adjoint Spalart–Allmaras model, requires extra computing time: In the presented cases, the solution with adjoint turbulence took roughly twice the time of frozen turbulence. Note, the flow and adjoint solutions were pre-converged with the same level of convergence, which influences the following solution process with frozen and adjoint turbulence differently. Because the numerous optimizations were done in parallel on the same computer, which would bias a fair comparison, the following comparisons use the number of function evaluations and not the computing time as measure.

3.4. Projection of the Gradients of the Objective Function

Using each airfoil coordinate as an individual design parameter can easily lead to kinks or unwanted bumps in the shape due to limited spatial discretization. In order to overcome such problems, additional smoothing approaches can be used, e.g., use of regularization methods [33–35]. The airfoil shape in this work is defined via a set of Catmull–Rom splines [36], which are connected to each other leading to a smooth airfoil representation. The splines are already available in OpenFOAM and a single spline is described by the following equation:

$$
\begin{aligned}
X(m) = C_{-1} &\left(-\frac{1}{2}m^3 + m^2 - \frac{1}{2}m \right) \\
+ C_0 &\left(\frac{3}{2}m^3 - \frac{5}{2}m^2 + 1 \right) \\
+ C_1 &\left(-\frac{3}{2}m^3 + 2m^2 + \frac{1}{2}m \right) \\
+ C_2 &\left(\frac{1}{2}m^3 - \frac{1}{2}m^2 \right) ,
\end{aligned}
\tag{12}
$$

where m is the spline index, C_i are the control points, and $X(m)$ is the resulting airfoil point. The adjoint approach, as it is implemented here, cannot handle discontinuities, which occur at the trailing edge corners [37,38]. Thus, the trailing edge is fixed and only the points of the suction and pressure side are allowed to move.

Since the use of splines is not a direct parametrization, the gradients of the objective function at the airfoil points have to be projected into a lower-dimensional space to the control points C_i of each spline. This smooths the initial gradient information and thus avoids kinks. For a given objective function $I = I\left(X_j(C_i)\right)$ the projection can be written as:

$$
\frac{\partial I}{\partial C_i} = \frac{\partial}{\partial C_i} I\left(X_j(C_i)\right) = \sum_{j=1}^{n} \frac{\partial I}{\partial X_j} \frac{\partial X_j}{\partial C_i} ,
\tag{13}
$$

where n is the number of airfoil points represented by each spline. $\frac{\partial I}{\partial X_j}$ are the computed gradients on each airfoil grid point and $\frac{\partial X_j}{\partial C_i}$ are the terms within the brackets of Equation (12). In the following section, different numbers of spline points are used in order to investigate their effects on the optimization result, but it must be noted that too few spline points cannot properly represent the initial airfoil shape. Hence, a minimum of 20 control points is used in this work.

3.5. Verification of Gradients

Before using the gradients from the adjoint approach in an optimization, it is a common procedure in the literature to verify the correct implementation of the gradients. Verification in laminar flow at a small Reynolds number was done by the authors [39], where an excellent agreement of the adjoint gradients against gradients by finite differences was presented. The reference in this work is also computed via forward finite differences (FDs). Another possibility to compute reference gradients is the complex step method [40], but this is out of the scope of this work and may be considered in future work.

Figure 3 shows a NACA 0012 and the 26 control points of the spline defining the airfoil shape, where 13 points are on the suction and pressure side, each.

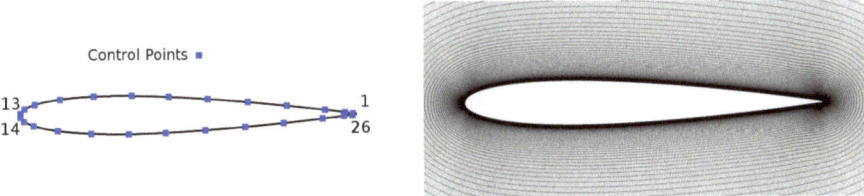

Figure 3. Control points of the verification case and close-up view of the mesh near the airfoil.

The Reynolds number of the verification case is $Re = 2 \times 10^6$, where the flow is fully turbulent. The angle of attack (AoA) is at $2°$ and the mesh consists of $208,000$ cells in total, with 800 faces on the airfoil. A hexahedral O-mesh is used and the domain has a radius of 45 chord lengths. The dimensionless wall distance is at $y^+ \approx 0.1$ in order to fully resolve the flow in the boundary layer and Figure 3 shows a close-up view of the mesh near the airfoil.

For the sake of brevity, a mesh independency study for this angle of attack and at $AoA = 12°$, as well as a validation with experimental results by Ladson [41], is presented in Appendix A.

The resulting gradients via the adjoint approach as in Equation (10) and by finite differences are shown in Figure 4 along the indices of the control points (labeled as in Figure 3). The objectives are the lift coefficient c_l and, respectively, the drag coefficient c_d. A step size study was done by using different step sizes for the computation of finite differences, which is presented in Appendix B. The step sizes with nearly no change in the gradients, representing optimal sizes in order to avoid round-off and truncation errors, were found to be between 5×10^{-8} and 1×10^{-7}. The gradients are computed with respect to the point motion in a normal direction. Using the adjoint approach, they are computed by the frozen turbulence assumption and by using the adjoint turbulence model, respectively.

The gradients are scaled in order to enable a better comparison, which is done for both the adjoint gradients and the gradients by finite differences (Kim et al. [42] showed that the step size can influence the size of the gradients, which could result from the non-linear nature of the Navier–Stokes equations). In general, it can be seen that the gradients using adjoint turbulence follow the trend of the finite differences better than the frozen turbulence approach, where some gradients even have a wrong sign. Still, a deviation is visible between the reference gradients by finite differences (FDs) and the adjoint gradients, which could possibly result from the complex flow due to high turbulence near the trailing edge.

However, it can be concluded that the implementation of the adjoint turbulence model leads to a better representation of the reference gradients than the frozen turbulence assumption. Further, it is not clear how the differences between these two approaches affect the optimization processes, which is the focus of this work and will be shown in the following section.

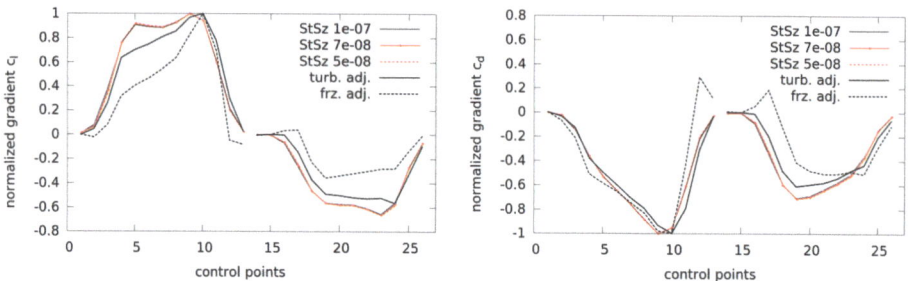

Figure 4. Comparisons of gradients obtained by finite differences (FsD) and gradients via the adjoint approach for lift objective ("gradient c_l") and drag objective ("gradient c_d"). Different step sizes (StSz) are used for finite differencing. Adjoint and frozen turbulence are used for gradients via the adjoint approach (labeled as "adj. turb" and "frz. turb", respectively).

3.6. Inverse Design

The optimizations in this work are gradient-based without any stochastic elements and can only find local optima [1,2,6]. This means that very different initial shapes converge to different optima, whereas more similar shapes converge to the same, but local, optimum (unless only one single optimum, the global one, exists). The adjoint approach is used for the gradient computation as previously discussed, and in order to increase the speed of the optimization process a quasi-Newton method is used, which approximates second-order derivatives. Here, the BFGS algorithm by Broyden, Fletcher, Goldfarb and Shanno [2] is used for updating the Hessian and the described set-up for the gradient computation is combined with the optimization module from SciPy [43], based on the programming language Python. This module offers a high flexibility for various applications and makes it easy to switch between different optimization algorithms or procedures.

All optimizations are unconstrained single-point optimizations for the lift and drag coefficients, respectively. In order to reach a certain lift coefficient $c_{l,aim}$ or drag coefficient $c_{d,aim}$, the objective functions are formulated in a quadratic form:

$$I_{l/d} = \frac{1}{2}\left(1 - \frac{c_{l/d}}{c_{l/d,aim}}\right)^2 , \qquad (14)$$

where the index $_{l/d}$ is used as a place holder for either the lift or the drag coefficient.

This formulation allows a clear convergence criterion of the objective function due to its convexity. In contrast, a pure maximization of lift or pure minimization of drag without any constraints or bounds is less suitable, since it would strongly depend on the number of control points and the mesh deformation would probably limit the process at some point, leading to wrong solutions of the primal flow field. Thus, the quadratic form of Equation (14) is used.

Although the posed optimization problem is unconstrained, it already gives insight into the effect of frozen and adjoint turbulence, as will be shown in the following section. Depending on the number of design parameters, the problem in Equation (14) may result in many possible solutions. However, for a gradient-based optimization with small shape deformations it is expected that the possible optima are close to each other. Furthermore, the resulting shapes indicate the distribution of the gradients, and thus give valuable information about the optimization process.

In order to provide a proof of concept of the optimization framework, a simple inverse study is conducted, where a known optimal geometry is reproduced.

The same mesh and geometry as in the previous gradient verification are used, again at $Re = 2 \times 10^6$ and $AoA = 2°$. Adjoint turbulence is used, and the airfoil is represented by a spline with 30 control points. First, the lift of the NACA 0012 is increased by 20%. Then, this geometry is optimized such that the aim is the lift coefficient of the initial NACA airfoil. The same procedure is followed for a drag optimization, where the initial NACA 0012 is optimized for a drag decrease of 3%.

The history of function values of forward and inverse design are shown in Figure 5 for the lift and drag objectives, respectively. Also in the same plot, the supremum norm of the gradient is shown and it can be seen that all optimizations converge well. During the optimization, the flow and adjoint equations are converged to residuals of at least 10^{-10} and 10^{-7}, respectively. First, the RANS equations are converged, then the adjoints are computed based on the solved RANS field, and afterwards the gradient information or function value is transferred to the optimizer. With this information, the mesh is moved accordingly, but not during the solution process of the primal or adjoint fields. This procedure is also used in the following optimizations.

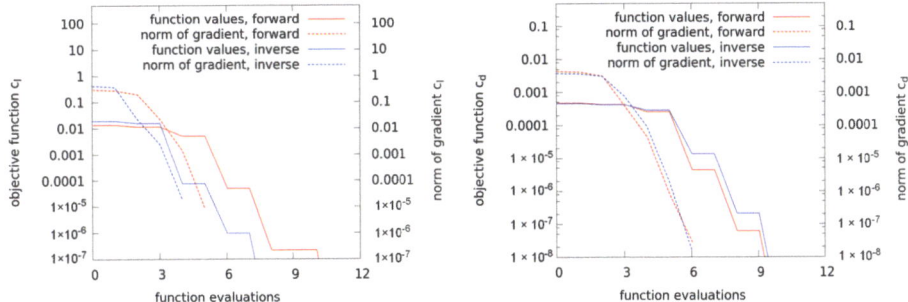

Figure 5. Objective functions as in Equation (14) and norm of the gradient for the lift objective and drag objective along the number of function evaluations.

Figure 6 shows the initial and corresponding optimized shapes of forward and inverse design. It can be seen that the initial NACA 0012 can be reproduced by the inverse design and thus, the optimization procedure works as expected.

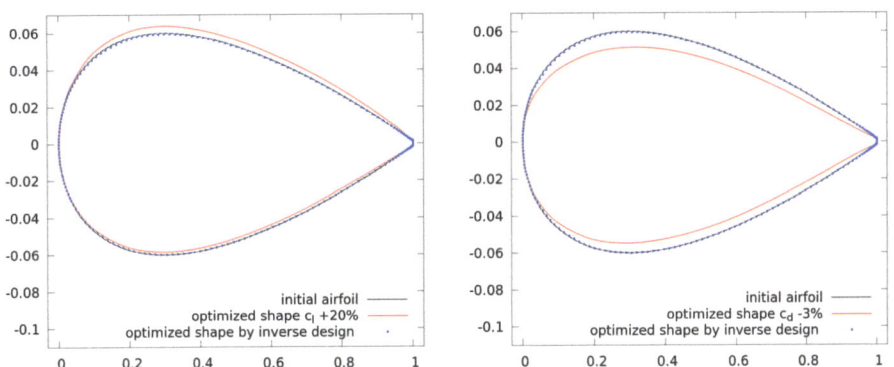

Figure 6. Shapes of inverse design study for the lift objective and drag objective. For a better visualization of the inverse design, only every third point is plotted.

4. Optimization of Airfoils

In the following optimizations, the design parameters are the coordinates of the spline control points, which are equally distributed along the airfoil. The trailing edge is fixed and the splines are parametrized by 20, 30, and 50 control points (abbreviated by "cp") in order to investigate their effect on the optimization process. As in the previous inverse design study, the optimizations aim at certain lift or drag coefficients, respectively, and the objective functions are formulated as in Equation (14). The flow solutions in the optimizations are pre-converged and the compared cases have the same level of pre-convergence.

4.1. NACA 0012 at $AoA = 2°$

The initial airfoil for the first comparisons is the NACA 0012 at a Reynolds number of $Re = 2 \times 10^6$ and an angle of attack of $AoA = 2°$. The mesh and general set-up are the same as for the verification of the adjoint gradients and the inverse design of the previous section. Different numbers of spline control points are used.

Figure 7 shows the convergence of the lift and drag optimizations. The objective for the lift is an increase of the lift coefficient by 20%. The lift optimizations all lead to a convergent solution. More control points (labeled as "XXcp") require more function evaluations.

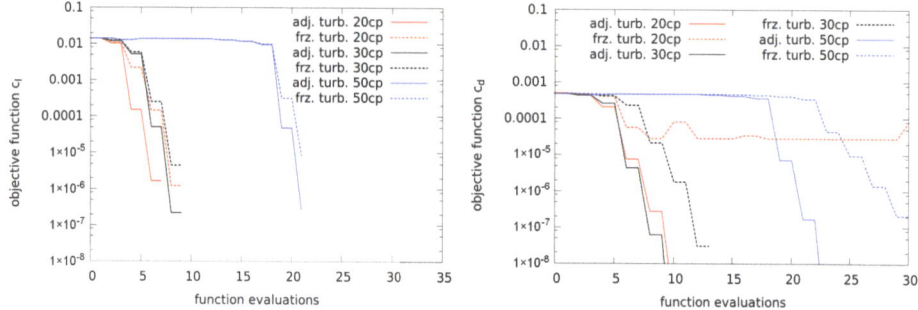

Figure 7. Objective functions for lift and drag as in Equation (14) along the number of function evaluations for the NACA 0012 at $AoA = 2°$. Frozen as well as adjoint turbulence are used. The number of control points is labeled as "XXcp".

The objective of the drag optimizations is a decrease of the drag coefficient by 3%. Most cases lead to a convergent solution and only the case with frozen turbulence and 20 control points does not converge well. In order to investigate this, the gradients of the first optimization steps are plotted in Figure 8. In order to be able to compare the gradients with a different amount of control points, the gradients by 20 and 50 control points are scaled in the x-direction to match the gradients by 30 control points.

Different conclusions can be drawn from the graph. Firstly, the size of the gradients depends on the number of control points. This follows from the summation during the projection from higher to lower-dimensional space (see Equation (13)) and fewer control points need to include more information of the gradients. Secondly, the gradients obtained by frozen turbulence are smaller than the ones by adjoint turbulence. Thirdly, compared to the highest values by 20 control points and adjoint turbulence, the use of frozen turbulence leads to slightly stronger gradients near the trailing edge (at low and high numbering of control points, respectively). This results into a different shape at the trailing edge, as shown in Figure 9 (see the shape with 20 cp and frozen turbulence), where the solution of the flow as well as the adjoints may be wrong and the optimizer is not able to generate a clearly better shape from this point.

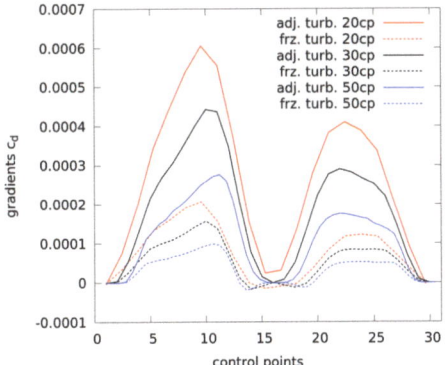

Figure 8. Gradients of the first optimization step for a decrease in drag by 3% at $AoA = 2°$. Frozen as well as adjoint turbulence are used. The number of control points is labeled as "XXcp". The control points start from the trailing edge on the suction side, pass the leading edge, and end at the trailing edge on the pressure side.

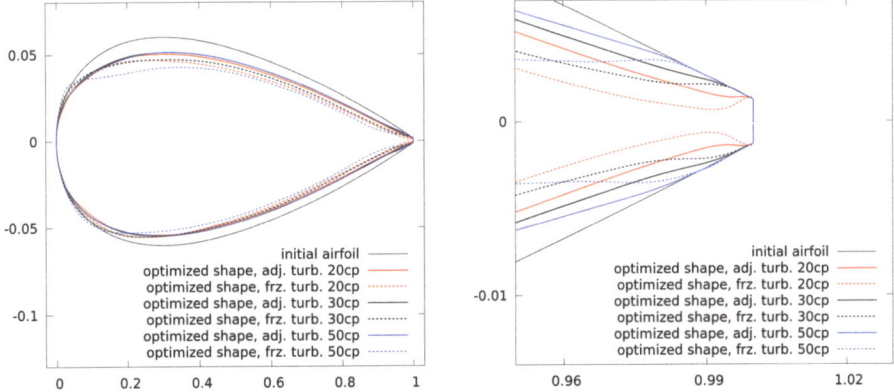

Figure 9. Airfoil shapes using adjoint and frozen turbulence for the NACA 0012 at $AoA = 2°$. The objective is a decrease in drag by 3%. Frozen as well as adjoint turbulence are used. The number of control points is labeled as "XXcp".

4.2. NACA 0012 at $AoA = 12°$

As a next step, the angle of attack is increased to $AoA = 12°$, which is closer to the stall, and flow separation becomes more dominant. The mesh and general set-up are the same as before. Since the initial lift and drag coefficients at this angle are much higher than in the previous case, an increase in lift by only 2% and a decrease in drag by only 1% is aimed for.

Figure 10 shows the convergence of the lift and drag optimization using the same nomenclature as before. For the lift objective, it can be seen that the cases using adjoint turbulence converge well, but the cases with frozen turbulence do not converge at all.

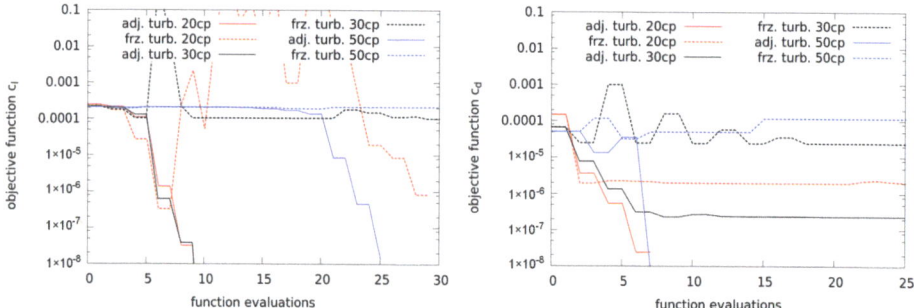

Figure 10. Objective functions for lift and drag as in Equation (14) along the number of function evaluations for the NACA 0012 at $AoA = 12°$. Frozen as well as adjoint turbulence are used. The number of control points is labeled as "XXcp".

The reason for this poorer behavior using frozen turbulence can be found in the gradients shown in Figure 11, where the gradients of the first optimization step are plotted. Again, in order to be able to compare the gradients with a different number of control points, the gradients by 20 and 50 control points are scaled in the x-direction to match the gradients by 30 control points.

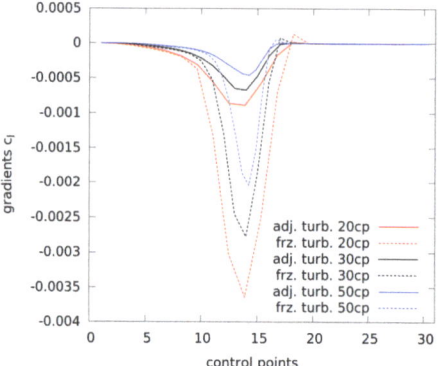

Figure 11. Gradients of the first optimization step for an increase in lift by 2% at $AoA = 12°$. Frozen as well as adjoint turbulence are used. The number of control points is labeled as "XXcp". The control points start from the trailing edge on the suction side, pass the leading edge, and end at the trailing edge on the pressure side.

As before, due to the summation during the projection of gradients (see Equation (13)), the gradients with more design variables are smaller than the ones with fewer design variables. Besides, it can be seen that the gradients obtained by frozen turbulence are clearly bigger than the ones computed by adjoint turbulence, and show a deviating trend. These stronger gradients appear near the leading edge on the suction side and lead to a larger deformation at this part of the airfoil, which is shown in Figure 12 for an intermediate step with 30 control points and frozen turbulence.

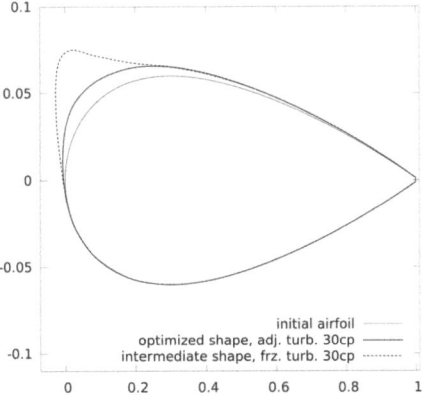

Figure 12. Intermediate airfoil shape during an optimization of lift at $AoA = 12°$ using frozen turbulence compared to the initial airfoil and the final shape using adjoint turbulence (all with 30 control points).

The intermediate shape shows a stronger deformation of the leading edge on the suction side and with this shape, the adjoint equations do not properly converge, which leads to even worse gradient information afterwards. The optimization cannot recover from this and it explains the poor convergence of the optimization processes using frozen turbulence in Figure 10.

Figure 10 also shows the convergence of the drag optimization and it can be seen that the cases using adjoint turbulence converge better than the cases using frozen turbulence, where some do not converge at all. Still, the distinction is not as clear as for the lift optimization. There is a stronger dependence on the number of design variables, which may result from a higher sensitivity of the drag coefficient on the mesh motion and a higher influence of friction forces. Also, this comparison shows that a drag optimization at this angle of attack with early beginning of flow separation seems to be more challenging than the previous cases. The deviation of gradients obtained by the adjoint approach from gradients by finite differences, presented in Section 3.5, leads to this problem, which can follow from the simplifications discussed in Section 3.3. However, these are required for stable convergence of the adjoint system, which cannot be simply solved by using finer meshes.

Figure 13 shows the final shapes from the lift and drag optimization at $AoA = 12°$. For the lift, it can be seen that the shapes using adjoint turbulence are similar, whereas the shapes using frozen turbulence all differ from each other, which is a result of the wrong initial and following gradients. For the drag optimization, the shapes are all a little different from each other. Since the drag has a higher sensitivity to the shape, even small differences lead to a relatively strong impact on the objective function.

It can be concluded that in more complex cases (an increased angle of attack is more complex because of the beginning of separation) the use of adjoint turbulence is beneficial and leads to a better convergence behavior than in cases when frozen turbulence is used. The negative influence of the frozen turbulence assumption could become even worse when constraints are used in multi-objective optimization or more precise approximations of the Hessians are needed.

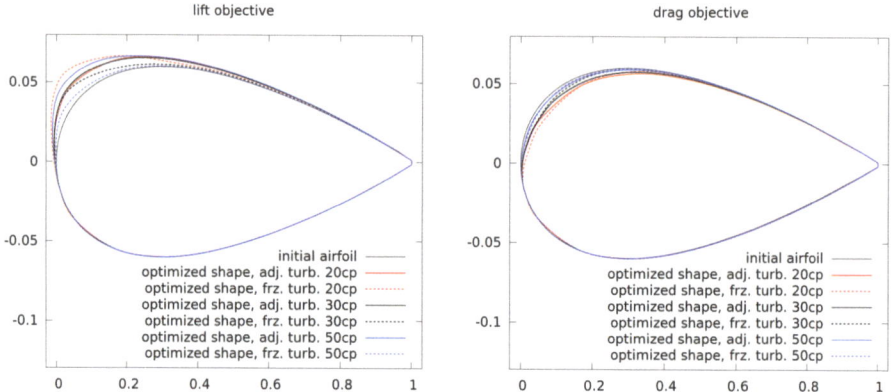

Figure 13. Airfoil shapes using adjoint and frozen turbulence for the lift and drag objective with NACA 0012 at $AoA = 12°$. Frozen as well as adjoint turbulence are used. The number of control points is labeled as "XXcp".

4.3. DU 93-W-210 at $AoA = 2°$

The following comparison uses a wind turbine airfoil DU 93-W-210 developed at TU Delft by Timmer and van Rooij [44]. It is specially designed for the use on wind turbines and has a stronger camber as well as a higher thickness (21%) than the previous shape. It is aerodynamically optimized for a high lift-to-drag ratio, which makes the airfoil an interesting object for optimization. The general set-up of the simulations is as before, the mesh has the same size and quality, and the Reynolds number is again $Re = 2 \times 10^6$. The angle of attack is at $AoA = 2°$, where this airfoil has a higher lift and drag than the previous NACA airfoil. Thus, the objective is to increase the lift coefficient by only 7% and to decrease the drag by 3%.

Figure 14 shows the convergence of the lift and drag optimization, where the convergence of frozen and adjoint turbulence is very similar. Only in the case of 50 control points is a clearly higher number of function evaluations required, which may result from more steps in order to compute the approximated Hessian, and this case does not scale linearly.

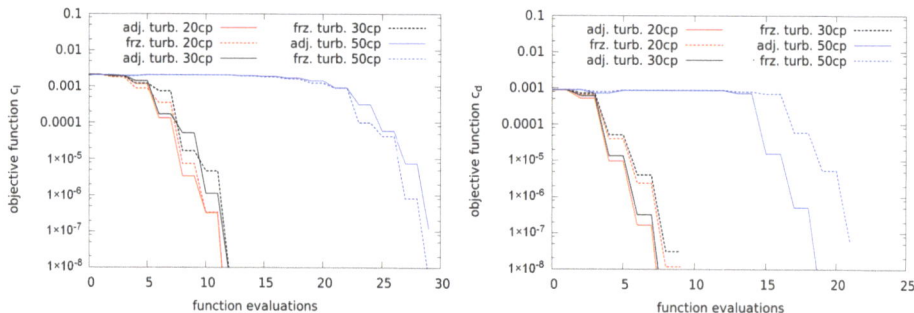

Figure 14. Objective functions for lift and drag as in Equation (14) along the number of function evaluations for the DU 93-W-210 at $AoA = 2°$. Frozen as well as adjoint turbulence is used. The number of control points is labeled as "XXcp".

The final shapes of the lift and drag optimizations are shown in Figure 15. The higher lift is gained by an increase in camber and thickness. The differences between shapes generated by adjoint and frozen turbulence are small. The lower drag is gained by a decrease in camber and thickness. Again, the differences between shapes generated by adjoint and frozen turbulence are small.

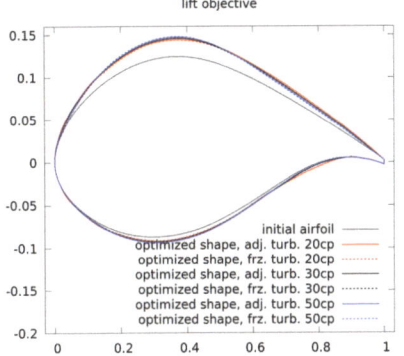
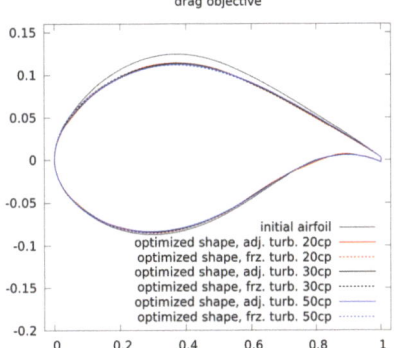

Figure 15. Airfoil shapes using adjoint and frozen turbulence for the lift and drag objective for DU 93-W-210 at $AoA = 2°$. Frozen as well as adjoint turbulence are used. The number of control points is labeled as "XXcp".

4.4. DU 93-W-210 at $AoA = 6°$

Due to a different curvature and thickness, the DU 93-W-210 has different aerodynamic characteristics than the symmetric NACA airfoil. The lift of the DU airfoil drops less strongly in the stall, but the airfoil stalls a few degrees earlier. That is why the following optimizations are conducted at $AoA = 6°$, which is little before the stall in fully-turbulent flow. The objectives are an increase in lift by 3% and a decrease in drag by 2%.

Figure 16 shows the convergence of the lift and drag optimization, where the convergence of frozen and adjoint turbulence is similar.

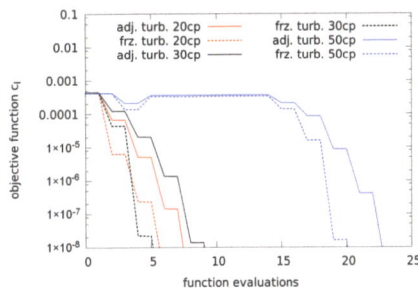
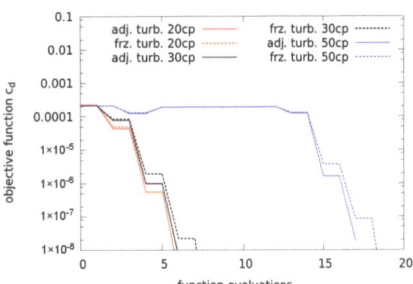

Figure 16. Objective functions for lift and drag as in Equation (14) along the number of function evaluations for the DU 93-W-210 at $AoA = 6°$. Frozen as well as adjoint turbulence are used. The number of control points is labeled as "XXcp".

As in the previous case, at a lower angle of attack, the use of 50 control points requires a higher number of CFD iterations. This may result from more steps in order to compute the approximated Hessian and does not scale linearly.

The final shapes of the lift and drag optimizations are shown in Figure 17. The higher lift is gained through an increase in camber and thickness. The lower drag is gained by a decrease in camber and thickness. As for the lower angle of attack, the differences between shapes generated by using adjoint and frozen turbulence are small.

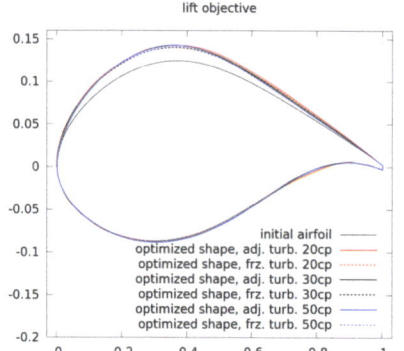
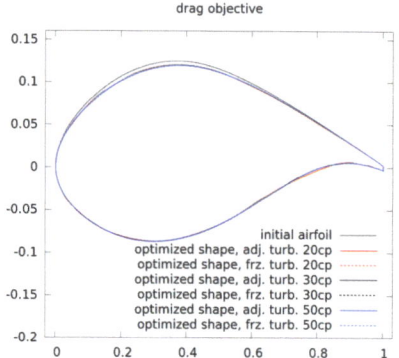

Figure 17. Airfoil shapes using adjoint and frozen turbulence for the lift and drag objective for DU 93-W-210 at $AoA = 6°$. Frozen as well as adjoint turbulence are used. The number of control points is labeled as "XXcp".

In order to investigate why the differences between frozen and adjoint turbulence are small in terms of convergence and shape, Figure 18 shows the gradients of the first optimization step for lift and drag objective, respectively. For the sake of a better comparison of the gradients using different numbers of control points, the abscissa is scaled to match 30 control points. Beside minor differences, it can be seen that the gradients are of similar size and show a similar trend. Although the gradients by frozen turbulence are a little larger than the ones by adjoint turbulence, the optimization processes are not influenced much. This is very different to the previous optimizations of the symmetric NACA airfoil and results from the different airfoil shapes. The shape of the DU airfoil leads to gradients which are the strongest on the central suction side. Thus, mainly thickness and camber are changed during the optimization, which has a positive effect on the convergence of the optimization. In contrast, the symmetric NACA airfoil has stronger gradients near the leading edge (especially at $AoA = 12°$) and subsequently, the leading edge is more strongly deformed and the use of adjoint turbulence is more important.

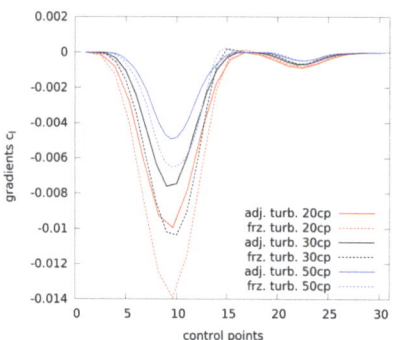
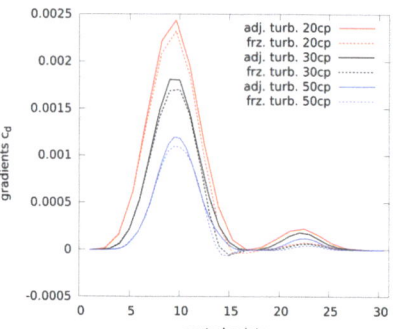

Figure 18. Gradients of the first optimization step for lift and drag objective of the DU 93-W-210 at $AoA = 6°$. Frozen as well as adjoint turbulence are used. The number of control points is labeled as "XXcp". The control points start from the trailing edge on the suction side, pass the leading edge and end at the trailing edge on the pressure side.

5. Summary and Conclusions

Airfoil shape optimization based on CFD and the adjoint approach is already an established method used by several authors. In this study, the effect of the so-called "frozen turbulence" assumption in incompressible flows is compared with the adjoints to a turbulence model, here the Spalart–Allmaras model. The simulations were conducted with the open-source CFD code OpenFOAM-2.3.0, which was extended by the authors for the presented purposes, i.e., external aerodynamics and the corresponding gradient computations as well as a robust, but precise mesh deformation. The implemented mesh motion technique is particularly suitable for shape deformations of airfoils, preserving the high mesh quality in the boundary layer. The solution procedure of the adjoint equations was improved in terms of stability and speed. The convergence time was reduced by half using the SIMPLEC algorithm. The objective functions of the single-point optimizations were quadratic functions in order to reach a certain target lift or drag coefficient, respectively. The function and gradient evaluations were coupled with the optimization module SciPy, written in the programming language Python. Unconstrained quasi-Newton optimizations were used, where the Hessian was approximated by a BFGS update.

The airfoils in the optimizations were represented by splines using different numbers of control points. In some cases, the convergence of the optimization and the resulting shapes depended on the number of control points, and it is recommended that at least 30 spline control points are used.

The presented cases showed that the adjoint turbulence is not always necessary, since some optimizations converged well with gradients obtained by the frozen turbulence approach. This strongly depends on the case itself and for some cases (which may be considered relatively simple), the significant effort for implementing or deriving an adjoint turbulence model can be saved. Besides, the additional PDE from the adjoint turbulence model leads to a higher computational time, which was roughly twice the time needed with frozen turbulence. The reader may evaluate this individually for his or her problem his- or herself, but in general, it is recommended that adjoints to the turbulence model be used, if available. In many cases it is useful, and in some even inevitable, as some airfoil shapes in complex flows may not be optimized without adjoint turbulence. This necessity may increase when a different optimizer is selected in order to use constraints and when the approximation of the Hessian has to be more precise. Noise in the gradients will be amplified using second-order derivatives, which leads to poorer convergence or even complete failure of the optimization.

Since unconstrained optimizations were conducted, other aerodynamic measures or thickness were not included in the optimization objectives, but thickness was clearly changed in the presented cases. Fulfilling the objective function, the shapes are mathematically correct, but for many engineering purposes they may not be useful. This can be considered as a negative side-effect of the presented single-objective optimization. Thickness or other aerodynamic constraints are important for many airfoil applications, e.g., in wind turbines, and hence, they shall be included in future work.

Acknowledgments: The authors would like to thank Martin Bünner (NTB, University of Applied Sciences Buchs, Switzerland) and Lena Vorspel (ForWind, University of Oldenburg, Germany) for the fruitful discussions about optimization and the adjoint approach. The authors appreciate the financial support of the project WIMS–Cluster (0324005), funded by the Federal Ministry of Economic Affairs and Energy, following a decision of the German Bundestag. The simulations were performed at the HPC Cluster EDDY, located at the University of Oldenburg (Germany) and funded by the Federal Ministry for Economic Affairs and Energy (Bundesministeriums für Wirtschaft und Energie) under grant number 0324005.

Author Contributions: M.S. performed the simulations and wrote the paper; B.S. and J.P. supervised the work, analyzed the data, and contributed to the general interpretation of the results.

Conflicts of Interest: The authors declare no conflict of interest.

Appendix A

A mesh study is conducted for a NACA 0012 at $Re = 2 \times 10^6$ and two angles of attack: $AoA = 2°$ and $AoA = 12°$. The Spalart–Allmaras turbulence model is used and in order to fully resolve the flow in the boundary layer the dimensionless wall distance is at $y^+ \approx 0.1$. The domains have a radius of 45 chord lengths and are spatially discretized as shown in Table A1. Hexahedral O-meshes are used and in order to be able to use these meshes for the computation of adjoint equations, they are finer than necessary for standard flow solutions with RANS.

Table A1. Number of cells used in the mesh study.

	Cells Around Airfoil	Cells in Radial Direction	Cells in Total
coarse mesh	400	130	52,000
medium mesh	800	260	208,000
fine mesh	1,600	520	832,000

The resulting changes in lift and drag coefficients are shown in the following Table A2, where the relative differences are computed based on the results of the finest mesh.

Table A2. Relative differences Δ_{lift}, Δ_{drag} in (%) of lift and drag coefficients compared to the coefficients resulting from the finest mesh.

	$AoA = 2°$		$AoA = 12°$	
	Δ_{lift}	Δ_{drag}	Δ_{lift}	Δ_{drag}
coarse mesh	−0.1	1.5	−0.6	5.0
medium mesh	0.4	0.4	0.1	1.5
fine mesh	0.0	0.0	0.0	0.0

Comparing the medium and the fine mesh, the differences at $AoA = 2°$ are below 1% and only for the drag at $AoA = 12°$, which is already near stall, the difference is above 1%. The medium mesh represents a compromise between mesh independency and fast primal and adjoint solutions, and as such is used within this work.

With this mesh for the NACA 0012, a validation is done at $Re = 2 \times 10^6$, comparing experimental results from Ladson [41] with the numerical predictions. Again, the simulations were conducted to be fully-turbulent with the Spalart–Allmaras model without transition. In the measurements, different levels of roughness are used and beside a clean configuration, boundary layer tripping is also used. The carborundum strips were placed at 5% of the chord on the suction and pressure side and had different grit sizes: 60-W and 80-W.

The resulting validation of the lift and drag coefficients is shown in Figure A1. In general, the CFD is able to reproduce the measurements, although the deep stall shows some deviations, which is a common effect from 2D-RANS simulations, but 3D wind tunnel measurements. Since the focus of this work is not a validation of OpenFOAM, but an investigation of frozen and adjoint turbulence, these results are considered to be good enough.

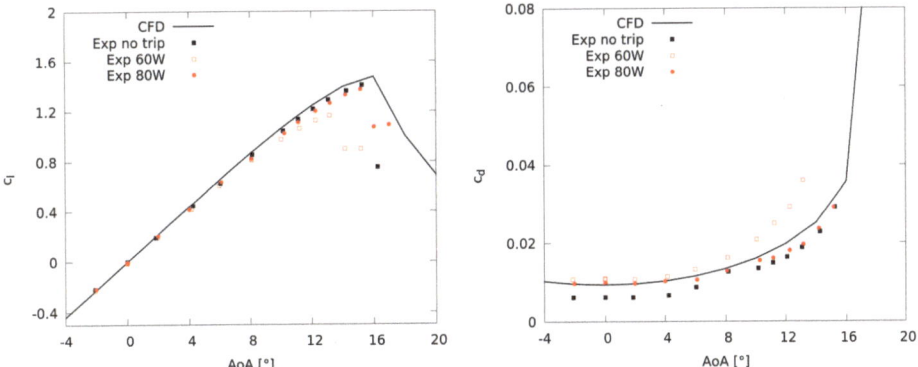

Figure A1. Validation of lift and drag coefficients of a NACA 0012 at $Re = 2 \times 10^6$ (experimental results by Ladson [41]).

Appendix B

A step size study for computing finite differences is conducted for the NACA airfoil at $Re = 2 \times 10^6$ and $AoA = 2°$. The airfoil is represented by a spline with 26 control points and different step sizes are used in order to search for an optimal range, where neither round-off errors nor truncation errors appear.

The resulting gradients are plotted in Figure A2 along the indices of the control points (labeled as in Figure 3) and it can be seen that the smallest changes in gradients are between 5×10^{-8} and 1×10^{-7}. Still, the gradients are not exactly the same and a promising approach to avoid the step size problem of finite differences is the complex step method [40]. However, this is not in the scope of this work, since the objectives in the optimizations are fulfilled when using adjoint turbulence. The complex step method may be used in the future for a better verification of the adjoint implementation when more complex objective functions are used, which require a higher accuracy of the gradients.

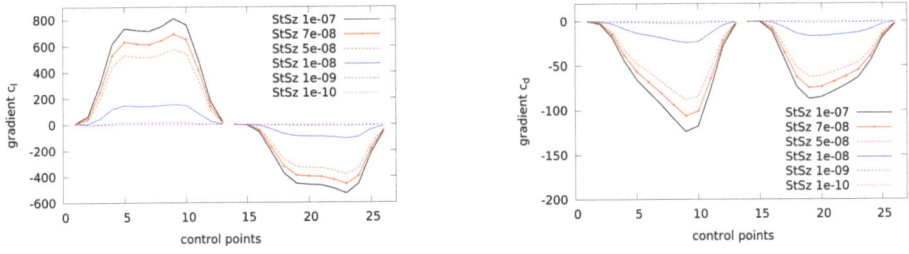

Figure A2. Gradients obtained by finite differences (FDs) for lift objective ("gradient c_l") and drag objective ("gradient c_d"). Different step sizes (StSz) are used for finite differencing.

Appendix C

The derivation of the adjoints to the Spalart–Allmaras turbulence model follows the description of Zymaris et al. [15]. However, our own derivation led to minor differences and for the sake of brevity only the finally resulting equations are shown here.

The adjoint momentum equation including adjoint turbulent viscosity is:

$$(\nabla u)^T \cdot \Psi_u - (u \cdot \nabla)\Psi_u - \nabla\Psi_p$$
$$- \nabla \cdot \left[(\nu + \nu_t) \left(\nabla\Psi_u + (\nabla\Psi_u)^T \right) \right] - \tilde{\nu}\nabla\tilde{\nu}_a$$
$$+ \frac{1}{S}\left[C_{D,S} - C_{P,S} \right] \left(\nabla \times \left(\tilde{\nu}_a (\nabla \times u) \right) \right) = 0 , \tag{A1}$$

where the derivatives $C_{D,S}$ and $C_{P,S}$ directly result from the Spalart–Allmaras model:

$$C_{D,S} = \frac{\partial}{\partial S}\left(c_{w_1} f_w \frac{\tilde{\nu}^2}{d^2} \right) = c_{w_1} \frac{\tilde{\nu}^2}{d^2} \frac{\partial f_w}{\partial g} \frac{\partial g}{\partial r} \frac{\partial r}{\partial \tilde{S}} \tag{A2}$$

$$C_{P,S} = \frac{\partial}{\partial S}\left(c_{b_1} \tilde{\nu} \tilde{S} \right) = c_{b_1} \tilde{\nu} . \tag{A3}$$

The adjoint continuity equation is:

$$-\nabla \cdot \Psi_u = 0 . \tag{A4}$$

The equation for the adjoint eddy-viscosity $\tilde{\nu}_a$ is:

$$(u \cdot \nabla)\tilde{\nu}_a + \left(\frac{\nu + \tilde{\nu}}{\sigma} \right) \Delta\tilde{\nu}_a$$
$$= \frac{2}{\sigma} \nabla\tilde{\nu}_a \cdot \nabla\tilde{\nu} + 2\frac{c_{b_2}}{\sigma} \nabla \cdot (\tilde{\nu}_a \nabla\tilde{\nu}) - \tilde{\nu}_a \left(C_{P,\tilde{\nu}} - C_{D,\tilde{\nu}} \right)$$
$$+ \frac{d\nu_t}{d\tilde{\nu}}\left(\nabla\Psi_u : \nabla u + \nabla u : \nabla\Psi_u \right) , \tag{A5}$$

where again some derivatives $C_{P,\tilde{\nu}}$ and $C_{D,\tilde{\nu}}$ directly result from the Spalart–Allmaras model:

$$C_{P,\tilde{\nu}} = \frac{\partial}{\partial \tilde{\nu}}\left(c_{b_1} \tilde{\nu} \tilde{S} \right) = c_{b_1} \tilde{S} + c_{b_1} \tilde{\nu} \frac{d\tilde{S}}{d\tilde{\nu}} \tag{A6}$$

$$C_{D,\tilde{\nu}} = \frac{\partial}{\partial \tilde{\nu}}\left(c_{w_1} f_w \frac{\tilde{\nu}^2}{d^2} \right) =$$
$$2 c_{w_1} f_w \frac{\tilde{\nu}}{d^2} + c_{w_1} \frac{\tilde{\nu}^2}{d^2} \frac{\partial f_w}{\partial g} \frac{\partial g}{\partial r} \frac{dr}{d\tilde{\nu}} . \tag{A7}$$

Standard Dirichlet and zero Neumann boundary conditions are used for the far-field boundaries, where the adjoint BCs are opposite to the primal BCs.

References

1. Arora, J.S. *Introduction to Optimum Design*, 2nd ed.; Elsevier Academic Press: Cambridge, MA, USA, 2004.
2. Nocedal, J.; Wright, S.J. *Numerical Optimization*, 2nd ed.; Springer Science+Business Media: Berlin, Germany, 2006.
3. Jameson, A.; Martinelli, L. Optimum Aerodynamic Design Using the Navier-Stokes Equations. *Theor. Comput. Fluid Dyn.* **1998**, *10*, 213–237.
4. Giles, M.B.; Pierce, N.A. An Introduction to the Adjoint Approach to Design. In *Flow, Turbulence and Combustion*; Kluwer Academic Publishers: Dordrecht, the Netherlands, 2000; Volume 65, pp. 393–415.
5. Papoutsis-Kiachagias, E.M.; Giannakoglou, K.C. Continuous Ajoint Methods for Turbulent Flows, Applied to Shape and Topology Optimization: Industrial Applications. *Arch. Comput. Methods Eng.* **2014**, *23*, 255–299.

6. Thévenin, D.; Janiga, G. *Optimization and Computational Fluid Dynamics*; Springer: Berlin/Heidelberg, Germany, 2008.

7. Nadarajah, S.K.; Jameson, A. A Comparison of the Continuous and Discrete Adjoint Approach to Automatic Aerodynamic Optimization. *Can. J. Earth Sci.* **2000**, *43*, 1445–1466.

8. Carnarius, A.; Thiele, F.; Özkaya, E.; Nemili, A.; Gauger, N. Optimal Control of Unsteady Flows Using a Discrete and a Continuous Adjoint Approach. In Proceedings of the 25th System Modeling and Optimization (CSMO), Berlin, Germany, 12–16 September 2011.

9. Othmer, C. A continuous adjoint formulation for the computation of topological and surface sensitivities of ducted flows. *Int. J. Numer. Methods Fluids Wiley InterSci.* **2008**, doi:10.1002/fld.1770.

10. Anderson, W.K.; Bonhaus, D.L. Airfoil Design on Unstructured Grids for Turbulent Flows. *AIAA J.* **1999**, *37*, 185–191.

11. Nielsen, E.J.; Anderson, W.K. Aerodynamic Design Optimization on Unstructured Meshes Using the Navier-Stokes Equations. *AIAA J.* **1999**, *37*, 1411–1419.

12. Lyu, Z.; Kenway, G.K.W.; Paige, C.; Martins, J.R.R.A. Automatic Differentiation Adjoint of the Reynolds-Averaged Navier-Stokes Equations with a Turbulence Model. In Proceedings of the 21st AIAA Computational Fluid Dynamics Conference, San Diego, CA, USA, 24–27 June 2013.

13. Osusky, L.; Buckley, H.; Reist, T.; Zingg, D.W. Drag Minimization Based on the Navier–Stokes Equations Using a Newton-Krylov Approach. *AIAA J.* **2015**, 53, 1555–1577.

14. Dwight, R.; Brezillon, J. Effect of various approximations of the discrete adjoint on gradient-based optimization. *AIAA J.* **2006**, 44, 3022–3031.

15. Zymaris, A.S.; Papadimitriou, D.I.; Giannakoglou, K.C.; Othmer, C. Continuous adjoint approach to the Spalart-Allmaras turbulence model for incompressible flows. *Comput. Fluids* **2009**, *38*, 1528–1538.

16. Spalart, P.R.; Allmaras, S.R. A one-equation turbulence model for aerodynamic flows. In Proceedings of the 30th Aerospace Sciences Meeting and Exhibit, Reno, NV, USA, 6–9 January 1992.

17. Bueno-Orovio, A.; Castro, C.; Palacios, F.; Zuazua, E. Continuous Adjoint Approach for the Spalart-Allmaras Model in Aerodynamic Optimization. *AIAA J.* **2012**, *50*, doi:10.2514/1.J051307.

18. Kavvadias, I.S.; Papoutsis-Kiachagias, E.M.; Dimitrakopoulos, G.; Giannakoglou, K.C. The continuous adjoint approach to the k-ω SST turbulence model with applications in shape optimization. *Eng. Optim. Taylor Francis Group* **2014**, *47*, doi:10.1080/0305215X.2014.979816.

19. OpenCFD. OpenFOAM®—The Open Source Computational Fluid Dynamics (CFD) Toolbox. Available online: www.OpenFOAM.org (accessed on 19 January 2018).

20. Towara, M.; Naumann, U. A Discrete Adjoint Model for OpenFOAM. *Proced. Comput. Sci.* **2013**, *18*, 429–438.

21. Önder, A. Active Control of Turbulent Axisymmetric Jets Using Zero-Net-Mass-Flux Actuation. Ph.D. Thesis, Katholieke Universiteit Leuven, Leuven, Belgium, 2014.

22. Petropoulou, S. Industrial Optimisation Solutions based on OpenFOAM Technology. In Proceedings of the 5th European Conference on Computational Fluid Dynamics (ECCOMAS), Lisbon, Portugal, 14–17 June 2010.

23. Othmer, C.; de Villier, E.; Weller, H. Implementation of a continuous adjoint for topology optimization of ducted flows. In Proceedings of the 18th AIAA Computational Fluid Dynamics Conference, Miami, FL, USA, 25–28 June 2007.

24. Jameson, A.; Reuther, J. Control Theory Based Airfoil Design using the Euler Equations. In Proceedings of the 5th Symposium on Multidisciplinary Analysis and Optimization, Panama City Beach, FL, USA, 7–9 September 1994.

25. Castro, C.; Lozano, C.; Palacios, F.; Zuazua, E. Systematic Continuous Adjoint Approach to Viscous Aerodynamic Design on Unstructured Grids. *AIAA J.* **2007**, *45*, 2125–2139.

26. Mohammadi, B.; Pironneau, O. Shape Optimization in Fluid Mechanics. *Ann. Rev. Fluid Mech.* **2004**, *36*, 255–279.

27. Soto, O.; Löhner, R. On the computation of flow sensitivities from boundary integrals. In Proceedings of the 42nd AIAA Aerospace Sciences Meeting and Exhibit, Reno, NV, USA, 5–8 January 2004.

28. Choi, H.; Hinze, M.; Kunisch, K. Instantaneous control of backward-facing step flows. *Appl. Numer. Math.* **1999**, *31*, 133–158.

29. Stück, A. Adjoint Navier-Stokes Methods for Hydrodynamic Shape Optimisation. Ph.D. Thesis, Technische Universität Hamburg-Harburg, Hamburg, Germany, 2012.

30. Palacios, F.; Alonso, J.J.; Jameson, A. Design of free-surface interfaces using RANS equations. In Proceedings of the 43rd Fluid Dynamics Conference, San Diego, CA, USA, 24–27 June 2013.
31. Patankar, S.V. *Numerical Heat Transfer and Fluid Flow*; Hemisphere Publishing Corporation: Washington, DC, USA, 1980.
32. Van Doormaal, J.P.; Raithby, G.D. Enhancements of the SIMPLE method for predicting incompressible fluid flows. *Numer. Heat Transf.* **1984**, *7*, 147–163.
33. Hojjat, M. Node-Based Parametrization for Shape Optimal Design. Ph.D. Thesis, Technische Universität München, Munich, Germany, 2015.
34. Jameson, A.; Vassber, J.C. Studies of alternative numerical optimization methods applied to the brachistochrone problem. *Comput. Fluid Dyn. J.* **2000**, *9*, 281–296.
35. Soto, O.; Löhner, R.; Yang, C. A stabilized pseudo-shell approach for surface parametrization in CFD design problems. *Commun. Numer. Methods Eng.* **2002**, *18*, 251–258.
36. Kropatsch, W.; Kampel, M.; Hanbury, A. *Computer Analysis of Images and Patterns—12th International Conference, CAIP 2007, Proceedings*; Springer: Berlin Heidelberg, 2007.
37. Anderson, W.K.; Venkatakrishnan, V. Aerodynamic design optimization on unstructured grids with a continuous adjoint formulation. In Proceedings of the 35th Aerospace Sciences Meeting and Exhibit, Reno, NV, USA, 6–9 January 1997.
38. Lozano, C. Discrete surprises in the computation of sensitivities from boundary integrals in the continuous adjoint approach to inviscid aerodynamic shape optimization. *Comput. Fluids* **2012**, *56*, 118–127.
39. Schramm, M.; Stoevesandt, B.; Peinke, J. Simulation and Optimization of an Airfoil with Leading Edge Slat. *J. Phys. Conf. Ser.* **2016**, *753*, 022052.
40. Martins, J.R.R.A.; Kroo, I.M.; Alonso, J.J. An Automated Method for Sensitivity Analysis using Complex Variables. In Proceedings of the 38th AIAA Aerospace Sciences Meeting, Reno, NV, USA, 10–13 January 2000.
41. Ladson, C.L. *Effects of Independent Variation of Mach and Reynolds Numbers on the Low-Speed Aerodynamic Characteristics of the NACA 0012 Airfoil Section*; NACA Technical Memorandum; NASA: Washington, DC, USA, 1988; Volume 4074.
42. Kim, S.; Alonso, J.J.; Jameson, A. A Gradient Accuracy Study for the Adjoint-Based Navier-Stokes Design Method. In Proceedings of the 37th AIAA Aerospace Sciences Meeting, Reno, NV, USA, 11–14 January 1999.
43. SciPy. Scientific Computing Tools for Python. Available online: www.SciPy.org (accessed on 19 January 2018).
44. Timmer, W.A.; van Rooij, R.P.J.O.M. Summary of the Delft University Wind Turbine Dedicated Airfoils. In Proceedings of the 41st Aerospace Sciences Meeting and Exhibit, Reno, NV, USA, 6–9 January 2003.

Article

Aerodynamic Optimization of Airfoil Profiles for Small Horizontal Axis Wind Turbines

Ali Cemal Benim [1,2,*], Michael Diederich [1] and Björn Pfeiffelmann [1]

[1]   Center of Flow Simulation (CFS), Department of Mechanical and Process Engineering,
     Düsseldorf University of Applied Sciences, Münsterstr. 156, D-40476 Germany;
     michael.diederich@hs-duesseldorf.de (M.D.); bjoern.pfeiffelmann@hs-duesseldorf.de (B.P.)
[2]   Institute of Thermal Power Engineering, Department of Mechanical Engineering,
     Cracow University of Technology, Al. Jana Pawła II 37, 31-864 Kraków, Poland
*   Correspondence: alicemal@prof-benim.com or alicemal.benim@hs-duesseldorf.de; Tel.: +49-211-4351-3504

Received: 2 March 2018; Accepted: 21 April 2018; Published: 25 April 2018

Abstract: The purpose of this study is the development of an automated two-dimensional airfoil shape optimization procedure for small horizontal axis wind turbines (HAWT), with an emphasis on high thrust and aerodynamically stable performance. The procedure combines the Computational Fluid Dynamics (CFD) analysis with the Response Surface Methodology (RSM), the Biobjective Mesh Adaptive Direct Search (BiMADS) optimization algorithm and an automatic geometry and mesh generation tool. In CFD analysis, a Reynolds Averaged Numerical Simulation (RANS) is applied in combination with a two-equation turbulence model. For describing the system behaviour under alternating wind conditions, a number of CFD 2D-RANS-Simulations with varying Reynolds numbers and wind angles are performed. The number of cases is reduced by the use of RSM. In the analysis, an emphasis is placed upon the role of the blade-to-blade interaction. The average and the standard deviation of the thrust are optimized by a derivative-free optimization algorithm to define a Pareto optimal set, using the BiMADS algorithm. The results show that improvements in the performance can be achieved by modifications of the blade shape and the present procedure can be used as an effective tool for blade shape optimization.

Keywords: CFD; RSM; RANS; BiMADS; HAWT; wind turbine; airfoil; aerodynamics; optimization

---

1. Introduction

Wind power has been receiving increasing attention as one of the most promising renewable energy sources. Wind turbine technologies for improved performance have been developed within the last two decades, where many aspects, including aerodynamics and aeroelasiticy, have been the subject of intensive theoretical, computational and experimental research [1]. As the airfoil profile shape has a crucial impact on the aerodynamic efficiency of a wind turbine, an important research area for wind turbine technology has been blade design. Within this context, automatic blade shape optimization procedures, which have a longer tradition in other areas such as compressors [2] and turbines [3] have also been used for the aerodynamic and structural optimization of wind turbine blades. The more classical intuition and experience based non-automatic optimization [4] has been used. In our study, we focus on Horizontal Axis Wind Turbines (HAWT).

Jureczko et al. [5] applied a genetic algorithm (GA) to optimize wind turbine blades, where the emphasis was put on structural stability. The aerodynamic loads were calculated by the Blade Element Momentum (BEM) theory. Genetic algorithms along with the BEM theory were used also by Mendez and Greiner [6] for aerodynamic optimization with respect to blade chord and twist angle. Burger and Hartfield [7] examined the feasibility of using the combination of the vortex lattice method with a GA for the optimization of the aerodynamic performance of horizontal axis wind turbine blades.

Clifton-Smith and Wood [8] applied differential evolution strategies to optimize numerically small wind turbine blades with the double purpose of maximizing power coefficient and minimizing starting time. Here, the power coefficient was calculated by the standard BEM theory.

Liu et al. [9] developed an optimization model based on an extended compact genetic algorithm to maximize the annual energy output of a 1.3 MW stall-regulated wind turbine. The flow field was computed by the XFOIL code [10], which is based on an inviscid linear-vorticity panel method, which can take viscous effects by superimposed sources into account. Compared to the original blades, the designed blades showed better aerodynamic performance.

A multidisciplinary design approach along with a gradient based optimization algorithm was used to solve the optimization problem of a wind turbine blade by Kenway and Martins [11]. The blade aerodynamics was modelled by the BEM theory. The blade was constructed using 7 design variables: chord, twist, spar (thickness, location and length), airfoil thickness and rotation rate. To demonstrate the potential for site-specific optimization, a 5 kW wind turbine case was used with results showing a possible output increase of 3–4%. In the analysis by Xudong et al. [12], the costs were also considered along with the aerodynamic/aeroelastic model and the cost of energy based on annual energy production was minimized, where the aerodynamic model was based on the BEM theory. Ceyhan et al. [13] studied the aerodynamic performance of horizontal axis wind turbine blades using the BEM theory and GA. The fitness function was based on the BEM theory, where two design variables, the chord and twist distributions, were optimized for optimum power production. An increase of 40–80% in power production was recorded on a 100 kW HAWT.

Li et al. [14] presented an improved optimization technique using response surface methods to optimize the lift-to-drag ratio for 2D wind turbine airfoils. Grujicic et al. [15] developed a two-level optimization scheme consisting of an inner and outer level. In the inner level, for a given aerodynamic design of the blade, which was based on a CFD analysis, the blade mass was minimized. Bottasso et al. [16] applied a complex multi-disciplinary approach for optimally sizing large, multi-MW wind turbines, seeking a compromise between the maximization of the annual energy production and the weight of the machine, assuming the weight is well correlated with the cost. The multi objective design is not formulated as a Pareto optimal problem but rather as a combined cost problem defined as the ratio of the annual energy production to the total weight.

An approach to optimizing the power factor and the power output of the wind turbine (bi-objective problem established by weights) using data-mining and evolutionary computation was presented by Kusiak and Zheng [17]. Song et al. [18] developed a MATLAB tool using BEM theory to perform aerostructural dynamic analysis of wind turbine blades on a 20 kW wind turbine. These authors optimized the chord length and twist angle at each blade element to maximize the wind energy utilization factor of each blade element. Wang et al. [19] presented a multi-objective algorithm where the maximum power coefficient at the design wind speed (9 m/s) and the minimum blade mass were chosen as two optimization objectives; a conflicting problem. The aerodynamic loads acting on the blade were calculated using the modified BEM theory.

Later in 2012, Graaso [20] focused on the airfoil design at the tip region of the blade using numerical optimization. Genetic and gradient based algorithms were used, on a hybrid optimization platform, to design a new family of airfoils dedicated to the root region of the wind turbine blade. This approach improved aerodynamic efficiency (lift-to-drag ratio) together with the sectional moment of resistance for the structural part of the problem. The flow was computed by the XFOIL code.

Chen and Agarwal [21] applied a GA for shape optimization of flatback airfoils, which was enhanced by combination with an artificial neural network algorithm. A considerable acceleration of the procedure by the use of artificial neural networks was reported, without, however, a quantification. For calculating the flow field, a CFD approach was employed. Ribeiro et al. [22] coupled CFD based flow analysis with an optimization algorithm for wind turbine airfoil design. Single and multi-objective GA were employed and artificial neural networks were used as a surrogate model. In the study, the effect of the domain size on the prediction and the effect of parallelization on speed-up were discussed. The use of artificial neural networks was shown to reduce the computational time by almost 50%.

Jeong et al. [23] minimized the fluctuations of the unsteady aerodynamic load under turbulent wind conditions. It was noted that the out-of-plane fluctuating unsteady aerodynamic load is more significant than the in-plane loads for structural fatigue of the blade. The RMS out-of-plane bending moment was reduced by about 20% and its mean was reduced by about 5%. Semi-empirical methods were used to estimate the sound pressure.

Ju et al. [24] developed a robust design optimization procedure for wind turbine airfoils by maximizing the lift to drag coefficient ratio and the lift coefficients of the airfoil, along with a sensitivity minimization of the roughness at the leading edge associated with the geometry profile uncertainty. The flow field information was obtained by a CFD approach.

The optimization of spar caps in wind turbine blades was examined by Liao et al. [25]. The thickness and the location of spars were chosen as the optimization variables. The FAST aero-elastic simulator was used along with unsteady BEM. Polat and Tuncer [26] optimized blade shapes for the maximization of power production at a specific wind speed, rotor speed and rotor diameter, applying a GA, within the framework of a parallel computing environment, using XFOIL as the flow solver.

Sessarego el al. [27] performed the multi-objective optimization of wind-turbine blades using a non-dominated sorting genetic algorithm. Annual energy production, flapwise root-bending moment and the mass of the turbine blade were considered as the objective functions. The aerodynamic model was based on BEM. Shen et al. [28] performed a multi-objective optimization of wind turbine blades using the lifting surface method as the aerodynamic model. Maximization of annual energy production and minimization of blade load including thrust and blade flap-wise moment were considered as the objective functions.

Hassanazadeh et al. [29] carried out the aerodynamic shape optimization and the analysis of small wind turbine blades using BEM and GA. Annual energy production was considered as the objective function. Porrajabian et al. [30] performed the aero-structural design optimization of a small wind turbine. Starting time of turbine and output power were considered simultaneously as the objective function. The design variables consisted of the chord, twist and the shell thickness. The aerodynamic model was based on the BEM theory. Dal Monte et al. [31] presented a procedure for aerodynamic-structural optimization of wind turbine blades, where the structural modelling was based on the finite element method and the aerodynamic part was based on the BEM theory. A more detailed survey of performance optimization techniques applied to wind turbines is presented in a recent review by Chehouri et al. [32].

Inspecting the previous work on the automatic optimization of wind turbine blade shapes, one can see that aerodynamic analysis has been most frequently based on the BEM method but rarely on the solution of the Navier-Stokes equations via CFD. Thus, a distinguishing feature of the present contribution from the majority of the previous work is the CFD based analysis of the flow field. In previous work on the automated optimization of wind turbine blade shapes, CFD based flow analysis was also reported by Bottasso et al. [16], Li et al. [14], Chen and Agarwal [21], Riberio et al. [22], Ju and Zhang [24]. Bottasso et al. [16] presented the applied the multi-disciplinary constrained optimization, however, hardy provided any detail information on the structural or flow (CFD) analysis. Li et al. [14] applied a CFD approach for the aerodynamic analysis. However, many details of the applied models and methods such as the turbulence model, discretization schemes were not provided and a grid independence study was not performed. In the work of Chen and Agarwal [21] a grid independence study was performed and the applied turbulence model was discussed. However, in conjunction with the latter, some important details are not sufficiently addressed such as the near-wall treatment that is crucial for prediction of the boundary layer development and flow separation.

Riberio et al. [22] and Ju and Zhang [24] presented a more detailed CFD analysis, where the details of the mathematical and numerical formulation were adequately addressed. A difference of the present mathematical CFD formulation compared to those of Riberio et al. [22] and Ju and Zhang [24] resides in the applied turbulence model. In [22,24] a one-equation turbulence model was used, where in the present study a principally more accurate two-equation turbulence model is employed. Furthermore, in References [22,24] only the angle of attack (AoA) was varied, while the approach velocity magnitude was kept constant. In the present study, the flow angle (FA) for the prevailing blade angle (BA) and the magnitude of the approach velocity, that is, the Reynolds number are varied independently from each other, which span a higher dimensional space from which an optimal blade shape is sought. Here, BA is the angle between the blade chord and the plane of rotation and FA is the angle between relative approach velocity vector and the plane of rotation (obviously the AoA results from the FA for a given BA). Considerable variations of FA are quite likely for small HAWT, as many of them use furling, whereby the rotor yaws out of the wind as a measure of protection against overspeed. In the previous studies [14,21,22,24], an essentially infinite domain size was considered, whereas in the present work, the effect of the domain size and the blade-to-blade interaction are addressed.

There are also differences in the applied optimization methods between the present and previous studies. In [14] the Response Surface Methodology (RSM) [33] was used as the optimization method. In [21,22,24] GA enhanced with artificial neural networks were used as the optimization procedure. In the present work the RSM is used to describe the effect of flow variables for the unmodified blade shape, which was an input for the subsequent optimization. The optimization of the blade shape was performed by a Biobjective Mesh Adaptive Direct Search (BiMADS) optimization algorithm. Furthermore, beyond high trust, a stable performance under varying wind conditions is considered as an additional goal within the present bi-objective optimization, whereas the latter objective was not addressed in the previous, comparable investigations.

2. Model Description

2.1. Overview of the Optimization Procedure

The optimization cycle is depicted in Figure 1. The blade shape is represented by a finite number of degrees of freedom (to be described, below, in more detail). They are denoted as "geometry parameters" in Figure 1. The optimization cycle is started by the optimization algorithm, which generates the geometry parameters and transfers them to the mesh generator to create a CFD grid. At the first cycle, the geometry parameters are, however, not generated by the optimization algorithm but stem from the original geometry. The Response Surface Methodology (RSM) module defines the aerodynamic operation points according to certain rules (to be defined later in more detail) that are fed to the computational flow solver (CFD) as boundary conditions, together with the computational mesh. Based on the CFD results, two values are calculated and passed over to the optimization module by the RSM module. These are the average thrust, that is, the tangential force (the force component in the direction of rotation that generates the power) and its standard deviation within the considered space of flow variables. The maximization of the former (maximum power) and the minimization of the latter are the objective functions (efficient and stable operation under varying wind conditions). The optimization algorithm (to be described later in more detail) proposes a new set of geometry parameters for the better fulfilment of these objectives, which closes the cycle.

2.2. Mathematical and Numerical Modelling of the Aerodynamics

The flow is assumed to be two-dimensional (2D) and statistically in the steady state. For a rotating turbine with fixed blades, this setting resembles a blade-to-blade surface at a fixed radial section, where the turbine rotational speed and the wind speed are constant in time, in a moving (i.e., rotating) reference frame. In the sense of a quasi-three dimensional procedure, which is also quite common in steam [34] and gas [35] turbines, a three-dimensional model can be constructed by an assembly of such blade-to-blade sections. It shall be noted that the resemblance is, however, approximate in so far, that a curved blade-to-blade surface resulting from a radial section is represented by a flat plane in 2D. The air flow is assumed to be incompressible, which is reasonable at the usually prevailing Mach numbers in HAWT applications. The Navier-Stokes equations along with the continuity equation are solved computationally.

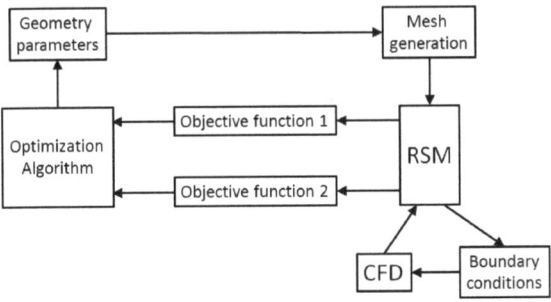

Figure 1. Optimization cycle.

The Computational Fluid Dynamics (CFD) analysis is based on the general-purpose code CFD ANSYS Fluent [36], applying the Finite Volume Method (FVM) for discretizing the governing differential equations. Flow turbulence is modelled within a RANS (Reynolds Averaged Numerical Simulation) approach [37], where the time-averaged equations are solved for the time-averaged variables in steady-state. A more accurate approach would be Large Eddy Simulations (LES) [38,39], which, being a three-dimensional and unsteady approach, would, however explode the frame in the present case. Turbulence is modelled by a two-equation turbulence model, that is, by the Shear Stress Transport (SST) model [36,40], which were shown to perform quite reliably especially for wall-driven turbulent flows with potential to predict transitional effects [41–43]. No wall-functions are used near the wall, resolving the near-wall layer. The coupling of the discretized Navier-Stokes and continuity equations are treated by a coupled solver [36,44]. The convective terms are discretized by a formally third-order accurate QUICK discretization scheme [36,45] for the Navier-Stokes equations and a second-order upwind scheme [36,46] for the transport equations of the two turbulence variables. Convergence criterion for the residual of each equation was set to 10^{-5}.

2.3. Flow Solution Domain and Boundary Conditions

The airfoil is positioned in a rectangular domain, with periodic boundaries on both sides in the circumferential direction, along with an inlet and an outlet boundary. The solution domain and the boundary definitions are sketched in Figure 2, where the velocity vector relative to the airfoil, the flow angle (FA) and blade angle (BA) are also indicated.

The inlet and outlet boundaries are placed ten and twenty chord lengths (C) away from the airfoil, respectively, which may be considered to be sufficiently far [47] that the boundaries do not influence the results. At the inlet, uniform distributions of the velocity components (the approach velocity V relative to the airfoil, Figure 2) and turbulence quantities are prescribed. The inlet values of the turbulence quantities are estimated assuming a turbulence intensity of 4% and a macro-mixing length [37] of 25% of the chord length. At the outlet, a constant static pressure is prescribed along with zero-gradient conditions for the remaining quantities. At the pair of periodic boundaries, obviously, periodic boundary conditions are applied. The extension of the domain between the two periodic boundaries (L) corresponds to the space between two neighbouring blades in a turbine wheel. In an application, in general, this size varies with the number of blades on the wheel, as well as the radial position of the considered blade-to-blade section.

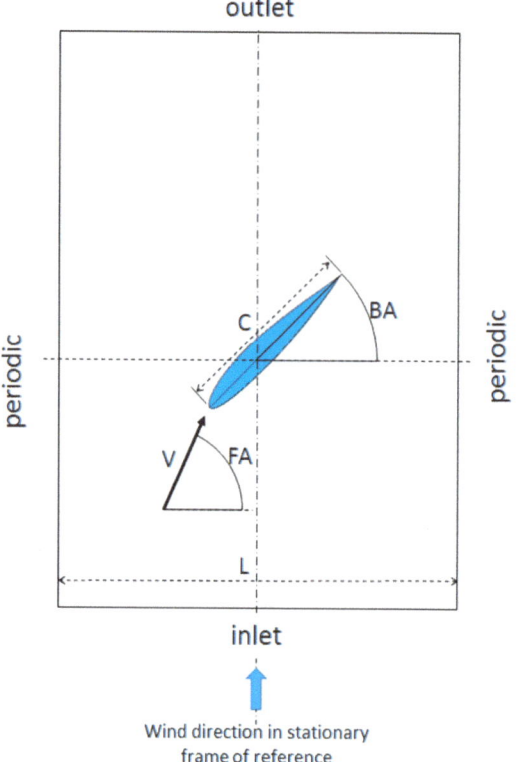

Figure 2. Solution domain and boundaries.

2.4. Generation of Computational Grid for Flow Simulation

A high-quality O-grid is generated around the blade, which interfaces with the essentially H-type block-structured grid in the outer domain. Via an in-house developed procedure based on the ANSYS ICEM grid generator [36] and replay scripts, different grids for different blade positions and different blade surface shapes can automatically be generated. Prompted by the optimization algorithm by the transfer of the geometry controlling parameters, the mesh generation module calculates the Hermite curves, manipulates the replay script (which stems from the previous grid) accordingly and prompts the ANSYS ICEM grid generator to generate the new mesh with the new replay script and transfers the mesh to the RSM module (Figure 1). These processes are controlled by scripts written in GNU Octave [48]. Since no-wall functions for turbulence modelling have been used, the grid resolution near the wall needs to be sufficiently fine. In generating the grids, it is ensured that the non-dimensional wall-distance y^+ [37] is everywhere smaller than 1 for the next-to-wall cells and at least 3 cells remain within the region $y^+ < 5$. The structure of a typical grid is displayed in Figure 3. From case-to-case, changes in the grid are confined to the O-grid surrounding the airfoil. The variations in the airfoil profile cause a grid modification only in this region and different BA can be obtained by the respective rotations of the O-grid connected to the airfoil.

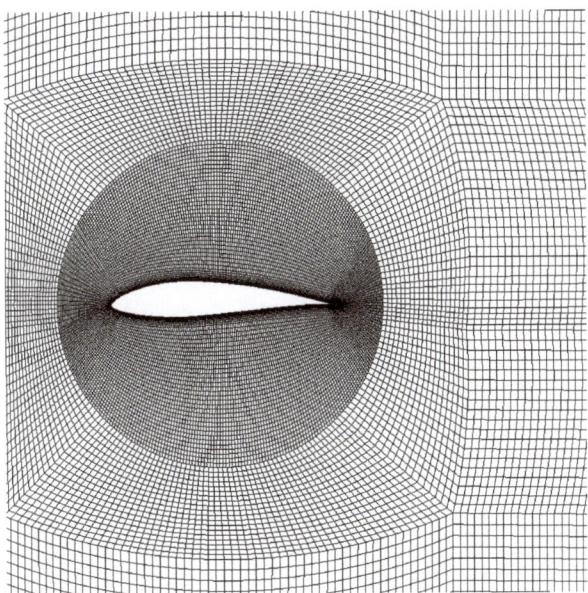

Figure 3. Detail view of a typical grid.

2.5. Parametrization of the Airfoil Shape

For the optimization, the airfoil geometry needs to be parametrized. Historically, different approaches have been used. For the present purposes, the Hermite curves, which are closely related with Bezier curves, are found to be most suitable for generating airfoil shapes with a limited number of parameters and with sufficient geometrical precision. A Hermite curve is defined by two points (P_i) and two tangent vectors (with lengths l_{ij} and directions α_i) on both its ends. With this function, the geometry of the airfoils has been generated by using four piecewise Hermite curves (HC_i), two representing the suction and two the pressure side, as shown in Figure 4.

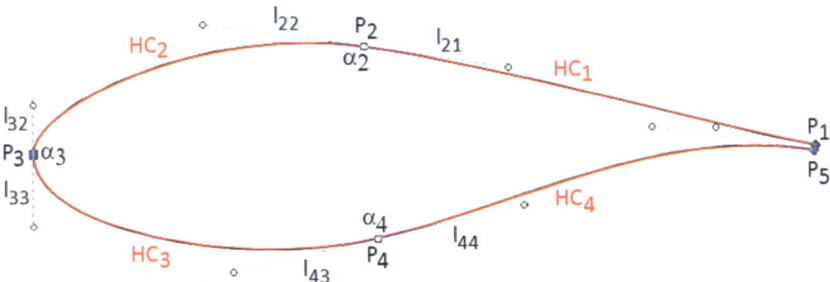

Figure 4. Parametric representation of airfoil shape by Hermite curves.

The Hermite curve segments are connected with each other in a continuous fashion at points P_2, P_3, P_4 by ensuring that the end-point of one curve is the same as the starting point of another and the local tangent vectors belonging to the curves that are joined at this point have the same direction for ensuring C^1 continuity. The mathematical expression of the Hermite curve i (HC_i), bounded by points P_i and P_j (with $j = I + 1$), is provided below (Figure 4).

$$\vec{x}_i(t) = \left(-\vec{P}_i + 3\vec{PI}_{ii} - 3\vec{PI}_{ji} + \vec{P}_j\right) t^3 + \left(3\vec{P}_i - 6\vec{PI}_{ii} + 3\vec{PI}_{ji}\right) t^2 + \left(-3\vec{P}_i + 3\vec{PI}_{ii}\right) t + \vec{P}_i$$

where the vector $\vec{x}_i$ contains the coordinate pair of any point on the curve HC$_i$, the variable t is a parameter varying along the curve between 0 (at P_i) and 1 (at P_j) and

$$\vec{PI}_{ii} = \vec{P}_i + \vec{e}_{11}(\alpha_i) \, l_{ii}; \vec{PI}_{ji} = \vec{P}_j + \vec{e}_{11}(\alpha_i) l_{ji}$$

with $\vec{e}_{11}(\alpha_i)$ denoting the unit direction vectors along tangents, pointing away from the corresponding edge points.

Assuming production by glass fibre-reinforced synthetic material moulding, a trailing edge with finite thickness is considered, which is defined by points P_1 and P_5 that are connected by a tiny straight line. In addition to the coordinates of the five points, the directions of the vector couples as well as their lengths describe the shape of the airfoil. The number of degrees of freedom can be reduced by introducing certain constrains on these parameters, which will be addressed below.

2.6. Response Surface Methodology and the Optimization Algorithm

Response Surface Methodology (RSM) [33] is a general approach to describe the response of certain output variables to the changes in the independent variables, that is, the influencing variables. For a well distributed number of "design points" in the space of the independent variables, a regression function, that is, an objective function, is created using the least-square approach, which can be used as basis for different optimization purposes. RSM can be used as an optimization scheme of its own [14]. However, in the present case, with a quite large number of influencing variables (when the airfoil shape parameters are also covered by the regression function), this would lead to a too complex formulation. Therefore, in the present work, RSM is used to describe the dependence of the objective function onto the wind conditions, while another approach is used to seek the optimal airfoil shape, as described below. Thus, in the present analysis, RSM is used to construct a functional relationship between the influencing variables (Re, FA) and the objective functions. The objective functions are the average thrust T (the force acting in the direction of blade motion) and its standard deviation σ within the considered space spanned by the influencing variables. The former (T) is to be maximized to achieve the maximum power and the latter (σ) is to be minimized to achieve a stable operation under varying wind conditions.

Based on the RSM, the dependence of the thrust on the two influencing variables is represented by a bivariate quadratic regression function. The coefficients of the function are obtained by a least-square fitting to a number of data points that are arranged in an orthogonal central composite design (OCCD) [33]. In two dimensions, that is, for two influencing parameters, the number of data points in OCCD is nine. Thus, for obtaining the functional representation of the thrust, nine CFD calculations are needed, for each new optimization cycle. Having obtained the functional relationship for the thrust, its average value and standard deviation are calculated, which are, then, the objective functions to be processed by the subsequent optimization step.

For the optimization, Biobjective Mesh Adaptive Search Algorithm (BiMADS) [49] is used, which is a derivative-free algorithm developed for black box optimizations. This is done within the framework of the optimization toolbox NOMAD [50]. The method iterates on a series of meshes with varying size in the space of influencing variables (in our case, the parameters that define the airfoil shape). The objective of each iteration of the algorithm, is to generate a trial point on the mesh that improves the current best solution. Depending on the success or the failure of the search, the mesh is coarsened or refined, along with a re-scaling of the search range to minimize the number of evaluations. A feature of the algorithm is its ability to handle failed evaluations of the objective function, what can happen in CFD based evaluations (e.g., due to convergence problems), which made the method attractive for the present application.

3. Results

3.1. Grid Independence

For ensuring grid independence in the CFD predictions, calculations have been performed for a typical airfoil shape and flow configuration, using different grid resolutions. The variation of the predicted lift coefficient (normalized by that of the finest grid with) with the total number of grid nodes (NGN), for the considered case is displayed in Figure 5. As it can be seen in the figure, a sufficient grid independence is achieved for grids with larger than 50,000 nodes. Following these findings, the grids are generated by the developed automatic grid generator, using the same grid topology and strategy, with an even finer resolution corresponding to number of nodes about 60,000, for assuring sufficient grid independence.

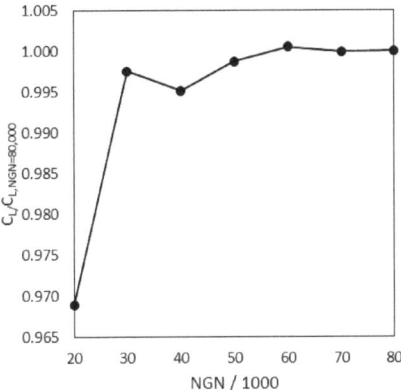

Figure 5. Variation of predicted lift coefficient with grid resolution.

3.2. Validation

For the validation of the applied CFD methodology, the flow over the airfoil NREL-S822 of Selig et al. [51] was calculated for Re = 400,000. The predicted lift and drag coefficients as function of AoA are compared with the measured values [51] in Figure 6. A quite well overall agreement between the predictions and measurements can be observed (Figure 6).

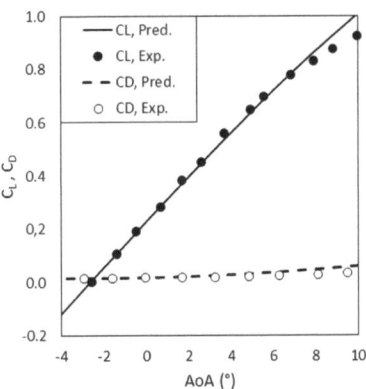

Figure 6. Comparison of predicted lift and drag coefficients with the measured values for the profile NREL-S822 of Selig et al. [51] (Re = 400,000).

3.3. Influence of the Domain Size, Blade to Blade Interaction

The flow around the NREL-S822 airfoil [51] is calculated for Re = 400,000, for BA = 5° and FA = 15° (AoA = 10°) for different circumferential domain sizes (L). The predicted lift coefficient as a function of dimensionless domain size (L/C) are shown in Figure 7.

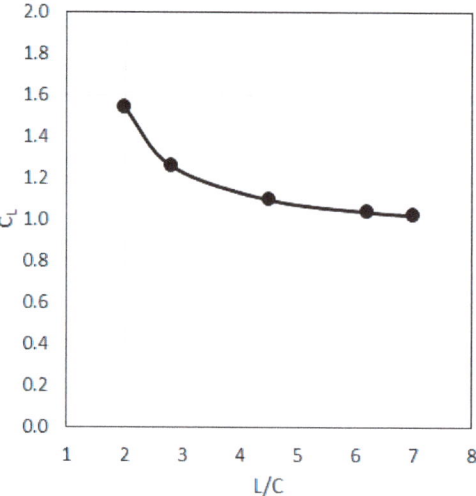

Figure 7. Variation of the predicted lift coefficient with circumferential domain size, for Re = 400,000, BA = 5°, FA = 15° (AoA = 10°).

As can be seen in Figure 7, the blade-to-blade interaction is negligible for L/C > 6 but becomes noticeable for lower values. The observed increasing trend of C_L with decreasing L/C is the reverse of what is implied by the classical, one-dimensional linear cascade theory, which predicts a decreasing C_L with decreasing L/C. This is because that the mentioned theory assumes a perfect flow deflection (which is reasonable for turbomachinery of gas and steam turbines with rather small L/C values), whereas in the present case with relatively large L/C values and, thus, non-ideal flow deflection on the average, a decrease of L/C improves the deflection of the passage flow, leading to an increase in C_L.

3.4. Optimization

The parametrization of the airfoil shape was discussed in Section 2.5 and depicted in Figure 4. In the present application of the optimization algorithm, some constraints are imposed on the shape parameters, to reduce the degrees of freedom and thus the computational effort and for improving the computational stability as well as considering issues related to structural aspects and manufacturing: The two points defining the trailing edge (P_1, P_5) and the associated vectors of the related Hermite curves (HC_1, HC_4) are fixed. The lengths of the vectors that are connected to P_2, P_4 and head towards the trailing edge (l_{21}, l_{44}) are additionally assumed to be constant. The point defining the leading edge (P_3) is also fixed in its position (Figure 4). Furthermore, the control points on the suction (P_2) and pressure (P_4) sides (Figure 4) are not allowed to move parallel to the chord but only in the perpendicular direction. An additional constraint was that the distance between P_2 and P_4 should not undershoot a certain value, to provide "too thin" blades, for structural reasons. Given these constraints and the continuity of the curves, the remaining degrees of freedom that define the profile shape are nine in total, that is, the vertical positions of the points P_2 and P_4, the directions (α_2, α_3, α_4) and the lengths of the vector pairs (each pair have a common direction) at the points P_2, P_3 and P_4 (l_{22}, l_{32}, l_{33}, l_{43}). The schematic of the resulting complete optimization loop is presented in Figure 8.

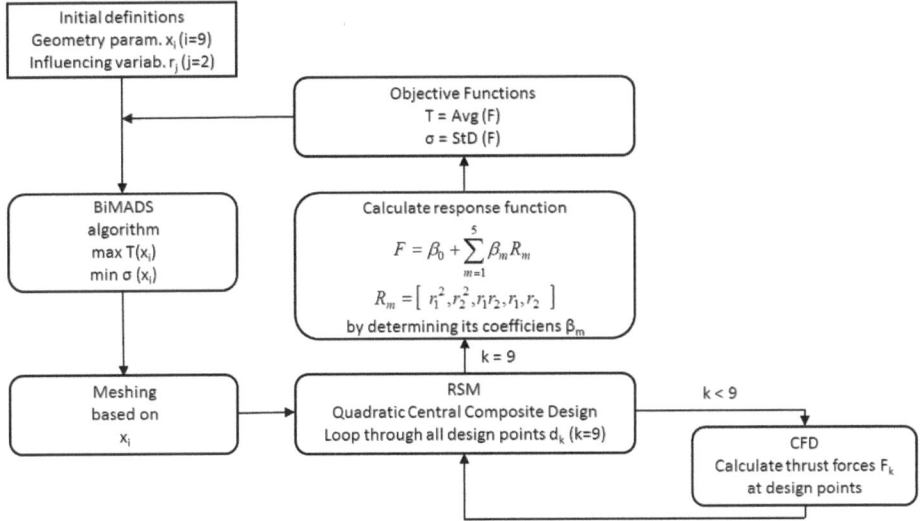

Figure 8. Detailed representation of the optimization cycle.

For the RSM, the applied factor levels and the natural values of the variables for the OCCD arrangement of the data points are provided in Table 1. Please note that the ranges covered in Table 1 are not necessarily meant to be realistic for a practical application but merely serve to an exemplarily demonstration of the procedure.

Table 1. Factor levels and the natural values of the variables (BA = 5°).

	Normalized Scale Parameters				
Variable	−1.414	−1	0	1	1.414
$Re/10^3$	90	92.93	100	107.07	110
FA (°)	10	11.46	15	18.54	20

The NREL-S822 [51] is profile is taken as the basis (the original, non-optimized profile) and optimized applying the procedure described above, for the different relative domain sizes, namely for L/C = 3 and L/C = 6. Doing so, the Reynolds number (Re), which based on the approach velocity magnitude V and the chord length C, is varied by varying V, keeping C and the air properties constant. The two objective functions, that is, the high average trust (T) and low standard deviation (σ) under varying wind conditions cannot be maximized simultaneously, without making a trade-off between the two goals. The feasible choices resulting from this trade-off can be represented by the so-called Pareto front [52]. The optimization is carried out for two cases, namely for L/C = 3 and for L/C = 6, with different levels of blade-to-blade interaction. The predicted Pareto fronts for two cases, that is, for L/C = 3 and L/D = 6, are presented in Figure 9 in terms of the average thrust coefficient C_T and the coefficient of thrust standard deviation C_σ that are obtained nondimensionalizing the variables by the dynamic pressure $1/2\rho V^2$ and the chord C.

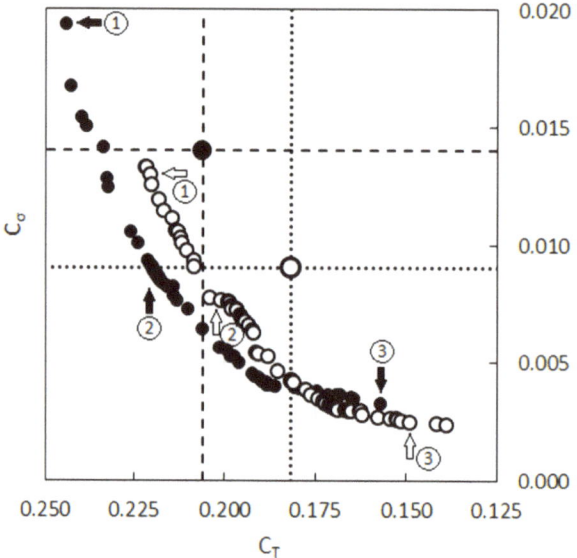

Figure 9. Predicted Pareto fronts of feasible solutions of optimization. Full circles: L/C = 3, Empty circles: L/C = 6.

The larger circles located at the intersecting broken lines in the figure indicate the performance of the original profile before optimization. The smaller circles are the results of different optimizations, which, altogether, build-up the Pareto front. Each circle is associated with a different profile with a slightly different shape. The numbers 1, 2, 3 indicate the profiles that are exemplarily chosen for a more detailed presentation, in the following. As can be seen in the figure, the performance of the profile changes with domain size. For the same operation range (Table 1) the original profile in the small domain (L/C = 3) delivers a larger thrust on the average (large full circle in Figure 9), whereas for the large domain (L/C = 6) it performs more stable (large empty circle, Figure 9). The Pareto fronts that result from the optimization are also different for both domain sizes (Figure 9). The dashed (L/C = 3) and dotted (L/C = 6) lines that cross the larger circles (marking the original profile) define four regions, for each domain size, with different qualitative behaviour compared to the original design. All points within the lower left quadrangle represent an improvement in both objectives, whereas the points in the upper right quadrangle (if any) would mean a worsening in both. In the upper left region, the thrust is improved at the expense of a larger standard deviation (less stability of operation under varying wind conditions), whereas the reverse is true in the lower right quadrangle.

The Pareto fronts of both domain sizes are quite close to each other in the lower right part of Figure 9, implying that the airfoil shapes that are optimized for stable operation (low standard deviation, low thrust) perform similarly, irrespective of the domain size. The Pareto fronts diverge towards the upper left direction (Figure 9), implying that for the blades optimized for high thrust, the domain size plays a greater role. In this region, for the same thrust coefficient, the optimized profiles for the smaller domain (L/C = 3) seem to exhibit a better stability (lower standard deviation) compared to those of the larger domain (L/C = 6).

The optimized profile shapes in comparison with the original profile are presented in Figures 10 and 11, for L/C = 3 and L/C = 6, respectively, for the three points indicated by arrows as 1, 2, 3 in Figure 9.

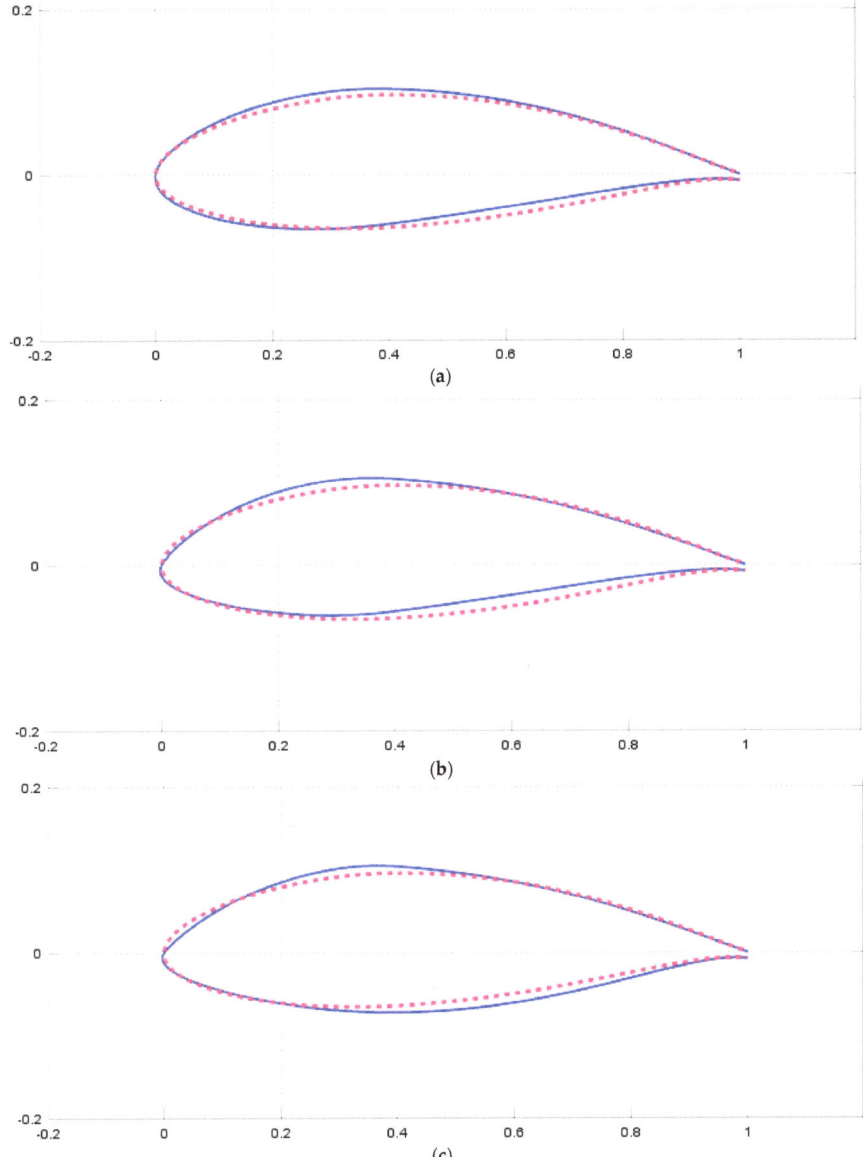

Figure 10. Optimized airfoil shapes for L/C = 3, for the points indicated by full arrows in Figure 9 (a) Point 1; (b) Point 2; (c) Point 3 (Figure 8), red dotted line: original, blue solid line: optimized (note that vertical scale is larger than horizontal scale).

One can observe (Figures 10 and 11) the differences in the optimization between the three considered points for each domain size, as well as between the two relative domain sizes. It is interesting to observe that rather small variations in the shape can have quite substantial impact on the performance.

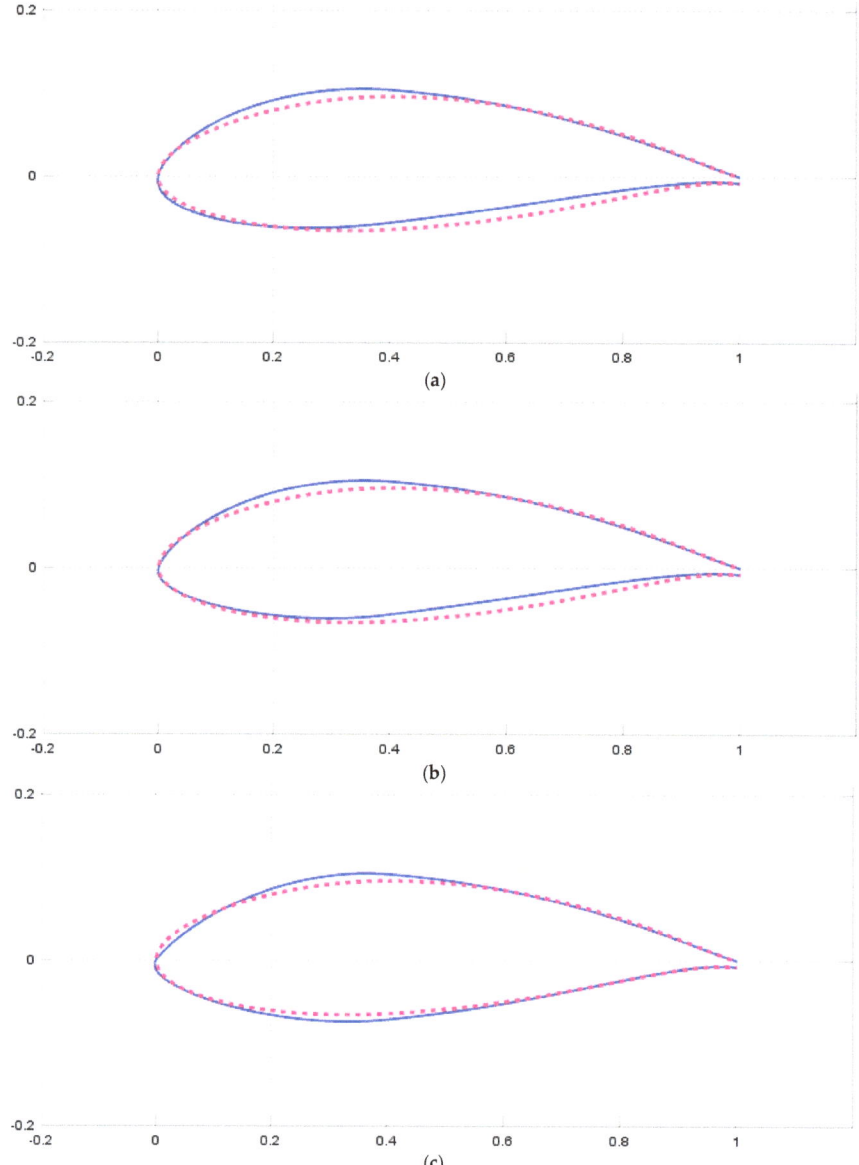

Figure 11. Optimized airfoil shapes for L/C = 6, for the points indicated by empty arrows in Figure 9 (a) Point 1; (b) Point 2; (c) Point 3 (Figure 8), red dotted line: original, blue solid line: optimized (note that vertical scale is larger than horizontal scale).

The predicted fields of non-dimensional velocity magnitude (velocity nondimensionalized by V) around the original airfoil and the three optimized airfoils corresponding to the three points (for each domain size) indicated in Figure 9 are presented in Figures 12 and 13 for L/C = 3 and L/C = 6, respectively, for Re = 100,000, BA = 5°, FA = 15° (AoA = 10°).

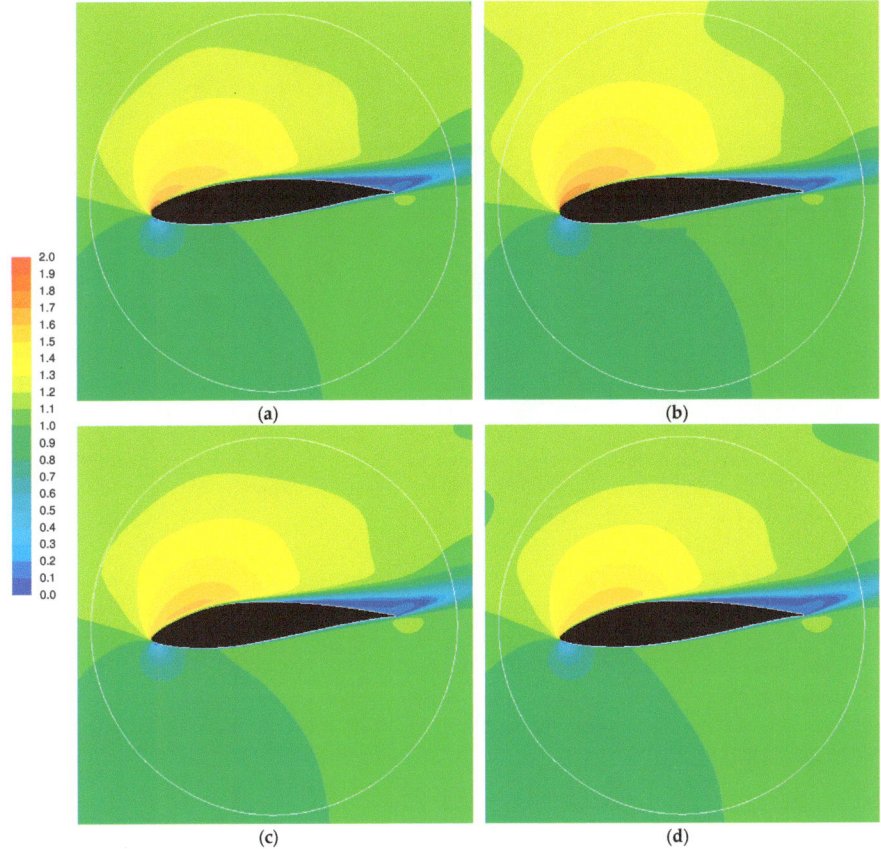

Figure 12. Predicted distribution of dimensionless velocity magnitude around the airfoil for Re = 100,000, BA = 5°, FA = 15° (AoA = 10°), for L/C = 3, (**a**) Original profile; (**b**) Point 1; (**c**) Point 2; (**d**) Point 3 (Figure 9).

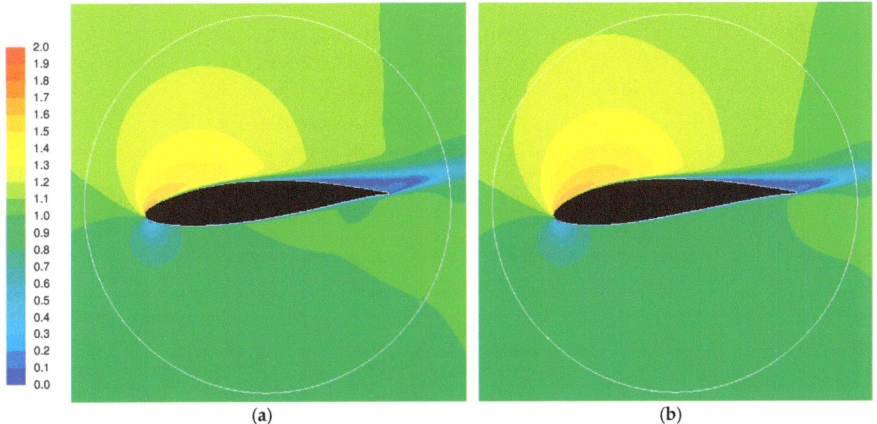

Figure 13. *Cont.*

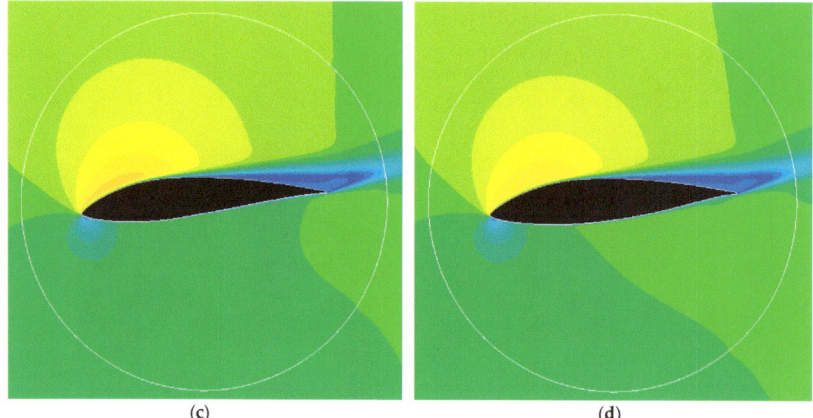

Figure 13. Predicted distribution of dimensionless velocity magnitude around the airfoil for Re = 100,000, BA = 5°, FA = 15° (AoA = 10°), for L/C = 6, (**a**) Original profile; (**b**) Point 1; (**c**) Point 2; (**d**) Point 3 (Figure 9).

Differences in the velocity fields with changing airfoil shape can be observed (Figures 12 and 13). Note that the performances indicated in Figure 9 for different profiles are the overall (average) performances for the considered range of operation (Table 1) but are not directly connected to a given operation point. Still, the predicted velocity fields imply that the relative performance of the profiles qualitatively correspond to the trend indicated in Figure 9, where moving from Profile 1 to Profile 2 and to Profile 3 a decreasing acceleration on the suction side can be observed, implying a decreasing trend for the lift, that is, thrust, agreeing qualitatively with the behaviour shown in Figure 9.

4. Conclusions

An automated two-dimensional airfoil shape optimization procedure for small horizontal axis wind turbines (HAWT) is presented, with emphasis on high thrust and aerodynamically stable performance. The procedure combines the Computational Fluid Dynamics (CFD) analysis with the Response Surface Methodology (RSM), the Biobjective Mesh Adaptive Direct Search (BiMADS) optimization algorithm and an automatic geometry and mesh generation tool. In the CFD analysis, a Reynolds Averaged Numerical Simulation (RANS) is applied in combination with a two-equation turbulence model. In the analysis, an emphasis is placed upon the role of the blade-to-blade interaction. The results show that improvements in the performance can be achieved by modifications of the blade shape, resulting in a Pareto front and the present procedure can be used as a tool for blade shape optimization. Prioritization of the properties while choosing a profile out of the Pareto front would depend on the purpose of the application. Profiles with high thrust may, for example, be preferred for a local, direct consumption of the generated electric power, while more stably operating profiles (with low standard deviation of thrust) may be preferred for feeding the power into the grid.

Author Contributions: All the authors contributed equally to this paper.

Acknowledgments: Stefan Rohr of RLE International GmbH, Cologne, Germany is gratefully acknowledged for valuable technical discussions.

Conflicts of Interest: The authors declare no conflict of interest.

Nomenclature

C	chord length
C_D	drag coefficient
C_L	lift coefficient
C_T	average thrust coefficient
C_σ	coefficient of thrust standard deviation
L	circumferential domain size (distance between periodic boundaries)
Re	Reynolds number
T	thrust
V	magnitude of approach velocity at Re = 100,000
y^+	distance to wall non-dimensionalized by wall shear stress, viscosity and density

Greek symbols

ϱ	density
σ	standard deviation of thrust

Abbreviations

AoA	Angle of Attack
BA	Blade Angle
BiMADS	Biobjective Mesh Adaptive Direct Search
BEM	Blade Element Momentum
CFD	Computational Fluid Dynamics
FA	Flow Angle
FVM	Finite Volume Method
GA	Genetic Algorithms
HAWT	Horizontal Axis Wind Turbines
LES	Large Eddy Simulations
NGN	Number of Grid Nodes
OCCD	Orthogonal Central Composite Design
RANS	Reynolds Averaged Numerical Simulations
RSM	Response Surface Methodology
SST	Shear Stress Transport

References

1. Hau, E. *Wind Turbines*; Springer: Berlin, Germany, 2013.
2. Oyama, A.; Liou, M.-S.; Obayashi, S. Transonic axial-flow blade shape optimization using evolutionary algorithm and three-dimensional Navier-Stokes solver. In Proceedings of the 9th AIAA/ISSMO Symposium on Multidisciplinary Analysis and Optimization (AIAA 2002-5642), Atlanta, GA, USA, 4–6 September 2002.
3. Semenova, A.; Chrikov, D.; Lyutiv, A.; Cherny, S.; Skorospelov, V.; Pylev, I. Multi-objective shape optimization of runner blade for Kaplan turbine. *IOP Conf. Ser. Earth Environ. Sci.* **2014**, *22*, 012025. [CrossRef]
4. Thumthae, C.; Chitsomboon, T. Optimal angle of attack for untwisted blade wind turbine. *Renew. Energy* **2009**, *34*, 1279–1284. [CrossRef]
5. Jureczko, M.; Pawlak, M.; Mezyk, A. Optimisation of wind turbine blades. *J. Mater. Process. Technol.* **2005**, *167*, 463–471. [CrossRef]
6. Mendez, J.; Greiner, D. Wind blade chord and twist angle optimization by using genetic algorithms. In Proceedings of the 5th Conference on Engineering Computational Technology, Las Palmas de Gran Canaria, Spain, 12–15 September 2006.
7. Burger, C.; Hartfield, R. Wind turbine airfoil performance optimization using the vortex lattice method and a genetic algorithm. In Proceedings of the 4th AIAA Energy Conversion Conference, San Diego, CA, USA, 26–29 June 2006.
8. Clifton-Smith, M.; Wood, D. Further dual purpose evolutionary optimization of small wind turbine blades. *J. Phys. Conf. Ser.* **2007**, *75*, 012017. [CrossRef]
9. Liu, X.; Chen, Y.; Ye, Z. Optimization model for rotor blades of horizontal axis wind turbines. *Front. Mech. Eng. China* **2007**, *2*, 483–488. [CrossRef]

10. XFOIL Subsonic Airfoil Development System. Available online: http://web.mit.edu/drela/Public/web/xfoil/ (accessed on 12 April 2018).

11. Kenway, G.; Martins, J.R.R.A. Aerostructural shape optimization of wind turbine blades considering site-specific winds. In Proceedings of the AIAA/ISSMO Multidisciplinary Analysis and Optimization Conference, Victoria, BC, Canada, 10–12 September 2008.

12. Xudong, W.; Shen, W.Z.; Zhu, W.J.; Sorensen, J.N.; Jin, C. Shape optimization of wind turbine blades. *Wind Energy* **2009**, *12*, 781–803. [CrossRef]

13. Ceyhan, O.; Sezer-Uzol, N.; Tuncer, I. Optimization of horizontal axis wind turbines by using BEM theory and genetic algorithm. In Proceedings of the 5th Ankara International Aerospace Conference, METU, Ankara, Turkey, 17–19 August 2009; pp. 17–19.

14. Li, J.Y.; Li, R.; Gao, Y.; Huang, J. Aerodynamic optimization of wind turbine airfoils using response surface techniques. *Proc. Inst. Mech. Eng. Part A J. Power Energy* **2010**, *224*, 827–838. [CrossRef]

15. Grujicic, M.; Arakere, G.; Pandurangan, B.; Sellappan, V.; Vallejo, A.; Ozen, M. Multidisciplinary design optimization for glass-fibre epoxy-matrix composite 5 MW horizontal-axis wind-turbine blades. *J. Mater. Eng. Perform.* **2010**, *19*, 1116–1127. [CrossRef]

16. Bottasso, C.; Campagnolo, F.; Croce, A. *Computational Procedures for the Multidisciplinary Constrained Optimization of Wind Turbines*; Scientific Report DIA-SR; Dipartimento di Ingegneria Aerospaziale, Politecnico di Milano: Milano, Italy, 2010.

17. Kusiak, A.; Zheng, H.Y. Optimization of wind turbine energy and power factor with an evolutionary computation algorithm. *Energy* **2010**, *35*, 1324–1332. [CrossRef]

18. Song, F.F.; Ni, Y.H.; Tan, Z.Q. Optimization design, modeling and dynamic analysis for composite wind turbine blade. *Procedia Eng.* **2011**, *16*, 369–375. [CrossRef]

19. Wang, L.; Wang, T.G.; Luo, Y. Improved non-dominated sorting genetic algorithm (NSGA)-II in multi-objective optimization studies of wind turbine blades. *Appl. Math. Mech. Engl. Ed.* **2011**, *32*, 739–748. [CrossRef]

20. Grasso, F. Hybrid optimization for wind turbine thick airfoils. In Proceedings of the 53rd AIAAJASME/ASCE/AHS/ASC Structures, Structural Dynamics and Materials Conference, Honolulu, HI, USA, 23–26 April 2012. AIAA Paper AIAA-2012.

21. Chen, X.M.; Agarwal, R. Optimization of flatback airfoils for wind-turbine blades using a genetic algorithm. *J. Aircr.* **2012**, *49*, 622–629. [CrossRef]

22. Ribeiro, A.F.P.; Awruch, A.M.; Gomes, H.M. An airfoil optimization technique for wind turbines. *Appl. Math. Model.* **2012**, *36*, 4898–4907. [CrossRef]

23. Jeong, J.; Park, K.; Jun, S.; Song, K.; Lee, D.H. Design optimization of a wind turbine blade to reduce the fluctuating unsteady aerodynamic load in turbulent wind. *J. Mech. Sci. Technol.* **2012**, *26*, 827–838. [CrossRef]

24. Ju, Y.P.; Zhang, C.H. Multi-point robust design optimization of wind turbine airfoil under geometric uncertainty. *Proc. Inst. Mech. Eng. Part A J. Power Energy* **2012**, *226*, 245–261. [CrossRef]

25. Liao, C.C.; Zhao, X.L.; Xu, J.Z. Blade layers optimization of wind turbines using FAST and improved PSO algorithm. *Renew. Energy* **2012**, *42*, 227–233. [CrossRef]

26. Polat, O.; Tuncer, I.H. Aerodynamic shape optimization of wind turbine blades using a parallel genetic algorithm. *Procedia Eng.* **2013**, *61*, 28–31. [CrossRef]

27. Sessarego, M.; Dixon, K.R.; Rival, D.E.; Wood, D.H. A hybrid multi-objective evolutionary algorithm for wind-turbine blade optimization. *Eng. Optim.* **2015**, *47*, 1043–1062. [CrossRef]

28. Shen, X.; Chen, J.E.; Zhu, X.C.; Liu, P.Y.; Du, Z.H. Multi-objective optimization of wind turbine blades using lifting surface method. *Energy* **2015**, *90*, 1111–1121. [CrossRef]

29. Hassanzadeh, A.; Hassanabad, A.H.; Dadvand, A. Aerodynamic shape optimization and analysis of small wind turbine blades employing the Viterna approach for post-stall region. *Alex. Eng. J.* **2016**, *55*, 2035–2043. [CrossRef]

30. Pourrajabian, A.; Afshar, P.A.N.; Ahmadizadeh, M.; Wood, D. Aero-structural design optimization of a small wind turbine blade. *Renew. Energy* **2016**, *87*, 837–848. [CrossRef]

31. Dal Monte, A.; De Betta, S.; Castelli, M.R.; Benini, E. Proposal for a coupled aerodynamic-structural wind turbine blade optimization. *Compos. Struct.* **2017**, *159*, 144–156. [CrossRef]

32. Chehouri, A.; Younes, R.; Ilinca, A.; Perron, J. Review of performance optimization applied to wind turbines. *Appl. Energy* **2015**, *142*, 361–388. [CrossRef]

33. Myers, R.H.; Montgomery, D.C.; Anderson-Cook, C.M. *Response Surface Methodology: Process and Product Optimization Using Designed Experiments*, 4th ed.; Wiley: Hoboken, NJ, USA, 2016.

34. Benim, A.C.; Brillert, D.; Cagan, M. Investigation into the computational analysis of direct-transfer pre-swirl systems for gas turbine cooling. In Proceedings of the ASME Turbo Expo 2004, Vienna, Austria, 14–17 June 2004; Volume 4, pp. 453–460, Paper No. GT2004-54151. [CrossRef]

35. Benim, A.C.; Geiger, M.; Doehler, S.; Schoenenberger, M.; Roemer, H. Modelling the Flow in the Exhaust Hood of Steam Turbines under Consideration of Turbine-Exhaust Hood Interaction. In Proceedings of the 1st European Conference on Turbomachinery—Fluid Dynamic and Thermodynamic Aspects: Computational Methods, Erlangen, Germany, 1–3 March 1995; Book Series: VDI Berichte; VDI Verlag: Duesseldorf, Germany, 1995; Volume 1185, pp. 343–357.

36. Engineering Simulations and 3-D Design Software. Available online: www.ansys.com (accessed on 17 October 2018).

37. Durbin, P.A.; Pettersson Reif, B.A. *Statistical Theory and Modeling for Turbulent Flows*, 2nd ed.; Wiley: Chichester, UK, 2011.

38. Benim, A.C.; Nahavandi, A.; Syed, K. URANS and LES analysis of turbulent swirling flows. *Prog. Comput. Fluid Dyn. An Int. J.* **2005**, *5*, 444–454. [CrossRef]

39. Benim, A.C.; Chattopadhyay, H.; Nahavandi, A. Computational analysis of turbulent forced convection in a channel with a triangular prism. *Int. J. Therm. Sci.* **2011**, *50*, 1973–1983. [CrossRef]

40. Menter, F.; Esch, T.; Kubacki, S. Transition modelling based on local variables. In Proceedings of the Fifth International Symposium on Engineering Turbulence Modelling and Measurements, Mallorca, Spain, 16–18 September 2002; Engineering Turbulence Modelling and Experiments 5. Rodi, W., Fueye, N., Eds.; Elsevier: Amsterdam, The Netherlands, 2002; pp. 555–564.

41. Benim, A.C.; Cagan, M.; Gunes, D. Computational analysis of transient heat transfer in turbulent pipe flow. *Int. J. Therm. Sci.* **2004**, *43*, 725–732. [CrossRef]

42. Benim, A.C.; Ozkan, K.; Cagan, M.; Gunes, D. Computational investigation of turbulent jet impinging onto rotating disk. *Int. J. Numer. Methods Heat Fluid Flow* **2007**, *17*, 284–301. [CrossRef]

43. Assmann, A.; Benim, A.C.; Gül, F.; Lux, P.; Akhyari, P.; Boeken, U.; Joos, F.; Feindt, P.; Lichtenberg, A. Pulsatile extracorporeal circulation during on-pump cardiac surgery enhances aortic wall shear stress. *J. Biomech.* **2012**, *45*, 156–163. [CrossRef] [PubMed]

44. Deng, G.B.; Ferry, M.; Piquet, J.; Queutey, P.; Visonneau, M. New fully coupled solutions of the Navier-Stokes equations. In *Notes on Numerical Fluid Mechanics (NNFM), Proceedings of the 9th GAMM Conference on Numerical Methods in Fluid Mechanics, Lausanne, Switzerland, 25–27 September 1991*; Vos, J.B., Ed.; Springer: Wiesbaden, Germany, 1992; Volume 35, pp. 191–200.

45. Leonard, B.P. A stable and accurate convective modelling procedure based on quadratic upstream interpolation. *Comput. Methods Appl. Mech. Eng.* **1979**, *19*, 59–98. [CrossRef]

46. Barth, T.J.; Jespersen, D. The design and application of upwind schemes on unstructured meshes. In Proceedings of the AIAA 27th Aerospace Sciences Meeting, Reno, NV, USA, 9–12 January 1989; Technical Report AIAA-89-0366.

47. Benim, A.C.; Pasqualotto, E.; Suh, S.H. Modeling turbulent flow past a circular cylinder by RANS, URANS, LES and DES. *Prog. Computat. Fluid Dyn. An Int. J.* **2008**, *8*, 299–307. [CrossRef]

48. GNU Octave. Available online: https://www.gnu.org/software/octave/ (accessed on 17 April 2018).

49. Conn, A.R.; Scheinberg, K.; Vincente, L.N. *Introduction to Derivative-Free Optimization*; SIAM: Philadelphia, PA, USA, 2009.

50. Le Digabel, S. Algorithm 909: NOMAD: Nonlinear Optimization with the MADS Algorithm. *ACM Trans. Math. Softw.* **2011**, *37*, 44. [CrossRef]

51. Selig, M.S.; Lyon, C.A.; Giguère, P.; Ninham, C.P.; Guglielmo, J.J. *Summary of Low-Speed Airfoil Data*; Soar Tech Publications: Virginia Beach, VA, USA, 1996; Volume 2.

52. Branke, J.; Deb, K.; Miettinen, K.; Slowinski, R. (Eds.) *Multiobjective Optimization*; Springer: Berlin, Germany, 2008.

MDPI AG
Grosspeteranlage 5
4052 Basel
Switzerland
Tel.: +41 61 683 77 34

Computation Editorial Office
E-mail: computation@mdpi.com
www.mdpi.com/journal/computation

www.ingramcontent.com/pod-product-compliance
Lightning Source LLC
LaVergne TN
LVHW072341090526
838202LV00019B/2458